— *The Unofficial Guide®* to Atlanta —

Also available from Macmillan Travel

The Unofficial Guide® to
Atlanta

3rd Edition

Fred Brown and
Bob Sehlinger

MACMILLAN · USA

To Martha Elizabeth Ramage Brown
who took me to Atlanta for the first time

A. W. B.

Every effort has been made to ensure the accuracy of information
throughout this book. Bear in mind, however, that prices, schedules,
etc., are constantly changing. Readers should always verify informa-
tion before making final plans.

Macmillan Travel
A Simon & Schuster Macmillan Company
1633 Broadway
New York, New York 10019-6785

Produced by Menasha Ridge Press
Design by Barbara E. Williams

ISBN 0-02-861243-4

ISSN 1071-6459

Manufactured in the United States of America

10 9 8 7 6 5 4 3 2 1

Third Edition

Contents

PART THREE: Hotels

PART FOUR: Visiting Atlanta on Business

PART FIVE: Arriving and Getting Oriented

List of Illustrations

Acknowledgments

Jane Garvey, an extremely talented writer and veteran food critic, prepared the dining section and restaurant profiles in this guide. Richard Gincel, an equally gifted journalist, stayed up late and evaluated dozens of Atlanta nightspots, reporting in depth on Atlanta's best. The input and contributions of these two professionals have enhanced this guide in countless ways. Holly Brown, Shane Kennedy, Patt Palmer, and Grace Walton inspected every lodging property in the greater Atlanta area and developed the hotel ratings and rankings.

Hundreds of Atlantans helped with the research for this guide, from MARTA bus drivers to restaurant owners to city government bureaucrats. Their aid is reflected in the extensive listings in the book.

In addition, we would like to thank the following individuals who provided assistance, insight, advice, and encouragement in many different ways: Barbara Baughman, Barbara Baughman & Associates; Christy Black, Galleria Centre; John Braden and Rhonda Copenny, Hartsfield Atlanta International Airport; Kellie Cannon, Georgia World Congress Center; Fernando Costa, Atlanta Bureau of Planning; Dorothy Etris, Historic Roswell Convention and Visitors Bureau; Carol Morgan Flammer, Atlanta Botanical Garden; Cynthia Fox, SCITREK; Franklin Garrett, Atlanta History Center; Makonnen Gebre-Hiwet, Metropolitan Atlanta Rapid Transit Authority; Cliff Graubart, Old New York Book Store; Chuck Gregory, Georgia Department of Natural Resources; Patti Hall, Gwinnett Civic and Cultural Center; Carolyn Boyd Hatcher and Lisa Patrick, The Georgia Conservancy; Susan Henderson, Tour Gals; Ron Hudspeth, the *Hudspeth Report*; Mark Johnson, Shepherd Spinal Center; I. Ney Lawson, Atlanta Bureau of Taxi Cabs and Vehicles for Hire; Rupert LeCraw, Oxford Bookstore; Sam Massell, The Buckhead Coalition; Karen McNeely and Rick Meyers, Atlanta Convention and Visitors Bureau; Carol Mumford, The Wren's Nest; Sylvia Ratchford,

Atlanta Market Center; Richard Rothman, Richard Rothman and Associates; Bill Smith, writer and publisher; Clint Smith, New World Communications; Don Smith, producer, director, writer; Michele Swann, Georgia International Convention and Trade Center.

Sherri M. L. Smith assisted with the research and editing of the book. Her contribution was invaluable.

Finally, many thanks to Barbara Williams, Holly Brown, Jude Grant, Robert Clay White, Brian Taylor, Tim Krasnansky, and The Marathon Group, Inc., the pros who managed to transform all this effort into a book.

— The Unofficial Guide® *to Atlanta —*

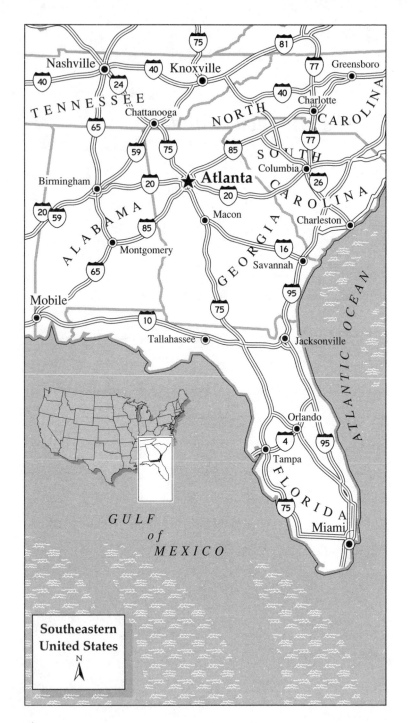

The Atlanta Experience

We have always had very definite ideas about what makes Atlanta an interesting city to visit. In the course of preparing this book, we had many conversations with individuals who know the city intimately—a wide spectrum of people representing a wide range of interests.

In our interviews we returned again and again to one core conversation. It goes like this:

"Suppose," we say, "you have some friends who are coming to visit Atlanta for several days. You want them to enjoy the best of the city and to leave feeling that they have discovered what is special about Atlanta. To go home with good memories. What would you tell them to do?"

Then we add this little caveat: "Remember, they will see just the things you recommend."

"Well," they say, "I would take them to . . ."

"You can't take them," we insist. "You have to direct them. Where would you tell them to go?"

"OK . . . I can't take them. I have to send them . . . OK . . . The Cyclorama . . . Underground . . . Stone Mountain . . . ."

Although the lists may vary slightly, they are generally pretty consistent: The Cyclorama, Stone Mountain, CNN, The King Center, the Coke Museum. When they get to the sixth or the seventh recommendation, they invariably slow down.

". . . The Wren's Nest . . . and . . . then . . ."

We wait expectantly.

Getting a little nervous, as though they had failed to fulfill a civic responsibility, they dive into another tier of attractions.

"SCITREK, Panola Mountain, the Puppet Museum . . ."

"Remember," we gently caution, "world-class attractions. Stuff special to Atlanta. Worth a special trip. The kinds of things that they will go home and tell their friends about."

Then comes the classic response. "You can't just see Atlanta," they say with a sigh of exasperation. "You have to experience it. You have to show them."

"This town," they say, "is not just a bunch of museums and roller-coasters. You have to show them the skyline. Go shopping. Tour neighborhoods . . ."

And so, inevitably, it goes. In the final analysis, you see, Atlanta is a city of experiences, not a city of attractions.

One person describes how she takes visitors on a tour through the shops, restaurants, and galleries of Peachtree Center's walkways and tunnels. It's a tour she has rehearsed, and her friends are always delighted.

Another has devised a very professional Olympics Venues tour that covers Olympic Stadium, Olympic Village, Centennial Olympic Park, and other sites familiar to millions of television viewers who saw these Atlanta landmarks on television during the summer of 1996.

Still another takes visitors to Oakland Cemetery where they wander among the tombstones of Margaret Mitchell, Bobby Jones, and Moses Formwalt with the Atlanta skyline prominent in the background. Friends write thanking her for sharing something unique about her city.

In fact, everybody who loves, tries to understand, and wants to show off Atlanta has their own little tour. They would not be caught dead packing someone off to Six Flags or Underground and letting it go at that.

This *Unofficial Guide* allows you to experience Atlanta as though you had a native holding you by the hand. In fact, if you explore Atlanta in some of the ways outlined in these pages, there will be plenty of residents asking you for advice on where to go and what to see.

The book does not ignore the traditional attractions. Indeed in some instances, the attractions are part of the experiences. But it does encourage you to see Atlanta as more than just a checklist of sights: we want you to experience the rich, diverse fabric that is the city of Atlanta.

Name another United States city that burned twice, was occupied once, and gave birth to the most important social revolution in the twentieth century. Atlanta is the home of Margaret Mitchell who wrote *Gone With The Wind*, a novel so powerful that most people cannot separate the real history of the city from the fiction of the book and movie. It is the city of Ralph McGill, Martin Luther King, Jr., and Gene Talmadge. W. E. B. DuBois, one of the main organizers of the National Association for the Advancement of Colored People, lived and taught here. The Student Non-Violent Coordinating Committee started here.

Atlanta was the first large American city with a black mayor. Within sight of his office, the Georgia flag, still bearing the Confederate battle emblem, flies on top of the state capitol.

It is the city that longtime mayor William B. Hartsfield called "too busy to hate," as well as the home of Coca-Cola, CNN, and the 1996 Centennial Olympic Games. A traditional southern city with a twist, Atlanta had to transcend many southern values to rise from the ashes of the Civil War.

To really get to know Atlanta you must walk over the battlefields at Kennesaw and read the historical markers at Peachtree Creek. Explore Auburn Avenue; go to a Braves game and join in the tomahawk chop. Visit The King Center and see what Martin Luther King, Jr., carried in his small handbag that last night in Memphis. Pick up a copy of *Creative Loafing* and shake your head over the weird personals. Tour the Cyclorama and the CNN Center. Walk along Peachtree Street, particularly between 14th and 16th. Stroll through Olympic Park. Take the elevator to the top of the 70-story Peachtree Plaza and drink a Dixie Daiquiri while the revolving lounge gives you a 360-degree panoramic view of the city. Walk to the top of Stone Mountain with its mammoth carvings of Confederate generals. Hear African folk tales at the Wren's Nest. Shop for shoes at the legendary Friedman's. Listen to jazz at Bennett Street or dance the two-step at Miss Kitty's. Wander around Buckhead at the midnight hour.

Savor Atlanta's personality while you're here, and you will leave Atlanta knowing that you have experienced one of the most historically profound and entertaining cities in America. This "unofficial" book is meant to be your personal guide.

Why Go to Atlanta

Post-Olympic Atlanta is different from the city that was here before the 1996 Summer Games. Thirty-acre Centennial Olympic Park extends north from the intersection of Techwood and Marietta Street giving a fresh open look to a section of town that was unsightly. Woodruff Park near Five Points in the center of town has been enlarged. Auburn Avenue, Marietta Street, International Boulevard, and Peachtree Street have been bordered with new sidewalks and trees.

The Olympics ushered in a building boom of apartments, condominiums, and lofts in the downtown area; the kinds of inner city residences that were almost nonexistent before. Olympics-related construction altered the profile of the city. The huge Olympic Village on the Georgia Tech Campus on North Avenue is now student housing. Olympic Stadium, modified for baseball and its seats reduced from 80,000 to 49,831, is the new home of the Atlanta Braves. Atlanta-Fulton County Stadium, an Atlanta landmark for 30 years, is gone, leveled.

There is more outdoor sculpture and artwork. Downtown is more open, interesting, and walkable.

A kind of "We really did it," civic pride pervades the city. The afterglow will last for a decade.

Yet even taking into account these substantial tangible and intangible changes, Atlanta is very much the same city it was before the Olympics.

Hospitality was, and is, Atlanta's number one industry, generating over $2 billion in revenue and employing over 200,000 people. But just like before the Olympics, the visitors are mostly business travelers and conventioneers, not the vacationing tourists who are attracted to New Orleans, Washington, DC, or San Francisco.

You can count all of Atlanta's main tourist attractions on the fingers of both hands—Stone Mountain, The King Center, Atlanta History Center, the Cyclorama, CNN Center, The World of Coca-Cola—and still have four fingers left over. Throw in Six Flags as a good amusement park and from that point on, as far as tourism is concerned, you're in Toledo. High on the "To Do" list posted in the offices of the Atlanta

Convention and Visitors Bureau is, "Transform Atlanta into a Destination City." Perhaps that will be another legacy of the Olympics.

In three important categories, however, Atlanta is irrefutably world class: sports, conventions, and shopping.

—— *Sports*

Atlanta has three major league teams: the Hawks (basketball), the Falcons (football), and the Braves (baseball). When the Braves are in a pennant race, a club-level seat is the hottest ticket in Atlanta.

Georgia Tech, which plays basketball in the Atlantic Coast Conference, routinely sells out the 14,000-seat Alexander Memorial Coliseum. Eighty miles away in Athens, the 80,000-seat Sanford Stadium is sold out for every University of Georgia home football game. Many of those thousands are Atlantans who make the drive as if it were a religious pilgrimage.

Each year on a hot, humid July 4th morning, 50,000 runners chug down Peachtree Street in the Peachtree Road Race. The race application appears in the paper on a Sunday in March, and nine days later the Atlanta Track Club closes out the race.

The long-range dream of Billy Payne, the man who brought the Olympics to Atlanta, and some of his close associates, is to make Atlanta the amateur sports capital of the world.

—— *Conventions*

There's a saying that dates back to Atlanta's railroad days: "whether you're going to heaven or hell, you've got to change trains in Atlanta." That has been updated to "changing planes," and it also holds true for "attending conventions." At one time or another business people from all over America find their way to Atlanta to attend a convention or trade show.

The Georgia World Congress Center (the busiest convention center in the world), the Georgia Dome, and the Omni create a convention and trade show complex that is awe-inspiring, even for the nonconvention-goer.

Combine it with the sprawling Merchandise Mart, Gift Mart, Inforum, and Apparel Mart, all just a few blocks away in Peachtree Center, and you have one of the great convention and trade show centers of America.

An entire city center of hotels, restaurants, entertainment, and transportation has sprung up around this ten-block area of downtown Atlanta.

Even Atlanta's fine restaurants, many of which are profiled in this guide, owe their prosperity over the last ten years to the convention business.

Shopping: The Number-One Attraction

Sporting events and conventions aside, without question, Atlanta's number one tourist attraction is shopping. Lenox Square Shopping Mall draws 14 million people yearly—40% of them from out of town. Compare this to Stone Mountain, the most popular traditional attraction, which draws 6 million a year, or The Martin Luther King Center, which draws 3 million.

The marketing people at Lenox Square fret because the Atlanta Convention and Visitors Bureau won't acknowledge what a powerful force shopping in Atlanta really is. The bureau insists on appealing to potential visitors by promoting more traditional attractions, when the Lenox people know from their marketing surveys that what people really want to do when they come to Atlanta is flex their credit cards.

When it comes to shopping, Lenox Square is just the tip of the iceberg. There's also Buckhead, Bennett Street, Miami Circle, the Chattahoochee outlets, Chamblee Antique Row, and Furniture Row . . . not to mention the huge shopping malls at every interstate interchange.

The annual boat show, the auto show, and the home and garden show at the World Congress Center draw more out-of-town residents than most traditional tourist attractions in the city. Why are these residents of Birmingham, Lexington, Columbia, and Jacksonville coming to Atlanta? Not to see the Telephone Museum. They are coming to shop. Shopping is to Atlanta what the Washington Monument is to Washington and what gambling is to Las Vegas.

The Ethnic Influence

Although it is not promoted, a crazy-quilt patchwork of Asian and Spanish-American cultures is growing like kudzu along Atlanta's Buford Highway. Up and down these seven miles, visitors can rent Chinese videos and CDs, buy Vietnamese newspapers, shop in a Korean retail center, purchase transparent fish at an 80,000-square-foot international market, and dine at some of the best restaurants in the Southeast. Atlanta's official International Boulevard runs from Courtland Street to the World Congress Center. Atlanta's *unofficial* international boulevard thrives between Lenox Road and the Gwinnett County line.

About This Guide

—— How Come "Unofficial?"

Most "official" guides to Atlanta tout the well-known sights, promote the local restaurants and hotels indiscriminately, and leave out a lot of good stuff. This guide is different.

Instead of pandering to the tourist industry, we'll tell you if a well-known restaurant's mediocre food is not worth the wait. We'll complain loudly about overpriced hotel rooms, and we'll guide you away from the crowds and congestion for a break now and then.

We sent in a team of evaluators who toured downtown and its outlying neighborhoods and popular attractions, ate in the area's best restaurants, performed critical evaluations of its hotels, and visited Atlanta's best night clubs. If a museum is boring, or a major attraction is overrated, we say so—and in the process, we hope, make your visit more fun, efficient, and economical.

—— Creating a Guidebook

We got into the guidebook business because we were unhappy with the way travel guides make the reader work to get any usable information. Wouldn't it be nice, we thought, if we were to make guides that are easy to use?

Most guidebooks are compilations of lists. This is true regardless of whether the information is presented in list form or artfully distributed through pages of prose. There is insufficient detail in a list, and prose can present tedious helpings of nonessential or marginally useful information. Not enough wheat, so to speak, for nourishment in one instance, and too much chaff in the other. Either way, these types of guides provide little more than departure points from which readers initiate their own quests.

Many guides are readable and well researched, but they tend to be difficult to use. To select a hotel, for example, a reader must study several pages of descriptions with only the boldface hotel names breaking up large blocks of text. Because each description essentially deals with the same variables, it is difficult to recall what was said concerning a particular hotel. Readers generally must work through all the write-ups before beginning to narrow their choices. The presentation of restaurants, nightclubs, and attractions is similar, except that even more reading is usually required. To use such a guide is to undertake an exhaustive research process that requires examining nearly as many options and possibilities as starting from scratch. Recommendations, if any, lack depth and conviction. These guides compound rather than solve problems by failing to narrow travelers' choices down to a thoughtfully considered, well-distilled, and manageable few.

—— *How* Unofficial Guides *Are Different*

Readers care about the authors' opinions. Authors, after all, *are* supposed to know what they are is talking about. This, coupled with the fact that the traveler wants quick answers (as opposed to endless alternatives), dictates that authors of travel guides should be explicit, prescriptive, and, above all, direct. The *Unofficial Guide* tries to do just that. It spells out alternatives and recommends specific courses of action. It simplifies complicated destinations and attractions and allows the traveler to feel in control in the most unfamiliar environments. The objective of the *Unofficial Guide* is not to have the most information or all of the information, but to have the most accessible, useful information.

An *Unofficial Guide* is a critical reference work; it focuses on a travel destination that appears to be especially complex. Our authors and research team are completely independent from the attractions, restaurants, and hotels we describe. *The Unofficial Guide to Atlanta* is designed for individuals and families traveling for the fun of it, as well as for business travelers and convention-goers, especially those visiting Atlanta for the first time. The guide is directed at value-conscious, consumer-oriented adults who seek a cost-effective, though not spartan, travel style.

—— *Special Features*

The *Unofficial Guide* offers the following features:

- Friendly introductions to Atlanta's most fascinating neighborhoods.

- "Best of" listings giving our well-qualified opinions on things ranging from bagels to baguettes, four-star hotels to 12-story views.

- Listings that are keyed to your interests, so you can pick and choose.

- Advice to sightseers on how to avoid the worst of the crowds; advice to business travelers on how to avoid traffic and excessive costs.

- Recommendations for lesser known sights.

- A zone system and maps to make it easy to find places you want to go to and avoid places you don't.

- Expert advice on avoiding Atlanta's notorious street crime.

- A Hotel Chart that helps you narrow down your choices fast, according to your needs.

- Shorter listings that include only those restaurants, clubs, and hotels we think are worth considering.

- A detailed index and table of contents to help you find things fast.

- Insider advice on crowds, best times of day or night to go places, and Atlanta's rail system.

What you *won't* get:

- Long, useless lists where everything looks the same.

- Information that gets you somewhere you want to go at the worst possible time.

- Information without advice on how to use it.

—— *How This Guide Was Researched and Written*

While other guides have been written about Atlanta, very few have been evaluative. Some guides practically regurgitate hotel and tourist office promotional material. In preparing this book, we took nothing for granted. Each museum, art gallery, hotel, restaurant, shop, and attraction was evaluated by a team of trained observers according to formal criteria. Interviews were conducted to determine what tourists of all ages enjoyed most *and least* during their Atlanta visit.

Although we are intimately familiar with the city, we assumed the mindset of a tourist or business traveler when compiling the information for this book. Atlanta offerings are marketed to the touring public; thus it is as the public that we have experienced them—noting our satisfaction or dissatisfaction.

The primary difference between the average tourist and the trained evaluator is the evaluator's skills in organization, preparation, and observation. The trained evaluator is responsible for much more than simply observing and cataloging. While the average tourist is being entertained by the deep-voiced narrator and the stirring music in the dimly lit, panoramic Cyclorama, for instance, the professional is rating the presentation in terms of content, historical accuracy, and entertainment value. He or she is checking out the physical arrangements: Is the sound system clear and audible without being overpowering? Is seating adequate? Can everyone in the audience see clearly? And what about the guide and host? Is he or she competent and professional? Is he or she compelling and engaging? Does the presentation begin and end on time? Were the lines long? Does the show contain the features described in the promotional literature?

These and many other considerations figure prominently in the rating and, in fact, the inclusion or exclusion of any attraction. They extend to the evaluation of the smallest museum or shopping experience. Observer teams used detailed checklists to analyze hotel rooms, restaurants, nightclubs, shopping, attractions, recreational opportunities, and convention facilities. Finally, evaluator ratings and observations were integrated with tourist reactions and the opinions of patrons for a comprehensive quality profile of each feature and service.

In compiling this guide, we recognize that tourists' ages, backgrounds, and interests will strongly influence their taste in Atlanta's wide array of activities and attractions. Our sole objective is to provide the reader with sufficient description, critical evaluation, and pertinent data to make knowledgeable decisions according to individual tastes.

—— *HOW INFORMATION IS ORGANIZED:*
By Subject and by Geographic Zone

To give you fast access to information about the best of Atlanta, we've organized material in several formats.

Hotels. Because most people visiting Atlanta stay in one hotel for the duration of their trip, we have summarized our coverage of hotels in charts, maps, ratings, and rankings that allow you to quickly focus your decision-making process. We do not go on page after page describing lobbies and rooms, which, in the final analysis, sound much the same. Instead, we concentrate on the variables that differentiate one hotel from another: location, size, room quality, services, amenities, and cost.

Restaurants. Because you will probably eat a dozen or more meals during your stay, and because not even you can predict what you might be in the mood for on Saturday night, we provide detailed profiles of the best restaurants in and around Atlanta.

Entertainment and Night Life. Visitors frequently try several different clubs during their stay. Because clubs and nightspots, like restaurants, are usually selected spontaneously after arriving in Atlanta, we believe detailed descriptions are warranted. The best nightspots and lounges are profiled by category in the "Nightspots" section of this guide.

Geographic Zones. Once you've decided where you're going, getting there becomes the issue. To help you do that, we have divided the Atlanta area into geographic zones and created maps of each zone.

- Zone 1. Southwest Atlanta
- Zone 2. Northwest Atlanta
- Zone 3. Buckhead/Sandy Springs
- Zone 4. Lenox/Chamblee
- Zone 5. Northeast Atlanta
- Zone 6. Southeast Atlanta
- Zone 7. Downtown West
- Zone 8. Downtown East

All profiles of hotels, restaurants, shopping, attractions, and nightspots include zone numbers. If you are staying at the Terrace Garden Inn, for example, and are interested in a good Italian restaurant nearby, scanning the restaurant profiles for restaurants in Zone 4 (Lenox/Chamblee) will provide you with the most geographically convenient choices.

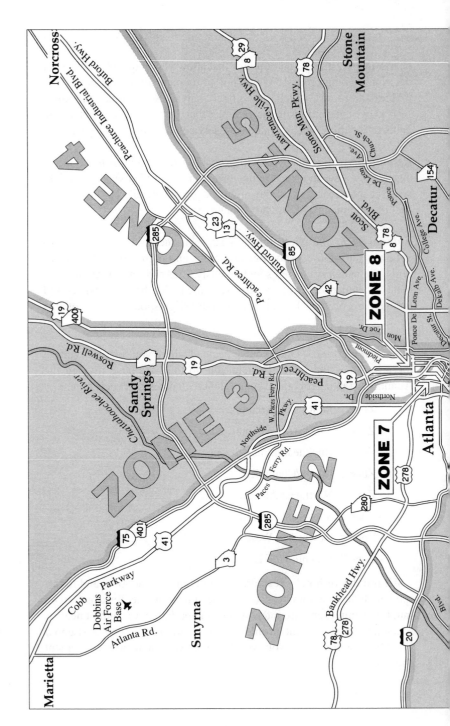

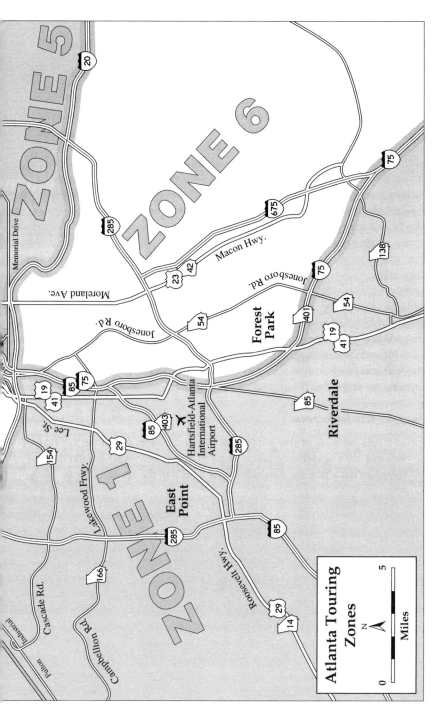

13

— *Letters, Comments, and Questions from Readers*

We expect to learn from our mistakes and from the input of our readers, and to improve with each book and edition. Many of those who use the *Unofficial Guide* write to us to ask questions, make comments, or share their own discoveries and lessons learned in Atlanta. We appreciate all such input, both positive and critical, and encourage our readers to continue writing. Readers' comments and observations frequently are incorporated in revised editions of the *Unofficial Guide,* and will contribute immeasurably to its improvement.

How to Write the Authors

Fred and Bob
The Unofficial Guide to Atlanta
P.O. Box 43059
Birmingham, AL 35243

When you write, be sure to put your return address on your letter as well as on the envelope—sometimes envelopes and letters get separated. And remember, our work takes us out of the office for long periods of time, so forgive us if our response is delayed.

Reader Survey

At the back of this guide you will find a short questionnaire that you can use to express opinions about your Atlanta visit. Clip the questionnaire out along the dotted line and mail it to the above address.

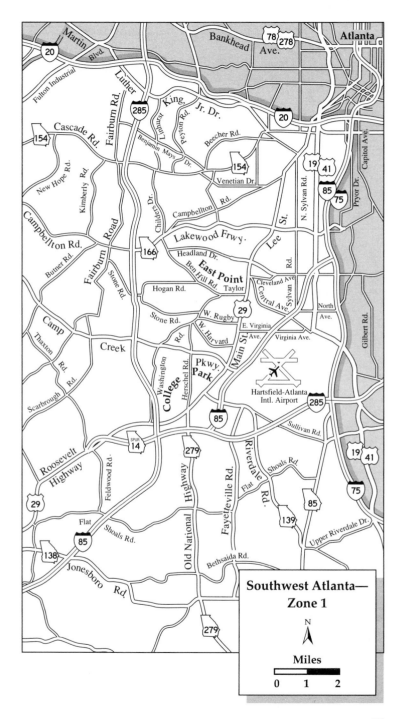

Southwest Atlanta—
Zone 1

N

Miles

0   1   2

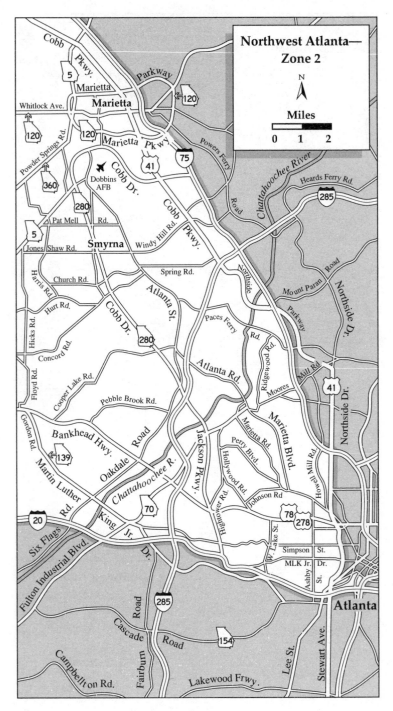

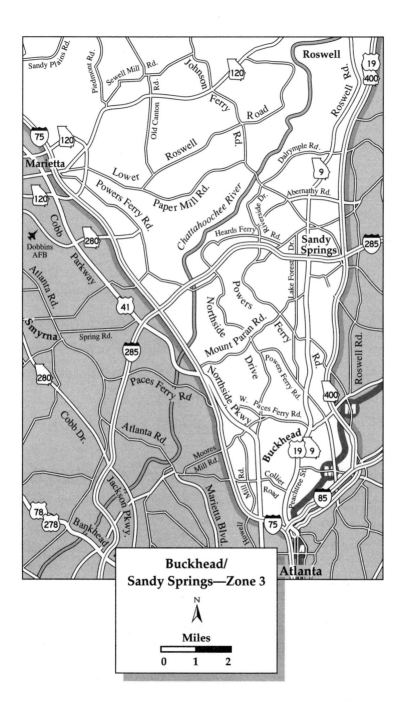

**Buckhead/
Sandy Springs—Zone 3**

N

Miles

0   1   2

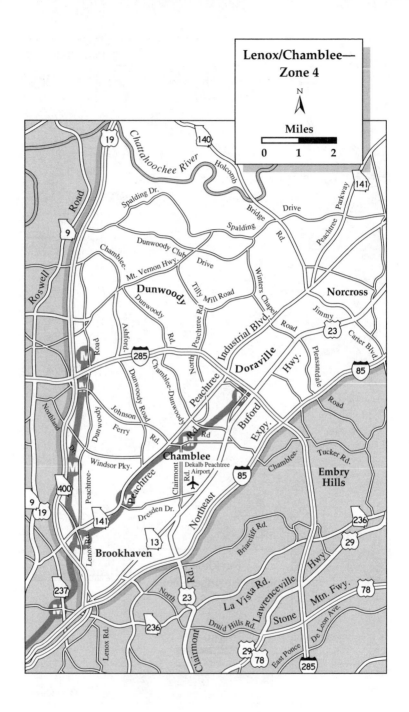

Lenox/Chamblee—
Zone 4

N

Miles

0   1   2

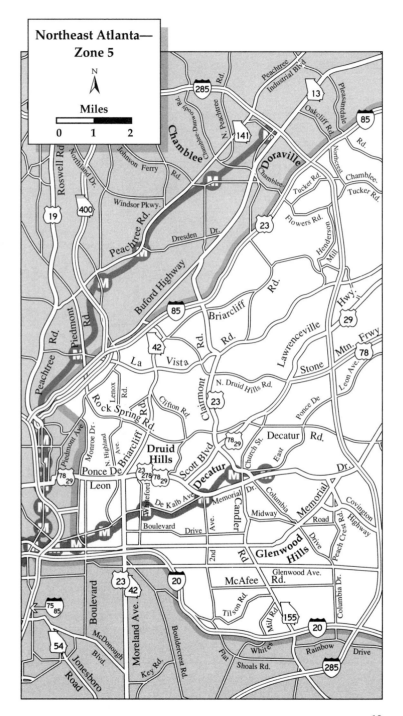

Northeast Atlanta—
Zone 5

N

Miles

0　　1　　2

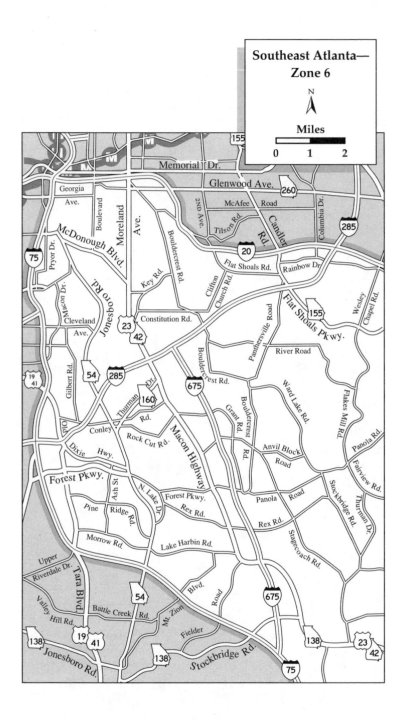

Southeast Atlanta—
Zone 6

N

Miles

0   1   2

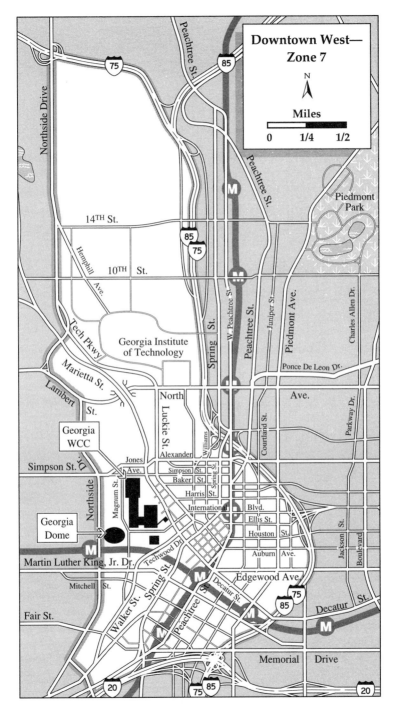

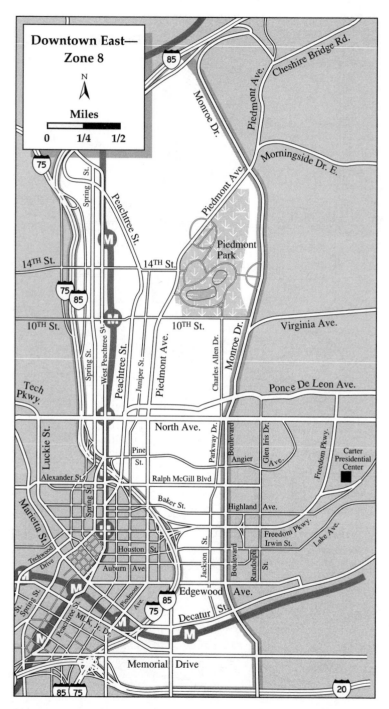

Downtown East—
Zone 8

N

Miles

0   1/4   1/2

PART ONE:

Understanding the City

A Capsule History of Atlanta

In the 1700s, a network of Indian trails crisscrossed what is now Georgia. At least two of those trails met where what is now called Peachtree Creek flows into the Chattahoochee River. Creek Indians lived up and down the river in a village called "Standing Peachtree."

During the war of 1812, the British built a small log fort on the site of the Indian Village and called it Fort Peachtree. Another similar fort was built on Hog Mountain in what is now northern Gwinnett County, north of Atlanta. The two forts were connected by a rough road called Peachtree Road. That was the beginning of Peachtree Street and the naming craze that has lasted to this day: the most recent Atlanta street atlas lists 42 streets, roads, trails, and circles prefixed by "peachtree."

Despite its roots in the eighteenth century, Atlanta was a latecomer to the stage of history. Marietta, 20 miles to the north, was laid out in 1833. Decatur, six miles to the east, got going in 1822. Savannah, Georgia's first city, was founded in 1733 and played an important part in the American Revolution.

While a few mule-drawn wagons were rattling along Marietta Street, no more than a dirt rut beside the railroad tracks, in New England, ships were unloading Chinese silks and spices at bustling Boston Harbor. When Atlanta's population finally reached 10,000 in 1860, the eve of the Civil War, over a million people lived in New York City.

Atlanta originated as a southern railroad hub. In 1837, Stephen Harriman Long, the locating engineer for the Western and Atlantic Railroad, drove a stake in the ground near the present Five Points. The post marked the southern end of a railroad from Ross Landing, Tennessee, later to be called Chattanooga. Long called the stake the "Terminus." So, before it was known as Atlanta, the city was called Terminus. When the city adopted its first seal in 1854, it showed a drawing of a steam locomotive.

During the Civil War, Atlanta's factories turned out cannons, tents, canteens, railroad cars, knives, belt buckles, saddles, pants, shirts, and Confederate gunboat armor. Thanks to its manufacturing muscle, the city became a prime target for the Union army.

In 1864, Union General William Tecumseh Sherman left Chattanooga. After a battle-punctuated march along the route of the Western and Atlantic Railroad laid out 27 years before, he laid siege to Atlanta and eventually set it afire. After the conflagration on November 14 and 15, only 400 structures remained.

In 1868, a post-war Union administration moved the capital of Georgia from Milledgeville to Atlanta as a kind of punishment for the state's conduct during the war. The next year, the Georgia Railroad Freight Depot was completed on old Alabama Street. Over the next 100 years bridges spanned the railroad tracks and eventually covered them. The bridges concealed the first floors of the buildings that fronted the tracks. In 1968 this area was rediscovered, restored, and tagged "Underground Atlanta," a bustling tourist attraction with restaurants, bars, and shops. The original freight depot, with significant modifications, still stands at the main entrance to the tourist attraction.

By 1881 the city had begun to grow again in earnest, spreading like spokes from its center at Five Points. That year's International Cotton Exposition in Atlanta not only launched the "New South" movement in America but defined the standard for it. In 1886, Atlanta pharmacist John S. Pemberton created a headache remedy he called Coca-Cola. In 1887, President Grover Cleveland and Mrs. Cleveland, along with 200,000 visitors, attended the Piedmont Exposition.

The 40 years from the 1880s through the 1920s were prosperous, booming years. Northern investment poured into the city. Railroads expanded. Ford built a Model-T plant. Coca-Cola prospered, generating astounding corporate and private profits. Personal wealth built grand Victorian houses and mansions along Peachtree Street.

After a lull during the Great Depression and World War II, annexation in 1952 extended the city limits from 35 to 118 square miles, placing Atlanta among the 25 largest cities in the United States. The 1960s saw continued, even phenomenal growth, with the building of 15 new skyscrapers.

Today the center of downtown has shifted north, from its origins at Five Points to the intersection of Peachtree and International Boulevard, the site of John Portman's 70-story Peachtree Plaza Hotel, the tallest hotel in the world. The hill on which the Peachtree Plaza stands, at an elevation of 1,070 feet, is the highest geographical point in the city.

The Atlanta Skyline

After the completion of One Atlantic Center in 1987, then known as the IBM Tower, Atlantans looked up and realized they had quite a skyline. The 50-story, pink granite building capped with a copper pyramid gave the city a point of reference in Midtown. It established a visual link between the development of downtown and the tall buildings going up around Lenox Square.

Since the completion of One Atlantic Center, many dramatic new skyscrapers have poked their heads above the horizon: GLG Grand, One Peachtree Center, 1100 Peachtree, and 191 Peachtree, to name four of the most exciting examples. In addition, Atlanta architects and developers seem to be in competition to see who can light the tops of the buildings in the most dramatic fashion. At night, driving south to north along the connector, the line of tall buildings from Five Points all the way out Peachtree Street to 14th Street looks like a strand of multicolored jewels.

There is no better illustration of Atlanta's "linear" nature than the way its skyscrapers extend in a curving line from downtown to Lenox Square. A surprising number of Atlanta's tallest, most dramatic structures are on, or a block or so to either side of, Peachtree Street.

As well as being a distinctive Atlanta address, Peachtree follows the crest of a ridge, which gives added height to buildings, making them appear more prominent from a distance.

—— Skyline Views

Thanks in part to the hilly piedmont terrain in north-central Georgia, the Atlanta skyline has a way of surprising you at unexpected moments, suddenly looming up as you drive over the crest of a hilltop in Ansley Park or as you approach the city from the west along I-20. Here are some particularly good views of the skyline that are easy to find:

1. Along the Connector. Driving south along the connector between Martin Luther King, Jr. Boulevard and Ralph McGill Boulevard, there is a good view of the skyline. On a clear night you can see some of the buildings clustered around Lenox Square.

2. *The Jackson Street Bridge.* Photographers, TV cameramen, and illustrators have long used this bridge on the east side of the city as a vantage point from which to view the skyline. Chances are, if you've seen a panoramic shot of the skyline, it has been taken from this bridge.

Margaret Mitchell, author of *Gone with the Wind,* was born in 1900 in her grandmother's house, which stood at this location, the intersection of Jackson Street and Cain Street. The house survived the Civil War but burned in the big Atlanta fire of 1917. Not only did Margaret Mitchell communicate her mental and emotional point of view about Atlanta to people all over the world through her writing, but long after her death the actual physical point of view she had of the city as a child has persisted via newspapers, magazines, and television.

From downtown, take North Avenue east to Parkway Drive. Turn right and follow Parkway a few blocks until it turns into Jackson Street. The bridge is in the first block of Jackson Street. Margaret Mitchell was born at 296 Cain Street, which dead-ends into Jackson at that point. It is best to visit this location during the day; unfortunately, it is not safe at night.

3. *The Exit #29 Bridge.* Driving south on I-85 take Exit #29, also marked "GA 13 South, Peachtree St." The bridge shoots you rapidly up and down giving you a roller coaster view of the city. The buildings around Lenox are visible on the far right.

4. *From Lindbergh.* From Peachtree take Lindbergh east to the intersection of Piedmont Avenue. Turn left on Piedmont then immediately left again on Lindbergh. Park free at the MARTA station on the right if you want to linger over the view.

— *More about Atlanta Architecture*

If you are interested in digging deeper into the architecture of Atlanta, an excellent book, *The American Institute of Architects Guide to the Architecture of Atlanta,* published in 1993, will help you do that. Its 365 pages are filled with informed text by Isabelle Gournay, recent photographs by Paul G. Beswick, and helpful maps prepared at Georgia State University under the expert direction of Jeff McMichael. It is an indispensable companion to a detailed exploration of Atlanta's architecture. It is available at bookstores throughout the city, but the most interesting place to buy it is at the Architecture Book Store run by the Atlanta Chapter of AIA in Peachtree Center (see "Shopping").

Atlanta Neighborhoods

Imagine that you are looking at Atlanta from a satellite miles above the city. There are at least three ways you can perceive the view below.

One is to see Atlanta circled by the perimeter highway and divided by interstate highways into pie-shaped slices. The zone map in this guide reflects that view. Another is to visualize Atlanta as a linear city following the winding seven-mile course of Peachtree Street. Both of these are accurate and helpful ways of understanding Atlanta. But the third—the most interesting—way is to see Atlanta as an interlocking series of neighborhoods, each neighborhood resembling a cluster of grapes on a meandering vine.

If you ask an intown resident where he or she lives, the answer is not, "On Morningside Drive," but, "In Morningside." A person does not live on Virginia Avenue. He or she lives in "Virginia-Highland." The Atlanta Department of Planning and Development has identified 230 neighborhoods inside the perimeter. Each is a source of pride for its residents. The 15 described here are the most commonly recognized and the most scenic.

Atlanta neighborhoods are clusters of trees and residential dwellings nestled among high-density urban development. In many ways they are like many small towns inside one big city. These neighborhoods are unique to Atlanta, and come as a genuine surprise to visitors more accustomed to the concrete grid patterns of other large cities.

The Atlanta visitor interested in getting a sense of what the city is really about should explore two or three of these neighborhoods. It makes an ideal driving tour for people who enjoy comparing different types of houses and lifestyles to those of their own hometowns. From the urban frontier where the restored Victorian homes of Inman Park border hip Little Five Points, to the reserved, enclave of Brookwood Hills, each neighborhood has its own personality. Here is a capsule summary of each.

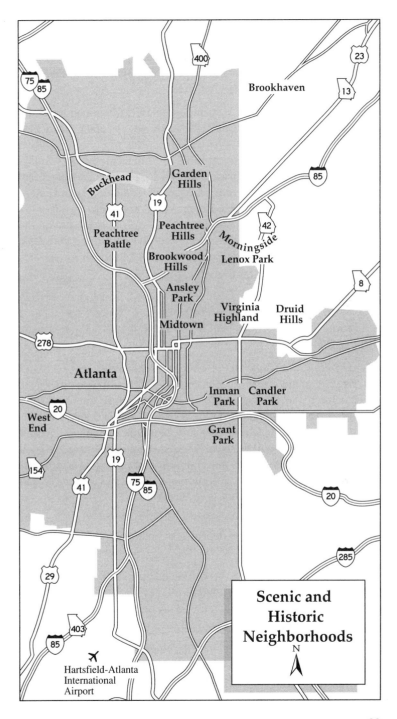

Scenic and
Historic
Neighborhoods

N

1. Brookhaven (Zone 4).   Definitely an upscale kind of place. A little staid, even. Expensive houses sit along the wandering Brookhaven Drive that borders Capital City Golf Club.

2. Buckhead (Zone 3).   An affluent, upscale neighborhood generally defined by W. Paces Ferry Road, Peachtree Road, and Habersham. Few residential neighborhoods in America surpass the beauty of the rolling dogwood- and magnolia-covered hills, the immaculate landscaping, and the grand houses that sit back from Northside Drive, Tuxedo Road, and Andrews Drive. The Governor's Mansion and the Atlanta History Center are in this neighborhood. Robert Woodruff, the patriarch of the Coca-Cola Company, lived here. Ivan Allen, mayor of the city in the 1960s, lives here. According to one real estate consulting company, there are 105 Buckhead residences valued at $1 million or more.

3. Garden Hills (Zone 3).   A settled, middle-class neighborhood between Peachtree, Piedmont, and Pharr roads. North Fulton High School, where many old-time Atlantans went to school, was located here. It was the high school featured in Anne Rivers Siddons's book *Peachtree Road.*

4. Peachtree Battle (Zone 3).   Could be considered a part of Buckhead, but this grand street (Peachtree Battle Avenue) with houses set well back has its own unique character. Definitely an Atlanta bastion of affluence, the neighborhood seems a little more approachable and welcoming than deepest Buckhead, maybe because the large houses are not set back quite so far from the street. The extension of the neighborhood to include Wesley Drive adds more modest houses and an interesting mix of younger residents. On nice afternoons Wesley is a circus of joggers, bicyclists, walkers, skaters, dogs, and kids.

5. Peachtree Hills (Zone 3).   Middle-range houses in a pleasant neighborhood of winding, tree-shaded streets, including Lindbergh and Peachtree Hills Avenue.

6. Brookwood Hills (Zone 3).   An affluent enclave hidden in a valley off Peachtree Street. Pat Conroy, author of *The Prince of Tides* and other novels, once lived in Brookwood Hills. This neighborhood is unique in that it has no through streets, making it extremely quiet and secluded.

7. Ansley Park (Zone 8).   Originally developed in 1904. Wide, curving streets meander among mature trees and small parks. Although none of the houses in this exclusive neighborhood are inexpensive, starting in the low $100,000s and going up to over $2 million, the wide range of house styles plus the well-tended parks and gardens make this one of the most attractive neighborhoods in the city.

8. *Morningside/Lenox Park (Zone 5).* A settled, pleasant neighborhood of houses in a wide range of styles and prices, around Morningside Drive and Rock Springs Road.

9. *Midtown (Zone 8).* These beautiful tree-lined streets, especially Myrtle and Penn, are popular with artists and writers. Midtown borders Piedmont Park and is a center of Atlanta's gay community.

10. *Virginia-Highland (Zone 5).* Centered around the colorful shopping intersection of Virginia Avenue and Highland Avenue, this is a neighborhood that brings together residents of many different lifestyles and incomes. Containing the most interesting mix of people in the city, it is a favorite neighborhood of writers. Atlanta's oldest bar, Atkins Park, and one of its most popular Sunday morning brunch spots, Murphy's, are located here.

11. *Druid Hills (Zone 5).* This tree-lined neighborhood lies between Emory University and Ponce de Leon Avenue. Oakdale, Springdale, and Lullwater are three of the prettiest streets in Atlanta, particularly in the spring when the dogwoods are in bloom. Frederick Law Olmstead designed some of the small parks that give the neighborhood a feeling of openness. The film *Driving Miss Daisy* was shot on location here. Miss Daisy's house is on Lullwater.

12. *Inman Park (Zone 5).* This was Atlanta's first suburb. Today, urban pioneers have restored Victorian houses built in the 1890s and the early 1900s. The city's first streetcar line ran out Edgewood Avenue to the Trolley Barn. The Barn still stands at 963 Edgewood Avenue.

13. *Candler Park (Zone 5).* Middle-class houses in a wide range of styles center on Candler Park golf course, given to the city by Asa Candler, founder of the Coca-Cola Company.

14. *West End (Zones 1, 2).* This is Atlanta's oldest neighborhood, as contrasted to its oldest planned suburb, Inman Park. The original building in West End was Whitehall Tavern on Whitehall Road, which led to Atlanta. Joel Chandler Harris, author of the Uncle Remus tales, lived here. His Victorian cottage is open as a museum (see "Attractions").

15. *Grant Park (Zone 6).* Restored homes circle the park where the Atlanta Zoo and Cyclorama are located.

PART TWO: Planning Your Visit to Atlanta

When to Go

Avoiding Crowds

In general, popular tourist sites are busier on weekends than on weekdays, and Saturdays are busier than Sundays. Big games draw many people to town, and weekends draw lots of regional out-of-towners making shopping pilgrimages.

If you're here to do business at a trade show or convention, you're in luck. Atlanta is one of the great convention cities of America, impressively equipped to serve your needs. The city's Georgia World Congress Center is the busiest convention center in the world. Repeat: the busiest.

If you're a nonconvention-goer and want to avoid convention madness downtown, check out the big meeting dates and schedule around them. The convention calendar includes the largest, most city-boggling conventions and shows, so you can choose to witness their spectacle or not.

The most monstrous crowds in Atlanta are those created by daily routine. Driving in weekday rush-hour traffic, among thousands of Atlanta's suburban residents, should be avoided at all costs.

If you're driving to Atlanta, try to arrive on a weekend or during nonrush hours—before 7 A.M. or between 9:30 A.M. and 3 P.M. Afternoon traffic doesn't begin to clear up until 6:30 P.M. or so.

One final note about avoiding crowds: Atlanta's MARTA public transportation system is a great way to get around, no matter how crowded the city may be (see "MARTA: An Introduction" page 113).

Choosing a Time to Visit

The best time to visit Atlanta is in the spring or fall, when the weather is most pleasant and nature puts on a show. With white dogwood blossoms and pink azaleas covering the rolling piedmont hills, Atlanta in the spring is a gloriously beautiful city. In the fall, mild temperatures along with colorful oak, hickory, and maple leaves hang on until just before Christmas.

But if you can't come in spring or fall, you may still enjoy mild, pleasant weather almost any time of year.

The most uncomfortable season is summer. Summers are hottest in July, August, and early September. But, even in the hottest months, Atlanta's relatively high elevation, 1,000 feet, saves it from the stifling heat and humidity inflicted on southern cities like Houston, New Orleans, and Washington.

Winters are mild. Atlanta will have one or two snowstorms a year, bringing the city to a halt and sending radio weather broadcasters into fits of hysteria. If you're from up North you'll be amused by the histrionics over a "big" snowstorm of one inch. But you still won't be able to get around.

Some of the prettiest days of the year come in mid-February when the sun is bright, the sky is blue, the temperature creeps up into the 60s. Here are the city's average monthly temperatures, in degrees Fahrenheit:

	High	*Low*
January	51	33
February	55	35
March	63	42
April	73	50
May	80	59
June	86	66
July	88	69
August	88	69
September	82	64
October	73	51
November	63	41
December	54	35

Warning: Population Explosion

Be forewarned that Atlanta is home to some of the largest conventions and trade shows in the world. If you attempt to visit Atlanta while one of these monsters is in progress, you will find hotel rooms scarce and expensive, restaurants crowded, rental car fleets sold out, and empty cabs impossible to find. To help you avoid the crowds, we have included a calendar of those conventions and trade shows large enough to affect your visit (see pages 99–102).

Getting to Atlanta

Atlanta is the transportation hub of the Southeast, so getting there is no problem whether you decide to fly, drive, or take the train.

If you fly, you'll arrive at Atlanta Hartsfield International Airport, one of the easiest airports to use in the world. Taxis, rental car companies, and Atlanta's rapid rail system, MARTA, connect the airport with downtown, a short seven miles away.

If you drive, you will most likely enter the city on one of the three interstate highways that converge in Atlanta: I-75, I-85, or I-20. These are linked by a 63-mile perimeter road, I-285, that circles the city. Try to plan your arrival so that you arrive at a time other than rush hour. Morning and evening traffic clogs all the freeways and there is no escape from it.

Parking in Atlanta is easy to find and relatively inexpensive. You shouldn't have to pay more than $8 per day. Some hotels have free parking for guests. This is usually the case if your accommodations are on the perimeter or along one of the interstate highways.

If you are arriving via rail, a MARTA bus stops just outside the Amtrak Station on Peachtree Street and connects conveniently to the city-wide rail system. Many of the city's best accommodations are within walking distance of MARTA stations

No matter how you choose to get to Atlanta, once you are there you'll find that if you want to venture very far away from MARTA's rail line, you'll need a car, your own or a rental. Atlanta is an odd mix of far-flung suburban developments growing like kudzu vine and settled intown neighborhoods connected by winding tree-lined streets. Attractions some distance from the central city like Six Flags and Stone Mountain Park can be reached by public transportation but not conveniently. Even those closer in like the Atlanta Zoo, Cyclorama, and Atlanta History Center are more fun when you can drive to them on your own schedule instead of spending hours waiting for trains and busses. To really see, enjoy, and understand the city, you'll have to do some driving.

How to Get More Information on Atlanta before You Visit

To receive information about Atlanta and the Atlanta area in advance of your trip, write or call the following:

The Metro Atlanta Convention and Visitors Bureau, 233 Peachtree Street, Atlanta, GA 30303; phone (404) 521-6688—for information on attractions, hotels, conventions.

The Atlanta Chamber of Commerce, 235 International Boulevard, NW, Atlanta, GA 30303; phone (404) 880-9000—for information on business statistics and population growth, relocation, and employment. When calling, ask for the public information department.

The Georgia Department of Industry, Trade, and Tourism, P.O. Box 1776, Atlanta, GA 30301; phone (404) 656-3590 or (800) 847-4842. Ask specifically for the publication *Georgia on My Mind,* which includes over 100 pages listing attractions, fairs, interesting side trips, accommodations, and state parks. Also request a Georgia state map.

Georgia Department of Natural Resources, Division of State Parks and Historic Sites, 205 Butler Street, SE, Suite 1352, Atlanta, GA 30334; phone (404) 656-3530. Ask for the free brochure titled *Georgia State Parks and Historic Sites.*

Forest Supervisor, Chattahoochee-Oconee National Forests, USDA Forest Service, 508 Oak Street NW, Gainsville, GA 30501; phone (770) 536-0541. Ask for the free *Recreation Directory,* which provides information about the forests and 40 recreation areas, including facilities, directions, and vicinity maps. It is an excellent initial planning tool for discovering outdoor recreation opportunities in Georgia's national forests.

Resource Managers Office, U.S. Army Corps of Engineers, Lake Sidney Lanier, P.O. Box 567, Buford, GA 30518; phone (770) 945-

9531. Ask for their brochure on Lake Lanier, which includes a fold-out map showing marinas, camping, and day-use areas.

In addition there are several information centers where you can pick up brochures, maps, and advice in person:

Atlanta Hartsfield International Airport. At the head of the escalator leading up from the passenger concourses between the north and south baggage claim areas. Operated by the Atlanta Convention and Visitors Bureau.

Underground Atlanta. On the upper level at the corner of Upper Alabama Street and Pryor next to Heritage Row. Operated by the Atlanta Convention and Visitors Bureau.

Lenox Square. In the concierge's area near the main Peachtree Street entrance. Operated by the Atlanta Convention and Visitors Bureau.

Peachtree Center. In the food court near the elevators across from Wolf Camera. Operated by the Peachtree Center Merchants Association, but distributes about the same information as is available from the Atlanta Convention and Visitors Bureau information centers.

Downtown. Welcome South, a consortium of tourism groups including the Atlanta Convention and Visitors Bureau and the Georgia Department of Industry and Trade, operates a large information center at the corner of International Boulevard and Spring Street. Here you will find information on Atlanta and Georgia as well as other states in the region.

A Calendar of Annual Events

Atlanta's Dogwood Festival in spring, and county fairs in and around the city in fall, make those seasons memorable times to visit. And as Atlanta matures, it is becoming a holiday kind of town. New Year's, St. Patrick's Day, July 4th, Halloween, and Christmas are times for parades and festivals. Each year the holiday events expand. In addition, certain months are big for conventions.

When planning your trip to Atlanta, consider working your schedule to include (or exclude) the following events. Note that for the convenience of the business traveler, a separate convention calendar is provided in "Part Four: Visiting Atlanta on Business." If you are a nonbusiness traveler and want to avoid the worst crowds downtown, check the convention calendar before planning your trip. For exact dates, times, locations, and admission fees for the following, call in advance.

January

New Year's Celebrations. New Year's is a big event in Atlanta—clubs, hotel lobbies, and bars fill to overflowing with celebrants. Popular nightspots like the rotating glass bar at the top of the 70-story Peachtree Plaza Hotel and the blue revolving dome of the Hyatt Regency Hotel are accessible by reservation only.

The biggest public celebration takes place at Undergound Atlanta, where 200,000 Atlantans and out-of-town visitors gather to mark the end of the old year and the beginning of the new by watching the Big Peach descend the light tower. Families and those interested in nonalcoholic celebration congregate in Midtown between 14th Street and Pershing Point.

CONSUMER TIPS Use the hotel listings in Part Three to select a hotel near Underground, and book a reservation well in advance.

ADDITIONAL INFORMATION Underground Atlanta, 50 Upper Alabama Street, Suite 007, Atlanta, GA 30303; phone (404) 523-2311.

Atlanta Boat Show. The biggest boat show between Miami and New York, this one draws potential buyers from 10-foot canoes to 85-foot yachts. Major houseboat manufacturers, SCUBA diving, salt and freshwater fishing, and water-related travel are represented by displays and demonstrations. Over 100,000 people attend to see $12 million in boats. Usually the first weekend in January. Admission fee.

CONSUMER TIPS Book a special boat show hotel package to save on both boat show admission and hotel room.

ADDITIONAL INFORMATION National Marine Manufacturers Association, 400 Arthur Godfrey Road, Suite 310, Miami Beach, FL 33140; phone (305) 531-8410.

King Week. A week-long series of speeches, films, seminars, and music celebrating the birth of civil rights leader and Nobel Prize recipient Dr. Martin Luther King, Jr. The week begins with an interfaith service and ends with a parade down Auburn Avenue. The second weekend in January. Most events free.

CONSUMER TIPS Use the hotel listings in Part Three to select a hotel near Auburn Avenue.

ADDITIONAL INFORMATION Martin Luther King, Jr. Center, 449 Auburn Avenue, NE, Atlanta, GA 30312; phone (404) 524-1956.

February

Goodwill Book Sale. The largest used book sale in Atlanta begins the first full week in February and lasts for a week. Over 300,000 books fill the lower level of Northlake Mall. Prices are cheap, starting at 50 cents.

CONSUMER TIPS Arrive early on the first day. People wait for this all year and leave pushing grocery carts loaded with paperbacks and hardbacks.

ADDITIONAL INFORMATION Northlake Mall, phone (770) 938-3564; Goodwill, phone (404) 377-0441.

Southeastern Flower Show. Gardens, landscaping, thousands of flowers in early bloom, trees, retail shops, lectures, and demonstrations are all part of this show. Organizers create elaborate landscaped gardens on three acres in the Town Hall Exhibition Center on North Avenue in

Midtown. Admission fee is in the $10 range. This event usually happens around the last week of February and extends over five days.

CONSUMER TIPS   Wear comfortable walking shoes and take a sweater.

ADDITIONAL INFORMATION   (404) 888-5638.

March

St. Patrick's Day Celebration.   The Hibernian Benevolent Society of Atlanta has been sponsoring the downtown St. Patrick's Day parade for 113 years, making it the oldest continuous civic event in Atlanta. This is a hometown type parade, with an easygoing, family atmosphere. The Buckhead parade, which begins at 2:30 P.M., is more of a hard-partying celebration that extends into the evening hours in this Atlanta entertainment center's bars and lounges. March 17th. Free.

CONSUMER TIPS   Free parking is available at the site.

ADDITIONAL INFORMATION   Call the Hibernian Benevolent Society of Atlanta, phone (404) 505-1208; Underground Atlanta, phone (404) 523-2311.

Spring Celebration at Callaway Gardens.   If this is not *the* top show of azaleas in the South, it certainly ranks among the very top. Visitors drive along a six-mile trail to "ooh" and "aah" at the banks of red, pink, white, and purple blooms.

CONSUMER TIPS   Make a weekend of it. Callaway Gardens is a beautiful Georgia resort, one-and-a-half hours south of Atlanta, with golf, tennis, good dining, and interesting places to see nearby. Book well in advance.

ADDITIONAL INFORMATION   Highway 27, Pine Mountain, GA 31822; phone (800) 282-8181.

Atlanta Home Show.   This is a consumer-oriented show with landscaping, pools, spas, architecture, fencing, furniture—anything that has to do with the southern good life. Show organizers build several new features each year, such as a 5,000-square-foot garden, a steel-frame house, or a log cabin. The show also features celebrity appearances and educational seminars. Usually takes place in mid-March at Georgia World Congress Center and in September at Cobb Galleria Centre. Admission fee.

CONSUMER TIPS   Take your charge card, there's plenty to buy here.

ADDITIONAL INFORMATION   113 Hightower Trail, Atlanta, GA 30350; phone (770) 998-9800.

Civil War Relic Show.   Civil War buffs and dealers display and sell relics, weapons, newspapers, books, clothing, and other artifacts. This event is held in the Exhibit Hall at the State Farmers Market, about 12 miles south of Atlanta. Over 300 tables. Admission fee.

CONSUMER TIPS   Come early for the best selection. Attend later to negotiate prices with dealers.

ADDITIONAL INFORMATION   102 S. Main Street, Jonesboro, GA 30236; phone (770) 477-9159.

Antebellum Jubilee.   Set around the Stone Mountain Plantation, which was imported from Dickey near Albany in south Georgia, this re-creation of life in the antebellum period includes a Civil War encampment.

CONSUMER TIPS   This would be a good time to plan a trip to Stone Mountain that would include a number of other attractions. See the Stone Mountain description under "Atlanta's Attractions." March or April. Admission fee to park.

ADDITIONAL INFORMATION   P.O. Box 778, Stone Mountain, GA 30086; phone (770) 498-5702.

April

Steeplechase.   Thoroughbreds race over brush jumps. With its affluent crowd dressed in tweed jackets and hats, driving antique autos, and tail-gating out of wicker baskets, the steeplechase is an opportunity to watch both people and horse racing. April 6.

CONSUMER TIPS   Advance tickets only.

ADDITIONAL INFORMATION   Atlanta Steeplechase, 3160 Northside Parkway, Atlanta, GA 30327; phone (404) 237-7436.

Kennesaw/Big Shanty Festival.   This festival focuses on re-enactments of the Battle of Kennesaw Mountain, which took place as Union General William T. Sherman marched from Chattanooga south to Atlanta. There are also crafts, food, and a downtown parade. Free.

CONSUMER TIPS   Visit Big Shanty Museum while you're in the area (see the description under "Atlanta's Attractions").

ADDITIONAL INFORMATION   P.O. Box 777, Kennesaw, GA 30144; phone (770) 423-1330.

Georgia Renaissance Festival.   A 16th-century English country fair is re-created on 30 acres of land about 20 miles south of Atlanta. Kings, queens, knights, court jesters, jugglers, minstrels, fire eaters, some 100 craftspeople, and demonstrations. Weekends April through June. Admission about $10 for adults.

CONSUMER TIPS   The earlier spring weekends are best, before it gets too hot.

ADDITIONAL INFORMATION   P.O. Box 986, Fairburn, GA 30213; phone (770) 964-8575.

Dogwood Festival.   A three-day weekend celebration that corresponds, everyone hopes, to the peak dogwood season. Even the most jaded veterans agree that the blooming of the dogwoods is a special time in Atlanta, a city known for its trees and intown neighborhoods. Held in Piedmont Park in Midtown Atlanta, the festival includes 120 artists, 50 crafters, live music on three stages, and a big children's area.

CONSUMER TIPS   Ride MARTA to the Arts Center Station and walk east on 14th Street to Piedmont Park. There is no more beautiful season to plan a trip to the city. This is a great time to take a walking tour of Atlanta.

ADDITIONAL INFORMATION   Atlanta Dogwood Festival, 4 Executive Park Drive, Suite 1217, Atlanta, GA 30329; phone (404) 329-0501.

Inman Park Festival and Tour of Homes.   About 15 restored Victorian homes in Atlanta's oldest planned suburb are open to the public. The dedicated house inspector can see most of the homes in one day. Many allow two days to enjoy what may be Atlanta's most interesting homes tour. Tickets are about $12.

CONSUMER TIPS   Ride MARTA to the Inman Park Reynoldstown Station and walk north on Hurt Street into the heart of the residential area.

ADDITIONAL INFORMATION   (404) 242-4895.

May

Prater's Mill Country Fair.   Two hundred artists and craftspeople display their handiwork in a rural setting around an operating grist mill. Take I-75 Exit #138 and follow the signs on GA Highway 2, about ten miles north of Dalton. Mother's Day weekend.

CONSUMER TIPS   With 150 manufacturers and 100 outlet stores, Dalton is known as the "Carpet Capital of the World." Combine the visit to Prater's Mill Fair with outlet carpet shopping. Outlets are easy to spot.

ADDITIONAL INFORMATION   For the fair call (706) 275-6455. For outlet info, contact Dalton Chamber of Commerce, 524 Holiday Avenue, Dalton, GA 30720; phone (706) 278-7373.

Cotton Pickin' Country Fair.   Antiques, crafts, and a country fair are set around an old cotton-ginning complex in the tiny community of Gay.

CONSUMER TIPS   Gay is about 30 miles from Callaway Gardens and Warm Springs (site of FDR's Little White House). Combine two or three destinations into one pleasant drive through middle Georgia.

ADDITIONAL INFORMATION   P.O. Box 1, Gay, GA 30218.

Atlanta Jazz Festival.   Names like Wynton Marsalis, Ron Carter, and Nancy Wilson perform in Atlanta city parks. Some events are free, others have an admission fee.

CONSUMER TIPS   For park concerts bring a picnic dinner and a blanket.

ADDITIONAL INFORMATION   Bureau of Cultural Affairs, 675 Ponce deLeon Avenue, NE, 5th Floor, Atlanta, GA 30308; phone (404) 817-6815.

June

Georgia Shakespeare Festival.   Three or four different Shakespearean plays, some traditional and some mounted in contemporary settings, are performed. Seating is for 400 under an open-sided tent. June through August. Admission fee.

CONSUMER TIPS   Picnic on the lawn before the performances.

ADDITIONAL INFORMATION   Oglethorpe University, 4484 Peachtree Road, NE, Atlanta, GA 30319; phone (404) 264-0020 (box office), (404) 688-8008 (administrative office).

National Black Arts Festival.   See listing for July.

July

July 4th.   The Fourth of July is an all-day celebration in Atlanta, starting with the Peachtree Road Race in the morning, continuing with the WSB-TV Salute to America parade that afternoon, and culminating in fireworks displays at locations throughout the city. The Road Race is a world-class event with 50,000 sweaty runners packed shoulder-to-shoulder, jogging down 6.2 miles of Peachtree Street. It's fun to run and fun to watch.

CONSUMER TIPS   Best place to watch the race is on Heart Attack Hill in front of Piedmont Hospital at Peachtree Street and Collier Road.

ADDITIONAL INFORMATION   On the road race, phone (404) 231-9064. On the parade, Salute America Parade, 1601 Peachtree Street, NE, Atlanta, GA 30309; phone (404) 897-7385. On the fireworks at Lenox Square Mall, probably the best display of explosions in the city, phone (404) 233-6767.

National Black Arts Festival.   A world-class event drawing participants and visitors from all over the United States and abroad, including 150 concerts, plays, films, dance performances, storytelling sessions, bookfairs, and workshops. Held biannually during the last week in July and the first week in August. In 1996, because of the Olympics, the festival will be held the last week in June and the first week in July.

CONSUMER TIPS   Be sure to make a visit to the Auburn Avenue area and Apex Museum part of your festival experience (see "Atlanta's Attractions").

ADDITIONAL INFORMATION   236 Forsyth Street, Suite 400, Atlanta, GA 30303; phone (404) 730-7315.

Civil War Encampment.   One hundred participants display and demonstrate Civil War weapons, uniforms, tents, command posts, camp life, and cooking. Firing of cannon is noisy and thrilling. This annual event marks the Battle of Atlanta, which took place on July 22, 1864.

CONSUMER TIPS   Participants are usually eager to talk about their interests in the Civil War; feel free to mingle and ask questions.

ADDITIONAL INFORMATION   Atlanta History Center, (404) 814-4000.

August

Georgia Mountain Fair.   The largest of Georgia's mountain country fairs, this one is something between a crafts fair and a county fair. Plenty of music, food, crafts, and clogging. Twelve days. Admission fee.

ADDITIONAL INFORMATION   Georgia Mountain Fair, US Highway 76, P.O. Box 444, Hiawassee, GA 30546; phone (706) 896-4191.

September

Arts Festival of Atlanta.   By far the biggest arts festival in the city, promoters claim it is attended by one million people each year. The celebration is centered in Centennial Olympic Park and extends throughout downtown. Artists and craftspeople from all over the country rent booth space to display and sell their work. Street performances throughout the park, site installations, and plenty of food. Some of Atlanta's best people-watching. Free.

CONSUMER TIPS   Parking here is impossible during this event. Take MARTA to the Arts Center station and walk, or take the MARTA special-event shuttle to the park.

ADDITIONAL INFORMATION   Arts Festival, 999 Peachtree Street, Atlanta, GA 30309; phone (404) 885-1125.

Powers Crossroads Country Fair and Arts Festival.   Popular for more than 20 years, this annual country fair has been the model for other fairs and festivals in the region. Three hundred craftspeople and artists show here. It takes all day to see it. Food, clogging, bluegrass music, blacksmithing, childrens' park.

About 35 miles south of Atlanta in Franklin. Take I-85 south to Georgia Highway 34 west to Franklin. Labor Day weekend. Admission fee.

CONSUMER TIPS   Another craft fair using a similar name sets up operation just off I-85 a few exits before the turn-off to Powers, on the same weekend. Keep going. Powers is the real thing.

ADDITIONAL INFORMATION   Coweta Festivals, Inc., P.O. Box 889, Newnan, GA 30264; phone (770) 253-2011.

Yellow Daisy Festival.   Four hundred craftspeople and entertainers at Stone Mountain Park make this one of the largest crafts fairs in the region. Admission fee to park.

CONSUMER TIPS   Stone Mountain Park itself is one of the area's best and largest attractions. Allow plenty of time to explore, and read up on the park (see "Atlanta's Attractions") before you go.

ADDITIONAL INFORMATION   P.O. Box 778, Stone Mountain, GA 30086; phone (770) 498-5702.

Atlanta Greek Festival.   Greek food including gyros and souvlaki, Greek coffee, wine, merchandise, and travel films are popular with the 40,000 people who attend this four-day festival, an Atlanta tradition for 20 years. The festival centers around the Greek Orthodox cathedral in the Clairmont/Briarcliff area. Begins the last Thursday in September. Admission fee.

CONSUMER TIPS   You can't get there on MARTA. Call the church for directions by car.

ADDITIONAL INFORMATION   2500 Clairmont Road, Atlanta, GA 30329; phone (404) 633-5870 or (404) 633-7358.

Atlanta Home Show.   See listing for March.

October

Folklife Festival.   Candle-making, weaving, blacksmithing, and soap-making are some of the folk arts of the 1840s Georgia Piedmont that are demonstrated at the Atlanta History Center's Tullie Smith House. Popular with school groups, this two-week program is of interest to anyone who wants to know what life was like in this section of Georgia in the last century. Admission fee.

CONSUMER TIPS   The History Center also offers a vast array of Civil War memorabilia and the grand neoclassical Swan House, all on the grounds with the Tullie Smith House. If history is your thing, allow plenty of time here.

ADDITIONAL INFORMATION   Atlanta History Center (404) 814-4000.

Great Miller Lite Chili Cook-Off.   A one-day event with hundreds of kinds of chili and Brunswick stew served in a festival atmosphere of country music and cloggers at Stone Mountain Park. Admission fee to park.

CONSUMER TIPS   Read up on Stone Mountain (see "Atlanta's Attractions") before you go.

ADDITIONAL INFORMATION (770) 498-5702.

Scottish Festival and Highland Games. One hundred clans and societies gather at Stone Mountain to pipe and drum, show off their kilts, folk dance, and throw tremendous logs and hammers. The three-day event is the third full weekend in October. Admission fee to park.

CONSUMER TIPS Read up on the many things to see and do at Stone Mountain before you go.

ADDITIONAL INFORMATION (770) 498-5702.

Halloween. Like New Year's, the Fourth of July, and St. Patrick's Day, Halloween gets big play in Atlanta. Business booms at costume rental stores, haunted houses spring up all over the city, and clubs and bars promote special costume contests. Little Five Points and Buckhead are centers of activity.

CONSUMER TIPS It takes a pretty hip spook to enjoy Halloween in Little Five Points. Check it out during the day before you try it under a full moon.

ADDITIONAL INFORMATION (404) 659-3522.

Cotton Pickin' Country Fair. See the listing for May.

November

Big Bethel's Heaven Bound. For 60 years the religious musical pageant "Heaven Bound" has been a community tradition at Big Bethel, one of the anchor churches on Auburn Avenue. Church members perform the roles and sing in the choir.

ADDITIONAL INFORMATION Big Bethel Church, 220 Auburn Avenue, Atlanta, GA 30303; phone (404) 659-0248.

Lighting of the Great Tree. The lighting of Atlanta's Christmas tree, accompanied by brass bands and colorfully robed choirs, has long been a tradition that officially begins the Christmas season in the city. The event is now held at Underground Atlanta on Thanksgiving night. Free.

CONSUMER TIPS Take MARTA to the Five Points station.

ADDITIONAL INFORMATION (404) 523-2311 or (770) 913-5551.

December

Eggleston Children's Christmas Parade.   Bands, floats, giant helium balloons, and life-size cartoon characters parade down Peachtree Street. Free.

CONSUMER TIPS   Best vantage point is in front of Macy's, but you need to get there early.

ADDITIONAL INFORMATION   3312 Piedmont Road, Suite 506, Atlanta, GA 30305; phone (404) 264-9348.

Festival of Trees.   Now in its 21st year, this popular event has spawned similar festivals all over the country. The festival is held at the Georgia World Congress Center, where designers, school groups, garden clubs, and a variety of other sponsors cover 200 trees in imaginative, colorful decorations. Proceeds from the sale of tickets ($8 for adults and $5 for children) go to Egleston Children's Hospital.

CONSUMER TIPS   It takes two hours to see all the trees and let the kids escape to the Pink Pig, Egleston Express Train Ride.

ADDITIONAL INFORMATION   3312 Piedmont Road, Suite 506, Atlanta, GA 30305; phone (404) 264-9348.

Callaway Gardens Fantasy in Lights.   Thousands of visitors ride through six miles of Christmas lights arranged into theme sections such as "Winter Wonderland" and "The Nutcracker."

CONSUMER TIPS   A very popular and crowded Christmas attraction. You must buy tickets in advance.

ADDITIONAL INFORMATION   (800) 282-8181.

Candlelight Tours.   Candlelight tours of a grand mansion, the 1928 Swan House, and the humble 1840s Tullie Smith farmhouse (both on the grounds of the Atlanta History Center) on the same evening for one admission price. Piano and violin music accompany the Swan House tour, visitors hear banjos and dulcimers playing in the Tullie Smith House. Hors d'oeuvres and cider come with the $15 admission, plus there's a cash bar.

ADDITIONAL INFORMATION   Atlanta History Center, (404) 814-4000.

Christmas at Callanwolde. Decorators and interior designers festoon the rooms of this Druid Hills mansion, the former home of the son of Coca-Cola founder Asa Candler. Admission $8 for adults; discount for children and seniors.

CONSUMER TIPS   Park in the Georgia Mental Health Facility lot on Briarcliff and take the shuttle to Callanwolde (no parking on the grounds).

ADDITIONAL INFORMATION   Callanwolde Fine Arts Center, 980 Briarcliff Road, NE, Atlanta, GA 30306; phone (404) 872-5338.

Peach Bowl. Now that it's played in the comfortable 70,000-seat covered Georgia Dome rather than outside on a cold December afternoon, the Peach Bowl has become a major event in the city, drawing people not only for the game but to the New Year's celebrations in Underground, Buckhead, and other entertainment spots. Tickets to the game are about $40 each.

CONSUMER TIPS   Take MARTA to the Dome (see "Riding MARTA").

ADDITIONAL INFORMATION   P.O. Box 1336, Atlanta, GA 30301; phone (404) 586-8500.

—— *Event Information Sources*

For more information on events compatible with your interests, contact one or more of these sources before you visit.

The Atlanta History Center
3101 Andrews Drive, NW
Atlanta, GA 30305
(404) 814-4000

Callanwolde Fine Arts Center
980 Briarcliff Road, NE
Atlanta, GA 30306
(404) 872-5338

Callaway Gardens
Highway 27
Pine Mountain, GA 31822
(800) 282-8181

Georgia Trust for Historic
   Preservation
1516 Peachtree Street
Atlanta, GA 30309
(404) 881-9980

Georgia World Congress Center
285 International Boulevard, NW
Atlanta, GA 30313
(404) 223-4000

Martin Luther King, Jr. Center
   for Nonviolent Social Change
449 Auburn Avenue, NE
Atlanta, GA 30312
(404) 524-1956

Stone Mountain Park
Highway 78
Stone Mountain, GA 30086
(770) 498-5702

Underground Atlanta
50 Upper Alabama Street
Suite 007
Atlanta, GA 30303
(404) 523-2311

PART THREE: Hotels

Deciding Where to Stay

Atlanta will belong (as it always has) primarily to business travelers. Major league sports and numerous attractions notwithstanding, Atlanta is not a destination city for tourists. This being the case, the economics of hotel room pricing are driven by business, state government, and convention trade. This translates to high rack rates (a hotel's published room rate) and very few bargains during the work week.

If room rates in Atlanta have not soared to the levels encountered in Washington DC or Chicago, it is because construction of new hotels has for the past decade stayed pretty much in step with demand. New properties that came on line for the Olympics still help increase supply and hold rates in check, at least in a relative sense.

The good news, if you are a discriminating traveler, is that Atlanta offers a surprising number of unusually fine hotels, including quite a few suite properties. The bad news, of course, is that you can expect to pay dearly to stay in them.

In Atlanta, as in most cities, the better and more expensive hotels are located close to the city center, with less expensive hotels situated farther out. If you are willing to stay outside the city center, off the interstate, and commute into downtown, you can expect to pay less for your Marriott suburban room than you would for a Marriott city-center room.

Lodging properties are situated in clusters around Atlanta. The finer hotels are located: (1) downtown, (2) near Atlanta Hartsfield International Airport, (3) in Buckhead near the Lenox Square shopping district, and (4) in the suburb of Vinings by the Galleria and Cumberland malls. Less expensive lodging can be found along I-75, I-85, and I-20 outside of the perimeter highway (I-285).

In the greater Atlanta area, every hotel is seemingly close to something. No matter how far you are from downtown, the Georgia Dome, and Underground Atlanta, you can bank on your hotel being within spitting distance of some state government office, airport, industrial complex, or convention site that funnels platoons of business travelers into guest rooms. Because many hotels have their own captive markets, it can be surprisingly difficult, especially for a leisure traveler, to reserve a nice room at a decent price in a specific preferred location.

—— *Some Considerations*

1. When choosing your Atlanta lodging, make sure your hotel is situated in a location convenient to your recreation or business needs, and that it is in a safe and comfortable area. Please note that while it is not practical to walk to Georgia World Congress Center (the major convention venue) from many of the downtown hotels, larger conventions and trade shows provide shuttle service.

2. Find out how old the hotel is and when the guest rooms were last renovated. Request that the hotel send you its promotional brochure. Ask if brochure photos of guest rooms are accurate and current.

3. If you plan to take a car, inquire about the parking situation. Some hotels offer no parking at all, some charge dearly for parking, and some offer free parking.

4. If you are not a city dweller, or perhaps are a light sleeper, try to book a hotel on a more quiet side street. Ask for a room off the street and high up.

5. The Atlanta skyline is quite beautiful. If you are on a romantic holiday, ask for a room on a higher floor with a good view.

6. When you plan your budget, remember that Atlanta's combined room and sales tax is 13%.

7. Atlanta is one of the busiest convention cities in the United States. If your visit to Atlanta coincides with one or more major conventions or trade shows, hotel rooms will be both scarce and expensive. If, on the other hand, you are able to schedule your visit to avoid big meetings, you will have a good selection of hotels at surprisingly competitive prices. If you happen to be attending one of the big conventions, book early and use some of the tips listed below to get a discounted room rate. To assist you in timing your visit, we have included a convention and trade show calendar in "Part Four: Visiting Atlanta on Business."

Getting a Good Deal on a Room

Special Weekend Rates

Although well-located Atlanta hotels are tough for the budget conscious, it's not impossible to get a good deal, at least relatively speaking. For starters, most downtown hotels that cater to business, government, and convention travelers offer special weekend discount rates that range from 15–40% below normal weekday rates. You can find out about weekend specials by calling individual hotels or by consulting your travel agent.

Getting Corporate Rates

Many hotels offer discounted corporate rates (5–20% off rack). Usually you do not need to work for a large company or have a special relationship with the hotel to obtain these rates. Simply call the hotel of your choice and ask for their corporate rates. Many hotels will guarantee you the discounted rate on the phone when you make your reservation. Others may make the rate conditional on your providing some sort of bona fides, for instance a fax on your company's letterhead requesting the rate, or a company credit card or business card on check-in. Generally, the screening is not rigorous.

Half-Price Programs

The larger discounts on rooms (35–60%), in Atlanta or anywhere else, are available through half-price hotel programs, often called travel clubs. Program operators contract with an individual hotel to provide rooms at deep discounts, usually 50% off rack rate, on a "space available" basis. "Space available," in practice, generally means that you can reserve a room at the discounted rate whenever the hotel expects to be at less than 80% occupancy. A little calendar sleuthing to help you avoid city-wide conventions and special events will increase your chances of choosing a time when the discounts are available.

Most half-price programs charge an annual membership fee or directory subscription charge of $25–125. Once you are enrolled, you receive a membership card and a directory listing participating hotels. Examining the directory, you will notice immediately that there are many restrictions and exceptions. Some hotels, for instance, "black out" certain dates or times of year. Others may only offer the discount on certain days of the week, or require you to stay a certain number of nights. Still others may offer a much smaller discount than 50% off rack rate.

Programs specialize in domestic travel, international travel, or both. More established operators offer members between 1,000 and 4,000 hotels to choose from in the United States. All of the programs have a heavy concentration of hotels in California and Florida, and most have a very limited selection of participating properties in New York City or Boston. Offerings in other cities and regions of the United States vary considerably. The programs with the largest selections of Atlanta hotels are Encore, Innovative Travel, Travel America at Half Price (Entertainment Publications), International Travel Card, Privilege Card, and Quest. Each of these programs lists between 4 and 50 hotels in the greater Atlanta area.

Encore	(800) 638-0930
Entertainment Publications	(800) 285-5525
Innovative Travel	(800) 446-8357
International Travel Card	(800) 342-0558
Quest	(800) 638-9819

One problem with half-price programs is that not all hotels offer a full 50% discount. Another slippery problem is the base rate against which the discount is applied. Some hotels figure the discount on an exaggerated rack rate that nobody would ever have to pay. A few participating hotels may deduct the discount from a supposed "superior" or "upgraded" room rate, even though the room you get is the hotel's standard accommodation. Though hard to pin down, the majority of participating properties base discounts on the published rate in the *Hotel & Travel Index* (a quarterly reference work used by travel agents) and work within the spirit of their agreement with the program operator. As a rule, if you travel several times a year, your room rate savings will easily compensate you for program membership fees.

A noteworthy addendum: deeply discounted rooms through half-price programs are not commissionable to travel agents. In practical terms this means that you must ordinarily make your own inquiry calls and reservations. If you travel frequently, however, and run a lot of business through your travel agent, he or she will probably do your legwork, lack of commission notwithstanding.

Preferred Rates

If you cannot book the hotel of your choice through a half-price program, you and your travel agent may have to search for a lesser discount, often called a preferred rate. A preferred rate could be a discount made available to travel agents to stimulate their booking activity, or a discount initiated to attract a certain class of traveler. Most preferred rates are promoted through travel industry publications and are often accessible only through an agent.

We recommend sounding out your travel agent about possible deals. Be aware, however, that the rates shown on travel agents' computerized reservations systems are not always the lowest rates obtainable. Zero in on a couple of hotels that fill your needs in terms of location and quality of accommodations, and then have your travel agent call the hotel for the latest rates and specials. Hotel reps almost always respond more to travel agents because travel agents represent a source of additional business. As discussed earlier, there are certain specials that hotel reps will disclose *only* to travel agents. Travel agents also come in handy when the hotel you want is supposedly booked. A personal appeal from your agent to the hotel's director of sales and marketing will get you a room more than 50% of the time.

If you want to do your own research, Travelgraphics, in Norcross, Georgia (phone (800) 644-8757) will sell you a directory of preferred rates just like one travel agents use. With the directory in hand you can make your own arrangements or have your agent make them for you.

Wholesalers, Consolidators, and Reservation Services

If you do not want to join a program or buy a discount directory, you can take advantage of the services of a wholesaler or consolidator. Wholesalers and consolidators buy rooms, or options on rooms (room blocks), from hotels at a low, negotiated rate. They then resell the rooms at a profit through travel agents, tour packagers, or directly to the public. Most wholesalers and consolidators have a provision for returning unsold rooms to participating hotels but are not inclined to do so. The wholesaler's or consolidator's relationship with any hotel is predicated on volume. If they return rooms unsold, the hotel may not make as many rooms available to them the next time around. Thus wholesalers and consolidators often offer rooms at bargain rates, anywhere from

15–50% off rack, occasionally sacrificing their profit margins in the process, to avoid returning the rooms to the hotel unsold.

When wholesalers and consolidators deal directly with the public, they frequently represent themselves as "reservation services." When you call, you can ask for a rate quote for a particular hotel, or, alternatively, ask for their best available deal in the area where you prefer to stay. If there is a maximum amount you are willing to pay, say so. Chances are the service will find something that will work for you, even if they have to shave a dollar or two off their own profit. Sometimes you will have to pay for your room with a credit card when you make your reservation. Other times you will pay as usual, when you check out. Listed below are several services that frequently offer substantial discounts:

Quikbook	(800) 789-9887
RMC Travel	(800) 245-5738 or (800) 782-2674
Hotel Discounts (on line)	www.hoteldiscount.com

Alternative Lodging

Bed-and-breakfasts, country inns, and youth hostels offer viable lodging options in Atlanta. For general information on various accommodations, call the Atlanta Convention and Visitors Bureau at (404) 521-6600. For B&Bs and youth hostels year round, call International Bed & Breakfast Reservations at (404) 875-2882. Another source for B&Bs is Bed & Breakfast Atlanta at (404) 875-0525. A second youth hostel operator is Atlanta Dream Hostels at (404) 370-0380.

—— How to Evaluate a Travel Package

Hundreds of Atlanta package vacations are offered to the public each year. Packages should be a win/win proposition for both the buyer and the seller. The buyer only has to make one phone call and deal with a single salesperson to set up the whole vacation: transportation, rental car, lodging, meals, attraction admissions, and even golf and tennis. The seller, likewise, only has to deal with the buyer once, eliminating the need for separate sales, confirmations, and billing. In addition to streamlining sales, processing, and administration, some packagers also buy airfares in bulk on contract like a broker playing the commodities market. Buying a large number of airfares in advance allows the packager to buy them at a significant savings from posted fares. The same practice is also applied to hotel rooms. Because selling vacation packages is an efficient way of doing business, and because the packager can often buy individual package components (airfare, lodging, etc.) in bulk at discount, savings in operating expenses realized by the seller are sometimes passed on to the buyer so that, in addition to convenience, the package is also an exceptional value. In any event, that is the way it is supposed to work.

All too often, in practice, the seller cashes in on discounts and passes none on to the buyer. In some instances, packages are loaded with extras that cost the packager next to nothing but inflate the retail price sky-high. As you may expect, the savings to be passed along to customers remain somewhere in Fantasyland.

When considering a package, choose one that includes features you are sure to use. Whether you use all the features or not, you will most certainly pay for them. Second, if cost is of greater concern than convenience, make a few phone calls and see what the package would cost if you booked its individual components (airfare, rental car, lodging, etc.) on your own. If the package price is less than the a la carte cost, the package is a good deal. If the costs are about the same, the package is probably worth buying just for the convenience.

If your package includes a choice of rental car or airport transfers (transportation to and from the airport), take the rental car. If you take the car, be sure to ask if the package includes free parking at your hotel.

—— *Helping Your Travel Agent Help You*

When you call your travel agent, ask if he or she has been to Atlanta. If the answer is no, be prepared to give your travel agent some direction. Do not accept any recommendations at face value. Check out the location and rates of any suggested hotel and make certain that the hotel is suited to your itinerary.

Because some travel agents are unfamiliar with Atlanta, your agent may try to plug you into a tour operator's or wholesaler's preset package. This essentially allows the travel agent to set up your whole trip with a single phone call and still collect an 8–10% commission. The problem with this scenario is that most agents will place 90% of their Atlanta business with only one or two wholesalers or tour operators. In other words, it's the line of least resistance for them, and not much choice for you.

Travel agents will often use wholesalers who run packages in conjunction with airlines, like Delta's Dream Vacations. Because of the wholesaler's exclusive relationship with the carrier, these trips are very easy for travel agents to book. However, they probably will be more expensive than a package offered by a high-volume wholesaler who works with a number of airlines in a primary Atlanta market.

To help your travel agent get you the best possible deal, do the following:

1. Determine where you want to stay in Atlanta, and if possible choose a specific hotel. This can be accomplished by reviewing the hotel information provided in this guide, and by writing or calling hotels that interest you.

2. Check out the hotel deals and package vacations advertised in the Sunday travel section of the *Atlanta Journal-Constitution* newspaper. Often you will be able to find deals that beat the socks off anything offered in your local paper. See if you can find specials that fit your plans and include a hotel you like.

3. Call the hotels, wholesalers, or tour operators whose ads you have collected. Ask any questions you have concerning their packages, but do not book your trip with them directly.

4. Tell your travel agent about the deals you find and ask if he or she can get you something better. The deals in the paper will serve as a benchmark against which to compare alternatives proposed by your travel agent.

5. Choose from the options that you and your travel agent uncover. No matter which option you elect, have your travel agent book it. Even if you go with one of the packages in the newspaper, it will probably be commissionable (at no additional cost to you) and will provide the agent some return on the time invested on your behalf. Also, as a travel professional, your agent should be able to verify the quality and integrity of the deal.

—— *If You Make Your Own Reservation*

As you poke around trying to find a good deal, there are several things you should know. First, always call the specific hotel as opposed to the hotel chain's national 800 number. Quite often, the reservationists at the national 800 number are unaware of local specials. Always ask about specials before you inquire about corporate rates. Do not be reluctant to bargain. If you are buying a hotel's weekend package, for example, and want to extend your stay into the following week, you can often obtain at least the corporate rate for the extra days. Do your bargaining, however, before you check in, preferably when you make your reservations.

— *Hotel/Motel Toll-Free 800 Numbers*

For your convenience, we've listed the toll-free numbers for the following hotel and motel chains' reservation lines:

Best Western	(800) 528-1234 U.S. & Canada
	(800) 528-2222 TDD
Comfort Inn	(800) 228-5150 U.S.
Courtyard by Marriott	(800) 321-2211 U.S.
Days Inn	(800) 325-2525 U.S.
Doubletree	(800) 528-0444 U.S.
Econo Lodge	(800) 424-4777 U.S.
Embassy Suites	(800) 362-2779 U.S. & Canada
Fairfield Inn by Marriott	(800) 228-2800 U.S.
Guest Doubletree Suites	(800) 424-2900 U.S. & Canada
Hampton Inn	(800) 426-7866 U.S. & Canada
Hilton	(800) 445-8667 U.S.
	(800) 368-1133 TDD
Holiday Inn	(800) 465-4329 U.S. & Canada
Howard Johnson	(800) 654-2000 U.S. & Canada
	(800) 654-8442 TDD
Hyatt	(800) 233-1234 U.S. & Canada
Loew's	(800) 223-0888 U.S. & Canada
Marriott	(800) 228-9290 U.S. & Canada
	(800) 228-7014 TDD
Quality Inn	(800) 228-5151 U.S. & Canada
Radisson	(800) 333-3333 U.S. & Canada
Ramada Inn	(800) 228-3838 U.S.
	(800) 228-3232 TDD
Residence Inn by Marriott	(800) 331-3131 U.S.
Ritz-Carlton	(800) 241-3333 U.S.
Sheraton	(800) 325-3535 U.S. & Canada
Stouffer	(800) 468-3571 U.S. & Canada
Wyndham	(800) 822-4200 U.S.

Atlanta Lodging for Business Travelers

The primary considerations for business travelers are affordability and proximity to the site or area where you will transact your business. Identify the zone(s) where your business will take you, and then use the Hotel Information Chart at the end of this book to cross-reference the hotels located in that area. Once you have developed a short list of possible hotels that are conveniently located, fit your budget, and offer the standard of accommodation you require, you (or your travel agent) can make use of the cost-saving suggestions discussed earlier to obtain the lowest rate.

—— Lodging Convenient to the Georgia World Congress Center

If you are attending a meeting or trade show at the Georgia World Congress Center, the most convenient lodging is downtown Atlanta, where a number of hotels, practically speaking, are within walking distance. From most downtown hotels, the Georgia World Congress Center is a five-minute cab or shuttle ride away. We recommend that you leave your car at home and use shuttles and cabs.

Commuting to the Georgia World Congress Center from the suburbs or the airports during rush hour is something to be avoided if possible. If you want a room downtown, book early . . . very early. If you screw up and need a room at the last minute, try a wholesaler or reservation service, or one of the strategies listed below.

—— Convention Rates: How They Work and How to Do Better

If you are attending a major convention or trade show, it is probable that the meeting's sponsoring organization has negotiated "convention rates" with a number of hotels. Under this arrangement, hotels agree to "block" a certain number of rooms at an agreed upon price for convention-goers. Sometimes, as in the case of a small meeting, only one hotel is involved. In the event of a large "city-wide" convention at the Georgia World Congress Center, however, almost all downtown and airport hotels will participate in the room block.

Because the convention sponsor brings a lot of business to the city and reserves a large number of rooms, it usually can negotiate a volume discount on the room rates, a rate that should be substantially below rack rate. The bottom line, however, is that some conventions and trade shows have more bargaining clout and negotiating skill than others. Hence, your convention sponsor may or may not be able to obtain the lowest possible rate.

Once a convention or trade show sponsor has completed negotiations with participating hotels, it will send its attendees a housing list that includes all the hotels serving the convention, along with the special convention rate for each. When you receive the housing list, you can compare the convention rates with the rates obtainable using the strategies covered in the previous section. If the negotiated convention rate doesn't sound like a good deal, you can try to reserve a room using a half-price club, a consolidator, or a tour operator. Remember, however, that many of the deep discounts are available only when the hotel expects to be at less than 80% occupancy, a condition that rarely prevails when a big convention is in town.

Strategies for Beating Convention Rates

There are several tactics for getting around convention rates:

1. Reserve early. Most big conventions and trade shows announce meeting sites one to three years in advance. Get your reservation booked as far in advance as possible using a half-price club. If you book well ahead of the time the convention sponsor sends out the housing list, chances are good that the hotel will accept your reservation.

2. Compare your convention's housing list with the list of hotels presented in this guide. You may be able to find a suitable hotel that is not on the housing list.

3. Use MARTA. If your meeting is at the Georgia World Congress Center, the Atlanta Market Center, or one of the large downtown hotels, you can travel to the meeting site quickly and economically on MARTA, Atlanta's mass transit system. Find a hotel

away from downtown, but on the MARTA system. This will often enable you to obtain a better room rate while providing convenient access to your meeting. At the Georgia World Congress Center particularly, your commuting time on MARTA will be less than for attendees walking or shuttling from downtown hotels (see "Hotels near MARTA Stations").

4. Use a local reservations agency or consolidator. This is also a good strategy to employ if, for some reason, you need to make reservations at the last minute. Local reservations agencies and consolidators almost always control some rooms, even in the midst of a huge convention or trade show.

5. Stay in a bed-and-breakfast, either downtown or near a MARTA line.

Hotels and Motels: Rated and Ranked

—— What's in a Room?

Except for cleanliness, state of repair, and decor, most travelers do not pay much attention to hotel rooms. There is, of course, a discernible standard of quality and luxury that differentiates Motel 6 from Holiday Inn, Holiday Inn from Marriott, and so on. In general, however, hotel guests fail to appreciate that some rooms are better engineered than others.

Contrary to what you might suppose, designing a hotel room is (or should be) a lot more complex than picking a bedspread to match the carpet and drapes. Making the room usable to its occupants is an art, a planning discipline that combines both form and function.

Decor and taste are important, certainly. No one wants to spend several days in a room where the decor is dated, garish, or even ugly. But beyond the decor, there are variables that determine how "livable" a hotel room is. In Atlanta, for example, we have seen some beautifully appointed rooms that are simply not well-designed for human habitation. The next time you stay in a hotel, pay attention to the details and design elements of your room. Even more than decor, these are the things that will make you feel comfortable and at home.

It takes the *Unofficial Guide* researchers about 40 minutes to inspect a hotel room. Here are a few of the things we check that you may want to start paying attention to:

Room Size.   While some smaller rooms are cozy and well designed, a large and uncluttered room is generally preferable, especially for a stay of more than three days.

Temperature Control, Ventilation, and Odor.   The guest should be able to control the temperature of the room. The best system, because it's so quiet, is central heating and air conditioning, controlled by the room's own thermostat. The next best system is a room module heater and air conditioner, preferably controlled by an automatic thermostat, but usually by manually operated button controls. The worst system is central heat and air without any sort of room thermostat or guest control.

The vast majority of hotel rooms have windows or balcony doors that have been permanently secured shut. Though there are some legitimate safety and liability issues involved, we prefer windows and balcony doors that can be opened to admit fresh air. Hotel rooms should be odor free, smoke free, and not feel stuffy or damp.

Room Security.   Better rooms have locks that require a plastic card instead of the traditional lock and key. Card and slot systems allow the hotel to change the combination or entry code of the lock with each new guest who uses the room. A burglar who has somehow acquired a room key to a conventional lock can afford to wait until the situation is right before using the key to gain access. Not so with a card and slot system. Though the largest hotels and hotel chains with lock and key systems usually rotate their locks once each year, they remain vulnerable to hotel thieves much of the time. Many smaller or independent properties rarely rotate their locks.

In addition to the entry lock system, the door should have a deadbolt and preferably a chain that can be locked from the inside. A chain by itself is not sufficient. Doors should also have a peephole. Windows and balcony doors, if any, should have secure locks.

Safety.   Every room should have a fire or smoke alarm, clear fire instructions, and preferably a sprinkler system. Bathtubs should have a nonskid surface, and shower stalls should have doors that either open outward or slide side-to-side. Bathroom electrical outlets should be high on the wall and not too close to the sink. Balconies should have sturdy, high rails.

Noise.   Most travelers have been kept awake by the television, partying, or amorous activities of people in the next room, or by traffic on the street outside. Better hotels are designed with noise control in mind. Wall and ceiling construction are substantial, effectively screening routine noise. Carpets and drapes, in addition to being decorative, also absorb and muffle sounds. Mattresses mounted on stable platforms or sturdy bed frames do not squeak even when challenged by the most passionate lovers. Televisions enclosed in cabinets, and with volume governors, rarely disturb guests in adjacent rooms.

In better hotels, the air conditioning and heating system is well maintained and operates without noise or vibration. Likewise, plumbing is quiet and positioned away from the sleeping area. Doors to the hall, and to adjoining rooms, are thick and well fitted to better keep out noise.

Darkness Control. Ever been in a hotel room where the curtains would not quite come together in the middle? In cities where many visitors stay up way into the wee hours, it's important to have a dark, quiet room where you can sleep late without the morning sun blasting you out of bed. Thick, lined curtains that close completely in the center and that extend beyond the dimensions of the window or door frame are required. In a well-planned room, the curtains, shades, or blinds should almost totally block light at any time of day.

Lighting. Poor lighting is an extremely common problem in American hotel rooms. The lighting is usually adequate for dressing, relaxing, or watching television, but not for reading or working. Lighting needs to be bright over tables and desks, and alongside couches or easy chairs. Since so many people read in bed, there should be a separate light for each person. A room with two queen beds should have an individual light for four people. Better bedside reading lights illuminate a small area, so if you want to sleep and someone else prefers to stay up and read, you will not be bothered by the light. The worst situation by far is a single lamp on a table between beds. In each bed, only the person next to the lamp will have sufficient light to read. This deficiency is often compounded by lightbulbs of insufficient wattage.

In addition, closet areas should be well lit, and there should be a switch near the door that turns on lights in the room when you enter. A seldom seen, but desirable, feature is a bedside console that allows a guest to control all or most lights in the room from the bed.

Furnishings. At bare minimum, the bed(s) must be firm. Pillows should be made with nonallergenic fillers and, in addition to the sheets and spread, a blanket should be provided. Bedclothes should be laundered with a fabric softener and changed daily. Better hotels usually provide extra blankets and pillows in the room or on request, and sometimes use a second topsheet between the blanket and the spread.

There should be a dresser large enough to hold clothes for two people during a five-day stay. A small table with two chairs, or a desk with a chair, should be provided. The room should be equipped with a luggage rack and a three-quarter to full-length mirror.

The television should be color, cable-connected, and ideally have a volume governor and remote control. It should be mounted on a swivel base and preferably enclosed in a cabinet. Local channels should be posted on the set, and a local TV program guide should be supplied.

The telephone should be touchtone, conveniently situated for bedside use, and should have, on or near it, easily understood dialing instructions and a rate card. Local white and yellow pages should be provided. Better hotels have phones in the bath and equip room phones with long cords.

Well-designed hotel rooms usually have a plush armchair or a sleeper sofa for lounging and reading. Better headboards are padded for comfortable reading in bed, and there should be a nightstand or table on each side of the bed(s). Nice extras in any hotel room include a small refrigerator, a digital alarm clock, and a coffeemaker.

Bathroom. Two sinks are better than one, and you cannot have too much counter space. A sink outside the bath is a great convenience when two people are bathing and dressing at the same time. Sinks should have drains with stoppers.

Better bathrooms have both tub and shower with a nonslip bottom. Tub and shower controls should be easy to operate. Adjustable shower heads are preferred. The bath needs to be well lit and should have an exhaust fan and a guest-controlled bathroom heater. Towels should be large, soft, and fluffy and provided in generous quantities, as should hand towels and washcloths. There should be an electrical outlet for each sink, conveniently and safely placed.

Complimentary shampoo, conditioner, and lotion are a plus, as are robes and bathmats. Better hotels supply their bathrooms with tissues and extra toilet paper. Luxurious baths feature a phone, a hair dryer, sometimes a small television, or even a jacuzzi.

Vending. There should be complimentary ice and a drink machine on each floor. Welcome additions include a snack machine and a sundries (combs, toothpaste) machine. The latter are seldom found in large hotels that have 24-hour restaurants and shops.

—— *Room Ratings*

To separate properties according to the relative quality, tastefulness, state of repair, cleanliness, and size of their **standard rooms**, we have grouped the hotels and motels into classifications denoted by stars:

★★★★★	*Superior Rooms*	Tasteful and luxurious by any standard
★★★★	*Extremely Nice Rooms*	What you would expect at a Hyatt Regency or Marriott
★★★	*Nice Rooms*	Holiday Inn or comparable quality
★★	*Adequate Rooms*	Clean, comfortable, and functional without frills—like a Motel 6
★	*Super Budget*	

Star ratings in this guide apply to Atlanta properties only and do not necessarily correspond to ratings awarded by Mobil, AAA, or other travel critics. Because stars have little relevance when awarded in the absence of commonly recognized standards of comparison, we have tied our ratings to expected levels of quality established by specific American hotel corporations.

Star ratings apply to *room quality only* and describe the property's standard accommodations. For most hotels and motels a "standard accommodation" is a hotel room with either one king bed or two queen beds. In an all-suite property, the standard accommodation is either a one- or two-room suite. In addition to standard accommodations, many hotels offer luxury rooms and special suites, which are not rated in this guide. Star ratings for rooms are assigned without regard to whether a property has a restaurant(s), recreational facilities, entertainment, or other extras.

In addition to stars (which delineate broad categories), we also employ a numerical rating system. Our rating scale is 0–100, with 100 as the best possible rating and 0 as the worst. Numerical ratings are presented to show the difference we perceive between one property and another. Rooms at the Omni Hotel at CNN, Atlanta Renaissance Hotel, and Atlanta Marriott Perimeter Center, for instance, are all rated as ★★★★. In the supplemental numerical ratings, the Omni Hotel and the Renaissance Hotel are rated 88 and 86, respectively, while the Marriott is rated 83. This means that within the four-star category, the Omni Hotel and the Renaissance Hotel are comparable, and both have somewhat nicer rooms than the Marriott.

—— *How the Hotels Compare*

Cost estimates are based on the hotel's published rack rates for standard rooms, averaged between weekday and weekend prices. Each "$" represents $30. Thus a cost symbol of "$$$" means a room (or suite) at that hotel will average about $90 a night (it may be more for weekdays or less on weekends).

Here is a hit parade of the nicest rooms in town. We've focused strictly on room quality and excluded any consideration of location, services, recreation, or amenities. In some instances, a one- or two-room suite can be had for the same price or less than that of a hotel room.

If you used a previous edition of this guide, you will notice that many of the ratings and rankings have changed. In addition to taking into account new properties, these changes also consider guest room renovations or improved maintenance and housekeeping. A failure to properly maintain guest rooms or a lapse in housekeeping standards can negatively affect the ratings.

Finally, before you begin to shop for a hotel, take a hard look at this letter we received from a couple in Hot Springs, Arkansas:

> We cancelled our room reservations to follow the advice in your book [and reserved a hotel room highly ranked by the *Unofficial Guide*]. We wanted inexpensive, but clean and cheerful. We got inexpensive, but [also] dirty, grim, and depressing. I really felt disappointed in your advice and the room. It was the pits. That was the one real piece of information I needed from your book! The room spoiled the holiday for me aside from our touring.

Needless to say, this letter was as unsettling to us as the bad room was to our reader. Our integrity as travel journalists, after all, is based on the quality of the information we provide our readers. Even with the best of intentions and the most conscientious research, however, we cannot inspect every room in every hotel. What we do, in statistical terms, is take a sample: we check out several rooms selected at random in each hotel and base our ratings and rankings on those rooms. The inspections are conducted anonymously and without the knowledge of the management. Although unusual, it is certainly possible that the rooms we randomly inspect are not representative of the majority of rooms at a particular hotel. Another possibility is that the rooms we inspect in a given hotel are representative, but that by bad luck a reader is assigned a room that is inferior. When we rechecked the hotel our reader disliked, we discovered our rating was correctly representative, but that he and his wife had unfortunately been assigned to one of a small number of threadbare rooms scheduled for renovation.

The key to avoiding disappointment is to snoop around in advance. We recommend that you ask for a photo of a hotel's standard guest room before you book, or at least get a copy of the hotel's promotional brochure. Be forewarned, however, that some hotel chains use the same guest room photo in their promotional literature for all hotels in the chain; a specific guest room may not resemble the brochure photo. When you or your travel agent call, ask how old the property is and when your guest room was last renovated. If you arrive and are assigned a room inferior to that which you had been led to expect, demand to be moved to another room.

How the Hotels Compare

Hotel	Zone	Quality Rating	Star Rating	Cost
Occidental Grand Hotel	7	97	★★★★★	$$$$$$–
Ritz Carlton Atlanta Downtown	7	95	★★★★½	$$$$$$$–
Hotel Nikko	3	94	★★★★½	$$$$$$–
Guest Quarters Suite Hotel	4	93	★★★★½	$$$$+
Ritz Carlton Buckhead	4	92	★★★★½	$$$$$$+
Marriott Suites Midtown	7	91	★★★★½	$$$+
French Quarter Suites	2	90	★★★★½	$$$$–
Stouffer Concourse Hotel	1	90	★★★★½	$$$$$$$–
Stouffer Waverly Hotel	2	90	★★★★½	$$$$$$–
Swissôtel Atlanta	4	90	★★★★½	$$$$+
Homewood Suites Cumberland	2	89	★★★★	$$$+
Sheraton Suites Cumberland	2	89	★★★★	$$$$$+
Hyatt Regency Suites	3	88	★★★★	$$$$$+
J.W. Marriott at Lenox	4	88	★★★★	$$$$$+
Omni Hotel at CNN Center	7	88	★★★★	$$$$$–
Sheraton Colony Square Hotel	7	88	★★★★	$$$$$
Suite Hotel at Underground	7	88	★★★★	$$$+
Atlanta Hilton & Towers	7	87	★★★★	$$$$$$$–
Biltmore Suites	7	87	★★★★	$$$+
Atlanta Renaissance Hotel	7	86	★★★★	$$$$–
Residence Inn Midtown	7	86	★★★★	$$$$$+
Doubletree Hotel at Concourse	4	85	★★★★	$$$$$–
Embassy Suites Buckhead	3	85	★★★★	$$$$$
Embassy Suites Galleria	2	85	★★★★	$$$+

How the Hotels Compare (continued)

Hotel	Zone	Quality Rating	Star Rating	Cost
Embassy Suites Perimeter Center	4	85	★★★★	$$$$+
Hyatt Regency Peachtree Center	7	85	★★★★	$$$$$$$–
Wyndham Midtown Atlanta	7	85	★★★★	$$$$
Marriott Atlanta Marquis	7	84	★★★★	$$$$–
Atlanta Marriott Perimeter Center	4	83	★★★★	$$+
Atlanta Renaissance Hotel Airport	1	82	★★★½	$$$$–
Embassy Suites Airport	1	82	★★★½	$$$$$
Marque of Atlanta	4	82	★★★½	$$$$–
Atlanta Airport Hilton	1	81	★★★½	$$$$$–
Atlanta Marriott Gwinnett Place	4	81	★★★½	$$$$+
Evergreen Resort at Stone Mountain	5	81	★★★½	$$$$$
Holiday Inn Crowne Plaza Ravinia	4	81	★★★½	$$$$$$–
Residence Inn	4	81	★★★½	$$$$–
Residence Inn Airport North	1	81	★★★½	$$$$
Residence Inn Cumberland	2	81	★★★½	$$$$
Summerfield Suites Buckhead	3	81	★★★½	$$$$$–
University Inn at Emory (new rooms)	5	81	★★★½	$$$+
Atlanta Marriott North Central	4	80	★★★½	$$$–
Courtyard Midtown	7	80	★★★½	$$$+
Sheraton Gateway Atlanta Airport	1	80	★★★½	$$$$$
Courtyard Airport North	1	79	★★★½	$$$–
Courtyard Airport South	1	79	★★★½	$$$–
Courtyard Executive Park	4	79	★★★½	$$$$–
Courtyard Gwinnett Mall	4	79	★★★½	$$$$–
Courtyard Medical Center	4	79	★★★½	$$$+
Courtyard Norcross	5	79	★★★½	$$$+
Courtyard North Lake	5	79	★★★½	$$$+
Courtyard Perimeter Center	4	79	★★★½	$$$$–
Courtyard Windy Hill	3	79	★★★½	$$$+
Atlanta Hilton Northwest	2	78	★★★½	$$$+
Courtyard Cumberland Center	2	78	★★★½	$$+
Hawthorn Suites Northwest	3	78	★★★½	$$$$
Marriott Atlanta Airport	1	78	★★★½	$$$–
Residence Inn Buckhead	3	78	★★★½	$$$$$+

How the Hotels Compare *(continued)*

Hotel	Zone	Quality Rating	Star Rating	Cost
Westin Peachtree Plaza	7	78	★★★½	$$$$$$+
Ramada Inn Northlake	5	77	★★★½	$$+
Wyndham Garden Hotel	4	77	★★★½	$$$$–
Stone Mountain Inn	5	76	★★★½	$$$
Terrace Garden Inn Buckhead	3	75	★★★½	$$$$$
Comfort Suites Atlanta Airport	1	74	★★★	$$$+
Harvey Hotel Airport	1	73	★★★	$$$
Holiday Inn Northlake	5	73	★★★	$$$+
Atlanta Marriott Northwest	3	72	★★★	$$$–
Best Western Bradbury Suites Windy Hill	2	72	★★★	$$$–
Holiday Inn Airport North	1	72	★★★	$$$$–
Holiday Inn at Lenox	4	72	★★★	$$$$
Travelodge Hotel Druid Hills	4	70	★★★	$$$–
Best Western Granada Suite Hotel	7	69	★★★	$$$+
Clubhouse Inn	5	68	★★★	$$+
Holiday Inn Airport South	1	68	★★★	$$$$–
La Quinta Stone Mountain	5	68	★★★	$$+
Holiday Inn Midtown North	7	67	★★★	$$–
Regency Suites Hotel	7	67	★★★	$$$+
Biltmore Peachtree Hotel	7	66	★★★	$$$–
Emory Inn	5	66	★★★	$$$+
Quality Inn Northeast	5	66	★★★	$$–
Ramada Atlanta Airport North	1	66	★★★	$$$+
Ramada Hotel Airport South	1	66	★★★	$$
University Inn at Emory (old rooms)	5	66	★★★	$$+
Best Western Bradbury Suites Northlake	5	65	★★★	$$$–
Fairfield Inn Midtown	7	65	★★★	$$+
Hampton Inn Atlanta Airport	1	65	★★★	$$+
Hampton Inn Druid Hills	4	65	★★★	$$$–
Hampton Inn Stone Mountain	5	65	★★★	$$$–
Days Inn Gwinnett Place	4	64	★★½	$$$–
Days Inn North Windy Hill	3	64	★★½	$$+
Days Inn Northlake Mall	5	64	★★½	$$–
Hampton Inn Northlake	5	64	★★½	$$+
Holiday Inn Central	3	64	★★½	$$$

How the Hotels Compare (continued)

Hotel	Zone	Quality Rating	Star Rating	Cost
Howard Johnson Cumberland	2	64	★★½	$$+
La Quinta Atlanta West	1	64	★★½	$$+
La Quinta Motor Inn Airport	1	64	★★½	$$+
La Quinta Norcross	5	64	★★½	$$+
Radisson Hotel Atlanta	7	64	★★½	$$$$
Ramada Inn Atlanta Six Flags	1	64	★★½	$$+
Travelodge Downtown	7	64	★★½	$$$–
Days Inn Airport West	1	63	★★½	$$
Days Inn Stone Mountain	5	63	★★½	$$
Fairfield Inn Airport	1	63	★★½	$$+
Fairfield Inn Gwinnett Mall	4	63	★★½	$$+
Fairfield Inn Northlake	5	63	★★½	$$+
Hampton Inn Buckhead	3	63	★★½	$$$+
Lenox Inn	4	63	★★½	$$$–
Amberly Suite Hotel	5	62	★★½	$$+
Best Western American Hotel	7	62	★★½	$$+
Budgetel Inn Atlanta Airport	1	62	★★½	$$–
Days Inn Downtown	7	62	★★½	$$$
Best Western Bradbury Inn Norcross	5	61	★★½	$$
Best Western Inn at the Peachtrees	7	61	★★½	$$$$–
Days Inn Clairmont Road	4	61	★★½	$$+
Castlegate Hotel	7	60	★★½	$$+
Comfort Inn Downtown Atlanta	7	60	★★½	$$$$–
Days Inn Airport	1	60	★★½	$$
Howard Johnson Airport	1	60	★★½	$$$
Travelodge Marietta	3	60	★★½	$+
Comfort Inn Buckhead	3	59	★★½	$$$–
Days Inn Six Flags	1	59	★★½	$$$–
Ho Jo Inn Airport West	1	59	★★½	$$–
Summit Inn	1	59	★★½	$$+
Budgetel Inn Atlanta Lenox	4	58	★★½	$$–
Comfort Inn Atlanta Airport	1	58	★★½	$$+
Days Inn Northwest	7	58	★★½	$$$–
Days Inn Peachtree	7	58	★★½	$$$+
Red Roof Inn Airport	1	58	★★½	$$+
Shoney's Inn Northeast	4	58	★★½	$$
Masters Economy Inn Six Flags	1	57	★★½	$$–

How the Hotels Compare (continued)

Hotel	Zone	Quality Rating	Star Rating	Cost
Travelodge Midtown	7	57	★★½	$$
Travelodge / Quality Inn Atlanta Airport	1	55	★★	$$+
Red Roof Inn Druid Hills	4	54	★★	$$+
Red Roof Inn North	2	54	★★	$+
Super 8 Motel Six Flags	I	52	★★	$$–
Red Roof Inn Six Flags	I	51	★★	$$–
Super 8 Airport	I	51	★★	$$–
Econo Lodge Airport	I	50	★★	$$$–
Atlanta West Hotel	I	33	★	$$+
Mark Inn Six Flags	I	31	★	$$
Executive Inn Six Flags	I	25	½	$+

—— Good Deals and Bad Deals

Having listed the nicest rooms in town, let's reorder the list to rank the best combinations of quality and value in a room. As before, the rankings are made without consideration of location or the availability of restaurant(s), recreational facilities, entertainment, and amenities. Once again, each lodging property is awarded a value rating on a 0–100 scale. The higher the rating, the better the value.

A reader recently complained to us that he had booked one of our top-ranked rooms in terms of value and had been very disappointed in the room. We noticed that the room the reader occupied had a quality rating of ★★½. We would remind you that the value ratings are intended to give you some sense of value received for dollars spent. A ★★½ room at $30 may have the same value rating as a ★★★★ room at $85, but that does not mean the rooms will be of comparable quality. Regardless of whether it's a good deal or not, a ★★½ room is still a ★★½ room.

Listed below are the best room buys for the money, regardless of location or star classification, based on averaged rack rates. Note that sometimes a suite can cost less than a hotel room.

The Top 30 Best Deals in Atlanta

Hotel	Zone	Quality Rating	Star Rating	Cost
Travelodge Marietta	3	60	★★½	$+
Atlanta Marriott Perimeter Center	4	83	★★★★	$$+
Courtyard Cumberland Center	2	78	★★★½	$$+
Marriott Suites Midtown	7	91	★★★★½	$$$+
Quality Inn Northeast	5	66	★★★	$$−
Ramada Inn Northlake	5	77	★★★½	$$+
Holiday Inn Midtown North	7	67	★★★	$$−
Homewood Suites Cumberland	2	89	★★★★	$$$+
Biltmore Suites	7	87	★★★★	$$$+
Embassy Suites Galleria	2	85	★★★★	$$$+
Suite Hotel at Underground	7	88	★★★★	$$$+
Marriott Atlanta Airport	1	78	★★★½	$$$−
French Quarter Suites	2	90	★★★★½	$$$$−
Ramada Hotel Airport South	1	66	★★★	$$
Atlanta Marriott North Central	4	80	★★★½	$$$−
Courtyard Airport South	1	79	★★★½	$$$−
La Quinta Stone Mountain	5	68	★★★	$$+
Courtyard Airport North	1	79	★★★½	$$$−
Swissôtel Atlanta	4	90	★★★★½	$$$$+
Guest Quarters Suite Hotel	4	93	★★★★½	$$$$+
Masters Economy Inn Six Flags	1	57	★★½	$$−
University Inn at Emory (new rooms)	5	81	★★★½	$$$+
Stone Mountain Inn	5	76	★★★½	$$$
Days Inn Northlake Mall	5	64	★★½	$$−
Ho Jo Inn Airport West	1	59	★★½	$$−
Marriott Atlanta Marquis	7	84	★★★★	$$$$−
Courtyard Medical Center	4	79	★★★½	$$$+
Budgetel Inn Atlanta Airport	1	62	★★½	$$−
Wyndham Midtown Atlanta	7	85	★★★★	$$$$
Courtyard Midtown	7	80	★★★½	$$$+

Hotels near MARTA Stations

Here is a summary of the hotels near MARTA stations, with maps showing streets. Walking times or distances are included when the distance from station to hotel is more than a couple of blocks. Most of these short walks are not only convenient and economical but take you through some of the most interesting and scenic parts of the city.

Especially noteworthy are the Lenox Square and Peachtree Center stations. Lenox puts you not only near a hotel but right next to the plush Lenox Square Shopping Mall, Atlanta's number one tourist attraction. Peachtree Center station is connected by escalators and tunnels to Peachtree Center, the Merchandise Mart, Atlanta Fulton County Library, and Peachtree Street. From here you could spend a half-day exploring downtown without setting foot on the street.

In any case, staying near a MARTA station can make transportation a whole lot easier. If your stay will be limited to within the perimeter area, locating near MARTA can even preclude renting a car. Use the following maps to locate your best lodging choices.

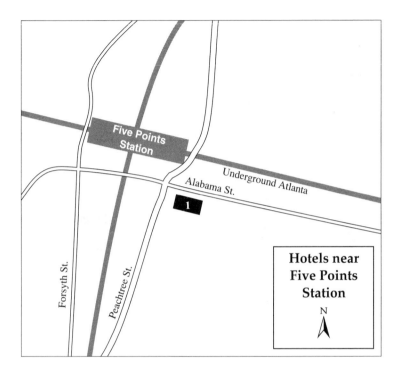

Five Points Station Hotels (Zone 7)

1. The Suite Hotel at Underground—just across the street from Underground Atlanta

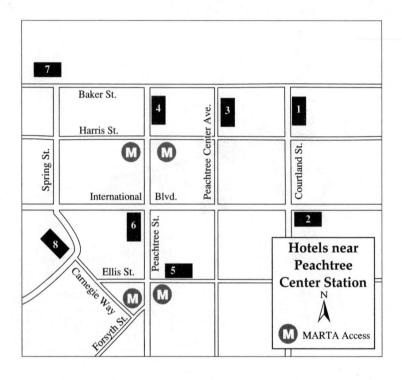

Peachtree Center Station Hotels (Zone 7)

1. Atlanta Hilton & Towers
2. Radisson Hotel Atlanta
3. Marriott Atlanta Marquis
4. Hyatt Regency Peachtree Center
5. Ritz Carlton Downtown
6. Westin Peachtree Plaza
7. Days Inn Downtown
8. Best Western American Hotel

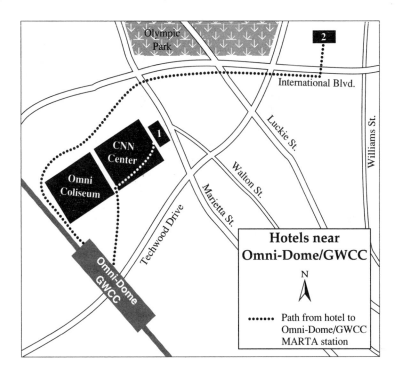

Hotels near Omni-Dome/GWCC

N

∧

••••••• Path from hotel to Omni-Dome/GWCC MARTA station

Omni / Dome / GWCC Station Hotels (Zone 7)

1. Omni Hotel—Equivalent of 2 blocks' walk through CNN Center
2. Comfort Inn Downtown—9-minute walk via International Boulevard

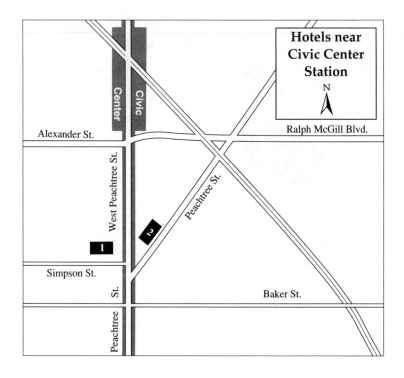

Civic Center Station Hotels (Zone 7)

1. Best Western Inn at the Peachtrees—1½ blocks
2. Biltmore Peachtree Hotel—1½ blocks

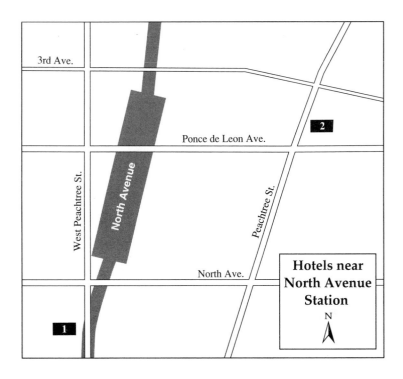

North Avenue Station Hotels (Zone 7)

1. Atlanta Renaissance Hotel
2. Days Inn Peachtree

Midtown Station Hotels (Zone 8)

1. Regency Suites Hotel
2. Residence Inn by Marriott Midtown
3. Wyndham Hotel Midtown

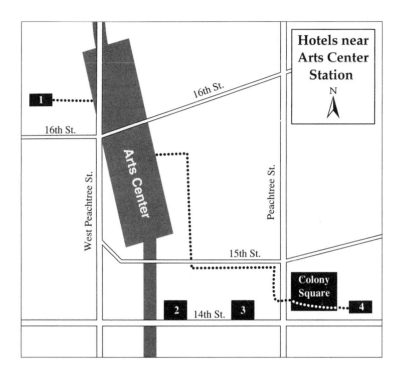

Arts Center Station Hotels (Zone 8)

1. Best Western Granada Suites
2. Marriott Suites Hotel
3. Grand Hotel
4. Sheraton Colony Square Hotel—3 blocks, 8-minute walk through Colony Square

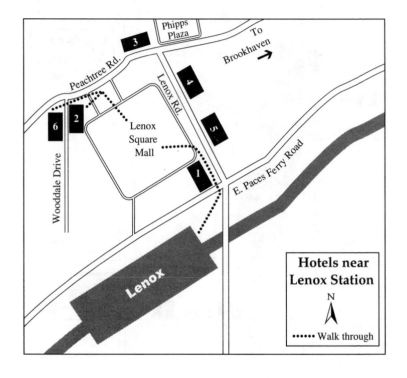

Hotels near Lenox Station

Lenox Square Station Hotels (Zone 4)

1. J. W. Marriott at Lenox—Across the street from station
2. Swissôtel—Walk through Lenox Square, 14 minutes
3. Ritz Carlton Buckhead—10 minutes
4. Lenox Inn—3 minutes
5. Terrace Garden Inn—5 minutes
6. Holiday Inn at Lenox—Walk through Lenox Square, 15 minutes

PART FOUR: Visiting Atlanta on Business

Meeting and Convention Facilities

Atlanta is a key convention, meeting, and trade show destination, offering convenient access to the business traveler via air, rail, and highway. The city offers no less than five major convention and trade show facilities capable of handling meetings with from 3,000 to 85,000 attendees. In addition, there are more than 120 hotels that can accommodate smaller groups.

—— The Georgia World Congress Center and Georgia Dome

The Georgia World Congress Center, located downtown adjacent to the Georgia Dome, is the third largest convention center in the United States (behind Chicago and Las Vegas). Ranked as the busiest (most occupied) convention facility in the nation, the Georgia World Congress Center hosts such mega–trade shows as the Super Show, COMDEX, and the National Association of Home Builders.

With the addition of two halls added in 1992, the facility now offers 950,000 square feet of exhibit space, 76 meeting rooms, and a ballroom and auditorium, the latter two equipped for multilingual, simultaneous translation. Food service is essentially self-contained and capable of catering banquets for as many as 3,300 persons. Finally, if the eight cavernous exhibit halls of the World Congress Center do not provide enough space, the floor of the Georgia Dome next door, home of the NFL Atlanta Falcons, can be pressed into service.

Any trade show exhibitor who has ever displayed at a union-controlled convention facility (like the Javits Center in New York) will appreciate the ease and simplicity of move-in and set-up at the Georgia World Congress Center. Because Georgia is a "right to work" state, exhibitors can make their own arrangements for delivery, move-in, and set-up without the hassle, interference, and persistent involvement of unions. Exhibitors who wish to erect their own displays may do so.

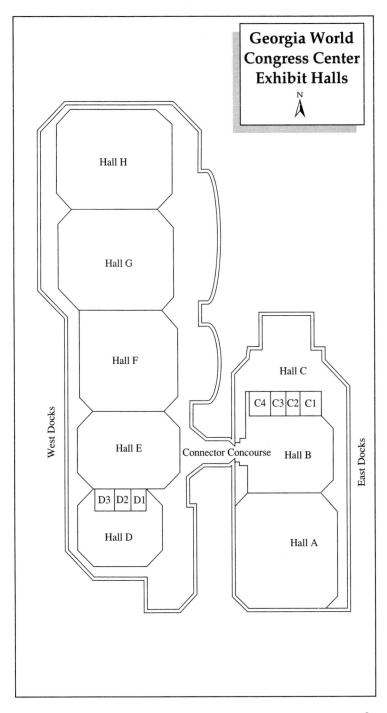

Georgia World Congress Center Exhibit Halls

N

Hall H

Hall G

Hall F

Hall E

Hall C

C4 C3 C2 C1

Hall B

Connector Concourse

D3 D2 D1

Hall D

Hall A

West Docks

East Docks

Georgia Dome,
Georgia World
Congress Center,
and
Omni Coliseum

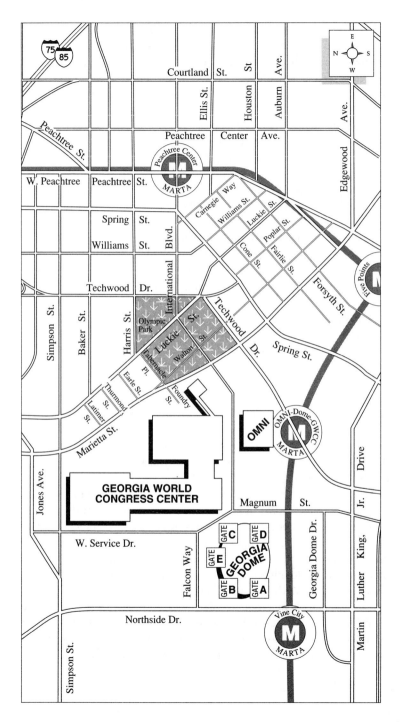

Likewise, exhibitors are free to handle their own unloading, move-in, breakdown, and move-out. The World Congress Center, of course, makes contractors available to those exhibitors who desire to contract for these services.

Trade show exhibitors who ship their exhibits to the World Congress Center will usually find their shipments handled efficiently and expeditiously. Smaller exhibitors, self-delivering their exhibits in cars, vans, and trucks, will also find the convention center user-friendly. If you are delivering your own exhibit, make sure you know which exhibit hall (A, B, C, D, E, F, G, or H) you will be in. The east docks serving halls A, B, and C can be reached via Foundry Street off Marietta Street, and for some shows through the A-5 door off International Boulevard. The west docks, for all other halls, are accessible via Falcon Way from Northside Drive. Specific arrangements for the loading and unloading of privately owned vehicles is determined by each trade show sponsor, so make sure you obtain final instructions from your show's organizer before attempting delivery.

Thanks to the development of Centennial Olympic Park and the landscaping along International Boulevard, the walk from the hotel center to the convention facility is aesthetically pleasing and interesting.

Another option for accessing the Georgia World Congress Center is via MARTA. The closest station to the convention facility is the Omni/Dome/GWCC Station, a four- to six-minute walk to the entrance of the convention center. Next to shuttle buses (provided by convention sponsors) and cabs, MARTA is probably the most convenient way to reach the World Congress Center, particularly if you are lodging in one of the hotels at Peachtree Center.

Though there are almost 17,000 parking places within the eight square blocks of the World Congress Center, no one lot or deck offers more than 2,000 spaces, with most lots offering considerably fewer. In other words, with the parking thus dispersed in small lots over a couple of square miles, finding a lot with available space is pretty hit or miss. If you are lodging far enough away to need a car, your best bet is to park near a MARTA station in the 'burbs and take the train in.

A more persistent problem associated with spending time at the World Congress Center is the scarcity of restaurants in the immediate area. By and large, show-goers are relegated to the food service at the convention center, or to taking a cab to an off-site restaurant.

—— *The Atlanta Market Center*

A second major downtown convention venue is the Atlanta Market Center, a multibuilding, high-rise complex of exhibit halls, meeting rooms, offices, and permanent showrooms spread over a four-block area. The conference and convention facilities of the Atlanta Market Center include the Inforum (Information Forum), the Apparel Mart, the Gift Mart, and the Merchandise Mart, all tied together by covered aerial walkways. Each building is a self-contained convention center with food service, loading docks, exhibit halls, and conference rooms. Two of the "Marts," Inforum and the Apparel Mart, also feature large theater/auditoriums.

Because the Atlanta Market Center is spread over so many floors in so many buildings, it tends to host smaller trade shows and conventions than the Georgia World Congress Center—shows that optimally can be fully contained in one of the four buildings. While occasional meetings occupy two or more of the "Marts," this arrangement disperses the exhibits into numerous halls ranging over several floors in different buildings—a bit confusing for attendees.

The one configuration that does provide for traffic continuity is the combination of the main exhibit level of Inforum with that of the Apparel Mart. These halls, though in separate buildings, are conveniently connected by aerial corridors large enough to accommodate ten-foot by ten-foot booths along both sides of the passageways.

Like the Georgia World Congress Center, the Atlanta Market Center is an efficient, well-administered meeting facility. Because it is situated in the congested center of downtown Atlanta, however, and because of its physically dispersed layout and dependence on elevators, the Atlanta Market Center is more logistically complicated for, and less accessible to, exhibitors transporting their own displays. Both exhibitors and attendees at the Atlanta Market Center should contact the meeting's sponsoring organization for precise directions to meeting and exhibit venues.

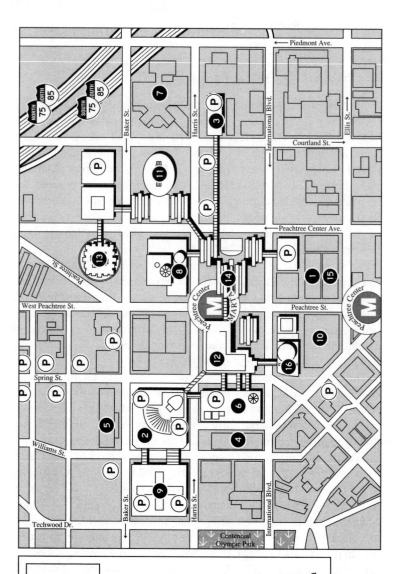

Atlanta Market Center

N↑

1. 191 Peachtree
2. Apparel Mart
3. Athletic Club
4. Comfort Inn
5. Days Inn
6. Gift Mart
7. Hilton Hotel
8. Hyatt Regency
9. Inforum
10. Macy's
11. Marriott Marquis
12. Merchandise Mart
13. One Peachtree Center
14. Peachtree Center
15. Ritz Carlton Hotel
16. Westin Peachtree Plaza

The Atlanta Market Center is much more convenient to major downtown hotels than the Georgia World Congress Center. All of AMC's meeting and exhibit facilities are within a 5- to 15-minute walk of the larger hotels. Several hotels (the Westin Peachtree Plaza, the Hyatt Regency, and the Marriott Marquis) are directly connected to the Atlanta Market Center by aerial walkways. Attendees using MARTA should disembark at the Peachtree Center Station and take the Harris Street exit. From there, all of the convention venues are a three- to eight-minute walk away.

As in the case of the Georgia World Congress Center, parking is available but spread over dozens of small to medium-sized decks and lots. We recommend walking or using MARTA to access the Atlanta Market Center.

On a happier note, restaurants within convenient walking distance from the Atlanta Market Center are plentiful, making an escape from the exhibit floor or a quiet meal with clients easy and practical.

— *Georgia International Convention & Trade Center*

Located a quick ten-minute cab ride away from Hartsfield International Airport on Atlanta's south side, the Georgia International Convention & Trade Center is a popular site for small to medium-sized conventions and trade shows. The facility offers 125,000 square feet of exhibit space in 5 separate halls, as well as 2 ballrooms and 35 meeting rooms.

Attached to the Sheraton Gateway Airport Hotel, the convention facility offers exceptional convenience to attendees arriving by commercial air or by car. In addition to the Sheraton, there are in excess of 30 lodging properties close by (but not within walking distance).

Among the better features of the GIC&TC are the simplicity of its design and layout and its easy logistical accessibility for exhibitor and show attendee alike. Move-in and move-out are a snap, and you are never more than five minutes from your van if you forget something. As you might have deduced, parking is plentiful, free, and in close proximity to the trade show floor.

The only problem with a meeting at the GIC&TC is its relative isolation. While the facility is convenient to the airport and interstate highway system, it is a long way from Atlanta's shopping, entertainment, and sight-seeing areas. Downtown, the Georgia Dome, Underground Atlanta, and Fulton County Stadium are about 30 minutes away by car if the traffic is not bad. Lenox Square and other prime shopping venues are farther. Fortunately, there are a number of passable to very good restaurants in the vicinity of the GIC&TC, so at a minimum you can eat well in your exile.

—— Galleria Centre and the Gwinnett Civic & Cultural Center

Atlanta has two new suburban convention centers, the Galleria Centre, inside I-285 to the northwest of Atlanta in Cobb County, and the Gwinnett Civic & Cultural Center off I-85 northeast of Atlanta. Both are full-service facilities with in excess of 100,000 square feet of exhibit space, auditoriums/theaters, ballrooms, and food service. The Galleria Centre is situated next to the Stouffer Waverly Hotel and Galleria Specialty Shopping Mall. Close by, but not within walking distance, are another ten hotels. Shopping, dining, and entertainment opportunities in the immediate vicinity of the convention center are plentiful. Downtown Atlanta is about 25 minutes away by car during nonrush hours.

The layout of the Galleria Centre is a little confusing at first but is user-friendly once you are oriented. Likewise, move-in for exhibitors transporting their own displays, is a bit of an intelligence test if you are winging it, but not bad at all if you obtain directions in advance. Once in and set up, you will find the Galleria Centre very accessible and convenient.

The name of the Gwinnett Civic & Cultural Center illustrates the facility's dual role. Spacious and modern, it is the most remote and isolated of Atlanta's five premier convention facilities. Located outside the perimeter highway off I-85, 40 minutes from downtown, the facility is best suited to small and medium-sized meetings where most exhibitors and attendees have cars. There is food service on site, but for the moment, no hotel. Lodging, however, is plentiful up and down I-85, restaurants somewhat less so. Efficiently managed and operated, the center is an easy place to exhibit in or attend a show. Parking is abundant and free.

—— Atlanta's Big Hotels

In addition to the dedicated convention facilities described above, almost all of Atlanta's larger hotels have exhibit and meeting space sufficient to accommodate meetings of 25 to 3,000 persons. When the meeting space available at the hotels is added to that of the five dedicated sites and coupled with the "right to work" law, Atlanta offers the business traveler more diversity, variety, and flexibility for meetings and trade shows than any other city we know.

Dining for Downtown Convention-Goers

Downtown Atlanta, unfortunately, is not a great place for dining out. There are, however, some places where you can feast mightily and, if you're on an expense account, like royalty. Half a block off Peachtree, at Peachtree Center Avenue and International Boulevard, is **Hsu's** (see profile, page 378), featuring Chinese artifacts, subtle lighting, polished service, and a kitchen that delivers excellent specials, including such lovelies as soft-shell crab in black bean sauce and Szechuan beans in spicy pork.

If you're after a mound of meat, try **Morton's of Chicago**, a chain restaurant, but a good one. Pricey as precious jewels, but knowledgeable about properly aged meat, Morton's is on Peachtree Center Avenue, on the ground level of the Marquis One Tower. They serve fish as well as prime grades of meat and have bartenders who know how to mix a good stiff drink without referring to a pocket manual. Don't overlook this place if you have a client in tow you want to impress. The live lobster paraded from table to table as part of the menu presentation always seems to have a tragic look on his face, but wouldn't you?

Dailey's, on International just down from Peachtree, can be rather noisy if you head upstairs to the ever-popular dining room. Getting a table can require a long wait. You may have better luck grabbing a booth downstairs in the bar (which is quieter) and diving into good burgers or other no-fuss dishes. This place sometimes ties itself in a culinary knot by combining all the latest trend foods into one single entree, so you'll fare better with sandwiches and simple chicken dishes, or even the New England–style crab cakes with remoulade, than with a dish that sounds like an advertisement for The Gourmet Club.

If you need an excellent breakfast for mere pennies, or decent deli sandwiches, seek out **Jack's Sandwich Shop** in the 230 Peachtree Tower building. With sublime cheese grits, fine eggs and bacon, bagels and toast, and a good juice selection, Jack's is a penny-pinching treasure. The atmosphere is no more than austere, but a zillion business deals have been closed over Jack's Reubens, chicken sandwiches, and early morning feasts.

The Cafe at the Ritz, on Peachtree, is another wonderful, but decidedly upscale, choice for breakfast, lunch, or dinner. The menu is trustworthy, with something for everyone. Count on it for unobtrusive service when business is being conducted or you just want to relax with a paper and decent coffee.

In the **Westin Peachtree Plaza** at Peachtree and International, rely on their **cafe** for good breakfast buffets and an excellent, properly served Japanese breakfast.

Thelma's Kitchen at 768 Marietta Street (one block north of the Salvation Army second-hand store) is a dreamy little place for a meat and three, and okra patties when they are available. This is soul food at its best and dirt cheap to boot, if you don't mind the rather shabby environment.

A Calendar of Annual Atlanta Conventions

The city's considerable convention business can make it hard to get a hotel room in and around the city. Use the following list of major 1997 convention dates to plan your trip to Atlanta.

Dates	Convention/Event	Attendees	Location/HQ
1996			
Dec. 8–11	American Medical Association	3,000	Marriott Marquis/ Hilton/Hyatt
Dec. 15–18	National Association of Insurance Commissioners	2,500	Marriott Marquis
Dec. 19–22	Church of God By Faith, Inc.	5,000	Hyatt
1997			
Jan. 9–13	Wholesale Florists & Florists Suppliers of America	6,000	GWCC
Jan. 11–15	International Gift and Accessories Market	35,000	Atlanta Apparel Mart/Atlanta Merchandise Mart/Inforum
Jan. 22–24	Southeastern Poultry & Egg Association	26,000	GWCC
Jan. 24–26	Gooch Enterprises	30,000	GA Dome/ Marriott Marquis
Jan. 30– Feb. 3	Atlanta Women's and Children's Market	10,000	Atlanta Apparel Mart

Dates	Convention/Event	Attendees	Location/ HQ
Feb. 1–4	National Automobile Dealers Association	18,000	GWCC
Feb. 14–17	The Super Show	110,000	GWCC
Feb. 26– Mar. 2	Southern Council of Optometrists	6,000	Atlanta Apparel Mart
Feb. 26– Mar. 2	National Council of Teachers of Mathematics	3,000	Hilton
Mar. 15–18	Atlanta Spring Gift, Accessories, & Holiday Market	10,000	Atlanta Gift Mart
Mar. 18–21	Pittsburgh Conference on Analytical Chemistry and Applied Spectroscopy	31,000	GWCC
Mar. 20–23	Hinman Dental Society of Atlanta	24,000	Atlanta Apparel Mart/Inforum
Apr. 4–8	National Propane Gas Association	4,500	Inforum/ Atlanta Apparel Mart/ Westin/Hyatt
Apr. 8–10	The Wire Association	10,000	TBA
Apr. 10–14	Atlanta Women's and Children's Mart	10,000	Atlanta Apparel Mart
Apr. 13–18	Risk and Insurance Management Society	8,000	GWCC
Apr. 14–17	True Value Hardware Stores	10,000	TBA
Apr. 26–30	American Association of Museums	5,000	GWCC/Hyatt
Apr. 29– May 1	International Intermodal Expo	8,500	GWCC/Hyatt
May 3	International Reading Association	12,000	Marriott Marquis
May 9–11	Southpak Exposition	5,000	TBA
May 9–17	International Business Machines	4,000	TBA
May 15–17	National Glass Association	9,000	Marriott Marquis

Dates	Convention/Event	Attendees	Location/ HQ
May 16–23	Associates of Clinical Pharmacology	2,000	Marriott Marquis
May 19–23	Environmental Industry Associations	12,000	Hilton
Jun. 1–4	SoftBank Comdex, Inc.	100,000	TBA
Jun. 7–13	Daughters of the Nile Supreme Temple	4,000	GWCC/ GA Dome
Jun. 8–12	Million Dollar Round Table	5,500	Hilton
Jun. 12–17	Atlanta Women's and Children's Market	10,000	Atlanta Apparel Mart
Jun. 19–26	National Sheriffs Association	3,500	Galleria Centre/ Stouffer Waverly
June 25–29	Dragon Con/Atlanta Comic Expo	20,000	Hyatt/Westin Peachtree
Jun. 30– Jul. 5	National Education Association	14,000	GWCC
Jul. 12–16	International Gift and Accessories Market	35,000	Atlanta Apparel Mart
Jul. 14–17	Christian Booksellers Association	10,000	GWCC
Jul. 20–24	American Association of Clinical Chemistry	7,000	GWCC
Jul. 31– Aug. 2	American Wholesale Marketers Association	9,500	GWCC
Aug. 1–3	Southern Nurserymen's Association	10,000	Marriott Marquis/ GWCC
Aug. 21–25	Atlanta Women's and Children's Market	10,000	Atlanta Apparel Mart
Sept. 13–16	Atlanta National Fall Gift & Accessories Market/Atlanta National Gourmet Show	10,000	Atlanta Gift and Merchandise Marts
Sept. 23–26	Bobbin Show/AAMA Convention	25,000	GWCC

Dates	Convention/Event	Attendees	Location/HQ
Sept. 28–Oct. 1	American Association of Textile Chemists & Colorists	3,000	Inforum/Hyatt
Oct. 21–24	American Chemical Society/Rubber Division	8,000	GWCC
Oct. 23–25	Amusement and Music Operators	8,000	GWCC
Nov. 5–7	Federation of the Societies for Coatings	9,000	Hyatt/Marriott Marquis
Nov. 8–10	American Society of Landscape Architects	3,500	GWCC
Nov. 9–19	American Academy of Physical Medicine	3,000	Marriott Marquis
Dec. 7–10	American Society of Health System Pharmacists	7,000	TBA
Dec. 18–21	The Mandrill Group	30,000	TBA

1998

Dates	Convention/Event	Attendees	Location/HQ
Jan. 21–23	Southeastern Poultry & Egg Association	26,000	GWCC
Feb. 22–24	Food Marketing Institute	4,500	GWCC
Feb. 24–Mar. 1	Southern Council of Optometrists	5,000	TBA
Mar. 12–15	Hinman Dental Society of Atlanta	25,000	GWCC
Mar. 14–15	Atlanta Phoenix Cat Society	5,000	Marriott Gwinnett
Mar. 29–Apr. 1	American College of Cardiology	28,000	TBA

PART FIVE: Arriving and Getting Oriented

Coming into the City

—— By Car

If you drive into Atlanta, you will most likely arrive by interstate: I-75 or I-85 from the north or south; I-20 from the east or west. These three routes converge on Atlanta like the spokes of a wheel, connected by the interstate perimeter that is I-285.

Any one of the three interstate routes will take you directly into and through the heart of the city. The perimeter essentially makes a big loop through Atlanta's sprawling suburban outskirts.

The main thing to know about driving into the city is to just drive straight in (don't get on I-285). That goes for passing through Atlanta, too. The quickest routes are straight through the city. Use the perimeter to get to suburbia, or to destinations right on or near I-285. As we've mentioned earlier, avoid interstates during rush hours.

—— By Train

Amtrak's Crescent connects Atlanta daily with New York, Philadelphia, Washington, Baltimore, Charlotte, New Orleans, and other eastern cities on its 1,380-mile route. Accommodations available include sleeping cars, slumbercoach, coach, dining car, and lounge car. The train arrives and departs from Brookwood Station on Deering Road and Peachtree Street. With its Palladian entrances, marble floors, and oak benches, the station has been an Atlanta landmark since it was built in 1917.

Upon arriving in the train station, you can either take a cab to your hotel or easily connect with Atlanta's efficient, inexpensive metro rail service—the Metropolitan Atlanta Rapid Transit Authority, known as MARTA. MARTA's #23 bus stops right outside the front door of Brookwood Station and connects to the rail system at the Arts Center station southbound and the Lenox station northbound.

Amtrak publishes a brochure about the Crescent route, including a simple map and brief sketches of the towns and cities the train passes through. For reservations, current schedules, fares, or a copy of the brochure, call (800) 872-7245. Locally, call (404) 881-3061 (tickets) or 881-3067 (baggage). Delivery time on the brochure is two to three weeks.

—— By Plane

If you are flying into Atlanta, you will probably arrive at Hartsfield International Airport, one of the world's largest and most convenient airports.

Since it opened on September 21, 1980, builders of new large terminals have looked to Hartsfield as a model. The airport has a central terminal connected to long concourses by a one-mile long, high speed, automated underground rail system, which for more than 15 years has operated at a 99.997 efficiency rate. Although the airport is spread out over a huge area, passengers at the curbside are within minutes of their departure gates. You can transfer easily from airline to airline without ever seeing the main terminal.

Atlanta's Hartsfield consistently ranks among the top five airports in the world in terms of airplane arrivals and departures. Well over 159,000 passengers pass through the terminal every day, many of them traveling on one of the 490 daily flights that the Atlanta-based Delta Air Lines runs out of Hartsfield. The terminal and concourses are spread over 50 acres, and the total airport area covers 3,750 acres. Yet, despite its awesome size and 24-hour revolving-door pace, one rarely hears a serious, well-founded complaint from knowledgeable travelers.

Airport Layout

The airport is located in Zone 1, ten miles south of Atlanta in a huge triangle formed by Interstate Highways 85, 75, and 285. As indicated on the diagram, the airport layout is quite simple. Five parallel concourses are connected to the main terminal by a 1.7-mile underground rail train and walkway that run perpendicular to the concourses. One domestic concourse is connected directly to the North Terminal. The train is easy to use and the signage is clear. The international concourse is the largest international concourse in the United States and has its own self-contained customs, immigration, and security. Ticket counters and baggage claim areas for the airlines that serve the airport are located in the terminal building.

Signs along the highway leading into the airport direct travelers to the North and South terminals as if they were two separate buildings,

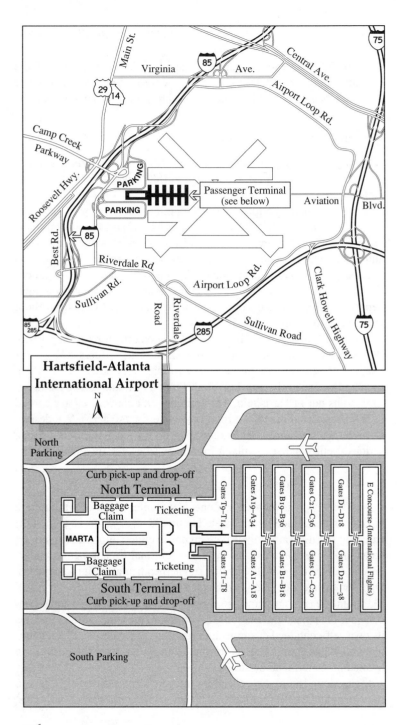

Hartsfield-Atlanta
International Airport

N

but they are actually two halves of the same building, as shown on the diagram.

Parking and Transportation

Airport parking is plentiful and reasonably priced. Economy: $1 per hour with a maximum of $5 for any 24-hour period. Park-Ride: $1 per hour with a $6 maximum for each 24-hour period. A free shuttle service takes departing passengers to the curbside check-in areas and picks up arriving passengers. West Autopark: $1 per hour with a maximum of $5 in any 24-hour period. Decks: $1 per hour with a maximum of $9 in any 24-hour period. Upper-deck: designed for hourly parking at a charge of $1 per hour for the first two hours and $2 per hour each additional hour with a $24 maximum for any 24-hour period The different parking areas are clearly marked on the routes into the airport.

The drive downtown from the airport (and vice versa) takes anywhere from 20 to 45 minutes, depending on traffic. Cab fares to downtown run about $15.

The Metropolitan Atlanta Rapid Transit Authority (MARTA) offers efficient, inexpensive rail service from the airport to downtown and connections to rail and bus routes throughout the city. One-way fare is $1.50. Travel time from the airport to Five Points in the middle of downtown Atlanta, 9 miles away, is 15 minutes; to Lenox Square, 16 miles away, is 28 minutes.

For more information about the airport write or call the Airport Commissioner's Office, Hartsfield Atlanta International Airport, Atlanta, GA 30320. Phone (404) 530-6834.

—— Getting from the Airport to Your Hotel

Your options are: hotel shuttle, taxi, rental car, private shuttle, limousine, or the airport train.

The Airport Train

One of America's really neat urban transportation tricks is the MARTA train from the Atlanta airport to downtown. Travelers who have discovered it love it.

The airport entrance to the train platform is near the baggage claim. It's adequately marked when you reach the claim area. From there, for $1.50, you can quickly reach any place on the rail system map. Five Points Station, the centerpoint of the rail system, is only 15 minutes away. Many hotels in the downtown area and along the Peachtree Street corridor are within easy walking distance of a MARTA station.

Hotel Shuttles

Some 42 hotels have shuttle service to and from the airport. If yours is one of these, a hotel shuttle bus will meet you at curbside outside the baggage claim area and transport you to your hotel. Generally, hotels in the airport area provide free service, but hotels downtown and in outlying areas charge for it.

Taxis

Taxis are easy to find at the west side of the airport near baggage claim. The bullpen holds 315 cabs. During busy times many drivers are waiting their turn. Ten or so line up by the dispatcher's booth on the sidewalk at any one time. The dispatcher is an employee of the city aviation department and is charged with keeping the taxi traffic flowing smoothly. Taxi fare from the airport to downtown is $15.

Rental Cars

Eight rental car companies have customer service counters at the Atlanta airport as well as other locations throughout the metro area. In addition, one off-airport rental company is listed. In each case, the companies have free pick-up and delivery to and from the Atlanta airport.

Auto rental companies with customer service counters at the Atlanta airport:

Alamo	(404) 763-5208
Avis	(404) 530-2700
Budget	(404) 530-3030
Dollar Rent-A-Car	(404) 766-0244
Hertz	(404) 530-2990
National	(404) 530-2800
Thrifty	(770) 996-2350
Value	(404) 763-0220

Off-site auto rental company:

Atlanta Rental Car	(404) 763-1110

Private Shuttles

A surprising number of vans, shuttle buses, and cars-for-hire carry passengers between Hartsfield Airport and destinations in and outside Atlanta. Each of these operators has at least one designated parking slot in the ground transportation area at the west end of the Atlanta airport. Atlanta Shuttle Service (formerly Northside Airport Express) is the biggest operator with regularly scheduled service between the airport and downtown and suburban hotels plus other destinations. A round-trip ride from the airport to downtown costs $14. For further information, call (404) 768-7600.

Other shuttle operators (and their scheduled destinations) include:

AAA Airport Express
(404) 767-2000
Duluth/Gwinnett, Lawrenceville, Norcross, Northlake/Tucker, Suwanee, Athens

A&M Limosines
(770) 919-8888
Perimeter, Windy Hill, Marietta, Galleria

Airport Connection
(770) 457-5757
Hotels along the I-285 perimeter including Perimeter, Norcross, Galleria, Marietta

Airport Express
(205) 591-7770
Birmingham, Alabama

Alabama Limousine
(205) 820-5990
Anniston and Fort McClellan, Alabama

Atlanta Airport Shuttle
(404) 524-3400 or (800) 842-2770
Downtown, Midtown, Lenox/Buckhead, Northeast/Northwest/Emory, Roswell

Atlanta Hotels Connection
(404) 312-2479
Cumberland-Windy Hill/Marietta, Roswell/Alpharetta, Perimeter

Center/Dunwoody, Norcross-Peachtree Corners/Gwinnett, Northlake/Tucker, Decatur/Stone Mountain

Daytime Transportation, Inc.
(770) 399-6069 or (770) 662-9787
Perimeter, Marietta, Roswell, Cumberland, Fulton Industrial, Norcross

Interstate Airport Jitney
(770) 932-6757
Galleria, Cumberland, Windy Hill, Delk Road, Dobbins AFB, Norcross, Duluth, Perimeter Center

Shuttle Trans
(800) 556-5466
Rome, Cartersville, Calhoun, Dalton

Limousines

Listed below are three limousine services. Rates vary, so call for information.

Cary	(404) 223-2000
Prestige	(404) 349-1231
Simon's	(404) 691-2101

A Geographic Overview of Atlanta

Atlanta is located in the southeastern United States in what has become known as the Sunbelt. It is the capital of Georgia, the last of the 13 original American colonies and the largest state east of the Mississippi River. Atlanta is in the northern half of the state, a region known as the "piedmont," a section of rolling hills between the rugged mountains and the flat coastal plain.

Atlanta got its start as a transportation town, and that has been its strong suit ever since. The site was originally selected because it was the first place south of the mountains flat enough to serve as a connecting point for railroads from the North, South, East, and West. The first name for Atlanta was Terminus. A stake in the ground designated where the Western and Atlantic Railroad from Chattanooga terminated. The city grew up around that stake. The geographical location that made it such a fortuitous location for railroads has also worked for airlines, highways, electronic communications, and, lately, for conventions and trade shows. Atlanta is, and always has been, a crossroads town.

Metropolitan Atlanta encompasses 20 counties and approximately 100 cities and towns. It covers over 5,000 square miles. Over 3 million people live in the area. It has no natural geographical boundaries. Connected by a network of interstate highways, it is similar to Los Angeles in its urban sprawl. Suburbanites think nothing of driving 40, 50, or 60 miles to work at an office building downtown or off I-285, the perimeter highway that circles the city.

Atlanta proper is a city of 136 square miles and 400,000 residents. Officially the city is divided into four quadrants: Northwest, Northeast, Southwest, and Southeast. Five Points is the center point. Lines extend in the four directions of the compass to the city limits. The designations (NW, NE, SW, SE), which are used on mail and shown in the telephone book, are useful in a city where several streets may have the same name. Street numbers begin at Five Points and increase as they get farther afield. Odd numbers are on the right-hand side of the street, even numbers on the left.

In addition to the major quadrants, common usage has divided the city into loosely defined sections that lie along Peachtree Street: Underground and Old Downtown, Downtown, Midtown, Buckhead, and Brookhaven. There is nothing sacred about these designations—they have evolved over the years. You will not find common agreement on exactly what these divisions are or the precise geographical boundaries that define them.

The city is further divided into neighborhoods. These tree-lined enclaves, each with its own style, have defined the city since its earliest days (see "Part One: Understanding the City").

One thing you will find confusing is that some neighborhoods and some sections of town have the same names. For example, a senior vice president of Georgia Pacific will tell you, "I live on Tuxedo Road in Buckhead." He means the neighborhood. A twenty-something waiter at Houston's may say, "When I get off tonight, I'm going to The Chameleon Club in Buckhead." He means the section of town. The distinction is significant.

Things the Natives Already Know

—— MARTA: An Introduction

Atlanta is a driver's town. If you are coming to the city for any length of time, our advice is to come here with your own car or rent one. If you are going to see the city's neighborhoods, enjoy attractions like Six Flags and Stone Mountain, or visit any suburban areas, a car is a must.

With that said, every visitor to Atlanta should understand that the Metropolitan Atlanta Rapid Transit Authority, known as MARTA, is a world-class, clean, efficient, safe, well-run transportation system. It can be the ideal way of getting around Atlanta for some types of visits (especially those limited to the area inside the perimeter).

For detailed information on using MARTA, see "Riding MARTA: A Really Good Idea." The following will give you a brief overview of the system.

A City-Wide Network of Rails and Buses

Many people think of MARTA strictly as a rail system—like the Metro in Washington or the Underground in London. But the rail system, as useful as it is to out-of-town visitors, is only a small part of the vast MARTA system. The grand network includes not only rail but more than 700 buses driving 150 routes. It is a spiderweb of lines that reaches into every corner of the city.

The entire system map is prominently displayed outside every MARTA station, so you don't have to pay a fare to study the rail and bus network. All rail timetables and some bus timetables are available at every rail station. RideStores (ticket and information centers operated by MARTA) are likely to have more bus route timetables, but the supply of timetables is often depleted. The best bet for acquiring a complete set of bus route timetables is to go to the RideStore at the Lindbergh Station. This is MARTA headquarters, and usually the rack displaying the

ledules is full. If you have the opportunity, write or call
dvance of your visit for information about the transit sys-
se it, and how it relates to the city.

For Advance Information on MARTA

To receive information about the MARTA system before you arrive in Atlanta, write to: Schedule Information, MARTA Headquarters, 2424 Piedmont Road, NE, Atlanta, GA 30324-3330. Or call (404) 848-4711, Monday–Friday, 6 A.M.–10 P.M. and Saturday and Sunday, 8 A.M.–4 P.M.

When inquiring, ask for:

1. The rapid rail system timetable.

2. The system map. In addition to showing all 150 bus routes in great detail, this map provides, on the reverse side, one of the best street maps of downtown Atlanta.

3. Three individual bus timetables: Numbers 10, 23, and 25. These are the schedules and routes for the Peachtree Street bus. The information in these schedules will open up for you a wonderful route running the length of Peachtree Street, from the state Capitol to the I-285 perimeter highway. This is an easy-to-use system of buses that few Atlantans know about.

By familiarizing yourself with the basic format of these few schedules and the system map, you can determine how extensively you would like to use MARTA on your Atlanta visit. All the schedules work basically the same way. After you have mastered one, you will know how to use them all. MARTA also has a web page on the internet at http://www. itsmarta.com. You can find fare information, schedules, maps, current MARTA news, and special promotions.

—— Walking in Atlanta

It is often alleged that Atlanta is "not a walking city." Thanks to thousands of convention attendees who have never been exposed to this axiom, attitudes about walking are changing. In this guide we offer a number of walking tours. Should you elect to try one or more of them, you may find they afford the most personal way of exploring and enjoying the city. PATH is a walking, jogging, and biking trail that extends 40 miles through Atlanta and some of its suburbs. It connects several of the most interesting neighborhoods and provides inspiring views of the city. PATH maps are available at Atlanta area bike shops for $3 or by calling (404) 875-7284. Thanks to PATH and to the development of Olympic venues and parks in downtown coupled with Peachtree Street, which is walkable the entire seven miles from Five Points to Buckhead, Atlanta may be considered one of the premier walking cities in America.

The Taxi Situation

Atlanta has long had a reputation as a dreadful taxi town. For years it seemed that everyone you talked to had a nightmare story about the city's taxis. Consequently, Atlanta has instituted policy reforms, insisted on owners cleaning up the appearance of taxis, tightened up rules for issuing permits, and enforced some basic rules for driver behavior, such as requiring that all drivers speak English. Atlanta's massive spruce-up for the 1996 Olympics had a positive effect on the taxi situation. We hope it will last.

The main thing you need to know for now is that you shouldn't plan on hailing a cab in Atlanta. Call for one, or get into one at your hotel.

Atlanta Customs and Protocol

Tipping

Is the tip you normally leave at home appropriate in Atlanta? The answer is yes. Just bear in mind that a tip is a reward for good service. Here are some guidelines:

Porters and Skycaps. A dollar a bag.

Cab Drivers. A lot depends on the service and the courtesy. If the fare is less than $8, give the cabbie the change and a dollar. On a $4.50 fare, in other words, give him the 50¢ change plus a buck. If the fare is more than $8, give the cabbie the change and two dollars. If you are asking the cabbie to take you only a block or two, the fare will be small, but your tip should be large ($3–5) to make up for his wait in line and to partially compensate him for missing a better-paying fare. Add an extra dollar to your tip if the cabbie does a lot of luggage handling.

Parking Valets. $2 is correct if the valet is courteous and demonstrates some hustle. A dollar will do if the service is just OK. Only pay when you check your car out, not when you leave it.

Bellmen. When a bellman greets you at your car with one of those rolling carts and handles all of your bags, $5 is about right. The more luggage you carry yourself, of course, the less you should tip.

Waiters. Whether in a coffee shop, a gourmet restaurant, or ordering from room service, the standard gratuity for acceptable service is 15% of the total tab, before sales tax. At a buffet or brunch where you serve yourself, it is customary to leave a dollar to two for the folks who bring your drinks.

Cocktail Waiters/Bartenders. Here you tip by the round. For two people, a dollar a round; for more than two people, two dollars a round. For a large group, use your judgment: Is everyone drinking beer, or is the order long and complicated?

Hotel Maids. On checking out, leave a dollar or two per day for each day you stayed, providing the service was good.

How to Look and Sound Like a Native

Fitting in is important in the South. It is easier in Atlanta because Atlanta is the least southern of any southern town, unless you count Florida as part of the South. Long an attractive investment for outside capital, a hub for transportation, and headquarters for Fortune 500 businesses, Atlanta has never cultivated its southernness like Charleston or Savannah. Most of the streets are paved. There is no Tara on Peachtree Street. Women don't wear hoop skirts, at least not to work. You will meet few native Atlantans. Nevertheless, there are some observances that those few natives and longtime residents admire in an outsider.

When ordering breakfast, order grits. When the grits arrive, resist the urge to cautiously probe them with your fork and say, "So. This is grits?" Simply put butter and salt and pepper on them and eat like you have grits for breakfast every day.

You may say "y'all," but use it correctly. "Y'all" is plural, never singular. When addressing a business associate, you do not say, "Y'all going to the Braves game tonight?" if you are referring to him alone. The question is perfectly phrased, however, if you are including his family in the inquiry.

Never say "You-all." This is a common and fatal mistake. Typically a couple from out-of-town having dinner with friends in Atlanta will amuse themselves by saying, "Do *you-all* want wine with dinner?" or,

"Will *you-all* pass the ceviche?" If they are very good friends, the Southerners may bear this with thin smiles, but it grates like a fingernail on a blackboard.

Do not say "fixin'" as in, "I'm fixin' to go to the airport." This is only for born Southerners. We have never seen a Northerner who could pull it off. Work on your "y'alls" and leave "fixin's" to the professionals.

Two individuals familiar to most first-time visitors are Margaret Mitchell and Martin Luther King, Jr. When you think about it, the essence of Atlanta, past and present, is personified in this fabled pair. The more you know about both of them, the better.

Oh yes, one more thing; there are 42 streets in Atlanta named "Peachtree." Good luck.

—— *Publications for Visitors*

Available at the front desk or concierge table at most hotels, the following publications provide a wealth of useful information on dining, entertainment, shopping, sports, tours and sightseeing, transportation, and special events. Most of them also contain coupons for discounts at local shops, restaurants, and attractions.

Creative Loafing is the best comprehensive entertainment guide available in the city. A thick weekly tabloid newspaper covering news, public issues, and arts and entertainment, its editorial content holds forth in that irreverent tone that distinguishes urban alternative newspapers. This one includes a healthy dose of articles, columns, reviews, and editorials, along with restaurant listings, concert and club calendars, a theater guide, attractions guide, special events calendar, and a fascinating classified section.

Creative Loafing is distributed free throughout the city. If you want to see a copy before you arrive in Atlanta, write the publisher:

Eason Publications, 750 Willoughby Way, Atlanta, GA 30312; or phone (404) 688-5623.

KEY Atlanta, the city's oldest visitor guide, is distributed in major hotels and prominent visitor locations throughout the metro area. The 34-page, pocket-sized publication provides a quick, weekly reference to shopping, restaurants, sightseeing, and entertainment. It also includes a calendar of weekly events; directory of Atlanta services; listings of shops, restaurants, and sights; and suggestions for going "out on the town." Each issue also includes maps of the metro area, MARTA, and Buckhead.

KEY Atlanta is free in hotels but does sell subscriptions. One copy per month for a year is $18. Fifty-two copies a year is $78. Write to:

KEY Atlanta, 550 Pharr Road, Suite 640, Atlanta, GA 30305; or phone (404) 233-2299.

WHERE Atlanta is a monthly magazine focusing on feature articles and directories of interest to the Atlanta visitor. It is distributed at no charge to hotels and attractions throughout the city. Each issue includes subjects that relate to visitor priorities, such as current art shows and trends, restaurants and food, profiles of local people, and business travelers' information.

The magazine also includes directories of art and antique sources, night life, useful phone numbers, restaurants, shops and services, museum events, theatrical productions, and maps of downtown, Buckhead, and Greater Atlanta. Subscriptions are available for $25. Write to:

WHERE Atlanta, 180 Allen Road, 302 North Building, Atlanta, GA 30328; or phone (404) 843-9800.

Leisure is the tabloid entertainment insert that appears each Saturday in the *Atlanta Journal-Constitution*. The publication includes a listing of key happenings for the week, as well as concert, club, arts, kids', theater/dance, movie, special events, and radio calendars. Also included are feature articles and food reviews. Write to:

The *Atlanta Journal-Constitution,* P.O. Box 4689, Atlanta, GA 30302; or phone (404) 526-5151.

The *Hudspeth Report*, a monthly tabloid paper, bills itself as "the pulse of Atlanta," and it certainly contains a large mixed-bag of entertainment listings, guides, and calendars. Slimmer than *Creative Loafing* but heavier on practical nuggets and lighter on editorials, this paper is fun-alternative rather than serious-alternative. Its upbeat, let's-party tone fills you in on everything from newly opened restaurants to freshly minted local gossip.

A long list of regular departments includes a restaurant guide, club guide, concert listings, movie guide, sports bar guide, and sports listings. Features provide close-up coverage of specific attractions and areas of town, such as Underground or Buckhead.

The paper is distributed free around the city. Annual subscriptions are available for $18. Write to:

The *Hudspeth Report,* 5180 Roswell Road, Suite 1, Courtyard South, Atlanta, GA 30342; or phone (404) 255-3220.

Atlanta is the official city magazine of Atlanta. This glossy monthly is better than most of its chamber-of-commerce type brethren across the United States. With its sharp graphic design and borderline investigative features, *Atlanta* gives an especially good look at the city for those who come here to do business or are contemplating doing so. Stories on local trends, leaders, companies, issues, and entertainment combine for a cross-sectional viewpoint of Atlanta culture.

Regular departments include "Dining Out," "Arts & Entertainment," "Style," and "Insider."

You can find the magazine in many hotels and office lobbies, or subscribe for a year for $15. Write to:

Atlanta, Two Midtown Plaza, 1360 Peachtree Street, Suite 1800, Atlanta, GA 30309; or phone (404) 872-3100.

— *Atlanta for Children*

Atlanta is a marvelous city to explore with children. In fact, many of the attractions, like Six Flags and White Water, are a lot more fun with children than without them.

Some of the inside-Atlanta things to do may not seem particularly kids-oriented. But, in fact, they have tremendous appeal to young people. Teenagers love Little Five Points. And what could be more entertaining for a family that enjoys the outdoors than a raft trip on the Chattahoochee? We have never met a child who did not think Lenox Square Shopping Mall was one of the most interesting places in Atlanta. When it comes to attractions, there are several museums designed especially for children—places like Fernbank and SCITREK—and at least two nature centers that have programs geared to young people.

The *Unofficial Guide* rating system for attractions includes an "appeal to different age groups" category indicating a range of appeal from one star (★), so-so, up to five stars (★★★★★), a hot ticket.

For starters, here are the 14 Atlanta attractions most likely to appeal to children.

Top Attractions for Kids

American Adventures
Center for Puppetry Arts
Chattahoochee River Rafting
CNN Studio Tour
Cyclorama

Fernbank
Lenox Square Shopping Mall
Little Five Points
SCITREK, The Science and Technology Museum of Atlanta
Six Flags over Georgia
Stone Mountain Park
Top of the Peachtree Plaza Hotel
White Water
The World of Coca-Cola Pavillion

—— *For People with Special Needs*

As a result of the passage of the Americans with Disabilities Act
on July 26, 1990, and the impact of the 1996 Olympics, the issue of
access for individuals with disabilities has become more and more
important in Atlanta. Transportation systems, hotels, entertainment and
arts centers, and virtually all other facets of the city are aware that
access is an important issue for their marketing and public relations.

Hartsfield International Airport is one of the most accessible airports
in the country. Well-traveled disabled individuals rate it a solid eight on
a scale of ten. Jetways, carpeting, the tram system, baggage retrieval,
and helpful airline employees all combine to give it high marks.

All of the MARTA train system is accessible. Approximately 70% of
the buses in the fixed-route fleet are lift-equipped, and as old buses are
retired, the new ones arrive with the lift feature. MARTA has 77 para-
transit vehicles in its fleet. Visitors must have proof of para-transit eli-
gibility from their home city to qualify for the service on a when-avail-
able basis. The cost of the service is $2.50 each way.

One hundred percent of the Cobb County Transit System buses
are lift-equipped. Call (770) 528-1610 for information.

Three companies in Atlanta rent lift-equipped vans: Wheelchair Get-
aways (770) 457-9851, rates about $89 per day; Adaptive Mobility Sys-
tems (770) 662-5242, rates about $89 per day; and Access Rent-A-Van
(770) 422-9674, rates about $95 per day. All three companies have spe-
cial fees for weekly and monthly rentals.

Special Audiences is compiling a database of the accessibility of arts
and cultural venues. If you have questions about the accessibility of the
High Museum, the Fox Theater, Chastain Park, or other locations where
arts and cultural events take place, call (404) 892-1123.

The Georgia Relay Service relays calls from "Hello" to "Good-bye"
between individuals who are deaf, hard-of-hearing, or speech-impaired

and people who can hear. The service operates 24 hours a day, seven days a week. Phone (800) 255-0135.

The Georgia Interpreting Services Network coordinates requests for sign language interpreters throughout the state. Inquiries should be made at least ten working days in advance; phone (800) 228-4992. Another private concern provides essentially the same service: The Interpreting Resource of Georgia, Inc., at (770) 928-6735.

The Center for the Visually Impaired has compiled a list of Atlanta services targeted specifically for the visually impaired. Call or write for information and a copy of the list: 763 Peachtree Street, NE, Atlanta, GA 30308; (404) 875-9011.

A Disability Coordinator in what is called the Mayor's Action Center can answer general questions about disability access in Atlanta; call (404) 330-6026. For general information about disability access in Fulton County, the county in which Atlanta is located, call the Fulton County Office on Disability, (404) 730-7390. The office should be able to tell you about access to county buildings, services, and programs. To obtain a disabilities *Access Guide* to Atlanta and selected attractions in Georgia, call the Atlanta Convention and Visitors Bureau at (404) 521-6600.

The Handi Hotline is an information source for wheelchair users. Call (770) 998-0211.

How to Avoid Crime and
Keep Safe in Public Places

Street crime in America's big cities is an unpleasant fact of life.
Atlanta has its share of crime, but it is no less safe than other cities of
comparable size. Most of the victims are young drug dealers in
shootouts with competitors, and people involved in violent domestic dis-
putes. Random murders are rare events that police say are haphazard
incidents that could happen anywhere. Furthermore, mayhem generally
occurs in sections of the city visitors do not frequent.

—— *Having a Plan*

Random violence and street crime are events to be reckoned with
in any large city. You've got to be cautious, alert, and plan ahead. Police
are rarely able to actually foil a crime in progress. When you are out and
about, you must work under the assumption that you must use caution
because you are on your own; if you run into trouble, it's unlikely that
police or anyone else will be able to come to your rescue. You must give
some advance thought to the ugly scenarios that might occur, and consider both preventive measures that will keep you out of harm's way and
an escape plan just in case.

Not being a victim of street crime is sort of a survival of the fittest
thing. Just as a lion stalks the weakest member of the antelope herd,
muggers and thieves target the easiest victim. Simply put, no matter
where you are or what you are doing, you want the felon to think of you
as a bad risk.

On the Street. For starters, you always present a less appealing target
if you are with other people. Second, if you must be out alone, act alert,
be alert, and always have at least one of your arms and hands free.
Felons gravitate toward preoccupied folks, the kind found plodding
along staring at the sidewalk, with both arms encumbered by briefcases
or packages. Visible jewelry (on either men or women) attracts the

wrong kind of attention. Men, keep your billfolds in
coat pocket, or in a fanny pack. Women, keep your
under your arm; if you're wearing a coat, put it on
bag strap.

Here's another tip. Carry two wallets: one inexpe
your hip pocket, containing about $20 in cash and some expired credit
cards. This is the one you hand over if you're accosted. Your real credit
cards and the bulk of whatever cash you have should be in either a
money clip or a second wallet hidden elsewhere on your person. Women
can carry a fake wallet in their purse, and keep the real one in a pocket
or money belt.

If You're Approached.   Police will tell you that a felon has the
least amount of control over his intended victim during the few
moments of his initial approach. A good strategy, therefore, is to
short-circuit the crime scenario as quickly as possible. If a felon starts
by demanding your money, for instance, quickly take out your billfold
(preferably the fake one), and hurl it in one direction while you run
shouting for help in the opposite direction. The odds are greatly in
your favor—the felon will prefer to collect your silent billfold rather
than pursue you. If you hand over your wallet and just stand there, the
felon will likely ask for your watch and jewelry next. If you're a
woman, the greater your vulnerability to personal injury or rape.

Secondary Crime Scenes.   Under no circumstance, police warn,
should you ever allow yourself to be taken to another location—a "secondary crime scene," in police jargon. This move, they explain, provides
the felon more privacy and consequently more control. A felon can rob
you on the street very quickly and efficiently. If he tries to remove you to
another location, whether by car or on foot, it is a certain indication that
he has more in mind than robbery. Even if the felon has a gun or knife, your
chances are infinitely better running away. If the felon grabs your purse, let
him have it. If he grabs your coat, come out of the coat. Hanging on to your
money or coat is not worth getting mugged, raped, or murdered.

Another maxim: Never believe anything a felon tells you, even if he's
telling you something you desperately want to believe, for example, "I
won't hurt you if you come with me." No matter how logical or benign
he sounds, assume the worst. Always, always, break off contact as
quickly as possible, even if that means running.

In Public Transport.   When riding a bus, always take a seat as close to
the driver as you can; never ride in the back. Likewise, on the MARTA

⌐ and buses, sit near the driver's or attendant's compartment. These ⌐ople have a phone and can summon help in the event of trouble.

In Cabs.   While it is possible to hail a cab on the street in Atlanta, you are somewhat vulnerable in the process. Particularly after dusk, call a reliable cab company and stay inside while they dispatch a cab to your door. When your cab arrives, check the driver's certificate, which must, by law, be posted on the dashboard. Address the cabbie by his last name (Mr. Jones or whatever) or mention the number of his cab. This alerts the driver to the fact that you are going to remember him and/or his cab. Not only will this contribute to your safety, it will keep your cabbie from trying to run up the fare.

If you are comfortable reading maps, familiarize yourself with the most direct route to your destination. If you can say, "Lenox Mall via Peachtree Street, please," the driver is less likely to run up your fare by taking a circuitous route.

If you need to catch a cab at the airport, always use the taxi queue. Taxis in the official queue are properly licensed and regulated. Never accept an offer for a cab or limo made by a stranger in the terminal or baggage claim. At best, you will be significantly overcharged for the ride. At worst you may be abducted.

—— *Personal Attitude*

While some areas of every city are more dangerous than others, never assume that any area is completely safe. Never let down your guard. You can be the victim of a crime and it can happen to you anywhere. If you go to a restaurant or nightspot, use valet parking or park in a well-lighted lot. Women leaving a restaurant or club alone should never be reluctant to ask to be escorted to their cars.

Never let your pride, or your sense of righteousness and indignation, imperil your survival. This is especially difficult for many men, particularly for men in the presence of women. It makes no difference whether you are approached by an aggressive drunk, an unbalanced street person, or an actual felon. The rule is the same: forget your pride and break off contact as quickly as possible. Who cares whether the drunk insulted you if everyone ends up back at the hotel safe and sound? When you wake up in the hospital with a concussion and your jaw sewn shut, it's too late to decide that the drunk's filthy remark wasn't really all that important.

Felons, druggies, some street people, and even some drunks play for keeps. They can attack with a bloodthirsty hostility and hellish abandon that is beyond the imagination of most people. Believe us, you are not in their league (nor do you want to be).

— Self-Defense

In a situation where it is impossible to run, you'll need to be prepared to defend yourself. Most policemen insist that a gun or knife is not much use to the average person. More often than not, they say, the weapon will be turned against the victim. In addition, concealed firearms and knives are illegal in most jurisdictions. The best self-defense device for the average person is Mace. Not only is it legal in most states, it is nonlethal and easy to use.

When you shop for Mace, look for two things. It should be able to fire about eight feet, and it should have a protector cap so it won't go off by mistake in your purse or pocket. Carefully read the directions that come with your device, paying particular attention to how it should be carried and stored, and how long the active ingredients will remain potent. Wearing a rubber glove, test-fire the device, making sure that you fire downwind.

When you are out about town, make sure your Mace is someplace easily accessible, say, attached to your keychain. If you are a woman and you keep it on a keychain, avoid the habit of dropping your keys (and the Mace) into the bowels of your purse when you leave your hotel room or your car. *The Mace will not do you any good if you have to dig around in your purse for it.* Keep your keys and your Mace in your hand until you have safely reached your destination.

— More Things to Avoid

When you do go out, walk with a minimum of two people whenever possible. If you have to walk alone, stay in well-lit areas that have plenty of people around. And don't walk down alleys. It also helps not to look like a tourist. Don't wear a camera around your neck, and don't gawk at buildings and unfold maps on the sidewalk. Be careful who you ask for directions. (When in doubt, shopkeepers are a good bet.) Don't count your money in public, and carry as little cash as possible. At public phones, if you must say your calling card number to make a long-distance phone call, don't say it loud enough for strangers to hear. Avoid public parks after dark.

— Carjackings

With the recent surge in carjackings, drivers also need to take special precautions. Keep alert when you're driving in Atlanta traffic, with your doors locked, the windows rolled up and the air conditioning or heat on. In traffic, leave enough space in front of you so that you're not blocked in and can make a U-turn. That way, if someone approaches your car and starts beating on your windshield, you can drive off. Store your purse or briefcase under your knees when you are driving, rather than on the seat beside you.

Though most police officials offer similar advice when it comes to personal safety on the streets, Detective J. J. Bittenbinder of the Chicago Police Department has consolidated professional opinion on the subject in an instructional audio cassette entitled "Street Smart: How to Avoid Being a Victim." Presented logically and forcefully, these are practical suggestions for safeguarding your body, possessions, and sanity in the city. The cassette can be ordered from the J Marc Group, (800) 888-5176, for about $15 (worth every penny, in our opinion).

— The Homeless

If you're not from a big city or haven't visited one in a while, you're in for a shock when you come to Atlanta. It seems that there are platoons of shabbily dressed people asking for money. Furthermore, along the interstates, near the state Capitol, on downtown sidewalks, and in parks you will see people sleeping in blankets and sleeping bags, their possessions piled up next to them. Homeless women with small children beg for money. Drivers in cars are approached at stop lights by men carrying Magic-Marker-on-cardboard signs reading "Homeless—Will Work for Food."

Who Are These People?   "Most are lifelong local residents who are poor," according to Joan Alker, assistant director of the National Coalition for the Homeless, an advocacy group headquartered in Washington. "The people you see on the streets are primarily single men and women. A disproportionate number of them are minorities and people with disabilities—they're either mentally ill, substance abusers, or have physical disabilities."

Are They a Threat to Visitors?   "No," Ms. Alker responds. "Studies done in Washington show that homeless men have lower rates of conviction for violent crimes than the population at large. We know that murders aren't being committed by the homeless. I can't make a blanket statement, but most homeless people you see are no more likely to commit a violent crime than other people."

Should You Give the Homeless Money? "That's a personal decision," Ms. Alker says. "But if you can't, at least try to acknowledge their existence by looking them in the eye and saying, 'No, I can't.'" While there's no way to tell if the guy with the Styrofoam cup asking for a handout is really destitute or just a con artist, no one can dispute that most of these people are what they claim to be: homeless.

Ways to Help. It's really a matter for your own conscience. We confess to being both moved and annoyed by these unfortunate people: moved by their need and annoyed that we cannot enjoy Atlanta without running a gauntlet of begging men and women. In the final analysis, we found that it is easier on the conscience and spirit to get a couple of rolls of quarters at the bank and carry an overcoat or jacket pocket full of change at all times. The cost of giving those homeless who approach you a quarter really does not add up to all that much, and it is much better for the psyche to respond to their plight than to deny or ignore their presence.

There is a notion, perhaps valid in some instances, that money given to a homeless person generally goes toward the purchase of alcohol or drugs. If this bothers you excessively, carry granola bars for distribution, or buy some inexpensive gift coupons that can be redeemed at McDonald's or other fast-food restaurants for coffee or a sandwich.

We have found that a little kindness regarding the homeless goes a long way, and that a few kind words delivered along with your quarter or granola bar brighten the day for both you and your friend in need. We are not suggesting a lengthy conversation or prolonged involvement, just something simple like, "Sure, I can help a little bit. Take care of yourself fella."

Those moved to get more involved in the nationwide problem of homelessness can send inquiries—or a check—to the National Coalition for the Homeless, 1612 K Street, NW, Suite 1004, Washington, DC 20006.

Keep It Brief. Finally, don't play psychologist. All the people you encounter on the street are strangers. They may be harmless, or they may be dangerous. Either way, maintain distance and keep any contacts or encounters brief. Be prepared to handle street people in accordance with your principles, but mostly, just be prepared. If you have a druggie in your face wanting a handout, the last thing you want is to pull out your wallet and thumb through the bills looking for a one-dollar bill. As the sergeant used to say on *Hill Street Blues,* "Be careful out there."

PART SIX: Getting around Atlanta

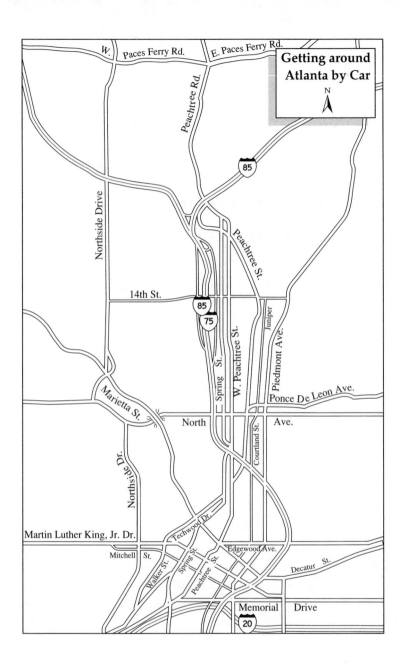

Getting around
Atlanta by Car

N

A Practical Guide to Driving in Atlanta

—— *Coping with the Sprawl*

Atlanta is a sprawling metropolis. Here's a guarantee: drive a car any length of time in this city, and you will soon have your own version of the "How I got lost in Atlanta" story. It's a great icebreaker. Everybody, resident and visitor alike, has one.

Atlanta streets began as Indian trails, ruts beside the railroad track, and cow paths. Many of Atlanta's winding streets and roads originally led to grist mills on creeks in and around the city, or to ferries over the Chattahoochee. That's why you will see Moore's Mill Road, Howell Mill Road, Paces Ferry Road, and Johnson Ferry Road, and many other similarly named roads as you tour the city.

Streets change names with no warning, and the number of one-way streets is maddening. Streets stop, then start up again a half-mile farther on. Broad, haphazardly marked boulevards—marked that way on purpose one finally realizes—wind through plush, tree-lined neighborhoods. No living human has ever driven the entire length of The Prado in Ansley Park. Back in the days before car phones, one longtime resident of the neighborhood tried it, beginning early one Saturday morning, and was out of touch with his family until after dark Sunday.

There was once an attempt at numbering Atlanta streets. The system starts at 3rd Street. It's not clear why there is no 1st or 2nd. There is a 4th, 5th, 6th, and so on up until 19th—a nub amputated by a freeway access. There are no streets numbered 20–24. The system picks up again at 25th. No one knows what happened to 27th. Twenty-Eighth Street is the last gasp at numbering Atlanta's streets.

Oh well, it's probably better to name streets, even if most of them are named Peachtree. In the current city atlas there are 42 streets with the word "Peachtree" in their names. In some places there are three or more streets named Peachtree on consecutive blocks. Peachtree Battle, Peachtree Memorial, Peachtree Hills, and Peachtree Road are all next to each other on the banks of Peachtree Creek.

No, driving in Atlanta is not simple. It is complicated and frustrating.

If you have time, it can be fascinating. If you don't have time to unravel the puzzle of Atlanta's street and highway network, here are a few tips to help you navigate in and around the city.

The Interstate System

Interstate 285 encircles Atlanta. Sixty-three miles in circumference, it is known as the "perimeter." I-75, I-85, I-20, and Georgia Highway 400 divide the rough circle created by the perimeter into six pie-shaped sections.

What locals refer to as the "connector" is a seven-mile section of interstate through the middle of town where I-75 and I-85 merge, "connecting" the north and south sides of town. The other interstate term that one hears regularly on morning traffic reports is "Spaghetti Junction." This is the tangle of concrete at the northeast intersection of I-285 and I-85. If and when you see Spaghetti Junction, you will acknowledge the name as apt.

Georgia Highway 400, the only toll road in Georgia, starts at I-85 in northeast Atlanta and heads north in a straight line to a point just south of Dahlonega. While this is not an interstate highway, it has all the characteristics of one: six high-speed lanes, interstate-type signage, and high-speed entrance and exit ramps. This is an important, high-volume commuter route for residents of the north suburbs of Roswell and Dunwoody. The toll is 50¢.

Traffic is heavy on all interstates during morning and afternoon rush hours, roughly 6:45–8:45 A.M. and 4:30–6:15 P.M., Monday through Friday. Traffic is particularly heavy in the triangle with a southern point formed by I-75 and I-85 and bordered by I-285. Traffic is also thick where I-75 and I-85 merge to form the south end of the connector. Generally speaking, traffic is lighter south of I-20. Even during rush hours, however, the interstate system is the best alternative for traveling from one side of town to the other.

Driving North and South in the City

Peachtree Street, which becomes Peachtree Road between 26th and 28th streets (there is no 27th Street), is Atlanta's main north/south noninterstate artery. Some of the city's most dramatic architectural development in the last 20 years follows the seven-mile corridor from Five Points to Lenox Square.

On either side of Peachtree are two other important north/south cor-

ridors: West Peachtree and Spring streets on the west side, and Courtland Street and Piedmont Avenue on the east side. You'll want to look
at the map to trace these streets because they are not simple straight
lines. Spring is one-way going north until it reaches the connector,
then changes to one-way going south, routing traffic over to West
Peachtree. Courtland changes names to Juniper on the north end and
Washington Street on the south end. Even with all the name changes
and odd routing, you will get around Atlanta easier if you become
familiar with these four north/south routes.

One additional handy north/south route is Northside Drive, also
marked on the map. This is an important corridor that runs along the
west side of the city all the way from West End to the Chattahoochee
River. Northside Drive can provide a handy route to the Georgia
Dome, or easy access to downtown via 10th, 14th, or Marietta Streets.

—— *Driving East and West in the City*

The important east/west routes are easier to master because they
all accommodate two-way traffic and they do not change names,
except in the case of Paces Ferry, which is West Paces Ferry Road on
the west side of Peachtree Street and East Paces Ferry Road on the
east side of Peachtree Street. The main east/west corridors are Martin
Luther King, Jr. Boulevard, North Avenue, 14th Street, and Paces
Ferry Road.

If you can locate and follow those important streets, you will be
able to navigate around Atlanta.

—— *Parking*

Generally speaking, parking in downtown Atlanta is plentiful
and reasonably priced. In fact, from an aesthetic standpoint there are
too many unsightly lots in Atlanta. Real estate developers use them as
land banks. In addition, the visitor will find numerous decked, covered parking garages. Expect to pay between $2.50 and $6 to park all
day and about $5–7 to park for a sporting event. During the madness
of a huge convention like the Sports Super Show at the World Congress Center, small surface lots near the GWCC overcharge, gouging
customers for $8–10 per day. But this is the exception rather than the
rule.

Here are some parking guidelines for other areas of the city. The
best advice is this: when given the choice of steering through the

streets of Atlanta looking for a free space and paying a reasonable fee to park in a secure place, pay the fee. For one thing, it's easy to get lost (or at least seriously turned around) in Atlanta's labyrinthine streets and intown neighborhoods. Second, police do ticket and wreckers do tow. Retrieving your car once it is towed in Atlanta is not an experience that will endear the city to you.

Piedmont Park.   Parking during the week usually is not a problem; on weekends during nice weather it's iffy; during special events such as the Arts Festival and Dogwood Festival it's impossible. MARTA is the answer. Ride MARTA to the Arts Center station and walk to the park or take the shuttle that MARTA provides during special events. Parking when it is available is free.

Intown neighborhoods such as Virginia-Highland and Little Five Points.   Parking is usually free during the week, but on weekends some business owners cordon off their spaces and charge a fee of $2–4.

Buckhead.   Although there are some pay lots in Buckhead, parking is usually available and free for patrons of businesses along Peachtree Street and Roswell Road. On weekends when large crowds of twenty-somethings congregate in the restaurants and bars of this entertainment district, business owners rope off their parking and charge for it. Expect to pay $4–6.

Omni/Dome/World Congress Center.   Parking is available at the large open lot called the "Decks" with entrances on Techwood Avenue and Spring Street, and at small surface lots scattered throughout the area. Expect to pay $1 each half hour with an $8 maximum up to 24 hours.

Midtown.   Parking is available at many lock box, pay-in-advance surface lots. Expect to pay $2–4. Colony Square has underground parking, and restaurants in the complex stamp tickets.

Underground Atlanta.   Parking is plentiful and reasonably priced at covered garages on Martin Luther King, Jr. Boulevard, Central Avenue, and Courtland Street. Expect to pay $2 for the first hour, $1 for each additional hour up to $8 per day maximum. Rates are $3 after 4 P.M. on weekdays, holidays, and all day weekends. Consider using Underground for your base when attending sporting events at either Atlanta Fulton

County Stadium or the Omni and Dome. Park at Underground, walk to the sporting event, then return to Underground for entertainment or food after the game.

Fox Theater area.   Expect to pay about $5 for parking during concerts and special events at the Fox.

MARTA stations.   MARTA offers free parking at most of its lots. Frequently the best way of getting downtown or to a sporting event is to park at a MARTA lot and ride the train. See "Riding MARTA: A Really Good Idea" for additional information on parking at MARTA lots.

—— *For the Advanced Driver*

For the visitor interested in a more intimate acquaintance with Atlanta's streets, here are some important roads and intersections that will come up again and again if you are driving around Atlanta.

Five Points.   This was the economic center of Atlanta until the last few years when the completion of the 191 Peachtree skyscraper and One Peachtree Center shifted the center of the city north to International Boulevard. Decatur Street, Edgewood Avenue, Marietta Street, and Peachtree Street intersect here. Underground Atlanta is one block away. Atlanta is divided into four quadrants: Southeast, Southwest, Northeast, and Northwest, with Five Points being the center point. Street numbers begin at Five Points and ascend as they move away. Odd numbers are on the right-hand side of the street and even numbers are on the left-hand side.

Marietta Street.   One of Atlanta's first streets, Marietta, along with Peachtree, Edgewood Avenue, Decatur Street, and Whitehall Street, formed the original Five Points in downtown Atlanta. Marietta Street led to Marietta, 22 miles north, following the railroad tracks out of Atlanta. Early in July of 1864, as Confederate troops under General Joseph Johnson retreated following the Battle of Kennesaw Mountain, they crossed the Chattahoochee River at Bolton and entered Atlanta along Marietta Street, known then as Marietta Road. On September 2, 1864, the Atlanta mayor, James Calhoun, surrendered the city to Union General William T. Ward on Marietta Street near where it now intersects with Northside Drive. A historic marker designates the spot.

International Boulevard. A key street for tourists and conventioneers. Easy walking distance from downtown hotels to the Georgia World Congress Center, the Omni, and the Georgia Dome.

Pershing Point. West Peachtree and Spring Streets merge into Peachtree Street. At this point, Spring Street is one-way going south, West Peachtree is one-way going north. Between 26th and 28th streets, Peachtree Street becomes Peachtree Road.

The Center of Buckhead. Here Roswell Road splits off Peachtree Road to begin its route to the Chattahoochee River and the town of Roswell. The Governor's Mansion is about one mile away on West Paces Ferry Road.

Boulevard. Becomes Monroe at Ponce de Leon.

Moreland. Becomes Briarcliff at Ponce de Leon.

Lenox Road. It stops for a half mile or so at Buford Highway and I-85, then begins again on its route to Virginia-Highland.

Peachtree and Lenox Roads. The combination of Lenox Square and Phipps Plaza at this intersection makes it the shopping capital of the Southeast.

Fork of Peachtree Road and Peachtree Industrial Boulevard. Peachtree Road runs parallel to Peachtree Industrial, then intersects with it and ends just inside the perimeter highway, I-285.

Riding MARTA: A Really Good Idea

As mentioned earlier, MARTA (the Metropolitan Atlanta Rapid Transit Authority) is Atlanta's clean, efficient, safe, and well-run public transportation system. It can be a great way to get around town—it can even be fun. If you have not read the introduction to MARTA in "Things the Natives Already Know," do so before diving into this chapter's nitty gritty on using the system.

Now for a few basics about this city-wide rail and bus network's routes, schedules, and fares.

—— Distances and Travel Times on the Rail System

It's 22.3 miles from the airport to Doraville at the far end of the North Line, and the train takes about 39 minutes to cover that distance. It's 15 miles from Hightower to Indian Creek at the end of the East Line, and it takes about 29 minutes for the train to cover that distance.

Here are other mileages and times between stations using the center of the system, Five Points Station, in the heart of downtown Atlanta, as the center point. For example, going from Five Points Station on the north line to Lenox, you will travel 7.1 miles in approximately 14 minutes.

Distances and Travel Times on the Rail System
(From Five Points Station)

Station	Miles	Minutes
North Line/Northeast Line		
Doraville	13.3	24.0
Dunwoody	13.1	24.0
Medical Center	12.1	22.0
Chamblee	11.3	21.0

Distances and Travel Times on the Rail System
(From Five Points Station) (continued)

Station	Miles	Minutes
North Line/Northeast Line		
Brookhaven	8.6	17.0
Lenox	7.1	14.0
Buckhead	7.4	15.0
Lindbergh Center	5.2	10.0
Arts Center	2.5	6.0
Midtown	2.0	4.0
North Avenue	1.4	3.0
Civic Center	1.0	2.0
Peachtree Center	0.5	1.0
South Line		
Garnett	0.4	1.0
West End	1.9	4.0
Oakland City	3.4	6.0
Lakewood	4.5	8.0
East Point	6.4	12.0
College Park	8.2	14.0
Airport	9.0	15.0
East Line		
Indian Creek	10.3	20.0
Kensington	9.0	18.0
Avondale	7.1	15.0
Decatur	6.3	13.0
East Lake	5.0	11.0
Edgewood	3.3	8.0
Inman Park	2.5	6.0
King Memorial	1.1	3.0
Georgia State	0.4	1.0
West Line		
Omni/Dome/GWCC	0.4	1.0
Vine City	0.8	2.0
Ashby	1.5	3.0
Bankhead	2.9	6.0
West Lake	3.2	6.0
Hightower	4.7	9.0

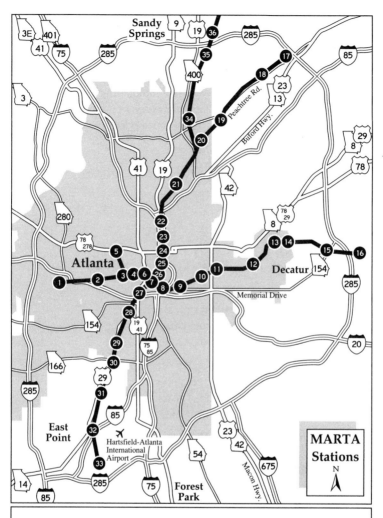

MARTA Stations

N

1. Hightower	12. East Lake	25. Civic Center
2. West Lake	13. Decatur	26. Peachtree Center
3. Ashby	14. Avondale	27. Garnett
4. Vine City	15. Kensington	28. West End
5. Bankhead	16. Indian Creek	29. Oakland City
6. Omni Dome/GWCC	17. Doraville	30. Lakewood/
7. Five Points	18. Chamblee	Fort McPherson
8. Georgia State	19. Brookhaven	31. East Point
9. King Memorial	20. Lenox	32. College Park
10. Inman Park/	21. Lindbergh Center	33. Airport
Reynoldstown	22. Arts Center	34. Buckhead
11. Edgewood/	23. Midtown	35. Medical Center
Candler Park	24. North Avenue	36. Dunwoody

Frequency of Service

Trains leave the stations every 4 to 8 minutes during the week and every 10 minutes on Saturdays. They run every 15 minutes on Sundays and holidays. Here is a summary of the rail service hours of operation:

Northbound from the Airport Station
    Weekdays from 4:35 A.M.–1:17 A.M.
    Saturday from 4:54 A.M.–1:04 A.M.
    Sunday from 5:32 A.M.–12:47 A.M.

Southbound from Doraville
    Weekdays from 4:57 A.M.–1:12 A.M.
    Saturday from 5:06 A.M.–1:44 A.M.
    Sunday from 5:06 A.M.–1:28 A.M.

Eastbound from Hightower
    Weekdays from 5:01 A.M.–1:13 A.M.
    Saturday from 5:15 A.M.–1:06 A.M.
    Sunday from 5:45 A.M.–12:05 A.M.

Westbound from Indian Creek
    Weekdays from 4:43 A.M.–12:44 A.M.
    Saturday from 4:55 A.M.–12:37 A.M.
    Sunday from 5:30 A.M.–12:20 A.M.

NOTE: Eastbound trains from Hightower and westbound trains from Indian Creek leave every 6 minutes on weekdays during the rush hours and through midday.

MARTA Fares

Following is a listing of fares you may expect to find for the MARTA rail and bus lines:

Single ride (cash or token)	$1.50 (one-way)
Tokens (roll of ten)	$15
Tokens (roll of twenty)	$25
Weekend TransCard	$8 (unlimited rides)
Weekly TransCard	$12 (unlimited rides)
Monthly TransCard	$45 (unlimited rides)

Single tokens are available at vending machines outside every call station. Rolls of tokens and TransCards are available at the five RideStores.

MARTA's Best Buy

For the tourist, the weekly TransCard for $12 is an outstanding value. It provides unlimited transportation for a seven-day period. Visitors can use it for multiple excursions up and down Peachtree Street via the train and the bus. Using this card, you can ride to a station, get off the train, walk outside, look quickly around the neighborhood and get right back on the train with no expense beyond your initial investment. In one week's time, we got $25 or $30 of transportation value out of an $12 card.

Purchase TransCards at any MARTA RideStore or at Kroger, A&P, and Wayfield grocery stores in Fulton and DeKalb counties.

Transfers

Transfers permit continuous one-way trips between two points not served by a single route. Bus-to-bus and bus-to-rail transfers are issued free by bus operators to cash and token riders upon request at the time of fare payment. Rail-to-bus transfers may be obtained at the fare gates when you enter a rail station. TransCard holders do not need any transfers.

A transfer may be used only by the person to whom it is issued. A transfer is valid for a continuous one-way trip and is not valid for a return trip. If it is necessary to transfer a second time to complete a one-way journey, this can be done at no additional charge by advising the bus operator upon boarding the second bus that you have to transfer to a third bus.

— Riding MARTA

Riding the Train

Station entrances are clearly marked outside. All stations have at least one entrance that is fully accessible to elderly and disabled passengers. Maps are located near the fare gates to provide information that will help you plan your trip.

You must pass through the fare gates to reach the boarding platforms. The gates will accept TransCards, bus-to-rail transfers, and the exact $1.50 one-way fare in coin or token.

Signs direct you to the correct platform for boarding the train. You must know whether your destination is northbound, southbound, eastbound, or westbound from the station.

On the train, each stop is announced prior to arrival. Maps will help you plan your trip. Be ready to leave the train before it stops. Signs will direct you to major streets, buildings, and bus transfer areas.

Riding the Bus

After you have selected a bus route and departure time, go to the nearest bus stop (white concrete post or pole-mounted sign) on the route you will be riding. The route name and number are displayed above the front windshield of the bus. As the bus approaches, signal to the operator that you wish to board. As you board the bus, drop the exact fare or token into the fare box, hand the operator your transfer, or pass your TransCard through the electronic farecard reader.

Operators do not carry change. If you need to transfer to another bus or the rail system, ask the operator for a bus-to-rail transfer or bus-to-bus transfer when you board the bus.

Using Cash or Token. Deposit exact fare or a token into the coin slot at the front of the fare gate. The fare gates do not accept half dollars or pennies. Token vending machines are available in all rail stations.

Using TransCard. Insert the TransCard, with your right thumb on the word MARTA, into the slot on the front of the fare gate (beside the coin slot). It will be returned at the top.

Using Bus-to-Rail Transfers. To transfer from bus to rail, obtain a bus-to-rail transfer from the bus operator as you board. Put this transfer into the card slot at the front of the fare gate. The bus-to-rail transfer expires 60 minutes after you receive it.

Using Rail-to-Bus Transfers. To transfer from rail to bus, you must obtain a rail-to-bus transfer when you enter the rail system. Push the transfer button on top of the fare gate after paying your fare or inserting your bus-to-rail transfer. A transfer will pop up. Hand this transfer to the driver of the bus you board after riding a train. The rail-to-bus transfer expires 1 hour and 40 minutes from the time of issue during nonpeak periods and 40 minutes after issue during the hours 6 to 9 A.M. and 3 to 6:30 P.M.

— MARTA Station Facilities

Rest Rooms

One of the few problems with MARTA is its rest rooms. All stations have rest rooms, but not all rest rooms are open all the time. The restrooms at Five Points Station are always open, and there is an attendant on duty to keep things clean. Generally speaking, stations at the end of the line have rest rooms open during the morning and afternoon rush hours. To get into a restroom that is locked, use the white MARTA assistance phone to ask that a MARTA employee open the door. Every employee has a key. All drivers have keys. Usually this system works.

Security

If MARTA suffers any image problem, it is that some people question the safety of the system. Nobody worries about the mechanical safety. What they are worried about is getting mugged. This apprehension, however, is not shared by regular MARTA riders. Virtually every regular rider we interviewed feels safe and secure on the system.

Just for the record, MARTA has 300 people in its police services division, 265 of whom are certified police officers. Four Atlanta police precincts are located in MARTA stations: Five Points, Lakewood/Fort McPherson, Indian Creek, and Doraville. Each rail station has a closed-circuit television camera system plus constant police surveillance and patrolling by uniformed and plain clothes officers. Statistics say that one in 2,461,216 passengers is likely to experience a bodily crime.

Parking

Parking is available at roughly two-thirds of the MARTA stations. Parking is free at all lots at all times. In addition, secured overnight parking and a 24-hour staff is available for $3 per night at Brookhaven and Medical Center stations, and covered parking decks at Lindbergh and Lenox cost $1 per day. Parking is limited at some stations (Arts Center, Vine City). If you are concerned about parking cost or availability, call MARTA information at (404) 848-4711.

Taxi Stands

Every station has an area designated for taxis and usually one or two are standing by. If that is not the case, use the white MARTA assistance phone and ask the person who answers to call a taxi for you.

Telephones

All MARTA stations have public pay telephones. Every station also has a white MARTA assistance telephone, a blue police telephone, and a red fire department telephone, all of which are free.

RideStores

RideStores are the ticket and information centers operated by MARTA. There are five stores, located at Lenox Station, Airport Station, Five Points Station, Lindbergh Station, and the Georgia World Congress Center during conventions. At the stores, you can buy rolls of tokens, weekly cards, weekend passes, and so forth in advance. Ride-Stores also have system maps and various brochures. Most stores are open at least from 7 A.M. to 7 P.M. on weekdays. The airport store is open until 10 P.M. on weekdays and from 11 A.M. until 10 P.M. on weekends.

—— The Dome, Omni, and Stadium via MARTA

Routes to the Dome, Omni, and Georgia World Congress Center (Zone 7)

Visitors to the Georgia World Congress Center, Georgia Dome, or Omni have a variety of ways to reach their destinations.

1. Ride MARTA to the Omni Station; walk the short distance to the Dome, Omni, or GWCC. Signs in the Omni Station show the way.

2. Ride MARTA to the Vine City Station; walk across Northside Drive.

3. Drive. In addition to the large parking lots, numerous small lots are located along Spring, Techwood, and International Boulevard. Parking rates for sporting events and concerts are between $5–8.

There are three alternate MARTA stations you may consider when departing from large events at the Dome, Omni, or Georgia World Congress Center, or when you expect the crowds to be unusually big and other routes congested.

1. Peachtree Center Station. Walking time on International Boulevard is 10 minutes from the Omni and GWCC, 18 minutes from the Dome.

2. Five Points Station. You'll have three good walking options:
   a. Take Martin Luther King, Jr. Boulevard from the Dome. Walking time is about 14 minutes.
   b. Take Mitchell Street from the Dome. Green and white signs on Mitchell Street designate it as an official "Dome Pedestrian Route." Walking time is about 15 minutes.
   c. Take International Boulevard, then Marietta Street from the Omni, GWCC, or Dome.

3. Civic Center Station. Take International Boulevard to Spring Street, then to Alexander. Green and white signs mark this as an official "Dome Pedestrian Route." Walking time is about 20 minutes.

Routes to Olympic Stadium (Zone 6)

The best method for getting to Olympic Stadium, where the Atlanta Braves play their home games, is on MARTA. Ride the train to the Five Points Station and take the shuttle to the stadium or ride the train to the Georgia State Station and walk four blocks south.

MARTA also operates a shuttle that picks up fans from hotels and restaurants around Peachtree Center and takes them directly to the ball park.

A Word about the Shuttle System

Using the shuttle bus system to a Braves game can be an anxiety-producing experience the first time you try it. Will I know where to catch the bus? Will it be clearly marked? Do I catch the return bus the same place I got off? How will I find my way back to that place? Will the last bus go without me?

Don't worry. The system works fine. The buses are well marked. Good signs in the stations direct you to the shuttle dock. Bus drivers are unbelievably patient and courteous. The bus won't leave you. The system works fine . . . Except.

It works better going to games and concerts than it does after the event. Going to the event, spectators are arriving at different times spread out over an hour or more. Leaving the game, it's a different story. Everybody is exiting at once, and the system inevitably jams up.

During a World Series game, for example, an occasion when the stadium was sold out and many of the fans were taking MARTA to the game, we parked at the Brookhaven Station on the north line and caught the train at 6:58 to get to the stadium for an 8:30 first pitch. We reached the Five Points Station at 7:13, got on the shuttle at 7:18, and were walking up the stadium steps at 7:28. There was never a line, never a wait.

Returning, however, we got to the shuttle stop at 11:25, jostled through a big crowd without any clear line patterns to get on the return bus, and arrived back at the Five Points Station at 12:05—35 minutes after the game compared with 10 minutes before the game. Not a bad experience. The ride back was filled with happy fans (the Braves won), but we could have walked the same distance in half the time.

While this experience occurred at the old Fulton County Stadium rather than the new ballpark, the timing would be about the same since the sites are adjacent.

The All-Purpose Peachtree Street Line

One of the most useful MARTA discoveries is the bus line that starts at the Georgia State Capitol and goes all the way to Lenox Square up Peachtree Street and Peachtree Road. This route roughly parallels the north-south train line but has more stops. It provides access to points along Peachtree that cannot be conveniently reached by train. It provides good access to the Buckhead area, for example.

The line really consists of two separate buses, #10 starts near the Capitol and goes to the Arts Center Station, and #23 connects at the Arts Center Station and goes north to Lenox Square. For the hard-core tourists, another bus, #25, connects with #23 at Lenox and goes all the way up Peachtree Road to I-285, the Atlanta perimeter highway.

The visitor who becomes familiar with these buses will have rapid, inexpensive access to shopping, historical sites, architecture, museums, restaurants, and hotels along Peachtree Street, Atlanta's main thoroughfare.

Buses begin operation between 5 and 6 A.M. and go throughout the day at intervals of about 10–20 minutes. The last bus is around 12 or 1 A.M. Schedules vary on weekends and holidays. Go to any MARTA RideStore and ask for the #10, # 23, and #25 schedules, or call (404) 848-4711 for specific route times and information.

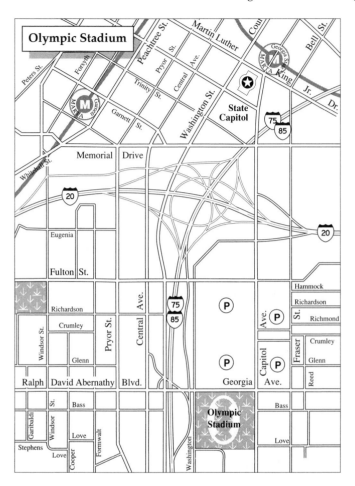

Atlanta Taxis

—— ## What to Know before You Go

Hailing a Cab

While it is possible to hail a cab in downtown or in Buckhead, it is not the common practice in Atlanta. Calling for a taxi or getting into one at a hotel is the accepted routine here. It would be practically impossible to hail a cab in the suburbs.

Cab Holding Areas

Cab holding areas are found at major hotels. In addition, cab waiting areas are located at Underground Atlanta, Grady Hospital, the intersection of Luckie and Forsyth streets, and the intersection of Pryor and Decatur streets.

Taxi waiting areas are designated at most MARTA stations, though not at the ones in the downtown area. Usually one or two cabs are waiting to meet the trains. If a cab is not waiting at the MARTA station, use the white assistance phone in the station and MARTA will call a taxi for you.

Taxis are always available at the west end of the Atlanta airport. At the airport or at a hotel, you'll have no choice regarding the cab company you ride with. You'll have to take the first of Atlanta's 1,800 licensed cars for hire that comes up next in line. Make sure the fares are posted on the side of the cab and that you and the driver are clear about the zone to which you are traveling.

The Minimum Standard for Atlanta Cabs

Here are four musts for taxi operators under the rules of the Atlanta Police Department. A cab must have a working meter. The taxi permit with the driver's photo must be displayed in the taxi. Rates and zones must be posted on the outside of the taxi. And the driver must speak English. If any of those simple rules is not followed, you should not get in the cab.

Complaints about Cab Service

Any complaints about taxi service in Atlanta should be directed to the Taxi Bureau at (404) 658-7600.

—— *Taxi Fares*

Metered and Zone Cab Fares

Under the rules of operation established and enforced by the Atlanta Police Department, taxicabs must charge fares based on a fixed schedule. In addition there are clearly defined "zones," and fares are fixed in and between those zones.

Metered Rates. The rates for Atlanta taxis are $1.50 for the first one-sixth of a mile, plus $.20 for each additional one-sixth mile. Add $1 per person for each passenger after the first, except that only one child accompanied by an adult will be charged the additional fee. You will be charged $12 per hour for waiting time.

There is a $5 charge for use of additional space for luggage, trunks, or cargo for which the trunk space of a four-door sedan is not adequate. This fee may be charged when a station wagon is requested by the passenger for its additional space, or when a driver and a passenger agree that luggage may be carried in the interior of a sedan after the trunk has been filled. But it may not be charged when the trunk doesn't work or is filled with something else that has no relation to the passenger.

Zone Rates. (Note that zones applicable to taxi fares have no relation to the zones used in this guide to designate different sections of the city.)

From the Airport to the Downtown Zone. One passenger $15, two passengers $8 each, three or more passengers $6 each. If passengers on the same trip need to get off at different stops in the same zone, the charge is $1 per passenger after the first stop.

From the Airport to the Buckhead Zone. One passenger $25; two passengers $13 each; three or more passengers $9 each. Just like in the Downtown Zone, if passengers on the same trip need to get off at different stops in the same zone, the charge is $1 per passenger after the first stop.

Trips within the Downtown or Buckhead Zones. Trips within the zones are $4 for the first passenger or $2 each for two or more passengers. Trips that start in the zone but end outside the zone are charged at the metered rate.

Drivers are required to have these metered and zone rates clearly posted on the outside of their cabs. If you do not find this to be the case, do not use the cab.

—— *Taxi Companies*

Listed below are several Atlanta taxi companies along with their phone numbers and the special areas of the city that they serve (when that applies). All of these are large, reputable companies with a dispatcher—that is, two-way communication between the driver and a central office. A record is kept of each fare.

Buckhead Safety	(404) 233-1152	Buckhead
Checker	(404) 351-1111	
Ealey Taxi	(404) 223-6000	
Day and Night	(404) 767-7464	East Point, College Park
Yellow	(404) 521-0200	

PART SEVEN: *Entertainment and Night Life*

The Performing Arts

From brave new dance works to the umpteenth Broadway revival, Atlanta's ever evolving performance arts scene is charged with passion.

Rare is the nationally touring drama troupe or ballet company that doesn't make a stop at one of the city's plentiful venues. However, if you are inclined to get a taste of home-based talent, the plate of offerings is brimming with choices.

Atlantans are especially proud of the **Atlanta Symphony Orchestra** under the direction of Yoel Levi, who steadily builds on the foundation established by Robert Shaw. Some publications have rated it one of the top ten American symphony orchestras. Accolades also go to the **Atlanta Ballet**, the nation's oldest continuously performing ballet company, in business for over 60 years.

The **Atlanta Opera** has grown into a very respectable company that stages three series of performances a year for purists and enthusiasts alike. There are also numerous light opera companies including the Buckhead Symphony Orchestra and the Southeast Savoyards that perform in various venues around town.

Atlanta has an exciting regional theater scene ranging from established traditional companies like the **Alliance**, under the direction of Kenny Leon, to more daring outfits that dot the city. "Diverse" and "visionary" describe some lesser known, avant-garde theater and dance companies. One such ensemble is the **Center for Puppetry Arts**, a rare institution of its kind in the country. During the week, the center stages imaginative children's works. But experimental yarns geared to adults fill the program on evenings and weekends.

Getting plugged in is a cinch. The best guides to current productions are in the *Atlanta Journal-Constitution*'s Friday "Preview" and Saturday "Leisure" sections. Both offer comprehensive listings and notes from the critics. *Creative Loafing*—a free, alternative weekly publication published on Wednesdays—also does a fine job. Both are available in street racks and bookstores.

Many advance tickets to concerts and fine arts events are available by phone through Ticketmaster. A service charge that varies by event is added to the price of each ticket. For concerts call (404) 249-6400; for fine arts events call (404) 817-8700; for general information call (404) 249-8300. Ticketmaster Southeast is located at One Georgia Center, 600 W. Peachtree Street, NW, Suite 2550, Atlanta, GA 30308.

—— *Music*

Atlanta Symphony Orchestra (Zone 8)

Types of Performances: Classical symphonic music. Additional symphony activities include free concert lectures on Thursday evenings, a Meet the Artist series, a Family Concert series, Champagne and Coffee Concerts, a Summer Pops series, and a summer festival of informal classical music.

Performances: The Master Season is 24 concerts performed on Thursday, Friday, and Saturday evenings at 8 P.M. during the season (September through May).

Ticket Prices: $18.50–45

Ticket Information: (404) 733-5000 (box office); (404) 733-4900 (administrative offices).

Seating: 1,762

Location: 1280 Peachtree Street, corner of 15th and Peachtree, in Symphony Hall in Woodruff Arts Center.

CONSUMER TIPS Tickets are usually available for most performances. Even if a performance is sold out, it's worth trying at the last minute since tickets frequently become available. MARTA Arts Center Station is a short, covered walk away.

Atlanta Opera (Zone 8)

Types of Performances: Classic operas such as *Carmen, La Bohème, The Marriage of Figaro,* and lesser-known works such as *Albert Herring* and *The Pearl Fishers.*

Performances: Three operas during the May to September season.

Ticket Prices: $16–107

Ticket Information: (404) 817-8700 (box office); (404) 355-3311 (administrative offices).

Seating: 4,500

Location: The historic Fox Theatre, 660 Peachtree Street, NE.

CONSUMER TIPS   Popular operas often sell out, but usually this does not occur until the day of the performance. Call as far in advance as possible. Advanced parking reservations may be picked up at the Fox box office ($4.50).

— Dance

Atlanta Ballet (Zone 7)

Types of Performances: From classical, full-length stories to contemporary premieres, including a holiday classic, *The Nutcracker.* Other recent productions include Ben Stevenson's *Cinderella,* Danny Ezralow's *Read My Hips,* Peter Martin's *Ash,* Lila York's *Rapture,* and David Rousseve's *Yellow-Tailed Dogs.*

Performances: Season runs September through May. Thursday–Sunday at 8 P.M., Saturday and Sunday at 2 P.M.

Ticket Prices: $10–42

Ticket Information: (404) 817-8700 or (404) 894-9600

Seating: 4,500 seats

Location: The historic Fox Theatre, 660 Peachtree Street, NE.

CONSUMER TIPS   Saturday and Sunday matinees are a popular option. Discounted tickets are offered an hour before the performance. Inquire about special savings for students, seniors, and children ages 16 and under. Come at 1 P.M. or 7 P.M. for "Footnotes," an educational and insightful discussion about the ballet you are about to see.

— Theater

Actors Express (Zone 5)

Types of Performances: An eclectic mix of classic and cutting-edge plays such as *Cloud 9, Hamlet, Jeffrey, Unidentified Human Remains,* and *The True Nature of Love.*

Performances: Thursday through Sunday throughout the year.

Ticket Prices: $14–17

Ticket Information: (404) 607-7469

Seating: 100 to 150, depending on the show.

Location: King Plow Arts Center, 887 W. Marietta Street.

CONSUMER TIPS   This is the place to experience exceptional theater in Atlanta. The plays are thoughtfully selected; the actors are consistently good. The setting is a brand new, custom-built theater space in a renovated plow factory along the Marietta Street corridor.

Alliance Studio Theatre (Zone 8)

Types of Performances: Contemporary drama with a polished cast and an intimate stage setting. Examples of performances include *Betrayal, Driving Miss Daisy, So Long on Lonely Street,* and *Blues for an Alabama Sky.*

Performances: Three series of plays are produced during the September through May season.

Ticket Prices: $21–26

Ticket Information: (404) 733-5000

Seating: 200, general admission.

Location: 1280 Peachtree Street in Woodruff Arts Center in the Studio Theater.

CONSUMER TIPS $10 RUSH tickets go on sale the day of the performance at 10 A.M. for matinee and evening shows.

Alliance Theatre Company (Zone 8)

Types of Performances: The Alliance produces a wide range of plays from classic to contemporary, including *A Street Car Named Desire, Once on This Island, Much Ado About Nothing,* and *Falsettos.*

Performances: Seven different shows, September through May.

Ticket Prices: $15–36

Ticket Information: (404) 733-5000

Seating: 864

Location: 1280 Peachtree Street in the Alliance Theatre in Woodruff Arts Center.

CONSUMER TIPS   This is the "Establishment" theater of Atlanta. In terms of funding, staging, and the level of sophistication, it is perhaps the top theater in the Southeast. $10 RUSH tickets go on sale the day of the performance at 10 A.M. for matinee and evening shows.

Atlanta Shakespeare Tavern (Zone 8)

Types of Performances: Three Shakespeare plays per year plus one other classical work.

Performances: Thursday through Sunday year-round.

Ticket Prices: $10–16, dinner is optional.

Ticket Information: (404) 874-5299

Seating: 175 in a dinner theater format.

Location: 499 Peachtree Street.

CONSUMER TIPS   Performances take place in an Elizabethan tavern setting so members of the audience can order food and drinks during the performance—although this is not a part of the ticket price, as in a dinner theater.

Center for Puppetry Arts (Zone 8)

Types of Performances: A variety of shows for children and adults.

Performances: Daily, Monday through Saturday.

Ticket Prices: $4.75 for students, seniors, and children under age 14; $5.75 for adults

Ticket Information: (404) 873-3391 (box office); (404) 874-0398 (recorded information)

Seating: Three different theaters seat from 100 to 340.

Location: 1404 Spring Street, NE at 18th Street in Midtown in the old Spring Street School.

CONSUMER TIPS   Don't make the mistake of thinking these plays are only for children. They are funny, imaginative, and a treat for all ages. Parking is free. The Center is within walking distance from the MARTA Arts Center Station.

Horizon Theatre Company (Zone 5)

Types of Performances: Atlanta premieres of outstanding contemporary plays, including comedies and dramas such as *Marvin's Room, Heidi Chronicles, Eastern Standard,* and *Frankie and Johnny in the Clair de Lune.*

Performances: Thursday through Sunday during the season (September through June).

Ticket Prices: $12–18

Ticket Information: (404) 584-7450

Seating: 165 to 200, depending on the show.

Location: Euclid and Austin Avenues in Little Five Points.

CONSUMER TIPS   Horizon has no walk-up box office so tickets must be ordered in advance over the phone. The theater is located on the edge of Little Five Points, Atlanta's answer to Greenwich Village. Eat at one of the small restaurants along Moreland or Euclid and walk to the theater. Free off-street parking is available.

Jomandi Productions (Zone 8)

Types of Performances: International plays that emphasize African-American cultural traditions. Examples include *Mr. Rainey's Black Bottom, Zoo Man and the Sign,* and *The Colored Museum.*

Performances: Wednesday through Sunday during the season (September through May).

Ticket Prices: $12–18

Ticket Information: (404) 876-6346

Seating: 400 seats at the 14th Street Playhouse.

Location: Most of the productions are at the 14th Street Playhouse at the corner of 14th Street and Juniper.

CONSUMER TIPS   A variety of price discounts and special offers are available to out-of-town visitors. Call Jomandi and ask what may apply at the time of your visit. Parking is available in the adjoining garage on 14th Street for $4. The MARTA Arts Center Station is an easy, two-block walk along a nice section of Peachtree Street.

Onstage Atlanta (Zone 7)

Types of Performances: An eclectic collection of musicals, dramas, and comedies including plays such as *Breaking Legs, Glass Menagerie, Little Shop of Horrors, Nunsense II, The Second Coming,* and *A Wonderful Life.*

Performances: Thursday through Sunday during the season (September through mid-June).

Ticket Prices: $14–18

Ticket Information: (404) 897-1802

Seating: 124

Location: 420 Courtland Street.

CONSUMER TIPS   A large population of homeless individuals who gather along Courtland Street for St. Luke's soup kitchen makes the option of taking MARTA to the Civic Center and walking to the theater less desirable than it might be. The theater makes a point of noting that parking behind the theater is free and a security guard is on duty.

Seven Stages (Zone 5)

Types of Performances: Adventurous theater, new plays, international premieres, local playwrights. Examples of recent works include *Angel Works, Waiting for Godot,* and *My Children My Africa.*

Performances: Wednesday through Sunday during the season (September through May).

Ticket Prices: $8–15

Ticket Information: (404) 523-7647

Seating: 220

Location: 1105 Euclid Avenue in Little Five Points.

CONSUMER TIPS   Not a place for the squeamish or easily offended.

Theatre Gael (Zone 8)

Types of Performances: Celtic and Celtic-American plays, music, and dance.

Performances: Run continuously.

Ticket Prices: $12, $15

Ticket Information: (404) 876-1138

Seating: Depends on the venue.

Location: Performances at the 14th Street Playhouse as well as other venues.

CONSUMER TIPS   The 14th Street Theater, where many productions are staged, is near good restaurants and adjoins a parking garage with reasonable rates.

Theatrical Outfit (Zone 8)

Types of Performances: Musical theater featuring plays such as *The Ladder, No Exit,* and *The Merchant of Venus,* plus the annual Christmas show, *Appalachian Christmas.*

Performances: Wednesday through Sunday during the season (September through June).

Ticket Prices: $12–26

Ticket Information: (404) 872-0665

Seating: 400

Location: 14th Street Playhouse at the corner of 14th Street and Juniper.

CONSUMER TIPS   Traditional plays are given a new twist here. *The Merchant of Venice,* for example, was turned into the *Merchant of Venus* and original music played by cast members was added. Whenever possible, the audience is brought into the action of the play. Parking is available in the adjoining garage on 14th Street for $4.

—— Venues

These concert venues are among the sites that also feature theater and variety entertainment. At most sites, tickets are available at the box office. Some venues offer tickets exclusively through Ticketmaster. If a phone number is not included with the venue listed below, call Ticketmaster at (404) 249-6400.

Atlanta Civic Center, 395 Piedmont Avenue, NE (Ralph McGill Boulevard and Piedmont Avenue); phone (404) 523-6275

Chastain Park Amphitheater, Powers Ferry Road at Stella Drive

Fox Theatre, 660 Peachtree Street, NE

Georgia Dome, 1 Georgia Dome Drive; phone (404) 223-9200

Georgia State University Recital Hall, Gilmer Street and Peachtree Center Avenue; phone (404) 651-4636

Georgia Tech Center for the Arts, 350 Ferst Drive, NW; phone (404) 894-9600

Lakewood Amphitheatre, 2002 Lakewood Way; phone (404) 627-6739

The Masquerade, 695 North Avenue, NE; phone (404) 577-8178

The Omni, 100 Techwood Drive, NW; phone (404) 681-2100

Rialto Center for the Performing Arts, at the corner of Forsyth and Luckie in downtown; phone (404) 651-1234

The Roxy, 3110 Roswell Road, NW; phone (404) 233-7699

Spivey Hall, North Lee Street on the campus of Clayton State College in Morrow; phone (770) 961-3683

Symphony Hall at Woodruff Arts Center, 1280 Peachtree Street, NE; phone (404) 733-5000

Variety Playhouse, 1099 Euclid Avenue, NE; phone (404) 524-7354

Dinner Theaters

Paris in springtime. Dinner with King Henry. An evening of light opera. Or perhaps you are in the mood to solve a not-so-mind-bending whodunit. These are a few of the offerings at Atlanta's dinner theaters, where patrons partake of delicious meals while being transported to places far and near.

Shakespeare fans will delight in fine acting staged in the rustic Elizabethan theater of the well-established **Shakespeare Tavern** (499 Peachtree Street). Artistic director Jeff Watkins is prone to stage the Bard's most beloved works, such as *Hamlet* and *Macbeth,* but doesn't shy away from directing some lesser-known productions. Food and drink are available, although the cost is not included in the ticket price. Shows are typically scheduled Thursday through Sunday. Cost is $8–16. Call (404) 874-5299 for reservations.

Devout Agatha Christie fans may be disappointed after viewing a show at **Agatha's—A Taste of Mystery** dinner theater (693 Peachtree Street, NE). Wacky, pun-filled whodunits fill the bill here, with titles such as *Peggy Sue Got Murdered* and *South by Southeast.* It's hammy, low-brow stuff, but mystery theater devotees usually leave satisfied. Shows center around a small cast of characters assisted by members of the audience who read from scripts (usually one-liners) distributed at the door. Participation isn't required, but enthusiastic guests perk up the evening. Cost is $39–45. Call (404) 875-4321 for reservations.

For many, the word *opera* is akin to snobbery, but the scene is quite different during "Tuesday Night at the Opera" in the banquet room of the **San Gennaro's Italian Restaurant** (2196 Cheshire Bridge Road). On the third Tuesday of each month, Capitol City Opera Company presents a lighthearted introduction to live opera interspersed with factual and humorous opera lore. A lively atmosphere is served up with a delicious Italian meal that includes antipasto, a salad, manicotti with spinach, grilled salmon, three different white wines, and for dessert, tiramisu and coffee. The cost is $39.50 per person. Call (404) 633-2848 for reservations.

A different show "must go on" at the **Whole World Theatre** (1214

Spring Street). The rapidly expanding actors' troupe offers an edgy blend of improv theater and comedy as well as safer, literary productions, such as Beth Henley's *Crimes of the Heart*. They no longer serve dinner but do have a cafe that offers beer, wine, coffee, and snacks. The cost is $10 per person or $5–7 for improv shows. Call (404) 817-7529 for reservations.

The dinner theaters listed in the *Unofficial Guide* accept major credit cards. Call ahead for show times and parking; early seating is recommended. Dress is evening casual.

Nightspots

When it comes to night life, no other city in the Southeast comes close to what Atlanta has to offer. Whether you have an urge to stage-dive at a rock concert (**The Wreck Room**) or a nostalgic itch to go ball-room dancing (**Johnny's Hideaway**), you can find it all here. The adrenaline rushes through town seven nights a week as live music roars into the night.

One way to go about creating just the right outing is to view Atlanta as a group of villages, each offering its own brand of late-night experiences. The city has several intown neighborhoods where diversity prevails from club to club. So, if one scene doesn't rattle your cage, you can dust off your boots and check out the scene next door.

Buckhead (Zone 3) is considered Ground Zero for the late-night party scene. Many places also get an early start, with the party beginning just after dinner. Club and restaurant owners like to claim that the area draws as many revelers as Underground Atlanta on weekends. That would amount to approximately 70,000 fun-seekers who swarm to the pricey strip of real estate where Peachtree Road bisects East Paces Ferry, to find the excitement of the next big thing or the familiarity of the same old song.

A slice of Buckhead night life might start around 9 P.M. in the East Village, the heart of which is at the corner of Buckhead Avenue and Bolling Way. At least a dozen restaurants just short walks away have bars (and desserts!) that beckon to the after-dinner crowd (**Metropolitan Pizza Bar, LuLu's Bait Shack**). You can then decide whether to roam with the singles crowd (**East Village Lodge, CJ's Landing**) or dive into the area's renowned glitz and glory and splash around with a martini (**Tongue and Groove, Otto's**).

Another Buckhead hub where you can safely park and hop from bar to bar is Tower Place, one block west of Peachtree Road on Piedmont Road, where national chains have opened their doors (**Sloppy Joe's, Dick's Last Resort, Fat Tuesday**). In each, you'll also find a stash of large-screen TVs for sports fans.

North of Buckhead, a few blocks north of I-285 and Roswell Road is a suburban party scene keen on a faux-beach-party theme. Weather permitting, **American Pie** has weekend deck parties with live rock on Sundays. Across the street, a bikini-clad "lifeguard" surveys the outdoor revelry from her throne at **Good Ol' Days**. Volleyball anyone? Step out back on a warm night and join the fun.

A few miles south of Buckhead you arrive in Midtown (Zone 8), where nightspots are plentiful and memorable. Regulars gravitate to the numerous neighborhood watering holes (**The Stein Club, Jocks and Jills**) and a few late-night eateries / lounges that attract an upscale clientele (**Martini Club, Occidental Grand Hotel**). Midtown is also the site for jazz, best served hot, at street level (**Yin Yang Cafe, Catfish Station**).

Unlike Buckhead, however, the nightspots in Midtown are more spread out. And because there are areas south of Tenth Street that beg caution, it's best to drive or take a taxi to get to and from destinations.

A few miles to the east is the eclectic and welcoming Virginia-Highland neighborhood where blues aficionados (**Blind Willie's**) blend with Irish music lovers (**Limerick Junction**) and spill onto North Highland Avenue with the neighborhood joint seat-warmers. On weekends post-college singles pack the ambient pubs that dot the area (**Atkin's Park, Dark Horse Tavern**).

Underground Atlanta (Zone 7) is alive with diverse entertainment ranging from live acoustic and jazz (**Dante's**) to the more rank-and-file watering holes (**Hooter's**). But those who prefer to walk on the wild side will probably find the area tame, since it attracts swarms of medium-starch business types and tourists.

Another center of late-night activity is located in the hip and colorful Little Five Points neighborhood (corner of Moreland Avenue and Euclid Avenue) in northeast Atlanta (Zone 5). The area rocks hardest on weekends and is a main artery for the city's live-music pulse. Several of the clubs (**Star Community Bar, The Point**) draw mainly a youngish, leather-jacket set on weekends, but once again, diversity is key, allowing for all types. For a break from the mainline surge, you can take in some chow and brew at the more cozy neighborhood gathering spots (**Bridgetown Grille, Euclid Avenue Yacht Club**).

And if the fat lady simply refuses to sing, the 24-hour clubs in Midtown provide an outlet for the blissed-out and bleary-eyed mobs. Nothing happens at **Club Anytime,** where the crowd is primarily straight, until 1 A.M. **Backstreet** is mostly gay and attracts a wilder, "anything goes" set.

In Atlanta, the gay community has more nightspots than there are colors in the rainbow. Bars and discos that cater mostly to men (**The Armory, Blake's, Burkhart's**) are located in Midtown a few miles apart. The women's bars (**Revolutions, The Otherside**) are equally lively.

Three excellent guides to live entertainment and the arts can be found in *Creative Loafing* (free) and Friday's and Saturday's "Leisure" sections of the *Atlanta Journal-Constitution.* For a comprehensive listing of gay culture and night life, pick up *Etc.* magazine, available for free in bookstores and street-corner racks.

If the mood calls for laughter, the **Punchline Comedy Club** provides the humor with marquee-name comedians. The **Uptown Comedy Club** caters mainly to an African-American clientele, headlining talents seen on Def Comedy Jam and Live at the Improv. Admission to comedy shows at nightclubs and cafes is less expensive, offering amateur stand-ups the chance to polish their act. Look for venues in the aforementioned entertainment guides.

Diners who prefer to eat early might want to leave the restaurant after the main course and sample coffee and dessert at one of the city's artful bistros. Accents are plentiful at **Cafe Diem** (642 N. Highland Avenue) in Virginia-Highland, affectionately known to locals as Eurotrash Cafe, where foreign languages buzz from all corners. Buckhead's **Cafe Intermezzo,** which mainly caters to fashionable urban go-getters, offers a full menu and bar as well as a feast of desserts.

When you go out on the town, remember there is little cause to be self-conscious as an out-of-towner because there is a lot of truth to the legendary southern hospitality. The nightspots featured in the *Unofficial Guide* are mainly casual environments where you are likely to meet plenty of "out-of-towners" who now call Atlanta home.

Finally, a word about safety. Like any major metropolitan area, Atlanta has its share of crime and violence. After dark, visitors who are unsure about finding their way around are advised to drive to destinations or hire a taxi, rather than walk. Generally speaking, the bustling, well-lit areas of Virginia-Highland, Buckhead, and the Peachtree Center downtown are safe to stroll at night, but unfortunately, those areas only span a few blocks. MARTA, the city's bus and rail system, is generally a safe mode of transportation, and many tourists use it to commute to and from Underground Atlanta; but some stations get shadier as the hours go by. As always, stay alert and remember there is safety in numbers.

American Pie

Bar and grill

Who Goes There: 23–35; mixed crowd

5840 Roswell Road, NW
(404) 255-7571

Zone 3   Buckhead/Sandy Springs

Hours: Every day, 11 A.M.–4 A.M.
(Saturday, until 3 A.M.)
Cover: $2–4 on weekends
Mixed drinks: $3.50–5
Wine: $3.75
Beer: $2.75–3.50
Dress: Casual.
Specials: None.
Food available: Burgers, salads, faji-
tas ($5–8).

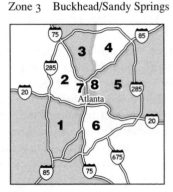

What goes on: Arching palm trees (the faux variety) and a multitiered waterfall (the Flintstone's variety) welcome you to "the Pie," where Sunday night's
live 80s rock music has become something of a suburban tradition. Friday and
Saturday nights are equally lively thanks to a strong local following, and perhaps—just perhaps—scantily clad cocktail waitresses. Groups tend to show up
gender-separate, but past the door there's plenty of mingling.

Setting & atmosphere: Who cares about atmosphere when there are two
hunky bouncers, a svelte hostess, and a barrel of beer bottles on ice to greet you
at the front door? Service is friendly, seating is plentiful, and diversions such as
air hockey, darts, and pool tables are short walks away. The dance floor generally stays empty until after 9 P.M.

If you go: Save some energy (and cash) to check out neighboring bars at this
suburban party square. Good Ol' Days, which boasts two sand-filled volleyball
courts, and Cabo Wabo, a bar and grill with a Southwestern flair, beckon from
across the street. Valet parking is free, but a gratuity of a dollar or two is
expected.

Atkin's Park

Neighborhood tavern
Who Goes There: 23–35; yuppies

794 N. Highland Avenue, NE
(404) 876-7249

Zone 5   Northeast Atlanta

Hours: Monday–Friday, 11 A.M.–
4 A. M.; Saturday, 10:30 A.M.–3 A.M.;
Sunday, 10:30 A.M.–4 A.M.
Cover: None
Mixed drinks: $3–4
Wine: $5.50–7
Beer: $2.50–4 draft; $2.50–3.50 bot-
tles; $7–14 pitchers
Dress: Casual.
Specials: The Bruno Burger.
Food available: Full menu: appetiz-
ers, salads, burgers, pasta, steaks, and
fish. Food served until 3:30 A.M.,
Sunday–Friday, and until 2:30 A.M. on Saturday.

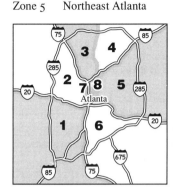

What goes on: A mainstay among the many Virginia-Highland taverns, Atkin's Park has held the city's longest-running liquor license. It's no wonder, then, that this establishment steadily attracts a neighborhood crowd of many ages who come to drink and dine in a friendly, social atmosphere. As one patron put it, "It's a lot like Cheers only busier."

Setting & atmosphere: Atkin's Park began as a deli in 1922 and has remained a local draw ever since. Tile floors, stained wood furnishings, and photographs of Atlanta's history on the walls add to the tavern's old-style charm. The dining area is placed separately from the bar, which gets rowdier as it gets later. The outside patio is narrowly enclosed by two brick walls and a bit cramped for open-air dining.

If you go: Weekends are packed, and music (top 40s and college rock) is turned up after 11 P.M., when the restaurant closes. Dress is come-as-you-are, but week-end crowds tend to upscale the threads a bit. Like all pubs in the area, unless you're a die-hard regular, IDs are a must. Parking and entrance in front and rear.

Backstreet

Gay disco

Who Goes There: 21–35; mixed crowd

845 Peachtree Street, NE
(404) 873-1986

Zone 8   Downtown East

Hours: Every day, 24 hours
Cover: No cover on weekdays; $3 on
weekends; membership fee is $10
Mixed drinks: $2.75–4.50
Wine: $2.75
Beer: $2.50–3
Dress: Evening casual to outrageous.
Specials: None.
Food available: Burgers, sandwiches,
and other bar fare.

What goes on: Just about anything goes at this tri-level disco and entertainment complex located in Midtown. A mainstay of Atlanta's gay night life for many years, on weekends Backstreet features a wild mix of gay, straight, and everything in between. Female impersonation shows start at 11:30 P.M. Thursdays, Fridays, and Saturdays (additional late-night shows) and 9 P.M. Sundays. Gay-couple country-western dances, 8 P.M.–midnight Wednesday, Friday, and Saturday. This is a members-only club.

Setting & atmosphere: The energy is nonstop on weekends. You must walk through the main bar to reach the balcony overlooking the massive dance floor below, or the staircase leading upstairs to the cabaret room. There are six separate bars throughout the club. The dance floor's impressively intense light show can't be missed. The cabaret room is kitschy and could use some serious remodeling (check out the waterfall area!) but most visitors are too lit to care.

If you go: Crowds tend to be thinner on weeknights, but then usually fuller after 2 A.M., when the club gets the spillover from surrounding clubs that close at 3. Off-street parking is $3. Straight couples who sit up front at the shows risk taking some heat from the emcee. Cash advance service on major credit cards. Entrance in rear. Coat check available.

Blind Willie's
Live blues club
Who Goes There: 21–40; mixed crowd

828 N. Highland Avenue, NE
(404) 873-2583

Zone 5   Northeast Atlanta

Hours: Nightly, 8 P.M.–closing varies
(call for specific times)
Cover: $5 Sunday–Thursday; $8
Friday–Saturday; more for national
acts
Mixed drinks: $3.75–5.50
Wine: $3.50
Beer: $2.50–3.50
Dress: Casual.
Specials: None.
Food available: Chicken wings,
sandwiches.

What goes on: A small stage in front accommodates live blues acts nightly.
Local icons Lotsa Poppa and Houserocker Johnson sometimes relinquish the
stage to national acts. The club hosts occasional acoustic and cajun entertainment
Sundays and Mondays (sets at 9 and 11 P.M.). A private-stock jukebox provides
the tunes between sets.

Setting & atmosphere: Blind Willie's is the closest thing to a Mississippi juke
joint this side of Alabama. Dimly lit and smoky (the ventilation isn't helped
much by the three ceiling fans), the interior is simple. Framed posters of blues
greats and assorted memorabilia are hung throughout. The club is very narrow,
but the 20-foot ceilings open the space somewhat. Three- and four-top tables are
crowded together to seat around 100 lively people who can clap, sing, and dance
in their seats.

If you go: Look for the neon alligator at the corner of North Highland Avenue
and Briarcliff Place. No reservations. Arrive before 9 P.M. on weekends for a
seat. Parking lot behind the club off Greenwood Avenue. Special parties can rent
the club from 6 to 9 P.M. The back of Blind Willie's T-shirts read "It Ain't Easy
Bein' Sleazy."

Buckboard Country Music Showcase

Live country music showplace

Who Goes There: 25–40; mostly casual suburbanites

2080 Cobb Parkway, Windy Hill Plaza, Smyrna
(770) 955-7340   Zone 2   Northwest Atlanta

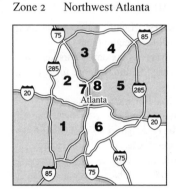

Hours: Monday–Wednesday, 4 P.M.–
2 A.M.; Thursday, 11 A.M.–2 A.M.;
Friday, 4 P.M.–3 A.M.; Saturday,
6 P.M.–3 A.M.; Sunday, closed
Cover: $4 Friday and Saturday; cover
on Thursday's showcase night varies
Mixed drinks: $3.25–5
Wine: $2.75–3.25
Beer: $2.75–3
Dress: Casual.
Specials: Women admitted free on
Friday before 10 P.M.
Food available: Burgers, nachos, sandwiches.

What goes on: This boot stompin' dance hall located north of the city offers some of Atlanta's prime country-western entertainment. Billy Ray Cyrus and Garth Brooks are just a couple of national celebrities to take the stage on Thursday's showcase night. Daron Norwood and the House Bandits keep the crowd twirlin' nightly (except Sunday) at 9 P.M. and take the stage every hour until closing. Recorded music plays between sets. The two pool tables are in high demand; you may want to opt for a game of darts.

Setting & atmosphere: Buckboard is massive (seating capacity tops 400). It's carpeted throughout and decorations are simple. Two bars—one in front and one at the back—seat around 30. The rest of the club is laid out with four-top tables and brown, vinyl-padded seats set up in tiers around the stage and dance floor. Beer signs, rebel flags, and western accents adorn the wood and stone walls.

If you go: Shows start at 9 P.M. Thursdays, and entertainment charge is usually around $10. Women admitted free before 10 P.M. on Fridays. Busiest nights are Thursday–Saturday. Free dance lessons 7:30 P.M. Mondays and 7 P.M. Tuesdays and Wednesdays. Reservations are honored any night of the week until 8:30. Parking is plentiful.

Catfish Station

Urban music club

Who Goes There: 21–40; crowd varies

618 Ponce de Leon Avenue
(404) 875-2454

Zone 5   Northeast Atlanta

Hours: Tuesday–Sunday, 11 A.M.–
2 A.M.; Monday, closed
Cover: Varies nightly
Mixed drinks: $4–6
Wine: $4
Beer: $3–3.50
Dress: Evening casual.
Specials: Sautéed catfish.
Food available: Catfish, calamari,
pasta, chicken. Lunch is available
11 A.M.–3 P.M.

What goes on: Jazz sizzles even hotter than catfish on the grill with a wide range of performers including Earth, Wind, and Fire drummer Sonny Emory; saxophonist Kyle Turner; and Atlanta jazz quintet Ten Til Two. Owners consistently cast a wide net that also brings in top-notch reggae, hip-hop, and rhythm and blues groups. In the mood to dance? There's plenty of room to groove.

Setting & atmosphere: Modeled after its sister store in Texas, the interior is vast with modern furniture and fixtures and tables galore. Showmanship is enhanced by an elevated stage, making performers visible from every corner of the restaurant, including the glass-enclosed VIP room upstairs.

If you go: Call ahead to see if the music suits your style. The sound level from the stage can get pretty loud, so diners who don't wish to shout over the music should request a table in the rear, or ask to sit at the bar. Music starts at 9 P.M. weekdays and 10 P.M. on weekends. Parking at Ponce Square is free and plentiful.

Cheetah Lounge
Strip club
Who Goes There: Convention crowd

---

887 Spring Street
(404) 892-3037

Zone 7   Downtown West

Hours: Monday–Friday, 11:30 A.M.–
4 A.M.; Saturday, 1 P.M.–3 A.M.
Cover: $7 after 7 P.M.
Mixed drinks: $4.25–7.50
Wine: $4.75–6.50
Beer: $3.50 and up
Dress: Casual to dressy.
Specials: Shift change at 8 P.M. is a
good time to be there.
Food available: Full service lunch and
dinner. One of the most popular lunch
spots in Atlanta. Late-night appetizers
available.

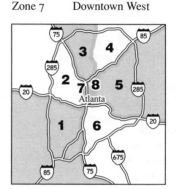

What goes on: Mostly male customers sit in a large showroom and watch beautiful leggy young women take off their clothes to the beat of rock music and with the encouragement of a live DJ. In addition, patrons can choose to be privately entertained in one of several theme rooms including a Board Room, a Jacuzzi Room, and a Dungeon Room. In the Dungeon Room, customers are tied up by naked women who will also take a Polaroid photo.

Setting & atmosphere: This is the class act of Atlanta strip clubs. The interior space is large and dramatically lighted to improve an already charged atmosphere. The main showroom has four elevated stages.

If you go: If possible, plan your visit around a shift change at the Cheetah. At those times during the day, up to 70 beautiful women strut out on the runway and waste little time shedding their clothes. During these shift changes, table dances are two for one, meaning that for the regular price of $10 a young lady will dance at your table for two records instead of the usual one. Boutique sells bikinis, lingerie, dance costumes, jewelry, souvenir hats, T-shirts, sweatshirts, calendars, and videos.

Club Anytime
High-energy dance club
Who Goes There: 21–35; mixed crowd

1055 Peachtree Street, NE
(404) 607-8050

Zone 8   Downtown East

Hours: 24 hours, 7 days
Cover: $5 Sunday–Thursday, after midnight; $10, Friday and Saturday, after midnight
Mixed drinks: $3.50–5.75
Wine: $3.50
Beer: $3.25–3.75
Dress: Anything goes.
Specials: None.
Food available: Hot dogs, burgers, deli sandwiches, and a full breakfast menu.

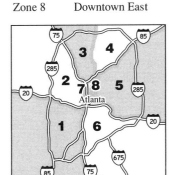

What goes on: All walks of life frequent this spacious Midtown dance club at all hours. It draws its largest crowd when nearby concerts let out, and after 3 A.M. when the surrounding bars close. High-energy dance music is the norm. It gets pumping after 9 P.M. nightly.

Setting & atmosphere: The energy of this club is bolstered by a nonstop party atmosphere. By 4 A.M. you can peel some of the patrons off the ceiling. It's a slice of the wild life and a genteel chap might find the place downright sleazy. The 15,000-square-foot interior is primarily black and is carpeted gray throughout. In addition to the five bars and 40-plus tables, there is a glass-enclosed VIP room and giant dance floor. Four pool tables, video games, and foosball are a plus.

If you go: Don't go before 11 P.M. unless you want to see how the place looks empty. The real action usually doesn't start until 2 A.M., when you should be prepared to let your hair down. Valet parking after 11:30 P.M. is $4, but street parking within a few blocks is plentiful.

Dante's Down the Hatch

Jazz lounge

Who Goes There: 25–40; tourists and business types

60 Upper Alabama Street, SW, Underground
(404) 577-1800   Zone 7   Downtown West

3380 Peachtree Road, NE
(404) 266-1600   Zone 4   Lenox/Chamblee

Hours: Sunday–Thursday, 1–11 P.M.;
Friday and Saturday, 1 P.M.–12:30 A.M.
Dinner served an hour before closing.
Cover: $6 on the ship; $1 on the wharf
Mixed drinks: $4–7
Wine: Extensive wine list; $3.75–5.25
glass; $14–100 bottle
Beer: $3.10–4.25
Dress: Casual; no torn jeans.
Specials: Mandarin fondue ($19.25 per
person).
Food available: Fondue, soups, and
salads.

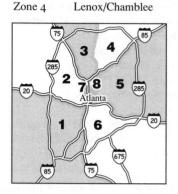

What goes on: Owner (and captain) Dante Stephenson is often on hand to welcome you aboard his ships. A cheerful crowd of regulars, tourists, and convention-goers gathers inside Dante's nautical-style nightclubs to enjoy a fondue "cheese tour of the world" and the cool sounds of live jazz, played nightly on the ship starting at 8 P.M. (7 P.M. Sundays). Easy-listening tunes and blues are played nightly.

Setting & atmosphere: Although it's nearly 200 miles away from the high seas, many authentic nautical touches make Dante's work. Captain's wheels, water wells, and ale kegs along with wood plank floors make an unexpected but pleasing setting for jazz.

If you go: Fondue dinners can get pricey ($17–24 per person), but there is an ample light-fare menu for smaller appetites. Dante's at Underground lets folks slip in after browsing in surrounding shops. Seating is plentiful. Parking is free at the Lenox location. At Underground, park in designated lots ($2–5).

Dark Horse Tavern

Neighborhood tavern

Who Goes There: 21–30; neighborhood crowd and yuppie mix

816 N. Highland Avenue, NE
(404) 873-3607

Zone 5   Northeast Atlanta

Hours: Monday–Friday, 5 P.M.–4 A.M.;
Saturday, 11:30 A.M.–3 A.M.; Sunday,
11 A.M.–4 A.M. Kitchen open until
2 A.M. weekdays, 3 A.M. weekends.
Cover: $1–4 for entertainment
downstairs
Mixed drinks: $3.50–5.25
Wine: $3.50–5.50 glass; $14–22
bottle
Beer: $3.25–3.50 draft; $2.50–3.25
bottle
Dress: Casual.
Specials: None.

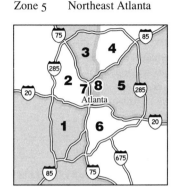

Food available: Appetizers, chicken, burgers, salads, steaks, pastas, seafood.

What goes on: Like many taverns in Virginia-Highland, this restaurant pub attracts a steady crowd of neighborhood regulars on weekdays, then packs in a younger mix of college types, artists, and young professionals on weekends. Evenings after six the crowd is lively and friendly with no shortage of singles. Local and national bands belt out diverse rock music nightly in the downstairs bar.

Setting & atmosphere: The dark wood furnishings, hunter green walls, red booths, and equestrian etchings and trophies make the Dark Horse reminiscent of an Ivy League riding club. For sports and special events, a 100-inch television screen rolls out from the ceiling. The small downstairs bar is still one of the best spots to catch bands on the way up, and the occasional slumming cult idol.

If you go: Compared to the expansive dining area, the bar is small, seating only 30 or so. But you may drink away the hours in the dining area, where eating is not required. After 9 P.M., a doorman checks ID. Parking in front or rear.

Dave & Buster's

Arcade, restaurant, and lounge

Who Goes There: Mostly families and couples

2215 Dave & Buster's Drive, SE, Marietta
(770) 951-5554

Zone 2   Northwest Atlanta

Hours: Monday–Thursday, 11 A.M.–
1 A.M.; Friday, 11 A.M.–2 A.M.;
Saturday, 11:30 A.M.–2 A.M.; Sunday,
11:30 A.M.–midnight
Cover: None
Mixed drinks: $3.25–5
Wine: $3–3.75
Beer: $2.75–3.50
Dress: Nice casual.
Specials: Specialty pizzas.
Food available: Sandwiches, salads,
burgers, pasta, steaks ($7–14).

What goes on: Though billed as a family entertainment complex, it could also be described as Chuck E. Cheese for adults. (Either way, expect plenty of children before 10 P.M.) There's a fern-bar restaurant, a billiards room, and a blackjack lounge where adults can buy $1,000 worth of just-for-play chips for $5. But most of the action goes on in the Midway, where visitors dart around like steel balls in a giant pinball machine. Whirring lights, sirens, and the bleep-bleep of video games hasten fun-seekers who ricochet from traditional venues like grip-the-fuzzy with the crane to hi-tech *Terminator II*–inspired video games and virtual reality machines. And, yes, there's plenty of pinball. Many of the machines, such as the roulette card games, dispense tickets redeemable for carnival prizes. D&B's Murder and Mystery Theater offers a three-act play and three-course dinner on Sundays for $32 per person (gratuity and cocktails not included; reservations required).

Setting & atmosphere: D&B's has dueling identities: part family arcade, part restaurant and watering hole for adults. Even though no one under 21 is admitted after 10 P.M., many youths linger until midnight. It's clean, safe, and chummy throughout. Blue-blazered "captains" direct the multitudes to rest rooms, token machines, and ticket counters.

If you go: Bring at least $10 if you only plan to sample the games for an hour or so. Expect to pay three times that or more if eating and drinking are in the game plan. Alcohol is served throughout, and the only nonsmoking section is in the restaurant. To get there, take I-75 to Exit 111 (Delk Road / Lockheed) and head west. Make a left at the first intersection (Franklin Road), then make a left at the first stoplight. Parking is free.

Dick's Last Resort

Bar and grill

Who Goes There: 21–40; mixed crowd

3365 Piedmont Road, NW
(404) 842-9300

Zone 3   Buckhead/Sandy Springs

Hours: Monday–Thursday, 11:30
A.M.–1 A.M.; Friday and Saturday, 11
A.M.–2 A.M.; Sunday, 11 A.M.–1 A.M.
Cover: None
Mixed drinks: $3.25–5.50
Wine: $2.75
Beer: $3–6.50 (for 32 ounces)
Dress: Casual.
Specials: None.
Food available: Chicken, ribs, shrimp
($8–12).

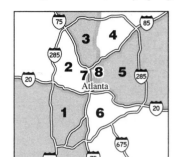

What goes on: Be sure to bring along your sense of humor because the bartenders and waiters are paid to be witty and sarcastic—all in the name of fun, of course. Ask about the wines, and you'll be told, " white, red, and off-white." Mention that $9.95 seems a bit high for roasted chicken and you get, "Hey, there's free entertainment." True enough. Revolving rock bands play nightly starting at 8 P.M., when things get rolling. But the real fun is in the lighthearted attitude of the employees and patrons.

Setting & atmosphere: The interior looks like three college dropouts pooled their life savings and opened a beer hall. Wooden tables stand in long rows from the entrance to the stage. As one waiter put it, "They spent a million dollars to make the place look like a hole-in-the-wall." A very large hole at that. Note the fun touches such as the Christmas lights no one bothered to take down and the socks and bras tacked to the walls.

If you go: Don't be surprised if a sneaky waiter slaps a "Call Me Stupid" sign on your back. For special events, the starring attraction gets to wear a "dick hat," which must be seen to be believed. Nonsmoking section available. Parking is free with validation.

Fadó

Irish pub and restaurant
Who Goes There: 25–50; eclectic

3035 Peachtree Road (at Buckhead Avenue)
(404) 841-0066   Zone 3   Buckhead/Sandy Springs

Hours: Every day, 5 P.M.–1:30 A.M.
Cover: None
Mixed drinks: $3.95–5.75
Wine: $5.50
Beer: $4.25–4.50 for a 20-ounce glass
Dress: Casual.
Specials: Smoked Irish salmon.
Food available: Corned beef, potato soup, oysters ($4–15).

What goes on: Styled after Dublin's cozy inns, *fado* means "long ago" in the ancient language of the Gaels. But here and now, patrons tap their feet to merry Irish songs, share stories over imported beers or Irish whiskeys, and sit by a peat fire and read Irish newspapers. Food is a minor player in the big beer and ale league, but both add comfort to the conversation and laughter that fills the pub almost any night of the week.

Setting & atmosphere: Designed to resemble a string of Irish pubs and shops with stone cobbled walkways; however, the actual effect is closer to the Irish pavilion at EPCOT in Walt Disney World. Walls and ceilings are painted with scenes from Gaelic myths, and seating is made from carved tree trunks. Nonetheless, five separate barrooms yield cozy nooks and corners for groups to settle in and cobblestone pathways to amble from bar to bar at leisure. Smoking is allowed throughout, but there's a stone-walled outdoor garden that beckons nonsmokers.

If you go: Drop by Monday night to hear local musicians play traditional Irish tunes. There's less elbow room but more friendly faces after 7 P.M. on weekends when the crowds pack in. On-street parking is scarce, but parking abounds in valet lots ($3–5) a block or two away.

Gold Club

Strip club

Who Goes There: Convention-goers, salesmen, locals

2416 Piedmont Avenue
233-5014

Zone 3   Buckhead/Sandy Springs

Hours: Monday–Friday, 4 P.M.–4
A.M.; Saturday, 4 P.M.–3 A.M.
Cover: $8 from 7 P.M. to closing
Mixed drinks: $4–7
Wine: $5
Beer: $4–5
Dress: Casual to dressy.
Specials: None.
Food available: Sushi bar.

What goes on: A half-dozen beautiful young women dance on stage to the accompaniment of rock music, then mix with the customers for conversation and table dances.

Setting & atmosphere: Customers watch the action from three levels in the cavernous Gold Club, which is attractively lighted with colored spots and strobes.

If you go: Take MARTA to the Lindbergh Station and walk across the street to the club. If you drive, park free in the MARTA lot. Otherwise parking is $2 self-park and $3 valet. Avoid purchasing champagne, which can range from $55–210 a bottle.

Gold Rush
Down-home, country boy's strip club
Who Goes There: Tourists and local mix

2608 Stewart Avenue
(404) 766-2532

Zone 1   Southwest Atlanta

Hours: Monday–Friday, 11:30 A.M.–
4 A.M.; Saturday, 11:30 A.M.–3 A.M.
Cover: Weekends, $6; weekdays, $5;
no cover before 7 P.M.
Mixed drinks: $3.25–5.25
Wine: $3.50
Beer: $2.25–3.75
Dress: Mostly casual.
Specials: None.
Food available: Full-service lunch and
dinner.

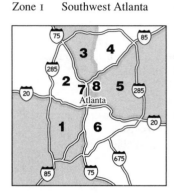

What goes on: Triple-X movie personalities like Nina Hartley, Sandra Scream, Crystal Storm, Tracy Tops, and Melissa Wolf appear on a regular basis. Attractive young girls dance nude on the runways, then mingle with the crowd for conversation and table dances.

Setting & atmosphere: The Goldrush is a good ol' boy's version of the strip club genre. The club draws a friendly blue-jeaned crowd of convention-goers, postgame Braves fans, and loyal locals.

If you go: Like other strip clubs, the standard table dance at the Goldrush is $10, but here you can expect to get 60 two-for-one specials per day, meaning that your basic table dance is effectively only $5. At night stay close to the well-lighted area around the club, which is located at the Stewart Avenue exit off I-85 South.

Have a Nice Day
Lounge and dance club
Who Goes There: 21–40; disco fans

857 Collier Road
(404) 351-1401

Zone 3   Buckhead/Sandy Springs

Hours: Wednesday–Saturday,
7 P.M.–3 A.M.
Cover: None
Mixed drinks: $2–3
Wine: $3
Beer: $3
Dress: Urban casual.
Specials: None.
Food available: None.

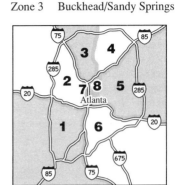

What goes on: Saturday Night Fever four nights a week. The lighted disco floor and twin-mirrored disco balls light up the night. The crowd ranges from blue-collar workers who stop in after work to shoot pool, to retro-chic nymphettes in bell-bottoms. Folks who lived through disco's first incarnation are given due respect when they saunter to the dance floor to lay down The Hustle and Bus Stop.

Setting & atmosphere: The name says it all. The familiar 70s smiley-face icon adorns every table in the joint as well as the Partridge family–style bus parked outside. One central bar and two "beer tubs" keep libations within easy reach when the dance floor fills up. Walls are plastered with posters of John Travolta, Andy Gibb, Farrah Fawcett, and other 70s luminaries. Those teethed on the sights and sounds of the decade will revel in the 90s update. For wannabes, it's a good place to get a taste of what you missed.

If you go: The action picks up after 10 P.M. and peaks after midnight. Parking is free and plentiful.

Jellyrolls
Dueling piano sing-along bar
Who Goes There: 25–35; singles, groups, and couples

295 E. Paces Ferry Road, NE
(404) 261-6866

Zone 3   Buckhead/Sandy Springs

Hours: Wednesday–Thursday,
7 P.M.–2 A.M.; Friday–Saturday,
7 P.M.–3 A.M.
Cover: $2 Wednesday and Thursday; $4
Friday and Saturday
Mixed drinks: $3.50–5
Wine: $4
Beer: $2.50–3.25
Dress: Preppy casual.
Specials: Birthdays and bachelorette
parties.
Food available: None.

What goes on: Hands clap, arms sway, and voices harmonize as dueling pianists raise the roof with a mix of Motown hits, foot-tapping classics, and geeky 70s rock tunes. The playlist changes nightly as eager patrons drop hand-written requests in jars atop the pianos. But don't expect that golden oldie to sound quite the same; the inspired pianists delight in twisting lyrics that are at times humorously clever, at other times downright corny. Audience participation is almost compulsory (one sign shouts "No Lounge Lizards") and joykills are frowned on.

Setting & atmosphere: Cheerful, upbeat, and shameless. Two grand pianos on the front stage are the main attraction for a standing-room-only weekend crowd who sing along to "Great Balls of Fire" or strut to the stage to saunter through a few moves of the Hokey Pokey. Seating is plentiful but tends to fill up fast.

If you go: Lay low if it's your birthday, unless you're prepared to have 100 or so well-wishers serenade you with an obscenely amusing rendition of "Happy Birthday to You." The order of the evening is roll: roll out the barrel, rock and roll, and just roll with it. Include the price of parking in a nearby lot ($4–6) as part of the evening's expense.

John Harvard's Brew House

Brew pub

Who Goes There: Young professionals and beer enthusiasts

3041 Peachtree Road
(404) 816-2739

Zone 3   Buckhead/Sandy Springs

1564 Holcomb Bridge Road, Roswell
(770) 645-BREW

Zone 3   Buckhead/Sandy Springs

Hours: Monday–Thursday, 4:30
P.M.–1 A.M.; Friday, 4:30 P.M.–2 A.M.;
Saturday, 11:30 A.M.–2 A.M.; Sunday,
11:30 A.M.–midnight (The Roswell
location closes slightly earlier, depend-
ing on the crowd)
Cover: None
Mixed drinks: $3.50–5
Wine: $3.50–6 by the glass; $15–25 by
the bottle
Beer: $2.75–3.50 for a pint; $2–2.75
for a 10-ounce glass
Dress: Evening casual.

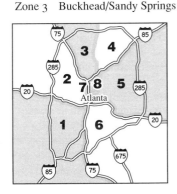

Specials: Seasonal ales; food specials including meat loaf, pot pie, and
sausage platters.
Food available: Full menu of upscale pub food featuring grilled specialties.

What goes on: Beer is the star of this scene where an overflow crowd gathers
to knock back an impressive selection of home-brewed beverages, ranging from
pale ales to hearty stouts. Try the Brewer's Sampler, which lines up five small
servings including each of the types served here such as Georgia Nut Brown ale
and Twelve Oaks porter. With all that beer, who needs food? Well, many folks
herd into the microbrewery's 350-seat restaurant for the upscale pub fare, which
includes salads, appetizers, entrees, and desserts. Grilled specialties such
as chicken Dijon and meat loaf are comforting, delicious, and thoughtfully
prepared.

Setting & atmosphere: The faux English pub setting is warm enough to be
relaxing, but is offset by the high-volume bustle of the crowds. Brew pubs on
this scale are probably better suited for lively groups than romance-seeking couples. Equally bustling is the traffic outside on the rear dining patio. Consider an
open-air table for a glimpse of Buckhead's colorful urban milieu.

If you go: Reservations are recommended; however, they are only accepted
Sunday–Wednesday. On other nights, expect to wait for a table after 6:30 P.M. A
spacious bar just a short walk from the restaurant awaits. Parking on nearby
streets is scarce, but there are plenty of attended lots in the area ($3–5).

Johnny's Hideaway

Ballroom dance lounge

Who Goes There: 30–60; locals, professional mix

3771 Roswell Road
(404) 233-8026

Zone 3   Buckhead/Sandy Springs

Hours: Daily, 11 A.M.–4 A.M. (until
3 A.M. Saturdays). Drinks served after
noon Sundays.
Cover: For special entertainment only
Mixed drinks: $4–4.50, $2.75 for
unescorted women until 7:30 P.M.
Wine: $3.75–4.50
Beer: $2.25–4.50 bottles
Dress: Evening casual; no jeans.
Specials: Food specials daily.
Food available: Full menu: appetizers,
salads, steaks, seafood, chicken, pasta.
Entree range $5.95–14.95.

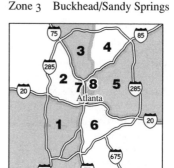

What goes on: By day it's a neighborhood bar and by night it transforms to a Vegas-style ballroom. Dancing to the big-band sounds of the 40s and 50s and golden oldies rock 'n' roll starts early and the years roll by with the hours. A happening place for singles, ladies can expect to be asked to dance. Owner Johnny Esposito is there most nights to greet customers.

Setting & atmosphere: Warm and lively. The establishment is carpeted red throughout, and red upholstered chairs are crowded together. The place seats around 200, but tables are sometimes in high demand. Black-and-white photographs of Hollywood celebrities adorn one wall and a mirrored ceiling hangs over the hardwood dance floor located in the center. When the time machine rolls back and the music's underway, you'd almost expect to see Frank and Nancy slumming after hours.

If you go: If you are under 30 you had better like golden oldies or you may feel like you are out with your parents. On the other hand, it's a great place to send the folks when they visit from out of town. Drink specials for women all night Tuesday. Most patrons are dressed up. Complimentary valet parking nightly except Monday.

The Lodge
Sports bar
Who Goes There: 21–30; yuppies

248 Buckhead Avenue, NE
(404) 233-3345

Zone 3   Buckhead/Sandy Springs

Hours: Every day, 11 A.M.–4 A.M.
Cover: $1 for upstairs entertainment;
no cover downstairs
Mixed drinks: $3–6
Wine: $3–4.75
Beer: $2.50 domestic, $3.50 imports,
$2.75–3.25 draft
Dress: Casual.
Specials: Dining until midnight from
the East Village Grille menu. Late-
night menu after midnight, Thursday
through Saturday.

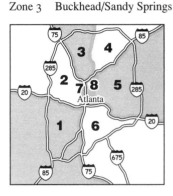

Food available: Traditional southern cuisine, rotisserie chicken, fresh
vegetables, and burgers.

What goes on: Whether or not you decide to enjoy the homestyle cooking at the
East Village Grille, you'll want to check out the action next door at the Lodge.
The crowds of yuppies have grown so much that the fire marshall cracked down,
so now short lines form at both ends of the club. Table shuffleboard, pinball
machines, and a basketball shoot are all part of the lively energy that makes this
a happening nightspot.

Setting & atmosphere: Formerly a fire station, the Lodge essentially remains
an empty cement shell. A main bar in the center, four-top wooden tables, and
arcade games have been added, but the only decorations are a few beer signs.
The main appeal is the hoards of attractive, single, noisy people. Plenty of folks
come alone and mate-scoping is noticeable. Jukebox music selections are anyone's guess.

If you go: Be sure to venture out of the club and take the stairs to the rooftop
patio for an awesome view of Atlanta's skyline. Upstairs, there is also a small bar
that seats around 15 people, where a more subdued crowd hangs out. Parking is
on-street or attended lot ($3–5).

Lou's Blues Revue

Blues bar and concert hall
Who Goes There: Blues fans, 25–30

736 Ponce de Leon Avenue
(404) 249-7311

Zone 5   Northeast Atlanta

Hours: Tuesday–Sunday, 4 P.M.–4 A.M.
(Saturday, until 3 A.M.)
Cover: Varies, $3–8
Mixed drinks: $3.50–5.50
Wine: $3.50
Beer: $3–4
Dress: Casual.
Specials: None.
Food available: Pastas, steaks, salads,
pizza.

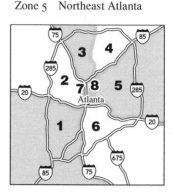

What goes on: Live blues with a rock-and-roll attitude on a large scale. The spacious basement hall has a top-notch sound system, a dance floor, and an elevated stage. The club is also the permanent home for Lou's Blues Revue, a homegrown outfit fronted by guitarist Lou Van Dora that delivers a polished string of standards and originals on Friday and Saturday.

Setting & atmosphere: The proprietor's cherished collection of instruments and music memorabilia reaching back to the 1930s is prominently on display. One of the more intriguing displays is the main bar, which encases numerous instruments under glass, including a Fender Stratocaster guitar. A blues theme even pervades the Neapolitan menu, which features a "Billie Holiday white pizza" and " Les Paul's revenge."

If you go: Expect marquee-name performers on weekends and local talent on other nights: Tuesdays and Sundays are reserved for jam sessions. If you bring an appetite, the menu isn't likely to disappoint. Parking is free.

Manuel's Tavern

Neighborhood tavern
Who Goes There: 21–50; mixed crowd

602 N. Highland Avenue, NE
(404) 525-3447

Zone 5   Northeast Atlanta

Hours: Monday–Saturday, 10:30
P.M.–2 A.M.; Sunday, 3 P.M.–midnight
(opens Sunday at 12:30 during football
season)
Cover: None
Mixed drinks: $2.65–4.55
Wine: $2.60–3.55
Beer: $1.75–3.10
Dress: Casual.
Specials: None.
Food available: Appetizers, burgers,
hot dogs, wings, steaks, salad.

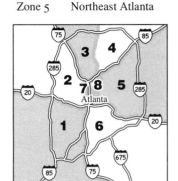

What goes on: Jimmy Carter occasionally comes here to drink a Moosehead
(while his Secret Service agents drink Coke). The mayor sometimes drops in to
grab some chow and check the local pulse. This corner taproom is owned by former DeKalb County chief executive officer Manuel Maloof, so it's heavy on the
political scene. An eclectic blend of reporters, politicos, cops, and clerks come to
roll up their sleeves, kick back, and call it a day at this favorite city hangout.
Sports rule on weekends.

Setting & atmosphere: The wild boar sign painted on the tavern's side proudly
declares that it has served up ale and burgers since 1956. And the somber, dark-
wood decor hasn't changed much since then. Although it's generally dark and
stuffy, the atmosphere never seems to hamper the revelry. The upbeat mood of
the patrons at the bar inevitably spills over into the adjoining dining areas as the
ale flows heavily throughout.

If you go: Before 6 P.M., it's usually calm enough to read the paper. After 7 P.M.,
the bar fills up and most folks are content to eat and drink in the restaurant.
Parking is free and plentiful.

The Martini Club

Cosmopolitan lounge

Who Goes There: Glamorous thirty-somethings

---

140 Crescent Avenue
(404) 873-0794

Zone 8   Downtown East

Hours: Every day, 4 P.M.–2 A.M.
Cover: None
Mixed drinks: $4.50–6.25
Wine: $5–8 by the glass; $20–35 by the bottle
Beer: $4
Dress: Upscale, dressy.
Specials: None.
Food available: Shrimp cocktails and Brie platters.

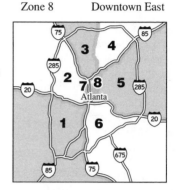

What goes on: Now that martinis are back in fashion, the M club goes all out with an updated approach to classic boozing. A stylish, thirtyish set languidly lounges about glamorous furnishings, enjoying The Scene, and taking in The Moment, while exalting that nifty triangular glass with pinkies raised. The glasses, by the way, are filled with the real thing for purists, or any one of 25 quasi-martinis, otherwise known as "shooters."

Setting & atmosphere: F-f-fabulous. The sophistication of art deco basks in a warm glow of Hollywood flash. The commercial conversion of this two-story house gives way to cozy rooms painted in lush hues of purple, red, and gold. Exquisitely upholstered chairs and sofas look like they might have been swiped from the set of a James Bond movie or, in some cases, "The Jetsons."

If you go: Dress the part. After-office attire is fine; pretheater swank will do nicely; anyone spotted in tennis shoes will be shot on-site. When the crowd packs in, which it does after 7 P.M. Thursday–Saturday, be prepared for a line outdoors and standing room only inside. For a more relaxing experience, visit early. Parking is free and plentiful in a nearby lot at the corner of Crescent Avenue and 14th Street.

Masquerade

Dance club and concert venue

Who Goes There: 18–25; urban clubbies

695 North Avenue, NE
(404) 577-7509

Zone 8   Downtown East

Hours: Wednesday–Sunday, 10 P.M.–3:30 or 4 A.M.
Cover: Cover in Heaven varies by act; cover in Hell and Purgatory is $5 Wednesday, Friday, and Saturday; $2 Thursday and Sunday
Mixed drinks: $2.75–4.50
Wine: $2.50
Beer: $2.50–3.25
Dress: Cool and casual.
Specials: Wednesday is Club Fetish, Thursday is Old Wave.
Food available: Burgers, sandwiches, french fries.

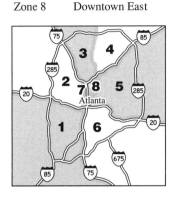

What goes on: This tri-level Midtown club is a major venue for international rock groups and dance bands. It's also a happening dance spot for the under-25 set. Heaven, on the upper level, has provided the concert space for groups like Public Enemy and the Village People. Gripping dance music fills the wide open space in Hell—the club's gothic-industrial dance space. Free pool, local bands, and a more casual atmosphere dominate Purgatory, located on the ground level.

Setting & atmosphere: Originally the Excelsior paper mill, renovations were kept simple: wood, brick, and open space dominate. Acoustics in Heaven are generally lousy, but the 1,250-capacity space is small enough (and the bands usually loud enough) to compensate. Purgatory is designed like a dungeon, and the stark design is conducive to the thunderous music generated by the DJs. No heat or air conditioning, so prepare to sweat or freeze, depending on the season.

If you go: Dress is creative casual, ranging from glitz to grunge. Most concerts are all ages (21 to drink). Admittance to Hell and Purgatory is free if you pay to attend a concert in Heaven. Crowds are generally young and vary widely, depending on the concert performers and the brand of music. Parking $2–3. Free, unsanctioned parking in the Kroger shopping center across the street.

Otto's

Elegant, upscale piano bar

Who Goes There: 28–50; white-collar business types

---

265 East Paces Ferry Road, NE
(404) 233-1133

Zone 3   Buckhead/Sandy Springs

Hours: Monday–Thursday, 5 P.M.–
1 A.M.; Friday, 5 P.M.–4 A.M.; Saturday,
7 P.M.–3 A.M.; Sunday, closed
Cover: $10 single men and couples;
$7 unescorted ladies, Friday and
Saturday, 9 P.M.–2 A.M.
Mixed drinks: $4.25–7.50
Wine: $4.75–6.75
Beer: $3.50–4
Dress: Dressy casual to formal.
Specials: Champagne by the bottle,
$49–195; cognac, $7.50–22; port,
$8.50–13.50.
Food available: Pizza.

What goes on: An older, dressy crowd frequents this Buckhead dance spot and lounge, which may come off at first as a rich man's singles club. Jazz pianist Ron Cooper plays Monday–Thursday, 9 P.M.–1 A.M. Jazz and swing pianist Tony Winston entertains Wednesday–Saturday, 9:30 P.M.–1:30 A.M. Contemporary jazz and easy-listening music ranges from Sinatra to Sade. Dancing here is the norm and ladies should expect to be asked.

Setting & atmosphere: Modern and elegant, Otto's is at once lively and intimate. The main bar in front seats 17, and mirrored walls open the narrow space. The larger carpeted lounge area is dimly lit by wall sconces and tabletop candles. Gray, upholstered couches for lounging line the walls. A piano bar located in front of the dance floor seats five. There is also a small bar at the back that is open on weekends.

If you go: Busiest nights are Thursday through Saturday, the best times to check out the singles action. Lines on weekends begin to form after 10:30, so arrive early to get a table. Attended lot parking is $2–5. Validate your parking ticket before leaving to receive a discount from the parking attendant.

Punchline Comedy Club

Comedy club
Who Goes There: 21–50

280 Hildebrand Drive, NE
(404) 252-5233

Zone 3   Buckhead/Sandy Springs

Hours: Show times:
Tuesday–Thursday, 8:30 P.M.; Friday
and Saturday, 8 and 10:30 P.M.; Sunday,
8 P.M.
Cover: Admission: $8
Tuesday–Thursday, Sunday; $10
Friday; $12 Saturday
Mixed drinks: $3.50–4.50
Wine: $3.25
Beer: $2.75–3.50
Dress: Casual to dressy.
Specials: Punchline punch in souvenir
glass, $6.95.

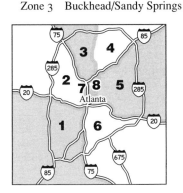

Food available: Appetizers, sandwiches, nachos, chicken wings, burgers.

What goes on: Nationally touring comics perform weekly, and talent ranges from the straight-shooting Pam Stone to the bizarre Emo Phillips. Count on local comics to warm up the audience, producing laughter and steady grins before the main act. The club's Amateur Night on Tuesdays showcases strictly local talent and one takes one's chances.

Setting & atmosphere: The setting is spacious and rustic, recalling a neighborhood tavern with wooden floors and furniture. Best seats to be close to the performers are front and center, but the club is small enough to allow for good views all around. Service is attentive and friendly. Thursday and early Friday shows are smoke-free.

If you go: The Punchline is located in The Balconies Shopping Center, and parking is tight in spaces near the entrance. Reserve tickets by phone (VISA, MC, AMEX). Seating is first-come, first-served, and reservations must be purchased at least 30 minutes before show time. Prepaid reservations are nonrefundable. Tickets may be purchased for same evening performances starting an hour before the show, but reservations are recommended because shows frequently sell out. Arriving at least 30 minutes before show time is also recommended, especially on weekends.

Three Dollar Cafe

Sports bar

Who Goes There: 21–30; yuppies

3002 Peachtree Road
(404) 266-8667

Zone 3   Buckhead/Sandy Springs

Hours: Sunday–Thursday, 11 A.M.–
1 A.M. (until 2 A.M. Friday–Saturday)
Cover: None
Mixed drinks: $3–5.25
Wine: $2.75–3.25
Beer: $2.75–10.95 bottles; $27 for
5-liter kegs
Dress: Casual.
Specials: Wings and beer selection.
Food available: Full menu: appetizers,
burgers, sandwiches, desserts.

What goes on: This lively sports bar in the heart of Buckhead is mainly a spot to go with friends, take in the game, and socialize over food and drink. A limited number of single barstools might make solitary first-comers feel a little out of step.

Setting & atmosphere: A boisterous roar pervades the expansive area of this popular Buckhead watering hole. Hundreds of beer bottles line the walls to boast an astounding array of brews offered. Beer and wine are specialties but a full bar flows. Bench booths and four-top wooden tables are packed together on a gray, cement floor. Suspended TV monitors are in every corner, offering an unobstructed view of the main event, even on the front patio.

If you go: The largest crowd congregates in the rear sports bar/theater, where a 250-inch video screen televises the main event. Thanks to the bar's 750 seating capacity, there is rarely a wait to be seated, except late night and weekends. Nonsmoking sections are available in the front bar only. The bar's parking lot is limited, so if you are already parked in the vicinity, it's a good idea to walk.

Tongue and Groove

Upscale lounge, dance club, and sushi bar
Who Goes There: 25–35; urban chic set

3055 Peachtree Street
(404) 261-2325

Zone 3   Buckhead/Sandy Springs

Hours: Every day, 8 P.M.–4 A.M. (give or take an hour)
Cover: $7 after 10 P.M.
Mixed drinks: $5 and up
Wine: $4
Beer: $3–3.50
Dress: Evening casual; no jeans or sneakers.
Specials: None.
Food available: Sushi ranges from $1 per piece to a sampler plate for $28. Wontons and Yakitori are also available.

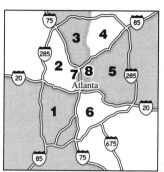

What goes on: Relaxed conversation is the mainstay in the lounge. Dancing and socializing take precedence in the dance area, where DJs spin a varying mix of globe-spanning rhythms.

Setting & atmosphere: The artful, carefully planned decor exudes elegance. Subdued lighting and modern furnishings are distributed throughout. The lounge, sushi bar, and dance space combine for an urban, tasteful appeal.

If you go: Be prepared to pay for parking or maneuver like a shark to find a free space within two blocks. Billed as an upscale lounge, jeans should be matched with a blazer. A dress code is enforced.

Yin-Yang Cafe
Acid jazz–Afro pop club
Who Goes There: 21–50; urban jazz enthusiasts

64 Third Street, NW
(404) 607-0682

Zone 7   Downtown West

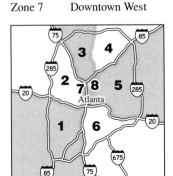

Hours: Tuesday–Thursday, 6 P.M.–
2 A.M.; Friday–Saturday, 6 P.M.–3 A.M.;
Monday, closed
Cover: $4–7
Mixed drinks: None available; beer
and wine only
Wine: $3.50–3.95
Beer: $2.75–3.25; $4 for pints of draft
Dress: Casual.
Specials: Tapas appetizers.
Food available: Soups, sandwiches,
salads, pasta, quiche, and vegetarian
dishes.

What goes on: Ears perk up as notable jazz musicians play their hearts out to rapt crowds. Acid jazz fills the club Thursdays during "Chocolate Soul" night, featuring a DJ and live music. Eric Vaughn and his band are the mainstays on Fridays. Saturday is dance night. During Sunday night jazz jams, regulars have learned to expect the unexpected, from musicians such as guitarist Joey Burns to nationally known performers such as Najee, Stephanie Mills, or Dionne Ferris, who might take the stage or merely blend in with the eclectic crowd.

Setting & atmosphere: The dimly lit, warehouse-like interior is an artful work in progress with funky wall decorations by Atlanta artists. Unlike jazz venues where bands play background music from a corner, the caliber of performers here commands full attention.

If you go: Pull up a chair, have a cup of Zen, and kick back. There's plenty of seating at four-top tables and the bar, but high-profile performers can mean standing room only. Music starts around 9 P.M., so arrive early or plan to dine at 7:30 or so to be assured a seat. Parking is plentiful a half-block away on Spring Street.

PART EIGHT: Exercise and Recreation

Working Out

Most of the folks on our *Unofficial Guide* research team work out routinely. Some bike, some run, some lift weights or do aerobics. While visiting Atlanta during the hot summer months, it didn't take long to figure out that exercising in the city's fearsome heat and humidity presented some problems.

The best months for outdoor exercise are March through June and October through December. In July and August, you must get up very early to beat the heat. January and February are unpredictable: you may run into a day of crisp, clear, fall- or spring-like weather or, almost as likely, very cold damp weather, with nasty bone-chilling rain and even the occasional snow or ice storm.

So during the dead of winter and during the summer months (unless you get up very early, as natives do, on hot days), we recommend working out indoors.

—— Walking

With its many parks and pleasant tree-shaded neighborhoods, Atlanta is a great place for walking. The following walks will not only provide exercise, but give you a great opportunity to enjoy the city's neighborhoods up close.

Walk: Old Peachtree

Significance: This is the heart of black, working-class Atlanta. Once known as Whitehall Street, this section of Peachtree was the center of the city. Some of the two- and three-story buildings along both sides of Peachtree date back to the last century.

Distance: About 1 mile round-trip.

Time: Between 45 minutes and an hour depending on how much window shopping you do.

Best MARTA Station: Five Points.

Route: From the Five Points MARTA Station near Underground Atlanta, walk south on Peachtree Street to Mitchell Street. Turn right and walk west on Mitchell as far as Friedman's shoe store at 209 Mitchell. Return using the same route, exploring the other side of Peachtree Street.

Cautions: Go during business hours during the week or on Saturday afternoon to see the street life at its most interesting (and at its safest).

Walk: Piedmont Park

Significance: Atlanta's biggest intown park.

Distance: Anywhere from a mile to 3 or 4 miles, depending on how extensively you explore the park and botanical gardens.

Time: Allow at least an hour.

Best MARTA Station: Arts Center.

Route: From Colony Square walk east on 14th Street to the intersection of Piedmont Avenue. This is one of the main entrances to Piedmont Park. From this point explore the park to the north and south using the sidewalks and roadways, most of which are closed to automobile traffic. Explore the Atlanta Botanical Garden, which is located on the northern end of the Park bordering Piedmont Avenue, and walk the 1.5-mile trail through the Garden's Stroza woods, one of the few remaining hardwood forests in the city. Return to Colony Square by the same 14th Street route.

Cautions: Explore the park during daylight hours.

Walk: Peachtree Street

Significance: This is Atlanta's most important and interesting street. Everything that Atlanta has to offer, good and bad, from high rise to homeless, will be found along this avenue.

Distance: A few blocks to 9 or 10 miles, depending on your interests and addiction to walking.

Time: Anywhere from an hour to an entire day.

Best MARTA Station: The MARTA rail line parallels much of Peachtree Street, but veers away to the east between the Arts Center and the Lenox stations. Use the #10 and 23 buses, which stop every block or so along Peachtree.

Route: You may walk the entire distance or any portion of Peachtree

Street from the Brookhaven MARTA Station to the Five Points MARTA Station. When you get tired of walking, use the #23 bus to leapfrog from one section of Peachtree to another. Note that many of the shopping experiences described in the shopping section are located along Peachtree Street. It is particularly rewarding to take short walks into the neighborhoods of Brookhaven, Peachtree Battle, and Ansley Park. Return by walking or by catching MARTA to your point of origin.

Cautions: Most of Peachtree is safe any time, night or day. Particularly good for nightime walking are the Buckhead area, Sobuck between 26th Street and Peachtree Battle Shopping Center, and downtown between Baker and Ellis Streets. Avoid Peachtree between Ralph McGill and North Avenue and between 5th Street and 8th Street. This area has a concentration of homeless characters who will almost certainly approach you for a handout.

Walk: Five Points to Oakland Cemetery

Significance: Still in use, this is Atlanta's oldest burying ground, located less than a mile from the center of downtown.

Distance: 1 mile

Time: Allow 30 minutes for the walk, an hour or so to explore Oakland Cemetery.

Best MARTA Station: Five Points or King Memorial.

Route: From Five Points walk east on Decatur Street about one mile to the intersection of Oakland Avenue (also the location of the King Memorial MARTA Station). The brick wall around the 88-acre Oakland Cemetery is visible from this intersection. Turn right and follow Oakland Avenue to the main entrance. Return by the same route or via MARTA from the King Memorial Station.

Cautions: This route passes along a fairly rough section of Decatur Street. Walk it during business hours only. Women will not be comfortable alone on this walk.

Walk: Inman Park to Colony Square

Significance: This walk passes through two of Atlanta's most interesting intown neighborhoods and along the edges of two more, to end at Colony Square, one of the prettiest parts of Peachtree Street. Few walks provide a more fascinating cross-section of Atlanta.

Distance: 6 miles.

Time: Plan at least a half-day for this interesting walk. Eat lunch either at Manuel's on the corner of Highland and North Avenue or in Virginia-Highland, the neighborhood at the intersection of those two streets.

Best MARTA Station: Begin at the Inman Park Reynoldstown Station and end at the Arts Center Station.

Route: From the Inman Park/Reynoldstown MARTA Station take Hurt Street to Euclid. Turn right on Euclid and follow it to the intersection of Euclid, Moreland, and McLendon, the center of the neighborhood known as Little Five Points. Take Seminole (it begins just behind Fellini's) to Cleburne. Turn left and follow Cleburne to the Carter Center. From the Carter Center return to Highland Avenue. Walk north on Highland to the intersection of Virginia. Turn left on Virginia and follow it to Monroe. At Monroe jog one street to the right and take 10th Street to Piedmont. Turn right on Piedmont and walk to 14th Street. Turn left on 14th and follow it to Peachtree Street. The Arts Center MARTA Station is on 15th Street between Peachtree and West Peachtree streets. Alternatively, if your sense of direction is reasonably good, cut diagonally across Piedmont Park from the intersection of Piedmont and 10th and reach 14th Street that way. It is a pleasant walk across the park. Return by taking MARTA to your point of origin.

Cautions: This is a long walk along a route that passes through many different parts of Atlanta. The adventurous and those in good shape will love it. Died-in-the-wool suburbanites will find it too diverse for their tastes. Stick to daylight hours on this route.

Walk: Candler Park to Jackson Street Bridge

Significance: This is a portion of PATH, a walking, jogging, and biking trail that extends 40 miles through Atlanta and some of its suburbs. This portion of the trail is handsomely paved and landscaped. It begins in Candler Park, one of Atlanta's most diverse and colorful neighborhoods, near the hip Little Five Points community, passes the Carter Center, and includes the Jackson Street Bridge, which offers one of the best views of Atlanta's skyline. (See "The Jackson Street Bridge," page 27.) From The Jackson Street Bridge you are within easy walking distance of Auburn Avenue and Martin Luther King, Jr., Memorial. PATH maps showing the entire 40-mile trail are available at Atlanta area bike shops for $3 or by calling (404) 875-7284.

Distance: About 3.5 miles.

Time: Between 2 to 3 hours.

Best MARTA Station: Edgewood Candler Park Station or the Civic Center Station (to walk west to east).

Route: From the Edgewood Candler Park MARTA Station walk north on Oakdale to the PATH trail at the intersection of Oakdale and North Avenue. Go left (west) on the 12-foot-wide PATH to the Jackson Street Bridge. Go right (north) on Jackson, which becomes Parkway Drive. Turn left (west) on Ralph McGill and follow it to the Civic Center MARTA Station.

Cautions: This is a route for enthusiastic walkers in good shape. It's best to take it during daylight hours.

Walk: CNN to the State Capitol

Significance: The route passes through the most historically significant part of Atlanta.

Distance: About 1.5 miles.

Time: Allow a half hour for the walk, more if you want to browse at Underground.

Best MARTA Station: Omni, Five Points, or Georgia State.

Route: From CNN Center walk east on Marietta Street to Peachtree Street. Turn right on Peachtree and go about one and a half blocks to the entrance of Underground Atlanta. Go in the "underground" entrance to Underground and turn left on Old Alabama Street. Walk about 300 feet along Old Alabama and exit Underground in front of the Old Freight Depot. Turn right and walk across Steve Polk Plaza in front of the Coke Museum to Martin Luther King, Jr. Boulevard. Turn left and walk one block to the Georgia State Capitol. Return via MARTA from the Georgia State Station or the Five Points Station.

Cautions: This interesting, culturally diverse route is safe anytime during daylight hours.

—— Running

Peachtree Street. If you want to squeeze in a run and you're staying anywhere inside the I-285 perimeter, the best thing to do is get out on Peachtree Street. Easily accessible, well lit along most of its length, lined with sidewalks, and featuring Peachtree Road Race mile markers, this route is hard to beat for convenient intown jogging.

Covering about a seven-mile distance from Lenox Square shopping mall to Underground Atlanta, Peachtree passes over varied terrain and through urban environments of every type, from streets lined with sleek skyscrapers to attractive upscale neighborhoods. The two biggest annual Atlanta road races, the Peachtree Road Race and the Atlanta Marathon and Half-Marathon follow this course.

No question about it, this is a high-density urban route with all the hazards associated with intown running. Drivers are accustomed to seeing runners all along Peachtree at all times of the day and night, but there is no reason to expect they will yield to runners or be especially courteous. So run defensively.

Men jogging alone or in a group would be safe running along Peachtree all the way from Lenox to Upper Alabama Street at Underground any time night or day. South of Alabama Street should be avoided at night. North of Lenox is safe enough but not as well lighted or as populated with pedestrians.

Women jogging alone or in a group will be comfortable along the entire 6.2-mile Peachtree Road Race route between Lenox Square and Piedmont Park during the day. (Look for big peaches with a mile number stenciled on them, on sidewalks on both sides of the road.)

The Peachtree Street running route is loaded with history: an important Civil War battle was fought along Peachtree Creek; Confederate defense lines were built at various places along the way. Margaret Mitchell, the author of *Gone with the Wind,* lived, wrote, and died on Peachtree.

Finally, MARTA rail and bus lines run parallel to the route, so you can easily catch a ride there and back.

Also of interest in town are the number of informal and loosely scheduled weekly runs around the city. For example, a group of mostly Atlanta Track Club members meets at Jocks and Jills across from the Brookhaven MARTA Station every Sunday morning at 8 A.M. for a run north or south on Peachtree Street. Runs are usually three to six miles in spring and summer, lengthening to 13 miles (half marathon distance) in the fall. For a list of other weekly runs call the Atlanta Track Club (404) 231-9064. For information on any upcoming race, including the Peachtree Road Race on July 4th and the Marathon and Half-Marathon on Thanksgiving, call the Track Club's race hotline at (404) 262-RACE. Phidippides, a popular Atlanta running store in Ansley Mall Shopping Center, is another good source of information at (404) 255-6149.

Kennesaw Mountain (Zone 2).   If you don't mind driving a short way out of town, this is the best hilly, rugged, cross-country system of trails for the serious jogger and runner in all of metro Atlanta. The trails are primarily hiking trails, but are popular and well used by runners in the Atlanta area.

Using a park map, you can design your own trail of 6, 7, 11, or up to 20 or more miles. Runners travel through woods and across battlefields where the Battle of Kennesaw Mountain was fought between Union and Confederate forces in June of 1864. National Park Service maps showing the various trails are available at the National Park Service Office. For maps, directions, and more information call (770) 427-4686.

Stone Mountain (Zone 5).   Also a short drive from town, this large park and Confederate memorial, with its Mt. Rushmore-like mountainside carvings of Confederate generals, is an attraction worth seeing in itself (see the more detailed listing under "Atlanta's Attractions"). Runners can jog all the way around Stone Mountain, or to the top of the mountain, on a system of hiking and walking trails. The trail around the mountain, called the Cherokee Trail, is a little over six miles; the trail to the top is about a mile one way. Maps showing the route are available at Confederate Hall, Memorial Hall, and the railroad station inside the park. For information call (770) 498-5702.

Cochran Mill Park (Zone 3).   A favorite jogging and walking track for Atlantans who live near the Chattahoochee River is the three-mile track at this park, located on the river between Johnson Ferry and Powers Ferry roads. Specifically designed for walking and jogging, the path is covered with M-10 fine compacted gravel. You'll find runners here at all times of the day. There is a short fitness course in the middle of the track oval. For information call (770) 399-8070.

—— Swimming

Dynamo Community Swim Center.   This facility has a 25-yard, ten-lane indoor pool; a 25-yard, five-lane indoor pool; and a 50-meter, eight-lane outdoor pool. Guests may use these for lap swimming for a $3 daily fee. Summer hours are Monday–Friday, 5:30–7:30 A.M.; 11 A.M.–4 P.M., and 6–10 P.M.; and weekends, noon–5 P.M. Fall and winter hours are Monday through Friday, 5:30–8 A.M., 10 A.M.–4 P.M., and 8–10 P.M.; and weekends, noon–5 P.M. 3119 Shallowford Road, Atlanta, GA 30341; phone (404) 451-3272.

For other swimming pools, see the health clubs listed below.

—— *Health Clubs*

City Athletic Club. Located in the CNN Center, this 50,000-square-foot health club is open to drop-in guests for a $12 per day fee. Facilities include a 20-meter, four-lane swimming pool, a one-tenth-mile track, Lifecycles, treadmills, Nautilus equipment, Badger Magnum, free weights, four racquetball courts, one squash court, sauna, steam, whirlpools, and showers. Hours are Monday–Thursday, 6 A.M.–9:30 P.M.; Friday, 6 A.M.–9 P.M.; Saturday, 9 A.M.–6 P.M.; and Sunday, 10 A.M.–6 P.M. One CNN Center, Suite 211, Atlanta, GA 30303; phone (404) 659-4097.

Peachtree Center Athletic Club. This is a 70,000-square-foot facility within easy walking distance of downtown. Guests at the Hyatt Regency, Ritz Carlton Downtown, Atlanta Hilton, Marriott Marquis, Radisson, Suites at Underground, and Travelodge Downtown may use the facility on a daily fee basis. Check with the hotel concierge. The $8 to $15 fee may be charged to your hotel room. Reciprocal membership privileges are also extended to members of Club Sports International and IRSA Association of Quality Clubs.

Facilities include a 25-meter, four-lane pool; track with 13 laps to the mile; over 60 pieces of cardiovascular equipment including Stairmaster, treadmills, rowing machines, and bicycles; sauna; steam; whirlpools; three racquetball courts; two squash courts; full-size basketball court; volleyball; showers; and lockers.

Guests not only get a great workout at this facility, but from its windowed location on the ninth and tenth floors of the Courtland Street Garage they can enjoy fine views of the city skyline. Open Monday, Wednesday, and Friday, 5:30 A.M.–10 P.M.; Tuesday and Thursday, 6 A.M.–10 P.M.; Saturday, 8 A.M.–6 P.M.; and Sunday 9 A.M.–5 P.M. 227 Courtland Street, 9th Floor, Atlanta, GA 30303; phone (404) 523-3833.

Buckhead YMCA. Facilities are open to YMCA members in other cities, and members may bring guests. A one-time guest pass is issued to prospective members. Facilities include a 25-yard, four-lane indoor pool, two racquetball courts, two basketball courts, a full set of Cybex equipment, Stairmasters, Lifecycles, free weights, steam, sauna, whirlpool, and showers. Guests can pick up a jogging map at the reception desk that shows jogging trails of one to five miles through attractive intown residential neighborhoods. Open Monday through Thursday, 6 A.M.–9:30 P.M.; Friday, 6 A.M.–8 P.M.; Saturday, 8:30 A.M.–6 P.M.; and Sunday, 2–6 P.M. 3424 Roswell Road, Atlanta, GA 30305; phone (404) 261-3111.

Downtown YMCA.   This modern workout facility in downtown Atlanta overlooks Peachtree Street and is just across from the Peachtree Center MARTA station and the Hyatt Regency Hotel. Facilities are open to YMCA members from other cities, and members may bring guests. A one-time guest pass can be purchased for $10. Facilities include Cybex equipment, Stairmasters, Wind-racer bicycles, treadmills, dumb bells and limited free weights, showers, steam, and lockers. Monday through Friday, 6 A.M. to 8:30 P.M.; Saturday, 9 A.M. to 2 P.M.; Sunday, closed. 260 Peachtree Street, Atlanta, GA 30309; phone (404) 527-7676.

Sporting Club.   This health club, the largest in the city, is open to drop-in guests for an $11 daily fee. The extensive facilities include a 25-meter, eight-lane pool, basketball court, four squash and six racquetball courts, Nautilus, Cybex, and Keiser machines, free weights, stationary bikes, and treadmills. There are nine tennis courts, four of which are covered in winter, and indoor and outdoor tracks. There is an outside, 50-foot rock-climbing wall, a full-service restaurant plus a sunbathing deck where wine and beer are served. Hours are Monday through Friday, 5:30 A.M.–10 P.M.; Saturday and Sunday, 8 A.M.–8 P.M. 135 Interstate North Parkway, Atlanta, GA 30339; phone (404) 953-1100.

—— Aerobics

Jeanne's Body Tech.   This workout parlor in Buckhead has nine aerobics classes a day, and guests are welcome to join any class for an $8 drop-in fee. Jeanne's also has step classes, Stairmasters, Lifecycles, and treadmills. Hours are daily, 6 A.M.–10 P.M. 334 East Paces Ferry Road, Atlanta, GA 30305; phone (404) 261-0227.

Australian Body Works.   This facility has a regular schedule of aerobics and step classes and guests may participate on a drop-in basis for a $10 fee. Call in advance for the schedule of classes. Other facilities at Australian Body Works include Stairmasters, stationary bikes, treadmills, and a 3,000-square-foot area with extensive free weights and Nautilus and professional trainers on duty. Hours are Monday through Thursday, 6 A.M. to 10 P.M.; Friday, 6 A.M. to 8:30 P.M.; Saturday, 9 A.M. to 6:30 P.M.; and Sunday, 10 A.M. to 6:30 P.M. 3872 Roswell Road, NW, Atlanta, GA 30342; phone (404) 365-9696.

Golf and Tennis

—— Daily Fee Golf Courses

If you visited Atlanta eight to ten years ago and your club did not have a reciprocal agreement with one of the fine private courses in the Atlanta metro area, your choices of four-star, daily fee facilities were very limited. All that has changed.

In the city of great golf traditions and great players like Bobby Jones and Larry Nelson, daily fee golf has come of age. In the past few years several golf management companies have bought and renovated existing courses or have developed golfing facilities from scratch for daily fee play. So much of a trend is this that five of the six daily fee courses recommended below were not in Atlanta in 1988. And the sixth, Stone Mountain, has undergone a dramatic facelift by George Cobb, protégé of John LaFoy. With a climate that invites year-round play and modern golfing facilities for the daily fee player, not packing your clubs when visiting Atlanta is a serious mistake.

Centennial Golf Course

Address: 5225 Woodstock Road, Acworth, GA 30101

Phone: (404) 975-1000

Tees:

Championship: 6,849 yards, par 72, USGA 73.1, slope 134.

Men's: 6,350 yards, par 72, USGA 70.8, slope 129.

Senior's: 5,893 yards, par 72, USGA 68.7, slope 125.

Women's: 5,095 yards, par 72, USGA 69.5, slope 122.

Fees: Tee times preferred. Weekdays, $25; weekends, $37. Cart fees: $13 per person (required until 4:30 P.M.). Proper attire required. Slow play rules in effect.

Facilities: Putting green, driving range, chipping green, practice bunker, lessons, pro shop, rental clubs, driving carts, snack bar, restaurant, locker room, showers, PGA teaching pro, USGA member.

COMMENTS   Larry Nelson has designed a spectacularly beautiful course. Each hole presents a scene seemingly more picturesque than the last. Across rolling hills, the lush Bermuda/419 fairways twist between the hardwoods to huge, sloping, bentgrass greens. Water comes into play on fifteen of the eighteen holes, but there are plenty of bail-out areas for the less aggressive player. From the opening hole—a long, tough par five— to the finishing hole—a great par four with water right and left—you will be delighted by the scenery and excited by the challenge. If you enjoy wonderful surroundings and a great test of golf, play Centennial.

DIRECTIONS   Take I-75 northwest of the perimeter to Exit #120, Highway 92. Turn left (west) and go .3 mile to Baker Road by the Waffle House Restaurant. Turn left and drive just over 1 mile to Woodstock Road. Turn left and go .8 mile to the course.

Champions Club of Atlanta

Address: 15135 Hopewell Road, Alpharetta, GA 30201

Phone: (404) 343-9700

Tees:
 Championship: 7,125 yards, par 72, USGA 71.5, slope 130.
 Men's: 6,001 yards, par 72, USGA 68.4, slope 124.
 Senior's: 5,471 yards, par 72, USGA 65.7, slope 118.
 Women's: 4,470 yards, par 72, USGA 64.9, slope 111.

Fees: Tee times required, taken three days in advance. Weekdays, $39; weekends, $45. Cart fees included and required.

Facilities: Putting green, driving range, chipping green, practice bunker, lessons, pro shop, rental clubs, driving carts, snack bar, cocktails, locker room, showers, meeting room, PGA teaching pro, PGA apprentice, USGA member.

COMMENTS   The Champions Club is a true champion, fulfilling a long-standing need for an upscale and challenging daily fee facility on the northside. Built by DeVictor and Melnyk on moderately steep terrain, the layout gets increasingly tighter and more difficult with each hole. Pines and hardwoods line the Tif/419 fairways and the tract is well bunkered. The bentgrass greens are large and undulating. Each hole has its own character. Hole number eight is a spectacular downhill par four. A balancing rock stands to your left near the tee. From there, the hole falls to a gorgeous lake, then takes you back up to an elevated green. The back nine is punctuated by a great finishing par five that will whet your appetite to play it again. As the course continues to mature, popularity will continue to soar. Call for early tee times.

DIRECTIONS Take Georgia Highway 400 north of I-285 to Exit #7, Windward Parkway. Turn left and go west 1.2 miles to Highway 9. Turn left and go .4 mile to Cogburn Road. Turn right and go 4 miles (Cogburn becomes Hopewell Road six-tenths of a mile before the entrance) to the course entrance on the right.

Chateau Elan Golf Club

Address: 6060 Golf Club Drive, Braselton, GA 30517

Phone: (770) 271-6050

Tees:
   Championship: 7,030 yards, par 71, USGA 73.5, slope 136.
   Men's: 6,484 yards, par 71, USGA 71.1, slope 125.
   Senior's: 5,900 yards, par 71, USGA 68.9, slope 119.
   Women's: 5,092 yards, par 71, USGA 70.8, slope 124.

Fees: Tee times required. Weekdays, $60; weekends, $65; includes range privileges, cart, and tax. Carts required on weekends. Dress code and fast play rules are enforced.

Facilities: Putting green, driving range, chipping green, practice bunker, lessons, pro shop, rental clubs, driving carts, snack bar, cocktails, restaurant, locker room, showers, meeting room, PGA teaching pro, PGA apprentice, USGA member.

COMMENTS   This Dennis Griffiths–designed course is the cream of the crop. An elegant golf course in an elegant setting, the layout winds along three lakes and two creeks. Water comes into play on ten holes. The 87 bunkers lend both definition and character to the Bermuda fairways and large bentgrass greens. Hole number 14 is a gem. Bordered on both sides by tall pines and hardwoods, the hole runs down and then up to a three-tiered green. Recently added is a picturesque waterfall, making this hole even more challenging, beautiful, and memorable. Evidence of great course design, there are plenty of bail-out areas and no forced carries, allowing the golfer to beat himself. A "Wee Links" practice area rents by the hour and invites you to perfect your short game. Don't miss the newly added spa and the winery.

   Chateau Elan is like a vacation retreat only 45 minutes from downtown and is well worth the trip.

DIRECTIONS   Take I-85 northeast to Exit #48, Highway 211. Turn left, and go 1.5 miles to Golf Club Drive. Turn left and go .5 mile to the club-house entrance on the left.

Eagle Watch

Address: 3055 Eagle Watch Drive, Woodstock, GA 30188
Phone: (404) 591-1000
Tees:

Championship: 6,896 yards, par 72, USGA 72.6, slope 136.
Men's: 6,458 yards, par 72.
Senior's: 6,044 yards, par 72.
Women's: 5,243 yards, par 72.

Fees: Tee times required and can be reserved four days in advance with Visa, Mastercard, or American Express. Weekdays, $40; weekends/holidays, $50. Cart fees $12/person (required).

Facilities: Putting green, driving range, chipping green, practice bunker, lessons, pro shop, rental clubs, driving carts, snack bar, restaurant, locker room, PGA teaching pro, PGA apprentice, USGA member.

COMMENTS   Eagle Watch is a premier course that demands careful management and shot-making skill. Arnold Palmer, the architect, skill-fully balances shot values from tee shot to approach, ensuring that the golfer has adequate area to land the ball. But don't be fooled. The care-less can be punished with sure bogeys or "others." The enormous bent-grass greens are filled with subtle breaks.

DIRECTIONS   Take I-575 north to Exit #5, Towne Lake Parkway. Turn left (west) and drive 1.5 miles. At this point Towne Lake Parkway makes a sharp right and meets Eagle Drive. Turn right and continue on Towne Lake Parkway 1.5 miles to Eagle Watch Drive. Turn right on Eagle Watch Drive and follow it .4 mile to the clubhouse.

Southerness Golf Club

Address: 4871 Flat Bridge Road, Stockbridge, GA 30281
Phone: (404) 808-6000
Tees:

Championship: 6,766 yards, par 72, USGA 71.5, slope 126.
Men's: 6,386 yards, par 72, USGA 69.8, slope 122.
Senior's: 5,838 yards, par 72, USGA 67.3, slope 117.
Women's: 5,008 yards, par 72, USGA 76.8, slope 114.

Fees: Tee times required and taken seven days in advance. Weekdays, $37; weekends, $45 including required carts.

Facilities: Putting green, driving range, chipping green, practice bunker, lessons, pro shop, rental clubs, driving carts, snack bar, cocktails, restaurant, locker room, meeting room, PGA member, USGA member.

COMMENTS   This course is rapidly joining the very best that the area has to offer. Architect Clyde Johnson uses the natural rolling terrain to present a dramatic and scenic look on each hole. Vistas abound, especially at the par threes. The rolling Bermuda fairways are lush and immaculately maintained. The bentgrass greens are large, undulating, and full of subtle breaks. The finishing holes rank with any in the area, with the highlight being number 16, a gorgeous gem over water, flanked by a wonderful burbling waterfall.

DIRECTIONS   Take I-20 east of the perimeter to Exit #36, Wesley Chapel/Snapfinger Road. Turn south on Wesley Chapel and go one block. Turn left on Snapfinger Road and drive 7.2 miles to Alexander Road (just south of Panola Mountain State Park.) Turn left, and go 2 miles to the dead end at Flat Bridge Road. Turn right, and go one block to the clubhouse.

Stone Mountain Stonemont (Zone 5)

Address: Stone Mountain Park, Stone Mountain, GA 30086
Phone: (404) 498-5717
Tees:
   Championship: 6,683 yards, par 72, USGA 72.6, slope 133.
   Men's: 6,094 yards, par 72, USGA 71.2, slope 128.
   Women's: 5,020 yards, par 72, USGA 69.1, slope 121.

Fees: Tee times available and taken on Tuesdays preceding the weekend. Weekdays and weekends, $36. Carts included in green fees.

Facilities: Putting green, driving range, chipping green, practice bunker, lessons, pro shop, rental clubs, driving carts, swimming pool, tennis, snack bar, cocktails, restaurant, meeting room, PGA teaching pro, USGA member, RV hookup.

COMMENTS   1992 will be remembered as the year great golf became even better at Stone Mountain Park. The newly defined Stonemont course is made up of nine holes of the original Robert Trent Jones course, integrated with a newly completed nine designed by George Cobb, protégé of John LaFoy. Thus for five holes you play the classic Rembrandt style of Trent Jones and then for nine holes, the Picasso style of La Foy, before returning to Jones on hole number 15. Hole number 14, the last in the sequence, will surely become one of the most talked-about holes in Atlanta. The approach shot on this relatively short hole is demand carry over an old stone quarry pond. The green sets hard against the edge of the quarry and is still surrounded by piers and other evidence of old rock-crushing equipment. This new course is exciting, demanding, and beautiful.

DIRECTIONS   Take I-285 (the perimeter) to Exit #30B, Stone Mountain Freeway/US 78. Turn east (outside the perimeter) and drive 7.7 miles to a Y where the right fork will lead to the park entrance. Immediately after entering the park turn left on Stonewall Jackson Drive and follow it to the clubhouse.

Stone Mountain Woodmont/Lakemont (Zone 5)

Address: Stone Mountain Park, Stone Mountain, GA 30086

Phone: (404) 498-5715

Tees:
    Championship: 6,585 yards, par 72, USGA 71.6, slope 130.
    Men's: 6,093 yards, par 72, USGA 69.0, slope 118.
    Women's: 5,231 yards, par 72, USGA 69.4, slope 120.

Fees: Tee times available and taken on Tuesdays preceding the weekend. Weekdays and weekends, $40. Green fees include carts.

Facilities: Putting green, driving range, chipping green, practice bunker, lessons, pro shop, rental clubs, driving carts, swimming, tennis, snack bar, cocktails, restaurant, meeting rooms, PGA teaching pro, USGA member, RV hookup.

COMMENTS   Like Stonemont, the Woodmont/Lakemont eighteen is half Jones and half LaFoy. The Woodmont nine-hole course by Robert Trent Jones has consistently been rated by *Golf Digest* as one of the top public golf courses in the world, but the John LaFoy Lakemont nine is quickly gaining its own fine reputation. Mr. LaFoy has made excellent use of the majestic beauty of the granite face of Stone Mountain and broad expanse of Stone Mountain Lake to create memorable golfing holes and wonderful sights. The most notable hole is the opening hole on the Lakemont nine, which features a carry over an arm of the lake and an approach straight into the face of Stone Mountain where Jeff Davis, General Robert E. Lee, and General Stonewall Jackson sit proudly, silently critiquing the goings-on. A definite must-play.

DIRECTIONS   Take I-85 (the perimeter) to Exit #30B, Stone Mountain Freeway/US 78. Turn east (outside the perimeter) and drive 7.7 miles to a Y where the right fork will lead to the park entrance. Immediately after entering the park, turn left on Stonewall Jackson Drive and follow it to the clubhouse.

NOTE: This golf section was prepared with the consultation and advice of Gene Kleese, author and publisher of the widely used and respected *Georgia Golf on My Mind,* a directory of 204 golf courses throughout the Atlanta metropolitan area and Georgia. The book is available free through the Georgia Department of Industry, Trade and Tourism. Call (800) 3-GOLF GA.

— Tennis Courts

With its temperate climate and enthusiasm for all outdoor sports, Atlanta offers no shortage of tennis facilities.

Bitsy Grant Tennis Center (Zone 7)

Address: 2125 Northside Drive, NW, Atlanta, GA 30305

Phone: (404) 351-2774

Outdoor Hard Surface Courts: 10

Outdoor Clay Courts: 13

Lighted: Six clay and four hard surface.

Fees: Clay, $2.50/hour; hard surface, $1.50/hour.

Facilities: Clubhouse with pro shop, lockers, showers, snack bar.

Days/Hours: Summer: daily, 9 A.M.–9 P.M. Winter: weekdays, 10 A.M.–8 P.M.; Saturday and Sunday, until 5 P.M.

Best Times to Get a Court: Any time except 4–7 P.M. on weekdays and Saturday and Sunday mornings in spring and summer, when courts are extremely busy.

Reservations: No

COMMENTS   Recently voted one of the top ten tennis facilities in the country by *Tennis* magazine. When he was alive, this was the home court and hangout of Atlanta tennis legend Bitsy Grant.

Blackburn Tennis Center (Zone 4)

Address: 3501 Ashford Dunwoody Road, NE, Atlanta, GA 30319
Phone: (770) 451-1061
Outdoor Hard Surface Courts: 18
Outdoor Clay Courts: None
Lighted: All
Fees: Day rate, $2/person/hour; night rate, $2.50/person/hour.
Facilities: Clubhouse with pro shop, showers, lockers, snack bar.
Days/Hours: Monday–Friday, 9 A.M.– 10 P.M.; Saturday, 9 A.M.–6 P.M.;
    Sunday, 10 A.M.–8 P.M.
Best Times to Get a Court: Before 6 P.M.
Reservations: Yes, two days in advance.

Dekalb Tennis Center (Zone 4)

Address: 1400 McConnell Drive, Decatur, GA 30033
Phone: (404) 325-2520
Outdoor Hard Surface Courts: 17
Outdoor Clay Courts: None
Lighted: Yes
Fees: $2/hour; $2.50/hour after 6 P.M.
Facilities: Clubhouse with showers and lockers, snack bar.
Days/Hours: Monday–Friday, 9 A.M.– 10 P.M.; Saturday and Sunday,
    9 A.M.–7 P.M.
Best Times to Get a Court: Between 1 and 4 P.M.
Reservations: Yes

Georgia Tech (Zone 8)

Address: 150 Bobby Dodd Way, NW, Atlanta, GA 30332
Phone: (404) 894-8371
Indoor Hard Surface Courts: 3
Outdoor Hard Surface Courts: 12
Outdoor Clay Courts: None
Lighted: Indoor courts and six outdoor courts.
Fees:
    Indoor: March–October, Monday–Friday, $15/hour before 5 P.M.,

$20/hour after 5 P.M.; weekends and holidays, $20. November–February, Monday–Friday, $20/hour before 5 P.M., $30/hour after 5 P.M.; weekends and holidays, $30/hour.

Outdoor: $2/hour or $2.50 for 2 hours.

Facilities: Vending area.

Days/Hours: Monday–Thursday, 6:30 A.M.– 10 P.M.; Friday, 6:30 A.M.–9 P.M.; Saturday, 8:30 A.M.–9 P.M.; Sunday, noon–9 P.M. The facility closes everyday at 9 P.M. June through August.

Best Times to Get a Court: During the week.

Reservations: Yes, one day in advance.

Hudlow (Zone 4)

Address: 2051 Old Rockbridge Road, Norcross, GA 30071

Phone: (770) 417-2210

Outdoor Hard Surface Courts: 16

Outdoor Clay Courts: None

Lighted: Yes

Fees: $2/hour singles, $2.50/1½ hours doubles.

Facilities: Soft drink machine.

Days/Hours: Monday–Thursday, 9 A.M.–9 P.M.; Friday, 9 A.M.–7 P.M.; Saturday, 9 A.M.–5 P.M.; Sunday, 10 A.M.–6 P.M. Lights stay on until midnight every day.

Best Times to Get a Court: Afternoons before 6 P.M.

Reservations: Yes, one day in advance.

North Fulton Tennis Center (Zone 3)

Address: 500 Abernathy Road, NE, Atlanta, GA 30328

Phone: (404) 303-6182

Outdoor Hard Surface Courts: 20

Outdoor Clay Courts: Four

Lighted: Yes

Fees: Clay, $2/hour (day), $2.75/hour (night); hard surface, $1.50/hour (day); $2/hour (night).

Facilities: Clubhouse, vending machines.

Days/Hours: Daily, 8:30 A.M.–9 P.M. Closed Christmas Day and New Year's Day.

Best Times to Get a Court: 1–4 P.M.
Reservations: Yes, up to three days in advance.

Piedmont Park (Zone 8)

Address: Located in Piedmont Park between 12th and 14th streets.
Phone: (404) 872-1507
Outdoor Hard Surface Courts: 12
Outdoor Clay Courts: None
Lighted: Yes
Fees: $1.50/hour.
Facilities: Clubhouse, snack bar.
Days/Hours: Daily, in summer, 9 A.M.–9 P.M.; in winter, 10 A.M.–8 P.M.
 Closes at 5 P.M. Saturday and Sunday in winter.
Best Times to Get a Court: Before 4 P.M.
Reservations: No

South Fulton Tennis Center (Zone 1)

Address: 5645 Mason Road, College Park, GA 30349
Phone: (770) 306-3059
Outdoor Hard Surface Courts: 20
Outdoor Clay Courts: Four
Lighted: Yes
Fees: Clay, $2/hour; hard surface, $1.50/hour, higher at night.
Facilities: Two-story clubhouse with large pro shop, showers, and
 lockers; vending machines.
Days/Hours: Daily, 8 A.M.–10 P.M.
Best Times to Get a Court: Anytime there is not a tournament.
Reservations: Yes, up to three days in advance.

For more information on tennis, call the Atlanta Lawn Tennis Association (ALTA) at (404) 399-5788.

Outdoor Recreation

Georgia is the largest state east of the Mississippi, and its terrain varies enormously. The Cumberland Plateau extends into the northwest corner of the state. A deep valley creases the middle of the northern quarter of Georgia. The rugged Appalachians rumple down into the northeast corner. Atlanta is typical of the piedmont section of the state, where the mountains taper off into rolling hills. Between Atlanta and the coast, those hills flatten out as they approach the sea.

While the coast may be too far away for a one-day or short weekend trip from Atlanta, the Georgia mountains are well within reach of the person who wants to spend a day hiking, trail biking, or canoeing in a Southeastern wilderness setting.

Some of the destinations described here are within a few minutes' drive of downtown. All are within reach of the day-tripper. For more distant destinations, such as the Cohuttas and the Chattooga River, an early start is necessary to get there and back in one day. And of course you wouldn't plan a 20-mile hike along Jack's River and expect to be back in Atlanta for dinner. But with a little planning, a real adventure in the beautiful north Georgia mountains is possible in the course of a one-day trip from the city.

—— *Bicycling*

The best sources of information on trail biking in Atlanta are **REI** (404) 633-6508 or (770) 901-9200 and **Outback** (404) 688-4878, both outdoor stores with a good inventory of bikes and good bike mechanics. REI has prepared a handout on three trail-bike routes in the Atlanta vicinity that is available in its stores.

The Chattahoochee River National Recreation Area has a few trails specifically set aside for trail biking. Contact the park or go by the park office for a map; phone (770) 399-8070.

The best trail-bike rides near Atlanta require a two-hour drive northwest to the **Cohutta National Forest.** Both REI and Outback usually carry Cohutta Forest Service maps.

— Hiking and Backpacking

If you plan to get out in the mountains, be sure to wear sturdy walking shoes and long pants. A hat, sunscreen, and sunglasses are also recommended. Carry a small daypack to hold items such as a first aid kit, lunch, water, a light jacket, and a flashlight. If you don't have the proper hiking gear with you, you can buy it from one of the outdoor outfitters listed at the end of this section.

Amicalola Falls State Park. This park contains Georgia's highest waterfall, which drops 729 feet in seven cascades. The 1,400-acre park sits at an elevation of 3,000 feet, 100 miles northwest of Atlanta (a two-hour drive). Here you can take the eight-mile approach trail to the beginning of the Appalachian Trail (see next entry). The eight-mile trek is an easy to moderate one. At the end of a one-mile hike, there's also a lodge that serves family-style meals. You can easily visit the park, take a hike, and return to Atlanta within a day. Free maps and brochures are available at the park. For more information call (706) 265-8888.

The Appalachian Trail. It begins (or ends, depending on your perspective) at Georgia's Springer Mountain, near Amicalola Falls State Park. The trail covers 75.6 miles within the state; over that length it crosses six highways, making for a combination of hikes that vary in length and difficulty from moderate to rugged. While the trail elevation in Georgia reaches 4,400 feet, most of the trail goes along ridges with elevations of about 3,000 feet. As described above, you can access the trail from Amicalola Falls State Park. For details on other access points and aspects of the trail, contact one of the outfitters listed at the end of this section.

Black Rock Mountain State Park. This area contains the highest state-park elevation in Georgia and is named for its steep cliffs of dark-colored biotite gneiss. In 1,803 acres, the park contains six different peaks over 3,000 feet high. The ten-mile trail system, which takes you along the cliffs, is moderate to rugged. The park is located 120 miles north of Atlanta, about a two-and-a-half-hour drive. For more information call (706) 746-2141.

Chattahoochee Nature Center. This represents one of the most convenient hiking options. Located just outside the I-285 perimeter, a short 25-minute drive from downtown, the center has an easy walking trail

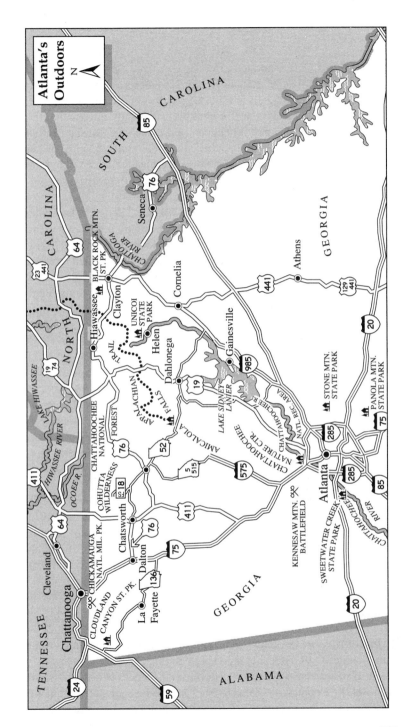

Atlanta's Outdoors

and boardwalk that wind along the banks of Bull Sluice Lake on the Chattahoochee River. A self-guided tour brochure available in the center tells how these wetlands are an integral part of the environment. A similar self-guided walk goes through the woodlands surrounding the center. The facility also has a small nature museum and gift shop with a good selection of outdoor books, particularly for children. Visitors can attend seminars, workshops, and field trips focusing on nature and the environment. For more information call (770) 992-2055.

Chattahoochee River National Recreation Area. Particularly for the visitor with limited time, this is the single best outdoor resource in the Atlanta area. On its course from the north Georgia mountains to the Gulf of Mexico, the Chattahoochee (Creek Indian for "painted rock" or "flowering stone") flows just north and west of Atlanta. The city's I-285 perimeter highway crosses the river in two places. Commuters stalled in rush-hour traffic can look down and see canoeists and rafters floating below.

Along a 48-mile stretch of the river between Lake Lanier and Cobb Parkway, the National Park Service has established a network of parks with hiking trails ranging in difficulty from easy to rugged. You can also picnic, canoe, and fish here.

Bottom line: just 25 minutes from downtown, you can find yourself in the wilderness, hiking a tree-canopied trail along a fast-flowing river. We recommend going by the park office to pick up the overall park map plus individual maps on each of the nine parks in the Chattahoochee system. For more information call (770) 399-8070.

Cloudland Canyon State Park. Here you'll find three moderate to rugged hiking trails winding through one of the largest and most scenic state parks in Georgia. Located 120 miles northwest of Atlanta (a two-and-a-half-hour drive), the park is set on rugged Lookout Mountain on the Cumberland Plateau and contains deep ravines that reveal the geology of the region. An excellent guidebook, *The Geologic Guide to Cloudland Canyon State Park,* by Griffin and Atkins, is available at the park office. For information call (706) 657-4050.

Cohutta Wilderness. This area contains 14 rugged hiking trails from 2 to 13 miles long. Trails often intersect, so hikers can spend a day or a week in this scenic wilderness 110 miles (two and a half hours) from Atlanta. The Cohuttas are home to black bear, wild boar, deer, and many varieties of birds. Four trails of four to seven miles in length are set aside for off-road vehicles. Access to the wilderness is via Forest Service road. Note that it's easy to get lost on these sometimes casually marked roads. For the most complete guide to the wilderness, see the *Georgia Conservancy's Guide to the North Georgia Mountains*, or contact the Cohutta Ranger District of the United States Forest Service at (706) 695-6736.

Kennesaw Mountain Battlefield. This isn't the place to go if you're looking for a rugged, challenging hike; but if you're interested in an easy and convenient one, and particularly if you are a Civil War buff, you'll enjoy Kennesaw. Just 25 miles (30 minutes) from Atlanta, Kennesaw's park trails follow battle lines and lead to sites of the Civil War Battle of Kennesaw Mountain, which took place in June 1864. A park brochure outlines hiking routes ranging from 2 to 20 miles in length. You can easily enjoy this place in half a day. For information call (770) 427-4686.

Panola Mountain. Here are six easy miles of hiking trails just 20 miles (25–30 minutes) from the city. At this 100-acre granite monadnock you'll also find a variety of programs taking place in the on-site interpretive center; films, slide shows, and storytelling are part of the program on Saturdays and Sundays during the summer months. Nature programs, workshops, and lectures are scheduled year-round. For information call (770) 389-7801.

Stone Mountain Park. Just 20 miles (25 minutes) from Atlanta, this multifaceted park features the world's largest granite outcrop. You can hike one of two trails around the base of the outcropping, or take another that leads to the top of the mountain, elevation 1,600 feet. All trails are easy to moderate. Trail maps are available at Confederate Hall, Memorial Hall, and the railroad station inside the park. For information call (770) 498-5702.

Sweetwater Creek State Park. Only ten miles from Atlanta, a 20- to 25-minute drive, this is the state park closest to the city. You'll find a particularly interesting (and easy) hiking trail that leads to the ruins of the New Manchester Manufacturing Company, a Civil War–era textile mill destroyed by Union troops during the siege of Atlanta. The 1,986-acre park also has a lake with bait shop and boat and canoe rentals (see Sweetwater Creek listing under "Fishing"). For information call (770) 732-5871.

Unicoi State Park. This park is located just two miles north of the Alpine-style village of Helen, a tourist center in the north Georgia mountains. It's a 90-mile drive to the park from Atlanta, a little over two hours. Unicoi contains 12 miles of easy to moderate hiking trails, as well as a lodge with buffet-style restaurant, 53-acre lake and beach, and tennis courts. For information call (706) 878-2201.

— Rock Climbing

For the best information on rock climbing and bouldering in the region go to **Mountain Ventures**, 3040 North Decatur Road, Scottsdale, (404) 299-5254, or **REI**, 1800 Northeast Expressway Access Road, NE, (404) 633-6508 and 1165 Perimeter Center West, (770) 901-9200. These outdoor stores can suggest climbing sites in the Atlanta metro area or direct you to more extensive climbing areas within a two-hour drive of the city. Both stores work well with beginning climbers. REI has a 12-foot, 3-inch wall good for traversing or trying out shoes. It's available to the public on Tuesday nights. More advanced climbers gravitate toward Mountain Ventures, where you will find more technical equipment and more detailed information.

Chris Watford at **Call of the Wild**, 425 Market Place, Roswell, (770) 992-5400, recently published a book on climbing sites in Alabama, Tennessee, and Georgia, which includes locations in the metro Atlanta area. The book is available at Call of the Wild, and Watford himself is happy to talk to interested climbers in person or over the phone.

The Sporting Club, at Windy Hill, has a 60-foot climbing wall that is open to the public on Tuesday and Thursday nights. The Sporting Club also offers periodic rock-climbing and bouldering courses. It is located at 135 Interstate North Parkway, less than one-tenth mile from I-75 North and Windy Hill Road; phone (770) 953-1100.

— Canoeing, Kayaking, and Rafting

Guided River Tours. You can choose from several outfitters that will take you on a one-day guided raft trip on the wild and scenic Chattooga River, made famous by the movie *Deliverance*. Rafters can expect rapids ranging in difficulty from Class II to Class V. So wear clothes you don't mind getting wet. It will take you an hour and a half to travel the 120 miles to the Chattooga, and the trip takes a full day. So consider spending the night in the charming Georgia mountain town of Clayton.

Safety equipment is provided by the outfitter. For more information call Southeastern Expeditions, (404) 329-0433; Wildwater, Ltd., (803) 647-5336; or the Nantahala Outdoor Center, (803) 647-9014.

The Chattahoochee Outdoor Center. For canoeists, kayakers, and rafters, the Chattahoochee River just north of the city is an important resource that can be accessed quickly and easily. During the summer when daylight savings time extends the usable sunshine, it's not unrealistic to spend a full workday in the city, drive to the river, and paddle an hour or two before dark. While not a difficult whitewater river, the Chattahoochee has plenty of shoals, Class I and II rapids, cliffs, eddies, and pools to satisfy most canoeists with average skills.

If you have your own canoe or kayak, go to the National Park Service office on Roberts Road, (404) 399-8070, and pick up a map of the river park showing put-in and take-out locations.

The Chattahoochee Outdoor Center rents canoes and rafts and provides a shuttle service for customers who rent from them or for those with their own rafts. A four-person raft is $36 per day, a six-person raft, $54 per day, and an eight-person raft $74 per day. Rental includes life jackets and paddles. Canoes are $30 per day with a $100 deposit. Shuttle service is $2.50 for adults and $1.25 for children. Those with their own rafts pay $3 for adults and $1.50 for children plus $3 for a deflated raft. Open May (weekends only) through mid-September, Monday–Friday, 10 A.M.–8 P.M.; Saturday, Sunday, and holidays, 9 A.M.–8 P.M. For more information call (404) 395-6851.

Canoe and Raft Rental. If you are interested in paddling the local rivers, but don't have a boat in tow, two area retailers may be able to help. **Go with the Flow** rents boats and is a good source of river information; phone (770) 992-3200.

—— *Snow Skiing*

Atlanta is four or five hours away from the nearest ski areas in Tennessee and North Carolina. These Appalachian mountain destinations, however, offer little to the serious skier. If you are interested in skiing in this region, call the Atlanta Ski Club for more information at (404) 255-4800.

—— Horseback Riding

Forty-five minute guided trail rides are available at Lake Lanier Islands, about 45 minutes north of Atlanta. Rides are $13 per person. Reservations are suggested; phone (770) 932-7233. To reach Lake Lanier Islands go north on I-85 to I-985, take Exit #2, turn left and follow the signs.

—— Fishing

Atlanta is the only American city of over a million population that has a river stocked with trout within minutes of downtown. Add the proximity of lakes Lanier and Allatoona, and you begin to understand why this southern city is popular with anglers.

Regardless of whether you are interested in lake, stream, or even saltwater fishing, your first stop in Atlanta should be the **Fish Hawk** in Buckhead. Gary Merriman and his laid-back staff can advise you on specific fishing locations and how to get there, supply you with books and maps, and sell you all the gear you could possibly need. The Fish Hawk can recommend a professional guide for lakes Lanier or Allatoona as well as for other lakes in the region. The store is at 279 Buckhead Avenue, NE, Atlanta, GA 30305; phone (404) 237-3473.

For those who just want to wet a hook without a lot of advanced planning or equipment, two small fishing lakes at state parks are easily accessible from downtown.

In addition to the main lake at **Stone Mountain**, there is a 38-acre lake where you can fish for crappie, bream, catfish, and bass. No license is required, but a $5 fee for adults and a $3 fee for children under 11 must be paid in addition to the $6 admission to the park. Small aluminum, flat-bottom boats with paddles or electric trolling motors are available for rent. You can rent or buy tackle and bait at the **Fish Hut** on the bank of the lake. Open daily, 8 A.M.–6 P.M. Call Stone Mountain Park, (770) 498-5690, for additional information.

Sweetwater Creek State Park has a 215-acre fishing lake stocked with bass, crappie, bream, catfish and carp. Boats and canoes without motors can be rented for $3 per hour, and good fishing spots are accessible from the bank. There is no fee for fishing, but Georgia state fishing license regulations apply. There is a $2 parking fee to enter the park. Bait and tackle are for sale in the bait shop, which is open Tuesday–Thursday, 8 A.M.–5 P.M.; and Friday–Sunday, 8 A.M.–6 P.M. Closed Monday. Phone (770) 732-5871.

—— *Pleasure Boating, Sailing, Waterskiing, Jet Skiing*

Ski boats, pontoon boats, houseboats, and party boats are available for rent at **Lake Lanier Islands**. It is best to call for detailed fees, restrictions, and availability. Excluding tax and gas, a 19-foot ski boat with 90-horsepower motor and a five-person capacity runs about $225 per day; a pontoon boat with eight-person capacity, $135 per day; a houseboat with ten-person capacity, $275 per eight hours; party boats that hold from 15 to 45 people are about $400–725 for a four-hour minimum. Call (770) 932-7255. Lake Lanier Islands is about 45 minutes from Atlanta. Take I-85 north to I-985; take Exit #2, turn left and follow the signs.

Lake Lanier Islands also has a one-mile white sand beach on popular **Lake Lanier** about 45 minutes from Atlanta. In addition to the artificial beach there are ten water slides, a wave pool, miniature golf, and paddle boats, sailboats, and canoes for rent. Admission is $13.99 and $6.99 for those under 42 inches tall. Hours are Monday–Friday, 10 A.M.–6 P.M.; weekends, 10 A.M.–7 P.M. Open daily the last weekend in May through Labor Day. Open weekends in May and the weekend after Labor Day. From Atlanta take I-85 north to I-985. Take Exit #2, turn left and follow the signs. Phone (770) 932-7200 or (800) 840-LAKE.

Jet skis are available from **The Grass Shack** on Lake Lanier for about $95 and up for two hours. Call the Grass Shack for detailed rates and directions to their dock on Lake Lanier, about 45 minutes from the city; phone (770) 271-7529.

Also see **Stone Mountain Park** under "Atlanta's Attractions."

—— *Outfitters*

For your convenience, we have listed several adventure sports outfitters in the area. We have found them to be good sources of information about outdoor activities in the Atlanta area.

The Fish Hawk. This is Atlanta's top fishing store. Located in Buckhead (Zone 3), this small store has the largest selection and highest quality fishing gear in the city. Owner Gary Merriman is an excellent source of information on local fishing, including Lake Lanier and the Chattahoochee River. 279 Buckhead Avenue, Atlanta, GA 30305; phone (404) 237-3473.

High Country Outfitters.   Here you'll find a good retail selection of outdoor merchandise and good advice about the out-of-doors of this region at two Atlanta locations. High Country is a good source of information about canoeing, kayaking, and sea kayaking, plus other outdoor sports such as hiking, climbing, and camping.

High Country also runs guided raft trips on the Class III and IV Ocoee River in Tennessee just north of the Georgia state line, the venue for Olympic whitewater paddling events in 1996. Other outdoor services include kayak touring, rope courses, and children's hikes. 3906-B Roswell Road, Atlanta, GA 30342 (Zone 3); phone (404) 814-0999 or 4400 Ashford-Dunwoody Road, Atlanta, GA 30346 (Zone 4); phone (770) 391-9657. Reserve raft trips at (800) 233-8594 or at either of the retail stores.

Outback Outfitters and Bikes.   Located in Little Five Points (Zone 5), this is the best local source of information on mountain bikes, equipment, and trails. The store has a good book section and professional, experienced bikers on staff. 1125 Euclid Avenue, NE, Atlanta, GA 30307; phone (404) 688-4878.

REI (Zone 4).   The largest outdoor stores in the city and Atlanta's rock-climbing headquarters. Here you'll find the best and most complete outdoor inventory in the Atlanta area. Boats, tents, bikes, backpacks, and sleeping bags each have a separate area of the store. Most gear is available for rental. REI also offers the city's best book and map section devoted specifically to the outdoors. In addition to stocking the city's most extensive inventory of rock-climbing gear, both stores offer a practice rock-climbing wall. 1800 NE Expressway Access Road, Atlanta, GA 30329; phone (404) 633-6508 and 1165 Perimeter Center West near Perimeter Mall; phone (770) 901-9200.

Spectator Sports

Spectator sports draw enthusiastic crowds in Atlanta. On a professional level, the Braves (baseball), Falcons (football), Hawks (basketball), and a minor league hockey team, the Knights, provide entertainment for residents and visitors. College sports, particularly football and Georgia Tech basketball, have a rabid following. This section will guide you to the spectator sports that suit your interests.

—— Baseball

Atlanta Braves (Zone 6)

Season: First week in April through the first week in October. Postseason play, if any, is concluded by the end of October. The Braves play 162 games, 81 home, and 81 away.

Site/Stadium: Home games are played in the 49,831-seat Olympic Stadium, which was modified especially for baseball after the 1996 games.

Game Times: Weekdays at 7:40 P.M., Saturdays at 7:10 P.M., Sundays at 1:10 P.M. Some business fans specials on weekdays at 1:10 P.M.

Ticket Prices: $20 dugout and club level, $17 field level, $12 lower pavillion, $10 upper level, $5 upper pavilion.

Where to Buy Tickets: The most convenient but most expensive method of buying single game tickets is through Ticketmaster, a telephone reservations system that will charge tickets to a major credit card. A service charge of $5 per ticket is added to the price. If tickets are bought ten days in advance, Ticketmaster will mail the tickets to you or they can be picked up the day of the game at the "will call" window near Gate G at the stadium. Call (404) 249-6400 or (800) 326-4000. Tickets can be purchased in person at Gate G at the stadium, Monday–Saturday, 8:30 A.M.– 5 P.M., during the season. For season ticket information call the Braves season ticket office, (404) 577-9100.

Parking: Atlanta Fulton County Stadium was leveled after the Olympics to provide 10,000 parking spaces for the 49,831-seat stadium. There are lots west of the stadium that charge between $5 and $7. Avoid the lots where neighborhood boys direct cars into vacant lots and backyards. They are unsafe and it is a nightmare getting out after a game.

The way to avoid the stadium parking hassle is to take MARTA to the Braves' games. Park free at a MARTA rail station, then ride to the Five Points Station and take the stadium shuttle; or ride to the Georgia State Station and walk to the stadium. For more detailed information on MARTA routes to the stadium see "Riding MARTA: A Really Good Idea" in Part Six.

CONSUMER TIPS   Given a solid team in a pennant race, the Braves are one of the hottest tickets in Atlanta. Many games are sellouts and yearly attendance can top 3 million, a number only a few teams reach. If you want to see a game, it's best to try as early as possible to get tickets.

—— Football

Atlanta Falcons (Zone 7)

Season: Preseason begins in early August; regular season begins in September and runs through December, with postseason play extending into January. The Falcons play 16 regular season games, eight home and eight away.

Site/Stadium: The 71,549-seat enclosed Georgia Dome opened in 1992.

Game Times: Sunday games begin at 1 P.M. The Falcons occasionally play Friday night and Monday night games.

Ticket Prices: $30 and $33

Where to Buy Tickets: Ticketmaster and Ticketmaster outlets, (404) 249-6400 or (800) 326-4000, or the Falcons ticket office, (404) 223-8000. All games were sold out last year, and it is chancey attempting to purchase a ticket on the day of the game. Ticket information is mailed out in June, and tickets go on sale around the middle of July. To be placed on the mailing list, call the ticket office, above.

Parking: Parking is limited at the Dome, although there are many small parking lots in the immediate neighborhood. The best parking is at the Omni Decks with entrances on Techwood Avenue and Spring Street.

CONSUMER TIPS   The best bet for getting to and from the Dome is to ride MARTA.

Georgia Tech (Zone 8)

Season: Early September until late November. Eleven games, six home and five away.

Site/Stadium: Bobby Dodd Stadium, 43,000 seats, natural surface.

Game Times: Generally Saturday afternoons about 1 P.M.

Ticket Prices: $21

Where to Buy Tickets: Call the Georgia Tech ticket office, (404) 894-5447, or Ticketmaster, (404) 249-6400 or (800) 326-4000.

Parking: Parking is limited. The best idea is to park free at a MARTA station, ride to the North Avenue Station, and walk the few blocks to the stadium.

CONSUMER TIPS   Tickets are readily available for most games. It is a tradition to stop by the Varsity, a local drive-in that's become an institution, at 61 North Avenue, for hot dogs or hamburgers before the game.

University of Georgia (Athens, Georgia)

Season: Early September through late November. Eleven games, six home games.

Site/Stadium: 86,117-seat Sanford Stadium.

Game Times: Saturdays at 1 P.M. when not moved to fit TV schedules.

Ticket Prices: $22

Where to Buy Tickets: Georgia Athletic Ticket Office, P.O. Box 1472, Athens, GA 30603; (706) 542-1231.

Parking: Plenty of spaces within walking distance of the stadium.

CONSUMER TIPS   To reach Athens from I-285, Atlanta's perimeter highway, take I-85 north to Georgia Highway 316. Bear right and stay on that road until it ends. Turn right on US 78, which will take you into downtown Athens. The stadium is on Lumpkin, which turns right off US 78 one block past the Athens Holiday Inn. Athens is normally an hour-

and-a-half drive from Atlanta, but on a football Saturday, allow at least three hours for the drive, plus time for parking and walking to the stadium. Games are usually at 1 P.M. but can vary. For a 1 P.M. game, traffic in Athens starts picking up by 10 A.M.

—— Basketball

Atlanta Hawks (Zone 7)

Season: Early November through the end of April, with playoffs beginning the first of May. 82 games, 41 home and 41 away.

Site/Stadium: The 16,400-seat Omni.

Game Times: 7:30 P.M., subject to change.

Ticket Prices: $10–33. Group discounts available for groups of 20 or more.

Where to Buy Tickets: Tickets are sold through Ticketmaster, a telephone reservation system that adds $3 to the price of each ticket. If tickets are bought 10 days in advance, Ticketmaster will mail the tickets to you, or they can be picked up the day of the game at the "will call" window across from Gate D at the Omni. Call Ticketmaster at (404) 249-6400 or (800) 326-4000. For season tickets call (404) 827-dunk.

Parking: Parking is available at many small lots around the Omni for between $3 and $8. The best, safest parking is at the Omni Decks with entrances on Spring Street and Techwood Avenue.

CONSUMER TIPS   Forget the parking and ride MARTA directly to the Omni Station.

Georgia Tech (Zone 8)

Season: Mid-November through early March.

Site/Stadium: 10,000-seat Alexander Memorial Coliseum.

Game Times: Varies

Ticket Prices: About $14

Where to Buy Tickets: As a rule, season ticket holders and student tickets sell out the small Alexander Coliseum. If tickets become available, they are put on sale at the coliseum the day of the game. Call the Georgia Tech ticket office, (404) 894-5447, for information on ticket availability.

Parking: Parking is limited around the coliseum. Ride MARTA to the Midtown Station and walk the few blocks to the coliseum.

CONSUMER TIPS   The best time to get tickets is during Christmas break, when students are away for the holidays.

— Golf Tournaments

BellSouth Classic (formerly the Atlanta Classic), a PGA Tour event (Zone 3)

Season: First week in May.

Site: Atlanta Country Club, named by *Golf Digest* as one of the 100 top courses in the country.

Game Times: Play lasts from Monday through Sunday.

Ticket Prices: $30 for the week.

Where to Buy Tickets: Call the BellSouth Classic office (770) 951-8777. Tickets are available at Atlanta Country Club during the tournament; call (770) 955-3850 from early April through tournament time.

Parking: At five lots with shuttle service to the tournament site; $5 fee.

CONSUMER TIPS   Wear comfortable shoes and comfortable clothes. Classic organizers are astounded by the ladies who show up in high heels.

Senior PGA Tournament Event (Alpharetta, Georgia)

Season: May.

Site: Golf Club of Georgia.

Game Times: Play (including practice rounds) lasts from Monday–Sunday.

Ticket Prices: $35 for the week.

Where to Buy Tickets: Call the tournament office, (404) 393-4567.

Parking: $5 includes a shuttle to the gate.

CONSUMER TIPS   Tickets are readily available for this event, which draws 30,000 to 40,000 spectators a year. Take Georgia Highway 400 north to Windward Parkway (Exit #11). Turn right and go 3 miles to a well-marked field for parking. Shuttle buses provide transportation to the course.

COMMENTS   With a purse of $1.2 million, this is considered one of the top five events on the Senior Tour. Players have included Jack Nicklaus, Arnold Palmer, Chi Chi Rodriguez, Raymond Floyd, and Isao Aoki.

Chick-fil-A Charity Championship at Eagle's Landing (Zone 6)

Season: April.

Site: Eagles Landing Country Club.

Game Times: Monday through Sunday. Actual tournament play, Friday through Sunday.

Ticket Prices: $20 for the week.

Where to Buy Tickets: Call the tournament office, (770) 474-4653.

Parking: Parking with shuttle available.

CONSUMER TIPS   Special tournament ticket promotions are available through Chick-fil-A restaurants. Watch from the top of the hill on the 18th hole. From there you can see both the 17th hole, a difficult par four which is bogeyed and double bogeyed frequently, and 18, a par five. A lot of scores change dramatically on these two holes.

COMMENTS   Nancy Lopez, Dottie Pepper, Betsy King, and Patty Sheehan are among the women golfers who have participated in this tournament. *Golf News* ranked Eagle's Landing one of the top five new golf courses in the country.

A Note about the Masters Tournament

Known all over the world as the grandfather of golf tournaments, the Masters is hosted by the Augusta National Golf Club in Augusta, Georgia.

Tournament tickets are sold to a "patron" list, which was closed due to demand in 1972. The "waiting list" to get on the patron list was closed in 1978. The bottom line is that now, and for the rest of your life, you will have to know someone to get a ticket to the Masters. However, if you would enjoy an opportunity to walk the famed course, write or call Augusta National Golf Club for information on Practice Round tickets. These tickets were limited for the first time in 1995 and were sold through the mail rather than at the gate. Cost is about $16 for Monday and Tuesday and $21 for Wednesday, which includes an informal par-three contest at 2 P.M. During the practice rounds, gates open at 8 A.M. and close at approximately 6:30 P.M. To obtain information about accommodations during practice days, call (800) 365-7273 (hotels and motels) or (800) 244-4709 (private homes).

The Masters is scheduled so that the tournament ends on the second Sunday in April. Future dates are: 1997, April 7–13; 1998, April 6–12; 1999, April 5–11; 2000, April 3–9.

To reach the Augusta National Golf Club, take I-20 east from Atlanta approximately 150 miles to Georgia Highway 28 (Washington Road) and go right (south) to the gate.

For additional information write or call the Augusta National Golf Club, Augusta, GA 30913; (706) 667-6000. Many Augusta area hotels and motels have lodging packages available. To obtain a list of properties approved by the Augusta Chamber of Commerce call the Chamber office at (706) 821-1300.

— Auto and Motorcycle Racing

Atlanta Motor Speedway (Hampton, Georgia)

Season: Two NASCAR Winston Cup races a year, one in the spring and one in the fall, plus accompanying races such as the Bush Grand National and the ARCA series on the same weekends.

Site: Races are held on the 1.522-mile track of the Atlanta Motor Speedway, on 870 acres about 30 miles south of Atlanta.

Days/Times: Races are on Saturday and Sunday, with workouts and time trials on Thursday and Friday. Races usually begin by 1 P.M.

Ticket Prices: $10–70 per day, depending on the event and seating.

Where to Buy Tickets: Call the track at (404) 946-4211 or Ticketmaster telephone reservation system at (404) 249-6400 or (800) 326-4000.

Parking: Plenty of free parking on the 870-acre site.

CONSUMER TIPS These races draw the biggest crowds of any paid sporting event in Georgia. When Richard Petty retired in November of 1992, 168,000 fans gathered here to witness his final race. Routinely, 100,000 people attend a race. Choice seats are in the East Turn Grandstand, which Speedway PR people modestly tout as "the best seats of any motor sports facility in the world." The infield was scooped out to bank the track. The positive result is a view from that vantage point that is like looking up from the bottom of a bowl at cars racing around the inside wall. "Public suite" tickets are available for $395 per person for three days, including food. Call four to six months in advance for these popular suites located at the top of the East Turn Grandstand. Here's a driving tip: Most people take I-75 to Exit #77 and follow US 19/41, 15 miles to the Speedway. Instead, take Exit #70 and then Georgia Highway 20/81. It's 2 or 3 miles longer, but there's much less traffic.

Road Atlanta (Braselton, Georgia)

Season: Twenty-five or more races from March to November.

Site: A 2.5-mile road racing course, plus a 1.3-mile off-road motor-cross course in Braselton, about 45 miles north of Atlanta.

Days/Times: All races are on weekends except for the Sports Car Club of America Road Race of Champions, which runs mid-week through the weekend, and the WERA motorcycle Grand National Finals, which runs for a full week.

Ticket Prices: $10–40, for single-day or weekend passes. All tickets are "super tickets," which allow spectators full access to the infield, grandstands, and paddock/garage areas.

Where to Buy Tickets: Tickets can always be purchased at the gate or can be purchased in advance by calling the Road Atlanta ticket office at (770) 967-6143.

Parking: Free parking at main entrance lot or infield.

CONSUMER TIPS   Free primitive campsites are always available, and nominal fees are charged for leveled graveled sites with electrical service. To reach the track, take I-85 north from Atlanta to Exit #49 and go west about 5 miles to Braselton.

COMMENT   The Sports Car Club of America holds its national championship on this track. With 600 race teams running in 22 different classes, it is the largest event of its kind in the world. Road Atlanta draws crowds of 25,000 to 30,000 for its biggest events.

—— Hockey

Atlanta Knights (Zone 7)

Season: October–April, with play-offs going through the end of May. The team plays a total of 82 games, 41 home and 41 away.

Site/Stadium: The Omni with 15,179 seats for hockey.

Game Times: Weekdays, 7:35 P.M.; weekend times vary from 1 P.M. to 7:35 P.M.; all Sunday games at 7:05 P.M.

Ticket Prices: $8–16

Where to Buy Tickets: Call the Knights ticket office at
(404) 525-8900 or Ticketmaster telephone reservation system
at (404) 249-6400 or (800) 326-4000.

Parking: The best parking is the Omni Decks with entrances on
Spring Street and Techwood Avenue, $8.

CONSUMER TIPS   Take MARTA to the Omni Station next to the
entrance.

COMMENTS   The team is in the International Hockey League, which is
to the National Hockey League what AAA baseball is to the major
leagues. Other cities with IHL teams include Cincinnati, Cleveland,
Phoenix, San Diego, Salt Lake City, and Kansas City.

PART NINE: Shopping in Atlanta

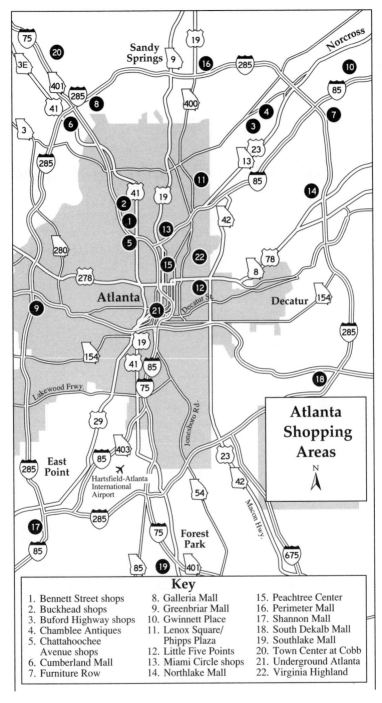

Atlanta Shopping Areas

N

Key

1. Bennett Street shops
2. Buckhead shops
3. Buford Highway shops
4. Chamblee Antiques
5. Chattahoochee Avenue shops
6. Cumberland Mall
7. Furniture Row
8. Galleria Mall
9. Greenbriar Mall
10. Gwinnett Place
11. Lenox Square/ Phipps Plaza
12. Little Five Points
13. Miami Circle shops
14. Northlake Mall
15. Peachtree Center
16. Perimeter Mall
17. Shannon Mall
18. South Dekalb Mall
19. Southlake Mall
20. Town Center at Cobb
21. Underground Atlanta
22. Virginia Highland

Nothing Like It Back Home

While transportation and business are the character of Atlanta and sports is its passion, Atlanta's personality is shopping. The city without shopping is unimaginable. Shopping is to Atlanta what a brass band and majorettes are to a parade, what ornaments are to a Christmas tree, what chocolate icing is to a devil's food cake.

The Buckhead Ritz Carlton's shopping weekend is the city's hottest package. Forty-five-passenger senior citizen tour buses roll into the Lenox Square Shopping Mall parking lot from Columbus, Macon, and Augusta. The passengers step off—and go shopping. Appropriately enough, the grandest retail space in the city—the high-ceilinged, chandeliered, Chanel-scented first floor of Macy's downtown—is located precisely at the highest geographical point in the city, the very pinnacle.

Shopping in Atlanta is recreation, people-watching, eating out, hanging out, companionship, something to talk about. It's a great way to see, understand, and enjoy the city.

For starters, Atlanta is home to some world-class shopping malls. The Lenox Square/Phipps Plaza complex (two plush malls across the street from each other in Zone 4) ranks as the number-one tourist attraction in the city. If you want to experience upscale indoor shopping in its maximum glory, this stop is a must. Then, when you think that can't be topped, head for Peachtree Center downtown (Zone 7).

If an eclectic, neighborhood-browsing experience is more your style, you'll find Atlanta to be a wealth of options. Buckhead shopping (Zone 3) is loaded with upscale color and personality, with more than 75 shops and art galleries. Little Five Points, the Haight Ashbury or Greenwich Village of Atlanta, is less upscale but even more eclectic.

Bennett Street (Zone 3), the Chamblee Antiques area off Peachtree Road (Zone 4), and Miami Circle (Zone 4) are the kinds of neighborhoods that art and antique lovers dream about. Chattahoochee Avenue (Zone 2) is discount heaven with its unparalleled collection of wholesalers, discounters, and liquidators.

The Atlanta area is also famous for its bargains on furniture and carpet. Shoppers from all over the region flock to Furniture Row (Zone 5) for deals on everything except antiques. And an hour north of Atlanta in Dalton, "the carpet capital of the world," you'll find over 100 carpet manufacturers' outlet stores.

The following pages will give you more insight into the malls, each prime shopping neighborhood, and each of Atlanta's leading shopping genres.

Malls

Lenox Square/Phipps Plaza (Zone 4)

When visitors come to Atlanta for any purpose other than business, they come most often to shop at Lenox Square. With 14 million visitors annually, Lenox Square, at the intersection of Peachtree and Lenox roads, could be called the number one tourist attraction in the city. Its 1,400,000 square feet make it Atlanta's largest shopping mall; and in terms of revenue, it consistently ranks as one of the top ten malls in the country.

Originally built as an open-air mall of modest proportion in 1959, it has been expanded, remodeled, enclosed, and double and triple decked.

A five-minute walk diagonally across the street from Lenox you'll find the 882,000-square-foot Phipps Plaza. Every materialistic impulse, every acquisitive instinct, that Lenox taps, Phipps takes and ratchets two notches higher. It is the ultimate concentration of upscale shops and merchandise in Atlanta. You won't find anything to beat it. Shoppers walk on marble floors, daylight pours through the arched atriums, and warm mellow cherry wood trim graces the walls. Columns throughout the mall and a grand staircase in the center convey the most elegant ideal of southern architecture.

Both malls contain multiplex movie theaters, plentiful fast food, and a number of upscale restaurants.

You can get to both Lenox and Phipps easily by hopping MARTA to the Lenox Station. Bus #23 also stops by the malls, on Peachtree Road.

Peachtree Center (Zone 7)

Walking through Peachtree Center is like driving through the streets of Atlanta. It defies logic. Anybody can lay out city streets in a grid. Anybody can build a mall with anchor department stores at both ends and a covered walkway connecting the two. It takes mad genius and hundreds of bright minds working in opposition to devise the delightfully labyrinthine confusion and surprise of a Peachtree Center.

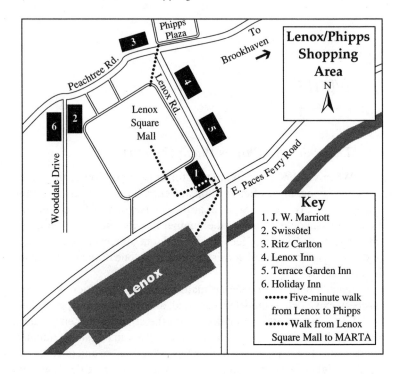

Lenox/Phipps Shopping Area
N

Lenox Square Mall

Phipps Plaza

Peachtree Rd.

Lenox Rd.

To Brookhaven →

E. Paces Ferry Road

Wooddale Drive

Lenox

Key
1. J. W. Marriott
2. Swissôtel
3. Ritz Carlton
4. Lenox Inn
5. Terrace Garden Inn
6. Holiday Inn
•••••• Five-minute walk from Lenox to Phipps
•••••• Walk from Lenox Square Mall to MARTA

So what is Peachtree Center? Loosely speaking, it is a network of downtown Atlanta hotels, shops, restaurants, food courts, and office space dominated by John Portman designed buildings, bordered by Piedmont Avenue, Ellis Street, Baker Street, and Techwood Drive; and connected by a maze of walkways and tunnels.

And in fact, if Macy's downtown is considered an "anchor" in the way that term is applied to the traditional shopping center, then Peachtree Center can be thought of as one of the most interesting, diverse shopping malls in Atlanta, rivaling even Lenox and Phipps for upscale merchandise.

MARTA, with its underground Peachtree Center Station, makes transportation to the Peachtree Center a snap. (Take the exit in the southeast corner of the station into the Peachtree Center Mall.) The system of bridges that link the different buildings are an attraction in themselves, fun to explore. If you're already downtown, Peachtree Center is just a short walk from Underground Atlanta.

If you're driving north on the I-75/85 Connector, exit on International Boulevard and park at the Cain Garage. From the bridge on the fifth floor of the parking garage, ride down to the "GL" level, which is the mall. If you're driving south on the I-75/85 Connector, exit at Courtland and park at the Courtland Street Garage. The bridge on the seventh floor of the garage leads directly into the mall.

—— *Other Malls*

Large, covered shopping malls with well-known department store anchors like Rich's, Macy's, Sears, and J.C. Penney dot the Atlanta perimeter and are convenient to northeastern, northwestern, and southern suburbs. Several of these malls have special features worth knowing about.

Greenbriar Mall.   Rich's clearance outlet, called Finale, for women's, men's, and children's fashion merchandise.

The Galleria Specialty Mall.   No anchors; mostly locally owned and operated one-of-a-kind retailers.

South DeKalb Mall.   Largest quality selection of African and African-American merchandise in the city.

Northlake Mall.   Annual February Goodwill Bookfair with 250,000 books—many priced at $1 or less.

Shopping Neighborhoods

—— Buckhead (Zone 3)

Buckhead, one of Atlanta's most exclusive residential neighborhoods, is also one of the most entertaining in which to walk, browse, and shop. Buckhead proper with its cluster of diverse, eclectic shops creates a counterpoint to the institutionalized nature of mall shopping found at the Lenox Square and Phipps Plaza shopping meccas only a mile north on Peachtree Road.

Along with a plethora of bars, restaurants, and clubs, there are over 75 shops and art galleries in and around Buckhead, ranging from **The Fish Hawk** (279 Buckhead Avenue; (404) 237-3473), with its top quality tackle and outdoor clothing, to **Cornelia Powell** (271-B East Paces Ferry Road; (404) 365-8511), where shoppers will find original Victorian lace dresses or can order custom-made dresses fashioned out of antique lace.

If you're shopping for Karl Lagerfeld or other couture designers, a sure bet is **Sasha Frisson** (3094 East Shadowlawn Avenue, NE; (404) 231-0393), owned by Ted Turner's daughter, Laura Turner-Seydel.

—— Little Five Points/Virginia-Highland (Zone 5)

San Francisco has Haight Ashbury, New York has Greenwich Village, and Atlanta has Little Five Points—a lively, young, diverse community on the edge of Inman Park, where clothing fads like hippy, punk rock, skinhead, and grunge erupt before they appear at Northlake Mall one year later as current fashion. The best shopping is concentrated at the intersection of Euclid and Moreland. **Urban Tribe** (1131 Euclid Avenue; (404) 659-1976) and **Junkman's Daughter** (464 Moreland Avenue; (404) 577-3188) appeal to teens with T-shirts, posters, black leather jackets covered with silver studs, and thick-soled combat boots.

Charis (1189 Euclid Avenue, NE; (404) 524-0304) is a first-rate feminist bookstore. **Wax N Facs** (432 Moreland Avenue, NE; (404) 525-2275) carries Atlanta's best selection of used records. **Stefan's** (1160

Euclid Avenue, NE; (404) 688-4929) was one of the first Atlanta stores to popularize quality antique clothes. **Sevenanda** (1111 Euclid Avenue, NE; (404) 681-2831) is one of the top organic and health food stores in the city.

A mile or so north, the purple crew cuts, multiple ear piercings, and skate boards of Little Five Points merge into the dirty bucks, polo shirts, khakis, and Volvos of Virginia-Highland. Like Little Five Points, this is not just a shopping district but a lively community rooted in an intown residential neighborhood.

You'll find the most concentrated shopping at the intersection of Virginia and Highland, with pear tree lined sidewalks, green and white striped awnings, and diners clustered around outdoor umbrella tables. **Murphy's**, with its *New York Times*–Sunday-morning-brunch crowd around one corner, and **Taco Mac**, with its satisfying collection of 300 foreign and domestic beers, enhance one of the most pleasant walking and shopping experiences in Atlanta. **Maddix Delux Flower and Chocolate** (1034 N. Highland, NE; (404) 892-9337) is the most popular shop. Other shops line Highland between Drewry and Ponce de Leon.

To get to Little Five Points and Virginia-Highland, take MARTA to the Inman Park Reynoldstown Station and walk to the heart of Little Five Points by going south on Hurt Street and east on Euclid. It's about a mile through scenic parts of Inman Park, Atlanta's oldest intown neighborhood. Or from the North Avenue Station take the #2 (Ponce de Leon) bus to Moreland and then the #6 bus to Little Five Points.

Where to Find . . .

—— Antiques

Bennett Street (Zone 3)

Forty-five of the best antique shops in the city, a dozen art galleries, and eleven sit-down restaurants of different ethnicity, all open for lunch, comprise the Bennett Street area. Rapidly becoming the city's most interesting collection of antiques and art, Bennett Street shops and galleries include **Out of the Woods** (22-B Bennett Street, NW; (404) 351-0446), **Bennett Street Gallery** (22-F Bennett Street, NW; (404) 352-8775), and **Red River Gallery** (22-G Bennett Street, NW; (404) 352-5163). Associations of dealers like those found at **Interiors Market** (55 Bennett Street, NW; (404) 352-0055) and **The Stalls** (116 Bennett Street, NW; (404) 352-4430) have made Bennett Street one of the hottest shopping streets in the city.

Tula (75 Bennett Street, NW; (404) 351-3551) is one large building housing a dozen or so galleries including photography, sculpture, textiles, pottery, and paintings. **Antique Row**, a five-minute walk down Peachtree Road from Bennett Street, is a strip of several shops and galleries that have been a center of antique trade in Atlanta for 40 years. Across the street at Twenty-Three Hundred Peachtree is a cluster of shops including **Oetgen Design and Antiques**, (404) 352-1112, and **Jane J. Marsden Antiques**, (404) 355-1288, acknowledged to be the most upscale and expensive in the city.

To get to Bennett Street, take the #23 bus from the Arts Center Station.

Chamblee Antiques (Zone 4)

The final scene of *Fried Green Tomatoes* is a nostalgic shot of a sign that says, "We Sell Crabs," that came from **Rust and Dust** (5486 Peachtree Road, (770) 458-1614), one of the many unusual antique shops in the Chamblee Antiques area off Peachtree Road. Shipments of rolltop desks, file cabinets, electric fans, and iceboxes go out by the truckload to movie and TV sets. **Moose Breath Trading Post** (5461

Peachtree Road, (770) 458-7210) does movies, too, but specializes in supplying nostalgic memorabilia to bars and restaurants. Ask to see the marvelous reproductions of neon signs of the 40s and 50s. Other unique shops in the Chamblee Antiques area include **Indiana's** (3519 Broad Street, (770) 455-8357), where you'll find items such as a complete 50s-style Coca-Cola bar and a beautiful Victorian Wooten desk from the 1870s.

There are two flea markets, one on Broad and the other larger one on Peachtree Industrial. At the latter, 150 dealers in 80,000 square feet of space sell everything from postcards to antique clothes to Boy Scout memorabilia to electronics. **Great Gatsby's Antiques** (5070 Peachtree Industrial Boulevard, (770) 457-1905) is famous for its large architectural antiques, including theater chandeliers, mantels, wrought iron fencing, and sculpture.

Miami Circle (Zone 4)

Miami Circle is home to one of the Southeast's largest concentrations of upscale antique and decorative accessory shops that are open to the public. Here among 70 diverse stores shoppers will find **Williams Antiques** (699 Miami Circle, (404) 231-9818), Georgia's oldest, largest, and some say most expensive antique dealer. At 711 Miami Circle, (404) 231-0734, is **The Gables,** specializing in country French furniture and oriental porcelain, lamps, tapestries, pillows, and mirrors. **Joseph Konrad** (693 Miami Circle, (404) 261-3224) features antique English furniture including sideboards, secretaries, hand-carved mirror frames, and custom-made classic reproductions. Fine 18th- and 19th-century French and English antiques are the main features of **William Word** (707 Miami Circle, (404) 233-6890), and wicker and pine furniture is the stock in trade of **Dearing Antiques** (709 Miami Circle, (404) 233-6333).

—— Art

These are the better fine art and craft galleries in the city, with Buckhead having the largest concentration.

Buckhead Galleries (Zone 3)

In business since 1965, **Heath Gallery** (416 East Paces Ferry Road, (404) 262-6407) is the oldest continuously operating gallery in the city. David Heath has carte blanche credibility with the knowledgeable art patrons and first-rate gallery owners of Atlanta. A long line of artists have shown here, including Jasper Johns, Andy Warhol, and Alexander Calder. Though gallery hours are limited and much of the business is done by appointment only, a visit to Heath is a touchstone for every serious art buyer.

Since opening in 1989, Jane Jackson has put together the top photography gallery in the city. **Jackson Fine Art** (3115 East Shadowlawn Avenue, (404) 233-3739) shows top national and emerging regional photographers, including Irving Penn, Ansel Adams, and John McWilliams.

Berman Gallery (3261 Roswell Road, (404) 261-3858) is the oldest and best primitive art gallery in the city. Rick Berman promoted the work of artists Howard Finster and Mose Tolliver long before this type of art was fashionable. Berman, an accomplished potter himself, shows the pottery of Athens, Georgia, potters Ron Myers and Michael Simon.

Eighty-something Blanch Reeves is an Atlanta institution in the fine crafts business. She was selling and promoting art and fine crafts in Atlanta when the market for that kind of merchandise was much thinner. Her **Signature Shop Gallery** (3267 Roswell Road, NW; (404) 237-4426) carries some of the top names in fine crafts, including Ed Molthroupe, an Atlanta native, and one of the top wooden bowl turners in the country.

Fay Gold Gallery (247 Buckhead Avenue, (404) 233-3843) is the hottest gallery in Atlanta at the moment. Fay's competitors don't see her as an aesthetic purist, but they begrudgingly acknowledge that she has the best eye and an on-target instinct for tomorrow's art trend. If it's going to be controversial, and marketable, expect to see it at Fay Gold.

Opened in early 1993, **Dorothy McRae Gallery** (3193 Roswell Road, (404) 266-2363) is the largest private gallery art space in the city. Visitors will find contemporary fine arts with a particular focus on figurative, narrative, personal works. The gallery also shows fine decorative glass, wood, jewelry, and some photography.

Martha Connell, owner of **Martha Connell Gallery** (333 Buckhead Avenue, (404) 261-1712), shows clay vessels and sculpture by Paul Soldner and Don Reitz, quilts by Pamela Studstill and Yvonne Porcella, and turned wood vessels by Bob Stocksdale and Rude Osoinik.

Other Atlanta Galleries

At 587 Virginia Avenue (Zone 5), midway between Downtown and Buckhead, is the large, comprehensive **McIntosh Gallery.** In business since 1981, Louisa McIntosh is an expert at helping clients build or expand a collection. Among nationally recognized artists represented are some of the finest African-American artists working in the United States. Ask to see the art stored in the loft that overlooks Piedmont Park. (404) 892-4023.

Within walking distance of the McIntosh Gallery is **Nancy Solomon Gallery** (Zone 5, 11037 Monroe Drive (404) 875-7100). The focus here is on conceptual and installation art, abstract painting and sculpture, and multimedia works involving photography, video, and CD-ROM.

Vesperman Gallery (Zone 8, 2140 Peachtree Street; (404) 350-9698) carries glass sculpture of a type that originated with the American Glass Movement of the 1960s. Shoppers will find figurative sculpture, human form and natural objects out of slump glass, and a derivative of an old Italian glass blowing technique known as "murrini." **The Craft Gallery** next door carries perfume atomizers, paper weights, jewelry, and ceramics.

Sandler Hudson (Zone 8, 1831-A Peachtree Road; (404) 350-8480) is a gallery that, in its own words, shows mostly "provocative psychologically motivated images." Many regional sculptors and painters show here.

Lowe Gallery (Zone 3, 75 Bennett Street, Space A-2 at Tula; (404) 352-8114) prides itself on picking talented but relatively unknown artists, promoting them, and sticking with them as their careers emerge. "Thought-provoking work by up-and-coming artists," is how the gallery likes to characterize the paintings and sculpture it displays.

—— *Bargains*

Chattahoochee Avenue (Zone 2)

Thanks to the predictable outlet malls along the interstate, we have come to think of outlet shopping as institutionalized—a cluster of familiar shops gathered under one roof and surrounded by acres of asphalt parking. Chattahoochee Avenue is nothing of the sort. There is no other place like this in the city.

Shoppers will dodge 18-wheelers coming and going from the warehouses and light manufacturing plants that are the natural inhabitants of this rough industrial park. Railroad yards are within sight of most stores. A car is a must for getting from one place to another. But despite these inconveniences, or maybe because of them, shoppers will find this to be the genuine article: discounters, wholesalers, and liquidators offering big savings off retail prices.

K&G (1777 Ellsworth Industrial Boulevard, (404) 352-3471) is a liquidator of men's clothing from top makers such as Polo, Calvin Klein, Adolfo, and Perry Ellis. **AJS Shoes** (1788 Ellsworth Industrial Boulevard, (404) 355-1760) carries 25,000 pairs of women's shoes with no seconds or off-brands. Ninety-five percent of the shoes are European-made and purchased directly from manufacturers. **Fashion Buys** (1600 Ellsworth Industrial Boulevard, (404) 355-1487) is a wholesale operation during the week and a discounter to the public on weekends, when it sells REO, Leslie Fay, and Giorgio at 35–50% off retail. **Forsyth Fabrics** (1190 Foster Street, (404) 351-6050) carries thousands of bolts of material and draws retail customers and decorators from all over Atlanta and the surrounding southeastern states. **Lighting Clearance Center** (1510 Ellsworth Industrial Boulevard, (404) 875-7637) is the manufacturer's closeout outlet for the well-known and highly regarded Georgia Lighting.

—— *Books*

The Oxfords (Zone 3)

Perhaps the cavernous Strand in New York has more used books, and the four-story Tattered Cover in Denver has more new books under one roof, but no city bookstore in America has in total more new and used books than Rupert LeCraw's pride and joy, **Oxford**. If LeCraw, whose father was mayor of Atlanta from 1940 to 1942, were not such a mild-mannered, self-effacing character, one would accuse him of being a proselytizing literary zealot, a kind of closet cult leader. Oxford is arguably the most important literary force and influence in Atlanta.

Oxford carries 150,000 new titles, over 100,000 used books, 3,500 magazine titles, the Sunday editions of 100 newspapers, and 15,000 video titles in four buildings located on or near Peachtree. More national and local authors sign books and do readings here than at any other place in the metropolitan area. The monthly tabloid newspaper, *Oxford Review,* goes out to a mailing list of 230,000. Performers sing and play in the *Acoustic Cafe* at the 360 Pharr Road store, (404) 262-3333, three nights a week and on Sunday afternoons. Oxford offers a long list of services including special orders, buying and selling books and records, binding, and appraisals.

The best advice for an out-of-towner is to go to the Pharr Road store and pick up a free copy of *Oxford Review.* It has a complete listing of upcoming book signings and readings as well as a detailed listing of the other services that Oxford offers.

Other Peachtree Street Bookstores

Directly across the street from the "Dump," the Victorian apartment building where Margaret Mitchell wrote *Gone with the Wind*, sits the **United States Government Bookstore** (Zone 8, 999 Peachtree Street; (404) 347-1900). Here, shoppers can tap into the vast and fascinating library of 15,000 publications put out by the U.S. Government Printing Office. These range from dull columns of county-by-county census data to colorful, large-format, hardbound books about the Grand Canyon. The 2,000–3,000 titles in the store include books on the American Civil War, aviation, education, nutrition, patents, and the American wilderness. Indexes available at this store show how to order any of the titles not carried.

The High Museum Gift Shop (Zone 8, 1280 Peachtree Street; (404) 733-4411) carries a good selection of art books as well as posters, cards, T-shirts, jewelry, and colorful Kindred Spirits masks designed by Gina Truex. **Barnes and Noble** (Zone 3, 2900 Peachtree Street; (404) 261-7747) carries over 100,000 volumes in a spacious well-lighted store. Its Premier Music department features hard-to-find CDs and tapes, particularly movie soundtracks no longer in print. A Starbucks coffee shop is open in the bookstore Sunday through Thursday, 9 A.M.–11 P.M., and Friday and Saturday until midnight.

In the refined, sedate environment of **Yesteryear Book Shop** (Zone 3, 3201 Maple Drive; (404) 237-0163), customers browse through rare, collectible, and autographed books. Specialties include the Civil War, southern history, modern first editions, architecture and decorative arts, and maps from the 1700s and 1800s.

Borders (Zone 3, 3637 Peachtree Road; (404) 237-0707) carries over 100,000 book titles, 50,000 music titles, and 8,000 videos. There is a cafe and espresso bar in the huge two-story store and plenty of nooks and crannies for leisurely browsing the merchandise.

These stores are located along a five-mile stretch of Peachtree Street and are all within walking distance of MARTA rail stations or bus stops. Using the train, the Midtown Station and the Arts Center Station get you within comfortable walking distance of the bookstores located between 10th and 15th streets.

While not on Peachtree Street, the **Engineer's Bookstore** (748 Marietta Street, NW; (404) 221-1669) warrants a special trip if you are interested in technical reference, building codes, or computer books. The bookstore opened in 1954 to serve Georgia Institute of Technology students and has grown over 40 years to a 10,000-square-foot, two-level store with the largest selection of engineering-related reference books in the Southeast.

The **Cyclorama Bookstore** (Zone 6, in the Cyclorama at 800 Cherokee Avenue next to Zoo Atlanta in Grant Park) has a first-rate collection of Civil War books and maps.

—— Ethnic Merchandise

Buford Highway (Zone 4)

Over the last ten years, the ethnic migration of Mexicans, Chinese, Koreans, and Vietnamese that is changing the personality and character of Atlanta has centered along Buford Highway from Lenox Road to the Gwinnett County line—a seven-mile-long quintessential American highway of strip shopping centers and urban pop culture.

Shoppers will find dozens of Asian shops, businesses, and food markets. Diners find many of the best ethnic restaurants in Atlanta on this avenue. For the kind of shopper who is as fascinated by the mix of people and cultures as the merchandise, this shopping adventure can be one of the most interesting experiences in the city. Some noteworthy stops for your ethnic shopping tour include the following:

Koreatown Mall (5302 Buford Highway, (770) 936-0969) contains 17 Korean businesses. For something different, check out the **Vietnamese Video Rental** (5150 Buford Highway in the Asian Square Shopping Center, (770) 986-7400). **Los Primos** (3287 Chamblee-Dunwoody Road, (770) 457-7210) is Atlanta's best Mexican market. **Chinatown Mall** (5379 New Peachtree Road, (770) 458-4624) offers newspapers, herbs, food, and a video rental.

The 80,000-square-foot **International Farmer's Market** (5193 Peachtree Industrial Boulevard, (770) 455-1777) is one of the top three international food markets in the city, carrying fish, poultry, vegetables, and fruit. **Buford Flea Market** (5000 Buford Highway, (770) 452-7140) features international dealers. **Outlet Square Mall** (4166 Buford Highway) contains 16 outlet stores.

The **Booknook** (3342 Clairmont Road, (404) 633-1328) has thousands of used paperback books and one of Atlanta's best inventories of CDs, tapes, records, and comic books. **Windfare** (3885 Buford Highway, (404) 634-9463) is one of the top three adult toy stores in Atlanta. **El Rinconcito** (2000 Cheshire Bridge Road, (404) 636-8714) is the premier Spanish market in the city.

—— *Furniture*

Furniture Row (Zone 5)

Shoppers from all over the Southeast converge on Furniture Row, a one-mile strip of I-85 access road between Jimmy Carter Boulevard and Pleasantdale Road. Dubbed the "Excess Access" by a local radio station, the road is lined with 47 furniture and home furnishing stores, mostly retail but with a few outlets. Shop here for traditional, contemporary, Scandinavian, leather, wicker, or unfinished pine furniture. You will also find La-Z-Boys, carpets, billiard tables, ceramic tile, and kid's outdoor swing sets. If it is furniture and anything besides fine antiques, it is here.

Atlanta Fixture (3185 NE Expressway Access Road, (770) 455-8844) supplies fixtures and equipment to the restaurant industry but is open to the public as well. It's all here: frying pans, colanders, ladles, knives, spatulas, glasses and dishes by the case, aprons, and measuring cups. There may be lots of big scale stuff, but you'll find plenty of items that the home cook can use. A special section of the store, Bargain Alley, has one-of-a-kind, discontinued sales merchandise.

Most Furniture Row stores are open 6 days a week, 9:30 or 10 A.M. until 6 P.M., half-day on Sunday.

—— *Rugs and Carpet*

Any shopper who has the slightest interest in antique rugs and textiles should head directly to the obscure storefront of **Afghanistan Nomadic Rugs** (Zone 3, 3219 Cains Hill Place; (404) 261-7259), where one can find museum-quality Afghani, Persian, Turkish, and American-Indian rugs, as well as other textiles. Ask to go downstairs where the real inventory is stacked around a yurt, a 16-foot-diameter wood-frame tent used in Mongolia.

Just one hour north of Atlanta on I-75 you'll find Dalton, Georgia, the "carpet capital of the world." Over 100 carpet outlet stores of leading carpet manufacturers sell to the public at tremendous savings. For more information, call the Dalton Chamber of Commerce at (706) 278-7373.

—— Shoes

Friedman's (Zone 7)

Even the relatively mundane task of buying men's shoes can be an eye-opening experience at Friedman's (209 Mitchell Street, SW; (404) 524-1311). You can find virtually any kind of shoe here: Wejuns, black wingtips, saddle shoes, brown cap-toe lace-ups to match Brooks Brothers suits. But where Friedman's shines is in its colorful history of service to celebrities and people with odd-sized feet.

Florida Marlins left fielder Gary Sheffield comes to Friedman's after hours and climbs three levels of narrow, creaky, fluorescent-lit stairs to buy a pair of shoes that cost $400 or even $850 or more.

Trailing an ESPN camera crew, Dominique Wilkins bought black patent leather and velvet shoes for himself and his father-in-law to be on the Saturday of his wedding. El Gigante, the seven-foot-seven Argentine wrestler, was fitted with a pair of size 20 Etonics in Friedman's and burst into tears over finally having shoes that fit. Shaquille O'Neal routinely calls to order five pairs of size 20s.

When a major league team comes to Atlanta, Friedman's sends its van to the hotel. Sometimes the team bus pulls up in front of the store. Superstars cart in signed jerseys, bats, and posters as tokens of appreciation for the shoes and service. Johnny Bench brought in a signed grey and red Cincinnati flannel shirt, number 5. Chili Davis's 1991 World Series bat leans in a corner behind some boxes of shoes. There are more framed jerseys, posters, autographed photographs, and bats in this place than in any Atlanta sports bar.

Friedman's has been an institution since 1929. From the peeling walls and the sagging, water-stained ceiling, it appears that the last coat of light green paint was applied the year they moved in. The decor otherwise is a combination of different kinds of metal storage bins lined with shoe boxes—about 80,000 of them.

While the men browse the cavernous, macho men's store, women can inspect the smaller inventory at Friedman's Store for Ladies six doors west of the main store (223 Mitchell Street, SW; (404) 523-1134). The women's division specializes in designer shoes in classic styles and larger sizes, 6–21. Slims and narrows are available in sizes 6–9. Both stores are open Monday through Saturday, 9 A.M.–5:30 P.M.

—— *Souvenirs of Atlanta and the Olympiad*

The visitor to Underground Atlanta (Zone 7) will find as good a selection of traditional tourist souvenirs as anywhere in the city: T-shirts, monogrammed ball caps, Atlanta Braves paraphernalia, Olympic souvenirs, books, cards, Georgia wines and food products like pecans and peaches, and *Gone with the Wind* books, posters, figurines, and music boxes.

PART TEN: *Sightseeing*

Atlanta's Attractions

Atlanta is a sports town, a convention town, a shopping town, a business town, and a residential neighborhood town before it is an attractions town. But that doesn't mean that there are no fascinating attractions to enjoy once you are here.

After all, Martin Luther King, Jr., the leader of the most important social revolution in the 20th century, was born here; Ted Turner's CNN, which has changed the way the world thinks about television news, is based here; Coca-Cola, an American cultural icon, got its start in Atlanta; and some of the most important battles of the Civil War, the most destructive war in American history, were fought in and around the city. Museums, memorials, tours, and parks commemorate these people and events. Also, there is a whole host of other attractions that will please visitors interested in everything from natural science to telephone technology to hand puppets. Add Six Flags, a fine family amusement park, and Stone Mountain Park, which draws over 6 million visitors a year, and you have an entertaining and diverse menu of attractions from which to choose.

This section provides you with a comprehensive guide to Atlanta's top attractions. We give you enough information so that you can choose the places you want to see, based on your own interests. Each attraction includes a zone number so you can plan your visit logically without spending a lot of time criss-crossing the city. Note that the greatest concentration of tourist attractions are in Zones 7 and 8, downtown.

Sights: Zone 1 — Southwest Atlanta

The Wren's Nest

Type of Attraction: Museum and storytelling in the home of Joel Chandler Harris, the creator of the Uncle Remus tales.

Location: 1050 Ralph David Abernathy Boulevard.

Best MARTA Route: Bus #71 (Cascade) from West End Station.

Admission: $4 adults, $3 seniors and teens, $2 children ages 4–12.

Hours: Tuesday–Saturday, 10 A.M.–4 P.M.; Sunday, 1–4 P.M.

Phone: (404) 753-7735

When to Go: Any time.

Special Comments: Because Joel Chandler Harris was white, the Wren's Nest was once considered a preserve of white culture and values. Ralph From Ben Hill, a controversial black radio talk show host, likes to relate the story of how he was once turned away at the door. But this is no longer the case. The creator of the Uncle Remus stories is now recognized as a person who helped preserve black culture through the recording of African folk tales. More and more the museum is involved with, and relates to, the West End community where it is located, an area developing a unique African-American personality.

Overall Appeal by Age Group:

Pre-school	Grade School	Teens	Young Adults	Over 30	Senior Citizens
★	★★½	★★	★★★	★★★	★★★

Authors' Rating: The only writer's house museum in Atlanta. ★★★

How Much Time to Allow: 45 minutes to one hour.

DESCRIPTION AND COMMENTS   This pretty, Victorian cottage was the home of Joel Chandler Harris, who worked as an editorial writer for an Atlanta newspaper and lived in West End, Atlanta's oldest neighborhood. Harris commuted to work via Whitehall Street's mule-drawn streetcars. He composed his tales about animals with human characteristics based on stories he had heard from slaves while growing up in Eatonton, Georgia. Dressed in a suit and string bow tie and wearing a large black hat, Harris liked to sit in a wicker rocker on his front porch and write his stories. The house, which is the most faithfully preserved of any Atlanta writer's, is very much as Harris lived in it until his death in 1908.

TOURING TIPS   Storytelling is an important part of the Wren's Nest touring experience. Call in advance to determine when a session is scheduled and plan your trip around it. Expect to pay an additional $2. Several good soul-food and home-cooking restaurants are within walking distance. Ask the Wren's Nest staff to direct you. A picnic area is available out back if you want to bring a lunch. Free parking is limited but usually adequate. There is one rest room inside the building, which is not disabled accessible, although the house is wheelchair accessible.

OTHER THINGS TO DO NEARBY   The staff at the Wren's Nest will give you a map that has directions to nearby sites, including the Herndon Home, the Hammond House with its fine African-American art collection, and the Shrine of the Black Madonna, which has an exceptionally good collection of African-American books.

Sights: Zone 2—
Northwest Atlanta

Kennesaw Mountain National Battlefield Park

Type of Attraction: Museum and self-guided tour of the Civil War battlefield.

Location: Old Highway 41 and Stilesboro Road in Marietta. Take I-75 north to Exit #116, Barrett Parkway, and follow the signs.

Admission: Free.

Hours: Daily, 8:30 A.M.–5 P.M. Closed Christmas Day.

Phone: (770) 427-4686

When to Go: Any time.

Special Comments: For the visitor interested in Civil War history, Kennesaw should be added to the Cyclorama and the Atlanta History Center as "must" stops.

Overall Appeal by Age Group:

Pre-school	Grade School	Teens	Young Adults	Over 30	Senior Citizens
—	★	★★	★★½	★★½	★★½

Authors' Rating: Essential touring for the Civil War buff, despite the out-of-date slide presentation in the museum. ★★★★

How Much Time to Allow: 45 minutes to one hour to see the museum and slide presentation. Up to a full day for touring battle sites in the surrounding national park.

DESCRIPTION AND COMMENTS   Kennesaw Mountain Battlefield was the site of the last battle between Union forces under General Sherman and Confederate troops under General Johnston before Johnston retreated to Atlanta. A small museum and slide show help the visitor place the battle into the perspective of the Atlanta Campaign. A self-guided tour directs visitors to Cheatam Hill, Kolb Farm, Pigeon Hill, and other places where fighting took place.

TOURING TIPS   Dennis Kelly, the former park historian, has written a book called *Kennesaw Mountain and the Atlanta Campaign*. The text and maps greatly enhance the visitor's understanding of this important Civil War memorial. It's on sale at the Visitor Center for $9.95.

This is a good location for picnicking, not only because there are no restaurants nearby (the closest food is about two miles away), but because the setting is beautiful and historic. Fine picnic locations can be found throughout the park either on tables or under shade trees within sight of the Civil War trenches and cannon. Rest rooms are available in the Visitor Center but no other place in the park. The Visitor Center is disabled accessible, but the trails are not. Free parking is available throughout the park.

OTHER THINGS TO DO NEARBY   Consider combining a visit to Kennesaw with a side trip to Big Shanty Museum and a driving tour of the antebellum homes in and around Marietta.

Marietta Walking and Driving Tour

Type of Attraction: A self-guided tour of Marietta's historic districts that recall life in pre–Civil War Georgia.

Location: Marietta Welcome Center, Number 4 Depot Street, Marietta. One-half block west of the square at the railroad depot.

Admission: The self-guided tour is free; guided tours are $8 adults and $4 children.

Hours: Welcome Center open Monday–Friday, 9 A.M.–5 P.M.; Saturday, 11 A.M.–4 P.M.; Sunday, 1–4 P.M. Guided tours each Thursday, except holidays, at 10:30 A.M. and 2 P.M. (April–November).

Phone: (770) 429-1115

When to Go: Self-guided tours can be taken at any time.

Special Comments: Houses still standing in Marietta served as headquarters for Confederate Generals Johnson and Loring during the Battle of Kennesaw Mountain.

Overall Appeal by Age Group:

Pre-school	Grade School	Teens	Young Adults	Over 30	Senior Citizens
—	★	★★	★★½	★★★	★★★½

Authors' Rating: Despite the fact that Marietta is a busy Atlanta suburb, the city square has the feeling of a small Georgia town. ★★

How Much Time to Allow: Two hours.

DESCRIPTION AND COMMENTS   Marietta, like Atlanta, existed because of railroads. Incorporated in 1834, Marietta was the last construction site of the Western and Atlantic Railroad before work crews moved into what was to become Atlanta. Marietta Street, one of young Atlanta's first streets, was the narrow dirt track running from the center of town parallel to the railroad tracks across the Chattahoochee to Marietta. In Marietta, the same road was called the Atlanta Road.

During the Civil War, Union troops marched from Chattanooga to Atlanta along the railroad tracks, destroying them as they went. On their way to Atlanta, the Yankees targeted Marietta because it was an important railroad town. Another big battle along the way was at Kennesaw Mountain near Marietta. Visitors who want to get a feel for what a lively 19th-century Georgia railroad town was like (and relive some Civil War history) will enjoy this tour.

TOURING TIPS   Brown-bag-lunch historic lectures are given at the Welcome Center the first and third Wednesdays in May, June, September, and October. Concerts on the square can be heard at noon on Thursdays in May and September and at 8 P.M. the last Friday evening of every month, April through August.

Parking is free in the paved lot adjacent to the Welcome Center. All-day parking passes are available at the Marietta Welcome Center. There is one rest room for both men and women in the Welcome Center. Rest rooms are also available in the Cobb County Courthouse across the square, open Monday through Friday, 8 A.M.–5 P.M. The Welcome Center is disabled accessible.

OTHER THINGS TO DO NEARBY   Kennesaw Mountain National Battlefield Park and Big Shanty Museum.

Sights: Zone 3 — Buckhead/Sandy Springs

Atlanta History Center

Type of Attraction: Museum and two styles of houses depict life in Atlanta between the 1840s and the modern era. Thirty-two acres of gardens.

Location: 130 West Paces Ferry Road. From the center of Buckhead, take West Paces Ferry Road west for about two blocks and turn left on Slaton.

Best MARTA Route: Bus #23 (West Paces Ferry) from Lenox Station.

Admission: $7 adults, $5 students and seniors, $4 children ages 5 and over, free under age 5. $1 additional to tour each of the two houses.

Hours: Monday–Saturday, 10 A.M.–5:30 P.M.; Sunday, noon–5:30 P.M. Closed Thanksgiving, Christmas Eve, Christmas Day, and New Year's Day; open noon–5:30 P.M. all other holidays.

Phone: (404) 814-4000

When To Go: Any time.

Special Comments: The History Center has a full schedule of annual events ranging from Civil War encampments to house tours to storytelling festivals. Call to learn what's scheduled during your visit.

Overall Appeal by Age Group:

Pre-school	Grade School	Teens	Young Adults	Over 30	Senior Citizens
★	★★	★★½	★★½	★★★	★★★½

Authors' Rating: An essential stop for the visitor interested in anything more than a once-over-lightly view of Atlanta history.
★★★★

How Much Time to Allow: One-half day.

DESCRIPTION AND COMMENTS   The Atlanta History Center with its museum, Tullie Smith House, and Swan House is a distillation of the cultural record of Atlanta from the 1840s to the present. For the visitor with limited time who wants a good overview of Atlanta history, this is the best place to find it.

The museum houses the region's most extensive collection of Civil War cannons, rifles, uniforms, projectiles, swords, maps, plates, and utensils. Twenty-five hundred individual items are rotated in and out of public view. For the visitor who wants to learn about the history of the Civil War in Atlanta, this is the second most important stop in the city, the Cyclorama being the first.

Also on the grounds of the 32-acre History Center is the Tullie Smith House, an 1840s farmhouse more characteristic of the "plantations" in the immediate vicinity of Atlanta in the years before the Civil War than the popular image of Tara conveyed in *Gone with the Wind*. The outbuildings include a kitchen, barn, well house, storage house, smokehouse, corn crib, log cabin, and blacksmith shop. Tours are given on the quarter-hour and sometimes include demonstrations of basketmaking, open-hearth cooking, and blacksmithing.

Also on the grounds is the neoclassical-style Swan House, a mansion designed by Phillip Trammel Shutz for Mr. and Mrs. Edward Inman in 1929. Grand landscaping, large-scale architecture, and elaborate furnishings illustrate the elegant lifestyle enjoyed by a handful of affluent Atlantans in the early years of this century and provide a thoughtful contrast to the humble, wooden Tullie Smith farmhouse nearby.

TOURING TIPS   The guided tours of each house take about a half hour, and the self-guided tour of the museum takes at least an hour. Disabled access is available to both houses and the museum. The Coca-Cola Cafe is located in the museum and offers counter service Monday–Saturday, 10 A.M.–5 P.M., and Sunday, noon–5 P.M.

OTHER THINGS TO DO NEARBY   Shop the fine boutiques and galleries of Buckhead. See "Part Nine: Shopping in Atlanta."

Big Shanty Museum

Type of Attraction: An exhibit featuring "The General," one of the two steam locomotives that participated in the Great Locomotive Chase during the Civil War.

Location: 2829 Cherokee Street, Exit #17 off I-75 North.

Best MARTA Route: Public transportation not available.

Admission: $3 adults, $1.50 children ages 7–15, free under age 6.

Hours: Monday–Saturday, 9:30 A.M.–5:30 P.M.; Sunday, noon–5:30 P.M. Closed Easter, Thanksgiving, Christmas, and New Year's.

Phone: (404) 427-2117, (800) 742-6897

When to Go: Any time.

Special Comments: The other locomotive that was part of the Great Locomotive Chase, the "Texas," is on display at the Cyclorama in Grant Park.

Overall Appeal by Age Group:

Pre-school	Grade School	Teens	Young Adults	Over 30	Senior Citizens
★★	★★★	★★	★★½	★★★	★★★

Authors' Rating: There's nothing like seeing the genuine article. ★★

How Much Time to Allow: 45 minutes to one hour.

DESCRIPTION AND COMMENTS   "The General," a steam locomotive stolen from this location by northern troops on April 12, 1862, is displayed. Disney Studios turned the incident, known to historians as Andrew's Raid, into a movie called *The Great Locomotive Chase.*

TOURING TIPS   For a sample of local dining, eat at the Burrell House, a 95-year-old building at 2689 Summers Street. Museum personnel will give you directions. The restaurant is open for dinner Tuesday through Sunday; for Saturday tea, noon–3 P.M.; and for Sunday brunch, 11 A.M.–2 P.M. Otherwise there are many fast-food franchises along busy Cobb Parkway nearby. Parking is free in the small lot adjacent to the museum. The site is disabled accessible.

OTHER THINGS TO DO NEARBY   For a real Civil War experience, combine a visit to Big Shanty Museum with a driving tour of the antebellum houses in Marietta. Also nearby, the Kennesaw Mountain National Battlefield is a must for Civil War buffs.

Roswell Walking and Driving Tour

Type of Attraction: Self-guided walking and driving tour of the Atlanta metro community that conveys a sense of the region's antebellum history.

Location: Roswell Visitors Center, 617 Atlanta Street, Roswell, Georgia.

Admission: Free self-guided tour; walking tour $3 per person.

Hours: Roswell Visitors Center open Monday–Friday, 9 A.M.–5 P.M.; Saturday, 10 A.M.–4 P.M.; and Sunday, noon–3 P.M. Walking tour 1 P.M. Saturdays and 10 A.M. Wednesdays, weather permitting.

Phone: (770) 640-3253 or (800) 776-7953

When To Go: Any time during daylight hours.

Special Comments: Compare Roswell, a pre–Civil War manufacturing village, to Marietta, a town of similar size to the west, which, like Atlanta, flourished before 1860 because of the railroads.

Overall Appeal by Age Group:

Pre-school	Grade School	Teens	Young Adults	Over 30	Senior Citizens
—	—	★	★★	★★★	★★★

Authors' Rating: ★★★

How Much Time to Allow: Schedule a half day.

DESCRIPTION AND COMMENTS In 1839, Roswell King, a successful plantation manager and businessman from the Georgia coast, founded the town of Roswell. He and several other families, the Dunwoodys, the Bullochs, and the Smiths, calling themselves "The Colony," moved from the coast to this section of the state. Their purpose: to build a cotton and woolen manufacturing industry on the banks of Vickery Creek, which flows into the Chattahoochee River.

During the 1840s and 50s, the mills prospered, the town grew, and the founders built a number of fine houses. During the Civil War, Roswell was the manufacturing center for Confederate Gray, the woolen material used in the manufacture of Confederate uniforms. As a result, it also became an important target for General Sherman's Union troops as they marched from Chattanooga to Atlanta. The woolen mill along Vickery Creek went up in flames. Four hundred women and children who worked in the mill were rounded up, shipped north, and charged with treason. Their fate was never fully learned. Union troops commandeered an apartment building for mill workers, called The Bricks, as well as the Presbyterian church, turning them both into Union hospitals.

Be sure to see Bulloch Hall, the antebellum home of Mittie Bulloch, Theodore Roosevelt's mother and Eleanor Roosevelt's grandmother.

TOURING TIPS Be sure you stop at the Visitors Center on the square at the corner of Atlanta Street and Sloan Street before beginning your tour of Roswell. The staff has done a good job of creating different mini-tours so you can choose to see different parts of the historic town without visiting everything. Rest rooms are in the Visitors Center and in many of the historic sites around town. The center is disabled accessible as are many, but not all, of the sites. Parking is plentiful and free in the paved lot directly behind the Visitors Center.

You can eat next door in the Public House, a building that at one time was the Roswell general store; lunch and dinner are served daily (lunch begins at 11:30 A.M. and dinner begins at 5:30 P.M. There are plenty of good restaurants in and around Roswell.

OTHER THINGS TO DO NEARBY   One of the ways to enjoy this area is to hike along Vickery Creek, which furnished the power for the Roswell Mills. The trails are part of the Chattahoochee National Park system, and maps are available at the park headquarters. Explore the natural history of the area at the Chattahoochee Nature Center. See the section "Outdoor Recreation" in Part Eight.

Sights: Zone 4— Lenox/Chamblee

Southeastern Railway Museum

Type of Attraction: Old railroad cars, in various states of restoration, scattered over 12 acres.

Location: 3966 Buford Highway, Duluth. Take I-85 north to Pleasant Hill Road; turn left and go to Buford Highway; turn left and go one-fourth mile.

Admission: $5 adults, $3 for senior citizens and children ages 2–12.

Hours: April–November, Saturday, 9 A.M.–5 P.M., plus third Sunday of each month, noon–5 P.M. Train rides included in admission price. December–March, Saturday, 10 A.M.–5 P.M., free, museum grounds only (no train rides).

Phone: (770) 476-2013

When to Go: Any time the museum is open.

Special Comments: Since railroad people founded Atlanta as the terminus of the Western and Atlantic Railroad, it seems appropriate to have a 12-acre outdoor museum of retired train cars here.

Overall Appeal by Age Group:

Pre-school	Grade School	Teens	Young Adults	Over 30	Senior Citizens
★½	★★★★	★★½	★★★	★★★	★★★

Authors' Rating: Unusual and fun. ★★

How Much Time to Allow: Two hours.

DESCRIPTION AND COMMENTS   Seventy pieces of rolling stock including passenger cars, dining cars, kitchens, cabooses, steam and diesel engines—some in dilapidated condition, some restored by the Atlanta Chapter of the National Railroad Historical Society. Visitors can take a free caboose ride around a three-quarter-mile track the third weekend of each month, March through November.

TOURING TIPS   Children can climb on many of the railroad cars, but be careful. Some of the cars are in such dilapidated condition that scrambling over them could be dangerous. There is a small snack bar in one of the train cars with coffee, soft drinks, candy and chips, and a few post-cards and souvenirs. Portable toilets are located around the 12-acre site. Free parking is available but not plentiful around the perimeter. The site is not readily accessible to the disabled.

OTHER THINGS TO DO NEARBY   Drive back to Atlanta along the ethnically diverse Buford Highway.

Sights: Zone 5—
Northeast Atlanta

Carter Presidential Center
The Museum of the Jimmy Carter Library

Type of Attraction: Presidential Museum.

Location: 411 Freedom Parkway.

Best MARTA Route: Bus #16 (Noble) to Freedom Parkway from Five Points Station.

Admission: $4 adults; $3 senior citizens; children under age 16 free.

Hours: Monday–Saturday, 9 A.M.–4:45 P.M.; Sunday, noon–4:45 P.M. Closed major holidays.

Phone: (404) 331-0296

When to Go: Any time, but spring is the best time to see the gardens.

Special Comments: Since the end of his presidency, Jimmy Carter has continued to garner respect as a man of strong principles and broad humanitarian concerns. This museum helps the visitor see how those attributes stem from his Georgia childhood and early political career.

Overall Appeal by Age Group:

Pre-school	Grade School	Teens	Young Adults	Over 30	Senior Citizens
★	★★½	★★½	★★★	★★★½	★★★½

Authors' Rating: Insightful look into the difficult problems and complex issues faced by American presidents. ★★★

How Much Time to Allow: One to two hours.

DESCRIPTION AND COMMENTS   Visitors see memorabilia from the life and presidency of Jimmy Carter, the 39th President of the United States, Georgia governor, state senator, and peanut farmer born in Plains, Georgia. There is a re-creation of the White House Oval Office and a half-hour film about the presidency and U.S. presidents. An interactive video allows visitors to pose questions to President Carter.

TOURING TIPS   The Copenhill Cafe in the museum sells soup, sandwiches, salads, and desserts at reasonable prices. Hours are Monday–Saturday, 11 A.M.–3 P.M., and Sunday, noon–2 P.M.

Parking is plentiful and free. Rest rooms are inside the museum. Disabled access is good, and wheelchairs are provided on request.

OTHER THINGS TO DO NEARBY   Before or after a visit to the Carter Library, shop Little Five Points or Virginia-Highland. Manuel's on Highland is a neighborhood tavern popular with politicians and journalists. Jimmy Carter and Bill Clinton met here when Clinton was campaigning in Atlanta.

Fernbank

Type of Attraction: Museum, science center, forest, and planetarium illustrating natural history, science, astronomy.

Location: The Science Center and the Planetarium are at 156 Heaton Park Drive; Fernbank Museum of Natural History is at 767 Clifton Road, NE.

Best MARTA Route: For the Science Center, Bus #2 (Ponce de Leon) to Artwood Road from North Avenue or Avondale stations. Walk one and one-half blocks.

Admission: Free for the Science Center; $2 adults, $1 students for the Planetarium; $9.50 adults, $8 students and seniors, $7 children ages 3–12 for the Museum of Natural History; $7 adults, $6 students and seniors, $5 children ages 3–12 for IMAX Theater; $14.50 adults, $12 students and seniors, $10 children ages 3–12 for Combination Museum/IMAX tickets.

Hours: The Fernbank Museum of Natural History is open Monday–Saturday, 10 A.M.–5 P.M.; Friday until 10 P.M. for IMAX Theater only; and Sunday, noon–5 P.M. The hours at the Science Center are Monday, 8:30 A.M.–5 P.M.; Tuesday–Friday, 8:30 A.M.–10 P.M.; Saturday, 10 A.M.–5 P.M.; Sunday, 1–5 P.M. For hours of the Planetarium and forest, call Fernbank. The Science Center, Planetarium, and forest are part of the DeKalb County school system and are closed for extended periods during holidays.

Phone: For the Science Center, Planetarium, and forest call (404) 378-4311; for the Fernbank Museum of Natural History call (404) 370-0960.

When to Go: Any time. (To avoid school groups on weekdays, arrive after 2:30 P.M.)

Special Comments: The 23,000-volume science reference library is an outstanding regional resource and is open to the public. For library hours call (404) 378-4311.

Overall Appeal by Age Group:

Pre-school	Grade School	Teens	Young Adults	Over 30	Senior Citizens
★★	★★★½	★★★	★★★½	★★★★	★★★★

Authors' Rating: ★★★★ for the Science Center; ★★★ for the Museum.

How Much Time to Allow: Two hours for the Science Center and one hour for the Museum of Natural History.

DESCRIPTION AND COMMENTS   This combination of public and private institutions provides the visitor with an unusual insight into the natural history of Atlanta and Georgia.

Fernbank Science Center.   The Center showcases taxidermy exhibits featuring wildlife in its natural environment (with particular emphasis on Georgia), dinosaur exhibits, and Apollo spacecraft. There are also 1.5 miles of paved trails with lookout points and instructional shelters in a 65-acre forest. The observatory's 36-inch reflecting telescope is available to the public on Thursday and Friday evenings, when the weather is clear, from 8 P.M. in winter and about 9:15 P.M. in summer. The Fernbank Greenhouse, which is part of the Science Center, is open 1–5 P.M. on Sunday afternoons. Each visitor receives a free plant; it could be a tomato, it could be a dogwood tree, whatever is in season.

Planetarium.   Fernbank Planetarium, with its 70-foot diameter projector dome, a Zeiss Mark V projector, and a 500-seat auditorium, is the largest in the Southeast.

Fernbank Museum of Natural History.   Visitors take a walk through time from the Georgia seacoast to the mountains in this 150,000-square-foot museum, opened in 1992. The museum features a popular large-screen IMAX Theater that rotates films during the year.

TOURING TIPS   If time allows, combine the Fernbank Science Center and the Fernbank Museum into one natural history day. They are not adjacent, but it is only a short drive between the two locations.

Parking at both locations is free. Restrooms are located in the buildings. Disabled access to the Science Center is poor. It is necessary to ride lifts to three levels. Disabled access to the Museum is good. There is a restaurant in the Museum of Natural History.

MARTA access for the Science Center and the Museum is not particularly good, and the visitor will enjoy both of these areas more if a car is available. On weekends, however, the bus stops right at the Clifton Road entry to the Museum.

OTHER THINGS TO DO NEARBY   Close by is the intown neighborhood of Virginia-Highland, fun for shopping, dining, and hanging out.

Martin Luther King, Jr. Historic District and Center for Nonviolent Social Change

Type of Attraction: Memorial to slain civil rights leader Martin Luther King, Jr.

Location: On Auburn Avenue between Jackson Street and Howell Street.

Best MARTA Route: Bus #3 (Auburn Avenue/MLK) from Five Points or Edgewood/Candler Park stations.

Admission: Free.

Hours: Daily, 9 A.M.–5:30 P.M. Open until 8 P.M. during daylight savings time.

Phone: (404) 524-1956

When to Go: Any time.

Special Comments: If you remember the turbulent days of the Civil Rights movement during the 1960s, and particularly if you were among those who supported or participated in it, you'll find it most interesting to visit this part of the city, where the movement's spiritual leader is enshrined.

Overall Appeal by Age Group:

Pre-school	Grade School	Teens	Young Adults	Over 30	Senior Citizens
★	★★	★★	★★★	★★★★	★★★★

Authors' Rating: King's simple humanity and awesome physical courage come through in this place. ★★★

How Much Time to Allow: Two hours to see The King Center, his birthplace, and walk along Auburn Avenue.

DESCRIPTION AND COMMENTS   In 1968, America's principal spokesman for racial equality, nonviolent activism, and radical social change completed the full circle of his life when his body was buried only a block from the house where he had been born 39 years earlier. The house, built in 1895, is now restored in its original Queen Anne style.

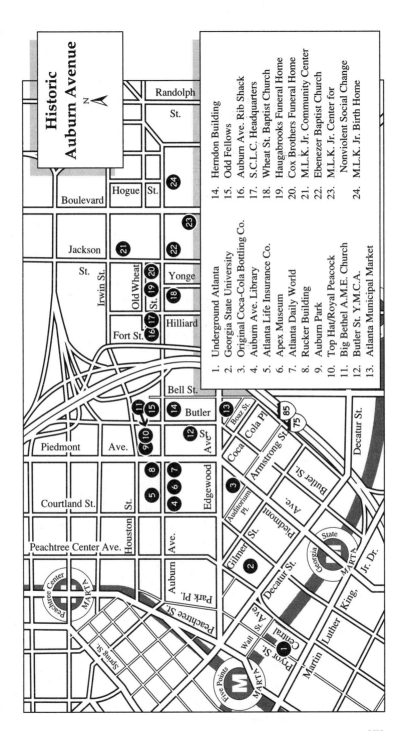

Historic Auburn Avenue

N

1. Underground Atlanta
2. Georgia State University
3. Original Coca-Cola Bottling Co.
4. Auburn Ave. Library
5. Atlanta Life Insurance Co.
6. Apex Museum
7. Atlanta Daily World
8. Rucker Building
9. Auburn Park
10. Top Hat/Royal Peacock
11. Big Bethel A.M.E. Church
12. Butler St. Y.M.C.A.
13. Atlanta Municipal Market
14. Herndon Building
15. Odd Fellows
16. Auburn Ave. Rib Shack
17. S.C.L.C. Headquarters
18. Wheat St. Baptist Church
19. Haugabrooks Funeral Home
20. Cox Brothers Funeral Home
21. M.L.K. Jr. Community Center
22. Ebenezer Baptist Church
23. M.L.K. Jr. Center for
    Nonviolent Social Change
24. M.L.K. Jr. Birth Home

Nearby sits Ebenezer Baptist Church, where Dr. King shared the pulpit with his father. Between the house and the church lies a memorial park, in the center of which is King's tomb, inscribed with his prophetic words: "Free at last." All of this, along with The King Center for Non-violent Social Change, lies within the five-block Martin Luther King Historic District (which overlaps Zone 8). It has proven to be one of Atlanta's major tourist attractions in recent years.

A 15-minute slide show about Auburn Avenue, a profoundly important part of Atlanta's history, is shown on request in the National Park Service Headquarters at 522 Auburn Avenue.

TOURING TIPS   In the summertime, plan your visit before noon to avoid crowds, which fill up the 15-person limit tours of King's birth home. Street parking is available on Auburn Avenue, and normally spaces are available. If the street is full, go to the National Park Service lot on Edgewood between Jackson Street and Boulevard, and you will find a space there. Parking is free.

There are no restaurants in the immediate area, but a small cafeteria, South Fork, in Freedom Hall, serves from 7:30 A.M.–7 P.M. weekdays and from 8 A.M.–7 P.M. on weekends.

Disabled access to the Visitor Center is circuitous but adequate. Rest rooms are available at the National Park Service Headquarters at 522 Auburn Avenue, and in The King Center.

OTHER THINGS TO DO NEARBY   Visit the Apex Museum at 135 Auburn Avenue, NE.

Michael C. Carlos Museum

Type of Attraction: Museum of archeology and antiquities.

Location: On the quadrangle of Emory University campus near the intersection of North Decatur and Oxford roads.

Best MARTA Route: Bus #36 (North Decatur) from Arts Center Station or Bus #6 (Emory) from Edgewood/Candler Park Station to Emory's Oxford Road gate.

Admission: Free, although a donation of $3 is appreciated.

Hours: Monday–Saturday, 10 A.M.–5 P.M.; Sunday, noon–5 P.M. Closed New Year's Day, Thanksgiving, and Christmas.

Phone: (404) 727-4282

When to Go: Any time.

Special Comments: You may be surprised at how school-age children enjoy this museum experience.

Overall Appeal by Age Group:

Pre-school	Grade School	Teens	Young Adults	Over 30	Senior Citizens
—	★★	★★	★★★	★★★	★★★

Authors' Rating: Well presented. ★★★
How Much Time to Allow: One hour.

DESCRIPTION AND COMMENTS Mummies, sculpture, pottery, coins, bronzes, glass vessels, cuneiform tablets, and everyday objects from the ancient civilizations of the Near East and Mediterranean can be found here.

TOURING TIPS Unless you are a student of ancient art you really need a guided tour to appreciate this place. For children, tours take place on weekdays at 10 A.M., 11 A.M., noon, and 1 P.M. by advanced reservation. Tours for the general public are available at 2:30 P.M. on the weekends. The children's tours must be booked in advance and are popular. The small cafe on the third floor serves breakfast and lunch.

Parking at the Emory University campus is and always has been a nightmare. The best bet is the commercial pay lot behind the Boisfeuillet Jones Center just off North Decatur Road at the main entrance to the campus. The rates are reasonable: $1 up to two hours and $2 for two or more hours. Reserved disabled access parking spaces are on the plaza level on South Kilgo Street. Rest rooms are available in the museum. Disabled access is good throughout the building.

OTHER THINGS TO DO NEARBY With its bike shops, pizza parlors, and book stores, Emory Village at the intersection of North Decatur Road and Clifton is a hangout of Emory University students. Druid Hills is one of the nicest Atlanta neighborhoods. Drive along Oakdale, Springdale, and Lullwater. *Driving Miss Daisy* was filmed in this neighborhood at a house on Lullwater.

Stone Mountain Park

Type of Attraction: Amusements, golf, historic attractions, and recreation centered around the world's largest mass of exposed granite.

Location: 16 miles east of Atlanta. From I-285 take Stone Mountain Freeway, US 78. From intown, take Ponce de Leon Avenue east and follow signs to US 78.

Best MARTA Route: Board bus #120 at the Avondale Station and ride to the Stone Mountain Village Park and Ride lot. From there, board the #119 bus into Stone Mountain Park. Buses run every hour on the hour weekdays from 6:15 A.M. to 7:40 P.M. and on weekends and holidays from 8:55 A.M. to 7:20 P.M. Buses enter the park through the west gate and stop at the following locations: Wildlife Trails, Antique Auto and Music Museum, Railroad Depot, Antebellum Plantation, Stone Mountain Park Inn, Memorial Hall, Skylift, Riverboat Marina, Grist Mill, Fishing Hut, Evergreen, Campground, The Commons and Golf Course, and the Training Center.

Admission: $6 per car, $25 annual pass. Individual attractions priced separately.

Hours: Daily, 6 A.M.–midnight. Attractions open June–August, 10 A.M.–9 P.M.; and September–May, 10 A.M.–5:30 P.M.

Phone: (770) 498-5690

When to Go: The park and most attractions are open year-round and events peak during the many colorful holiday festivals. Or plan your visit around the laser show, which begins at dark during the summer.

Special Comments: This is the most popular tourist attraction in Georgia. Two of Atlanta's best daily fee golf courses are within the park's borders.

Overall Appeal by Age Group:

Pre-school	Grade School	Teens	Young Adults	Over 30	Senior Citizens
★★★	★★★★	★★★★½	★★★★	★★★★	★★★½

Authors' Rating: There's something here for everybody. ★★★★

How Much Time to Allow: Two hours–all day, depends on your interests.

DESCRIPTION AND COMMENTS   Stone Mountain is the world's largest exposed mass of granite, rising dome-shaped some 825 feet above the central Georgia piedmont. Carved across the mountain's sheer face, Mount Rushmore–style, are monumental sculptures of Confederate President Jefferson Davis, General Stonewall Jackson, and General Robert E. Lee, all on horseback. Larger than a city block, the rock carving is the centerpiece of a 3,200–acre park. Other attractions in the park include a 19-building antebellum plantation, steam locomotive and paddlewheel riverboat rides, a bell tower, an antique auto and music museum, and two golf courses. It's a many-faceted tourist attraction, drawing vacationers and locals alike. So don't let crowds or lines surprise you.

You may want to join the many native Georgians taking advantage of breezy summer recreation on Stone Mountain Lake: seasonal fishing in a stocked lake (March 19–October 31), canoe and pontoon rental, riverboat rides and swimming. A beach is open daily from Memorial Day through Labor Day.

During winter, the riverboat does not run and there are no canoe, paddle boat, or pontoon boat rentals. But if you own a canoe, rowboat, or motorboat of ten horsepower or less, you can launch it at the ramp by the dam. During the week, you can spend the entire day on Stone Mountain Lake, but on weekends you must be off the lake by 11 A.M.

The golf courses open at 8 A.M. weekdays, 7 A.M. weekends and holidays. Call (770) 498-5715 for reservations and tee times. A miniature golf course offers hole-in-one fun for the family ($3.50 adults, $2.50 children). (For more detailed information about the golf courses, see "Part Eight: Exercise and Recreation.")

Leisure athletes will also find tennis courts, batting cages, and bicycle rentals.

A free laser light show is set to recorded pop music and projected on the north face of the mountain. Bring chairs or a blanket. Show times are at 9:30 nightly (May 24–September 8); and Fridays and Saturdays (April 15–May 24), 8:30 P.M.

Overnight accommodations are available at Evergreen, a 250-room conference center and resort, (770) 879-9900 or (800) 722-1000. The Stone Mountain Park Inn, (770) 469-3311 or (800) 277-0007, offers comfortable guest rooms, Southern-style buffets, and warm hospitality. A 400-site family campground provides the scenic alternative for back-to-nature overnighters; reservations accepted, (770) 413-5420.

A stash of picnic tables at every turn offers scenic, lakeside views for open-air and gazebo picnics. Bring your own grill for barbecues. Restaurants are plentiful but heavy on meat selections. Snack bars and concessions are located throughout.

TOURING TIPS   Plan at least a few hours to tour the mountaintop and visit a few of the park's main attractions, a full day or more if you plan to take advantage of Stone Mountain's wealth of recreational activities.

Visitors are given a map and attraction information guide upon entering the park. Making the scenic, five-mile drive around the mountain is helpful for getting your bearings and locating attractions and accommodations. Take some notes, then head to the centrally located Railroad Depot. An excellent place to start, the Depot is where you'll find a ticket and information center, restaurants and concession stands, scenic horse-and-carriage rides, and Stone Mountain Memorial Railroad.

The train makes a complete loop around the mountain and departs every 40 minutes, beginning at 10 A.M. (last ticket sold 5:20 P.M., or 8

P.M. in summer.) The trip lasts 25 minutes and tickets are good for return to Memorial Depot.

The train stops at Walk-Up Trail, Whistle Stop Barbecue, and the Wildlife Trail. Disembark at Walk-Up Trail only if you are wearing comfortable shoes and are prepared to make the 1.3-mile trek to the mountaintop. The walk takes approximately 40 minutes. Stay aboard to grab a sit-down, smoky barbecue meal or move on to the wildlife trails and petting farms where exotic snake shows are staged on some Sundays during the summer at various times. Call for details.

Scenic Railroad tickets are $3.50 adults, $2.50 children. Children under age three are admitted free. If time permits and you plan to visit more than three attractions, consider buying a ticket good for entrance to seven attractions: $15 adults, $10 children.

Back at Railroad Depot, it's a short walk to the skylift. An 825-foot ascent in a fully enclosed cable car provides thrilling aerial views perfect for camera enthusiasts. You can remain on the summit as long as you wish. Many folks ride the Swiss-made cable cars to the top, then walk down. Last tickets are sold at 5 P.M. (8:30 P.M. during summer). A beverage bar and rest rooms are located atop the mountain.

After returning to the base of the mountain, a jaunt to the park's other main attractions is in order. Since some attractions are miles apart, driving is recommended, but paved sidewalks are there for hoofers. Parking is available at all attractions.

Antebellum Plantation, a complex of 19 restored and authentically decorated buildings, offers a glimpse of the pre–Civil War South. Southern belles and Confederate soldiers stroll the grounds in period garb, eager to answer queries. Here you will find three nineteenth-century houses, a cookhouse, coach house, barn, formal gardens, country store, and more.

A half mile from the plantation is the marina, where paddlewheel riverboats take guests for an open-air, 25-minute ride on Stone Mountain Lake.

Antique buffs should be sure to stop at the Antique Auto and Music Museum.

During the Christmas holiday, you can be whisked away in a horse-drawn carriage down magical "Snowflake Lane" that leads into the Antebellum Plantation. The spectacle of 2 million twinkling holiday lights can be toured by carriage, train, or car. The South's largest "Tree of Lights" adorns the top of the mountain. The sing-along caroling train (Scenic Railroad) departs Railroad Depot at 6, 7, and 8 P.M.

Adding color and excitement to the year are the park's many festivals such as the Antebellum Jubilee in April, Springfest in May, Yellow Daisy Festival in September, and the Scottish Festival and Highland Games in October.

Tune to the park's travel information service on AM station 530 for up-to-date information on festivals and special events.

Sights: Zone 6—
Southeast Atlanta

Cyclorama

Type of Attraction: Civil War history.

Location: 800 Cherokee Avenue. Located next to Zoo Atlanta in Grant Park. From I-20 East, take the Boulevard exit, go east and follow the signs.

Best MARTA Route: Bus #97 (Atlanta Avenue/Georgia Avenue) or Bus #32 (Eastland) from Five Points Station.

Admission: $5 adults, $4 seniors and children over 12, $3 children ages 6–12, free for children under 6.

Hours: Daily, 9:30 A.M.– 5:30 P.M. June 1–Labor Day; 9:20 A.M.–4:30 P.M. Tuesday after Labor Day–May 31. Closed New Year's Day, Martin Luther King, Jr. Birthday, Thanksgiving, and Christmas.

Phone: (404) 658-7625

When to Go: Any time.

Special Comments: The video show before the actual viewing of the Cyclorama provides background information about the Civil War Battle of Atlanta.

Overall Appeal by Age Group:

Pre-school	Grade School	Teens	Young Adults	Over 30	Senior Citizens
★★	★★★	★★½	★★★	★★★★	★★★★

Authors' Rating: Among the top five "what to do in Atlanta" choices. ★★★★

How Much Time to Allow: One to two hours.

DESCRIPTION AND COMMENTS The Cyclorama is a huge, circular painting of the Civil War Battle of Atlanta, 42 feet high and 358 feet in circumference. Viewers sit in a steeply banked theater-style auditorium and are rotated in a circle to view the entire canvas while listening to a dramatic, well-written narrative. A diorama-style landscape of red clay, cannons, tree stumps, and battling soldiers connects the foreground to the canvas. There is also a museum, the steam locomotive "Texas," and a good Civil War bookstore.

TOURING TIPS   The only source of food near the Cyclorama is the fast-food Safari Cafe just outside the front entrance. Hours are 9:30 A.M. until 4 or 5 P.M., depending on the crowds at the nearby zoo. So you may want to bring a picnic and eat in Grant Park.

Parking is free and plentiful. Disabled access is good. Six wheelchairs are available for patrons at no charge. Rest rooms are available inside the Cyclorama and at a Grant Park public rest room about 100 yards from the entrance to the building.

OTHER THINGS TO DO NEARBY   Combine your Cyclorama visit with a trip to the zoo, also in Grant Park.

Zoo Atlanta

Type of Attraction: Zoo.

Location: 800 Cherokee Avenue, SE, at Grant Park.

Best MARTA Route: Bus #97 from Five Points Station.

Admission: $7.50 adults, $6.50 senior citizens, $5.50 children ages 3–11, free for children age 2 and under.

Hours: Monday–Friday, 10 A.M.–4:30 P.M.; Saturday and Sunday, 10 A.M.–5:30 P.M. Visitors are allowed to stay in the park one hour after the gate closes.

Phone: (404) 624-5600 or 624-WILD

When to Go: Nice weather is best.

Special Comments: Once a laughing stock, or more accurately a crying stock, the Atlanta zoo hit its low point when the resident veterinarian was accused of butchering and eating the zoo rabbits. Over the last few years this Atlanta institution has rebounded remarkably, thanks to aggressive leadership in the city parks department, a creative zoo director, and some financial assistance from the Ford Motor Company. Now it is regarded as one of the top ten zoos in the country.

Overall Appeal by Age Group:

Pre-school	Grade School	Teens	Young Adults	Over 30	Senior Citizens
★★★★	★★★★	★★★½	★★★★	★★★★	★★★½

Authors' Rating: ★★★

How Much Time to Allow: One-half day.

DESCRIPTION AND COMMENTS   Zoo Atlanta's animal collection represents six continents. Explore the Ford African Rain Forest where four
families of lowland gorillas reside. Visit the Masi Mara, home to
African elephants, black rhinos, lions, zebra, and ostriches. Go on a
safari to Sumatra and see the high-swinging orangutans and Sumatran
tigers. Other highlights include Chilean flamingos, drill baboons, and a
great reptile collection. Don't miss the petting zoo, elephant demonstrations, wildlife show, zoo express train, and animal feedings. Feeding
times vary, so call ahead to be sure you don't miss them. If you are so
inclined, Zoo Atlanta offers an overnight program called "Night
Crawlers," which includes an exclusive night-hike, animal diet kitchen
tour, animal encounters, and more. Call for more information.

TOURING TIPS   Parking is free and plentiful for zoo visitors. Wheelchairs are available at no cost at the security office near the main gate.
Strollers rent for $2 plus a $3 deposit; find these near the entrance ticket
booth.

Food is available in the zoo but is limited to bland fast-food choices.
The Okefenokee Cafe inside the zoo boundary invites visitors to use the
pleasant outside tables and chairs for picnics. Rest rooms are available
around the property.

OTHER THINGS TO DO NEARBY   The Cyclorama is also in Grant Park.

Sights: Zone 7—
Downtown West

The APEX Museum

Type of Attraction: An African-American history museum that contains exhibits on local, national, and international black history.

Location: 135 Auburn Avenue.

Best MARTA Route: Bus #3 from Five Points Station.

Admission: $3 adults, $2 students and senior citizens, free for children under age 4.

Hours: Tuesday–Saturday, 10 A.M.–5 P.M. Open on Sundays from 1–5 P.M. in February, June, July, and August. Closed major holidays.

Phone: (404) 521-APEX

When to Go: Any time.

Special Comments: This museum is an essential stop for anyone wanting to develop a deeper understanding of Atlanta's black history and culture.

Overall Appeal by Age Group:

Pre-school	Grade School	Teens	Young Adults	Over 30	Senior Citizens
★	★★★	★★★	★★★½	★★★½	★★★½

Authors' Rating: Insightful journey into the history of black Atlanta.
★★★

How Much Time to Allow: 45 minutes to one hour.

DESCRIPTION AND COMMENTS   Visitors see a recreation of Yates and Milton Drug Store, which was a center of community life on Auburn Avenue beginning in 1922. Cicely Tyson narrates a 15-minute video, *Sweet Auburn, Street of Pride.* Photographs and displays illustrate other aspects of black history in Atlanta.

TOURING TIPS   There is parking adjacent to the museum. If this lot is full, as it often is, circle the block bounded by Courtland (one-way southbound), Edgewood, Piedmont (one-way northbound), and Auburn until you find a spot in one of the pay-in-advance lockbox lots. Rates are $2.75 to $3. For the hardy, it is not a bad walk from the Five Points MARTA Station. Getting the feel for Auburn Avenue that only walking can give you is an interesting experience in itself. Rest rooms are available in the museum and disabled access is good.

OTHER THINGS TO DO NEARBY   The Martin Luther King, Jr. birthplace and The Martin Luther King, Jr. Center for Nonviolent Social Change are located a few blocks east, within walking distance. Directly across the street, at the Atlanta Life Insurance Company, you can view one of the nation's best African-American art collections. Also, there is a small museum honoring the company's founder, Alonzo Herndon, a key figure in the economic development of black Atlanta. For an extensive walking tour of black Atlanta, ask at the APEX Museum for the Freedom Walk brochure.

Atlanta Heritage Row: The Museum at Underground

Type of Attraction: Photographs, large dioramas, and recordings illustrate Atlanta history.

Location: Underground Atlanta on Upper Alabama Street between Central and Pryor streets.

Best MARTA Route: Two blocks east of the Five Points Station.

Admission: $3 adults; $2 seniors, students, and youth ages 6–17; children under age 6 free.

Hours: Tuesday–Saturday, 10 A.M.–5 P.M.; Sunday, 1–5 P.M. Closed Monday.

Phone: (404) 584-7879

When to Go: Any time.

Special Comments: Five exhibition areas illustrate six periods in Atlanta history, from the earliest days up to the present.

Overall Appeal by Age Group:

Pre-school	Grade School	Teens	Young Adults	Over 30	Senior Citizens
★	★★	★★	★★★	★★★	★★★

Authors' Rating: The exhibits depend on photographs and recordings of voices from the past. ★★

How Much Time to Allow: 45 minutes

DESCRIPTION AND COMMENTS   The museum includes exhibits, sound effects, and videos about Atlanta's past, including the Civil War, Hartsfield Atlanta International Airport, and Martin Luther King, Jr. Spend enough time with the excellent historical photographs in this linear museum to get an idea of the locations of some of the old Atlanta landmarks, particularly the route of the original railroad tracks, the site of the original passenger depot, and the spot where the old freight depot still stands. If you can get oriented here, your entire visit to Atlanta will be more enjoyable and meaningful.

TOURING TIPS   Visit the nearby World of Coca-Cola Museum first and your ticket stub is worth $1 off admission to Heritage Row. Rest rooms are next door at the Atlanta Convention and Visitors Bureau Visitor Center. All of Heritage Row is disabled accessible. The most convenient parking is on Central Avenue in the covered, decked garage; costs about $3.

OTHER THINGS TO DO NEARBY   Complement your visit to Heritage Row by taking the self-guided tour of Underground Atlanta. Inquire at the Underground information booth.

Atlanta Preservation Center

Type of Attraction: Guided walking tours of some of Atlanta's most interesting architecture and neighborhoods.

Location: Tours leave from a variety of locations. Call the Preservation Center at the number listed below for specific departure points. The local address of the Preservation Center is The Desoto, Suite 3, 156 Seventh Street, NW, Atlanta, GA 30308.

Best MARTA Route: Varies depending on the tour.

Admission: $5 adults, $4 senior citizens, $3 students, $4.50 for adult groups of 20 or more; $6 per person with a minimum of $60 for custom tour groups.

Hours: Days and hours vary by tour and sometimes by season. Call for specific information.

Phone: (404) 876-2041; tour hotline (404) 876-2040

When to Go: Tours sometimes vary by season. Check with the Preservation Center for an exact schedule.

Special Comments: The Atlanta Preservation Center is the authority on this kind of intown tour. Volunteers have been satisfying visitors' and residents' curiosity about the city for years.

Overall Appeal by Age Group:

Pre-school	Grade School	Teens	Young Adults	Over 30	Senior Citizens
★	★	★	★	★★★	★★★

Authors' Rating: New insights into the architectural diversity of the city and its neighborhoods. ★★★

How Much Time to Allow: Depends on the particular tour.

DESCRIPTION AND COMMENTS   The Atlanta Preservation Center is a nonprofit, membership organization dedicated to promoting historic preservation in Atlanta through education and advocacy. The center offers walking tours of Atlanta's historic districts as a means of generating public awareness of preservation and appreciation for the city's architectural heritage. There are ten regularly scheduled tours.

1. Downtown Atlanta.   Visit Atlanta's earliest high-rise district with historic commercial buildings representing architectural styles from Victorian to Art Deco to modern.

2. West End and the Wren's Nest.   See the various styles of Victorian architecture, recent renovation efforts, and neighborhood churches of Atlanta's oldest neighborhood, which dates back to 1835. The focal point of the tour is the Wren's Nest, former home of Joel Chandler Harris, author of the Uncle Remus tales.

3. Fox Theater District.   Tour the Fox Theater inside and out, and learn how Atlantans refused to lose this exotic Moorish and Egyptian revival movie palace.

4. Historic Underground/Birth of Atlanta.   This tour features Atlanta's most significant older buildings and three of its oldest churches. It describes the city's growth from a 19th-century railroad town to a 20th-century metropolis.

5. Walking Miss Daisy's Druid Hills.   Experience the gracious ambience of Druid Hills, laid out in 1893 by Frederick Law Olmsted, one of America's preeminent landscape designers. Fine homes of diverse architectural styles, created by notable architects such as Neel Reid, W. T. Downing, and Philip Shutze, sit in a lush parklike setting of curving streets and mature plantings. This was the setting for Alfred Uhry's play and Academy Award–winning film, *Driving Miss Daisy.*

6. Inman Park.   Tour Atlanta's first garden suburb, today a nationally recognized example of neighborhood preservation. This sidewalk tour of Atlanta's most celebrated Victorian district features elegant homes such as those built by Coca-Cola magnates Asa Candler and Ernest Woodruff.

7. Sweet Auburn. Visitors learn how Atlanta's black entrepreneurs developed "Sweet Auburn" Avenue into a prosperous hub of commercial activity and entertainment. Tour includes the avenue's historic African-American churches where Martin Luther King, Jr. and other prominent ministers gave birth to the Civil Rights movement.

8. Ansley Park Neighborhood. With its diverse styles of houses, many priced at well over a million dollars, and its wide curving streets, its parks and mature trees, Ansley is the epitome of Atlanta's intown neighborhoods.

9. Piedmont Park. This city park in the heart of Atlanta was a farm, Civil War encampment, and the grounds for expositions and international fairs important in the development of Atlanta.

10. Atlanta University Center. Tour historic Atlanta University Center, the largest concentration of African-American colleges in the United States, including Morris Brown College, Atlanta University, Clark Altanta, Spelman, and Morehouse. Vine City is where many civil rights strategies and political leaders were born. The classically styled Herndon Home was constructed by Alonzo Herndon, a former slave and founder of the Atlanta Life Insurance Company.

TOURING TIPS If you have to choose just one of these tours, pick Inman Park. Its restored Victorian houses help visitors conjure up a sense of Atlanta at the turn of the century.

OTHER THINGS TO DO NEARBY The guides on these tours are experts on Atlanta. They will be able to give you tips on nearby sights, restaurants, and watering holes.

CNN Studio Tours

Type of Attraction: Guided tour of television production and technology studios.

Location: One CNN Center at the corner of Marietta Street and Techwood Avenue.

Best MARTA Route: Near the Georgia World Congress Center and the Omni Station.

Admission: $7 adults, $5 seniors, $4.50 children age 12 and under. Not recommended for children under age 6.

Hours: Guided tours daily every half hour, 9 A.M.–6 P.M. Ticket office opens at 8:30 A.M. Closed Thanksgiving, December 24 and 25, New Year's Day, Easter, Memorial Day, July 4, and Labor Day.

Phone: (404) 827-2300

When to Go: Any time, but it is wise to purchase tickets early in the day.

Special Comments: Ted Turner's CNN has become one of the most important news-gathering and dissemination organizations in the world.

Overall Appeal by Age Group:

Pre-school	Grade School	Teens	Young Adults	Over 30	Senior Citizens
—	★★★	★★★★	★★★★	★★★★	★★★★

Authors' Rating: One of Atlanta's top tours. ★★★★

How Much Time to Allow: 45 minutes to one hour for tour.

DESCRIPTION AND COMMENTS   You will tour the 24-hour network's studios and witness the production of a live newscast from news gathering to on-air presentation. TBS Collection features memorabilia from the superstation, the Atlanta Braves, and the Atlanta Hawks—all part of Ted Turner's empire. The tour lasts approximately 45 minutes. Tickets are available on a first-come, first-served basis on the day of the tour. Reservations are accepted for groups of 30 or more.

TOURING TIPS   This has become one of the most popular tours in Atlanta. Purchase your tickets early in the day even if you plan to take the tour later. The tour is not readily disabled accessible. Disabled individuals must notify CNN 24 hours in advance of a tour.

CNN Center is an easy walk from the downtown hotels or from Underground Atlanta. If you are parking a car, use the Decks lot with entrances on Techwood and Spring streets. Rates are $3 to $4. Rest rooms are located near the beginning of the tour.

OTHER THINGS TO DO NEARBY   Walk down Marietta Street to International Boulevard to see the Celebrity Walk in front of the Atlanta Chamber of Commerce Building. Plaques set in the sidewalk honor famous Georgians. Tour Centennial Olympic Park. Walk east on Marietta Street to Underground Atlanta.

Georgia State Capitol Building

Type of Attraction: Guided and self-guided tour of displays highlighting the state's history.

Location: At the intersection of Washington Street and Martin Luther King, Jr. Boulevard.

Best MARTA Route: One block south from the Georgia State Station.

Admission: Free.

Hours: The Capitol is open and the museum available for self-guided tours Monday–Friday, 8 A.M.–5 P.M.; Saturday, 10 A.M.–4 P.M.; and Sunday, noon–4 P.M.

Phone: (404) 656-2844

When To Go: Any time.

Special Comments: Sherman's troops camped on the land where the Capitol sits as they prepared for the famous "March to the Sea."

Overall Appeal by Age Group:

Pre-school	Grade School	Teens	Young Adults	Over 30	Senior Citizens
★	★★½	★★½	★★★	★★★	★★★

Authors' Rating: The building itself is inspiring. Museum includes an important wildlife exhibit. ★★★½

How Much Time to Allow: Guided tours last 30 minutes, but give yourself an hour to an hour and a half to see the museum on your own.

DESCRIPTION AND COMMENTS   Not as widely recognized as it should be for its extensive collection of Georgia wildlife, this is the second best natural history museum in Atlanta and all of Georgia—the powerful one-two punch of Fernbank Science Center and the Fernbank Museum being first . . . but not by much. Excellent taxidermy exhibits allow visitors to view Georgia's mammals, birds, and fish. Thoughtful displays allow the visitor to see these animals in their natural habitats. This is no small undertaking since Georgia is the largest state east of the Mississippi and contains an extremely wide range of geographical areas, including two different mountain ranges, a rolling piedmont, and an environmentally diverse seacoast. Anyone interested in the wildlife or natural environment of Georgia will want to schedule a visit to this museum.

TOURING TIPS   Don't worry if you cannot plan your visit to coincide with one of the scheduled tours. Self-guided tours are available at the tours/information desk near the west (Washington Street) entrance. In fact, there are definite advantages to being able to move at your own pace. Tours can be crowded with schoolchildren during the school year. The best tour to take is the 2 P.M. one that avoids most of the school kids.

Rest rooms are available on the first and third floors. The best parking is at the covered Underground Atlanta lots with entrances on Courtland, Central, or Martin Luther King, Jr. Boulevard.

OTHER THINGS TO DO NEARBY   You're within easy walking distance of Underground Atlanta and the Coca-Cola museum. To get there, you'll walk by Atlanta's oldest church, Immaculate Conception Catholic Shrine (1869) and the city's oldest commercial building, the Georgia Railroad Freight Depot (1869).

The Margaret Mitchell House

Type of Attraction: Historic house and museum where Margaret Mitchell wrote much of *Gone with the Wind.*

Location: At the corner of Peachtree and 10th streets in Midtown.

Best MARTA Route: The house is next to the Midtown Station.

Admission: Not available at press time

Hours: Not available at press time

Phone: (404) 249-7012

When To Go: Any time

Special Comments: Because of a fire in 1996, the house will not open back up until May 1997. From 1925 to 1932 Margaret Mitchell lived with her husband John Marsh in a small apartment on the first floor of this converted Victorian house. It was here that she wrote most, if not all, of *Gone with the Wind,* the most popular book in the world aside from the Bible. The book continues to sell more than half a million copies worldwide each year.

Overall Appeal by Age Group:

Pre-school	Grade School	Teens	Young Adults	Over 30	Senior Citizens
—	—	★	★★	★★★	★★★

Authors' Rating: For anyone who has read *Gone with the Wind*, this is a must-see Atlanta site. Exhibits provide insight into the writing of the book and Atlanta history. ★★★

How Much Time to Allow: About 45 minutes.

DESCRIPTION AND COMMENTS   For many years this Victorian structure, circa 1899, stood on the corner of Peachtree and 10th streets neglected and slowly deteriorating. The City of Atlanta granted it "landmark" status in 1989. Fires in 1994 and 1996 threatened its existence. Daimler-Benz, the parent company of Mercedes Benz, provided the funds to underwrite the restoration and renovation. Margaret Mitchell's apartment has been restored to its original state. Exhibits highlight the author's life and the writing of the book. The third floor of the building is available for meetings and small-scale special events.

TOURING TIPS   Read (or re-read) *Gone with the Wind.* Then supplement it with *The Road to Tara,* an excellent biography of Margaret Mitchell by Anne Edwards published by Ticknor & Fields. Both of these books are required reading for anyone who really wants to understand what Atlanta is all about.

OTHER THINGS TO DO NEARBY   Walk north on Peachtree Street. This part of Peachtree Street between 10th and 17th streets is one of the most pleasant and interesting sections of the famous thoroughfare. It is also rich in Margaret Mitchell history. On August 11, 1949, she and her husband John Marsh were crossing Peachtree from west to east to enter a movie theater at the corner of Peachtree and 13th streets when she was hit by a taxi. She died from the injuries five days later in Grady Hospital. A little farther on, at 1401 Peachtree, a historic marker designates the site of the Mitchell home where she lived from the age of 11. Return to your starting point by retracing the route or via the Arts Center MARTA Station. Visit the Road to Tara Museum in the Georgian Terrace Hotel at 659 Peachtree Street across from the Fox Theater; phone (404) 897-1939. Hard-core *Gone with the Wind* fans will want to visit the site where Margaret Mitchell was born. See The Jackson Street Bridge in the "Atlanta Skyline" section in Part One.

Monetary Museum at the Federal Reserve Bank of Atlanta

Type of Attraction: Displays illustrating the history of currency.

Location: 104 Marietta Street just west of Five Points.

Best MARTA Route: Roughly halfway between the Five Points and Omni stations.

Admission: Free.

Hours: Monday–Friday, 9 A.M.–4 P.M.

Phone: (404) 521-8764

When to Go: Any time.

Special Comments: See $100,000 bills and a solid gold bar.

Overall Appeal by Age Group:

Pre-school	Grade School	Teens	Young Adults	Over 30	Senior Citizens
★	★★½	★★½	★★½	★★½	★★½

Authors' Rating: Limited appeal. ★★

How Much Time to Allow: Half hour.

DESCRIPTION AND COMMENTS   This museum shows the evolution of currency through history, the development of money in America, and the evolution of the private banking system. Visitors leave with a free souvenir package of shredded money.

TOURING TIPS   Not the place to drop by for a quick peek in the door, even though the tour is free. Unless you intend to spend some time here, it's not worth the trouble going through the strict security system. And this is no place for kids unless they are doing a report. A parking garage is located directly across the street. Rest rooms are located on the same floor as the museum. Disabled access is good. Guided tours for groups must be arranged in advance. Call (404) 521-8784.

OTHER THINGS TO DO NEARBY   This is the heart of old downtown. Walk from here along Marietta Street to Underground Atlanta.

Underground Atlanta

Type of Attraction: Shopping, entertainment, dining in restored downtown area.

Location: Underground Atlanta is at the intersection of Alabama and Peachtree streets in downtown Atlanta across from the Five Points MARTA Station.

Best MARTA Route: The entrance to Underground is directly opposite the Five Points Station. The station has a special access tunnel that leads directly to old Alabama Street.

Admission: Free.

Hours: Restaurants and nightspots keep their own hours. The information booth in Underground at the intersection of Pryor and Alabama is open Monday–Saturday, 10 A.M.–9:30 P.M.; and Sunday, noon–6 P.M.

Phone: (404) 523-2311

When to Go: Any time.

Special Comments: If you are a first-time visitor to Atlanta, you should have Underground Atlanta on your "must see" list.

Overall Appeal by Age Group:

Pre-school	Grade School	Teens	Young Adults	Over 30	Senior Citizens
★	★★★	★★★★	★★★★	★★★★	★★★★

Authors' Rating: Fun for browsing, shopping, people watching. ★★★

How Much Time to Allow: One hour at least—more if you're planning to eat or go to one of the nightspots.

DESCRIPTION AND COMMENTS Underground Atlanta is the name given to the oldest part of Atlanta, an area where, in the early days of the city, a line of buildings along Alabama Street faced the railroad tracks. Other streets—Pryor, Whitehall, and Broad—met the tracks at perpendicular angles, much like streets in a seaport town would come down to the harbor. As the city grew, more and more trains clattered through the middle of town. Buggy traffic and then auto traffic went back and forth across the tracks. The city fathers devised a system of bridges and viaducts that spanned the tracks and streets. As the system of bridges expanded, the first floors of many of the original buildings along this section of town disappeared "underground." This covered-up section of town was rediscovered in the 1960s. It was revitalized and restored by the A.L. Rouse Company in the 1980s to become a popular shopping, dining, and entertainment destination for visitors and local residents.

Brenda McAvoy's excellent book, *The Tracks of Underground*, contains information about Underground and early Atlanta history hard to find any other place. It will increase your enjoyment of this interesting and entertaining Atlanta location. Available for $7.95 at locations in Underground.

TOURING TIPS If you're going to Underground to be entertained, go at night when the magicians, tarot card readers, musicians, and other street entertainers are out and all the shops, restaurants, and clubs are open. If you're a history buff, go during the day, pick up a self-guided tour of Underground from the information booth at the intersection of Old Alabama and Old Pryor streets, and visit the 18 sites it describes. Anyone with a family in tow trying to shop, eat, and learn some history may be trying to take on too much in one visit.

There is plenty of reasonably priced covered parking for Underground. One large garage has entrances on Central Avenue and Courtland, and another has an entrance on Martin Luther King, Jr. Boulevard.

OTHER THINGS TO DO NEARBY   This is the heart of Old Atlanta. Go "above ground" and walk south on Peachtree Street observing the old buildings that date back to the late 1800s and early 1900s. Many tourists tend to shy away from this part of town. It is one of the most interestingly textured parts of the city. During the day it's as safe as any other part of Atlanta. Turn right on Mitchell Street and right again on Broad Street to head back to the Five Points MARTA Station and Underground.

Ride the underground trolley shuttle between Underground and downtown hotels; it's $3 for an all-day pass.

The World of Coca-Cola Pavilion

Type of Attraction: History and lore of the world's most popular soft drink.

Location: 55 Martin Luther King, Jr. Boulevard, at the intersection of Martin Luther King, Jr. Boulevard and Central Avenue near the entrance to Underground Atlanta.

Best MARTA Route: Go to the Five Points Station and walk through Underground to the museum.

Admission: $4.50 adults, $3.50 seniors, $2.75 children ages 6–12, free for children under age 6.

Hours: Monday–Saturday, 10 A.M.–9:30 P.M.; Sunday, noon–6 P.M. Last admission is one hour before closing. Closed Easter, Thanksgiving, Christmas Eve, Christmas Day, and New Year's Day.

Phone: (404) 676-5151

When to Go: Any time.

Special Comments: Coca-Cola got its start in Atlanta in 1886 when pharmacist John S. Pemberton dispensed the first one at Jacob's Pharmacy, at the corner of Peachtree and Marietta streets.

Overall Appeal by Age Group:

Pre-school	Grade School	Teens	Young Adults	Over 30	Senior Citizens
★★	★★★	★★	★★★★	★★★★	★★★★

Authors' Rating: Celebration of an American institution. ★★★

How Much Time to Allow: One to two hours.

DESCRIPTION AND COMMENTS   More than 1,000 items of memorabilia in a 45,000-square-foot pavilion trace the history of Coca-Cola, an American icon that was first marketed in Atlanta. Visitors hear and see old radio and television commercials for the product and a soda fountain of the future. This, along with the guided tour of the CNN Center, is one of the most popular tourist stops in Atlanta.

TOURING TIPS   Every weekend during the school year waiting lines may be from 30 minutes to two hours long. During summer months, the visitor may find long lines every day. A limited number of reservations are taken for groups of 25 or more. Plenty of covered parking is available nearby on Courtland Street and on Martin Luther King, Jr. Boulevard. Parking rates are about $3.

OTHER THINGS TO DO NEARBY   You are right next to Underground Atlanta and within sight of the oldest church in the city, Immaculate Conception Shrine, and the oldest commercial structure, the old Freight Depot. The Georgia State Capitol is one block away.

Sights: Zone 8 —
Downtown East

Atlanta Botanical Garden

Type of Attraction: Botanical garden and conservatory in Piedmont Park.

Location: 1345 Piedmont Avenue, on the north end of Piedmont Park.

Best MARTA Route: Bus #36 from Arts Center Station (Tuesday through Saturday). Bus #31 (Morningside/Lindbergh) from Lindbergh, Five Points, or Peachtree Center stations.

Admission: $6 adults, $5 senior citizens, $3 students and children ages 6–12, free for children under age 6. Free admission on Thursdays after 3 P.M.

Hours: April–October, Tuesday–Sunday, 9 A.M.–7 P.M.; November–March, Tuesday–Sunday, 9 A.M.–6 P.M. Closed Monday and major holidays.

Phone: (404) 876-5859

When to Go: Any time — spring, summer, and fall are best.

Special Comments: The $5.5 million Dorothy Chapman Conservatory adds to the year-round appeal of the gardens.

Overall Appeal by Age Group:

Pre-school	Grade School	Teens	Young Adults	Over 30	Senior Citizens
★★	★★★	★★★	★★★½	★★★★	★★★★

Authors' Rating: ★★★

How Much Time to Allow: One to two hours.

DESCRIPTION AND COMMENTS The 16,000-square-foot Dorothy Chapman Fuqua Conservatory houses tropical and desert plants, as well as free-flying tropical birds, fish, and a terrarium containing poison dart frogs. The 60-acre garden includes a Japanese garden and sections for roses, herbs, vegetables, and fountains. There is also a gift shop with a very good selection of garden and bird books. *Atlanta* magazine once voted the shop "Best Unusual Gift Source."

TOURING TIPS   Wear comfortable shoes and bring sunglasses or a hat. Remember to bring a pad and pen. Visitors invariably see plants and flowers they want to try in their own gardens and need to make notes. Kids love the carnivorous plants like the pitcher plants and Venus fly traps. They will remember the kid-size terrarium labeled, "Please Touch," with the meat eaters inside.

The best time to visit the garden is the first thing in the morning when the weather is coolest and the visitor traffic low. Parking is free. Disabled access is good throughout the garden. Several wheelchairs are available on a first-come, first-served basis. Rest rooms are in the Visitor Center. Guided tours are available for groups of ten or more with advance reservations.

OTHER THINGS TO DO NEARBY   Drive through the winding, tree-shaded avenues of Ansley Park, perhaps the epitome of Atlanta intown neighborhoods. Walk up 14th Street to Peachtree Street and the High Museum between 15th and 16th streets.

Center for Puppetry Arts

Type of Attraction: Large collection of puppets.

Location: 1404 Spring Street, NW.

Best MARTA Route: Go the the Arts Center Station and walk three blocks north on West Peachtree Street to 18th Street.

Admission: Call the ticket office at (404) 873-3391 for current admission prices.

Hours: Museum: Monday–Saturday, 9 A.M.–5 P.M. Puppet shows: Monday–Friday, 10 A.M. and 11:30 A.M. plus a 1 P.M. matinee on Wednesday; Saturday, 10:30 A.M. and 12:30 P.M. Summer hours vary slightly, with shows Monday–Saturday, 11 A.M. and 1 P.M., and the Wednesday matinee at 2:30 P.M.

Phone: (404) 873-3089; box office (404) 873-3391; 24-hour information line (404) 874-0398.

When to Go: Any time.

Special Comments: The puppets here are not just for children.

Overall Appeal by Age Group:

Pre-school	Grade School	Teens	Young Adults	Over 30	Senior Citizens
★★★½	★★★½	★★	★★	★★	★★

Authors' Rating: Demonstrates the imagination and craftsmanship
   that goes into the creation of puppets. ★★★

How Much Time to Allow: 45 minutes (more if you see performance).

DESCRIPTION AND COMMENTS   World's largest private collection of
puppets. Anybody with an ounce of imagination will be entranced by
the pretend world that unfolds on the Puppet Center stage. But the
biggest appeal is for kids from kindergarten age through the third or
fourth grade. To visit with a child in that age range is reward in itself.

TOURING TIPS   Be absolutely sure to schedule your visit here around one
of the performances in the puppet theater. The shows are immensely popular with schoolchildren, and yellow school buses fill the parking lot
almost every day. The best times for individuals or families to visit the
museum and see one of the imaginative shows is the Wednesday matinee
or the Saturday show. Summer is also a good time to avoid the school
crowds. But it is always advisable to call the center in advance to find out
if seats are available in the 350-seat theater. Parking is free and secure in
the lot behind the center. Disabled access is good.

OTHER THINGS TO DO NEARBY   The High Museum of Art is on
Peachtree Street between 15th and 16th streets, an easy walk.

High Museum of Art

Type of Attraction: Atlanta's best collection of fine art in an inspiring
   architectural setting.

Location: 1280 Peachtree Street between 15th and 16th streets.

Best MARTA Route: A covered walk from the Arts Center Station
   leads directly to the museum.

Admission: $6 adults, $4 students and senior citizens, $2 children ages
   6–17, free for children under age 6.

Hours: Tuesday–Saturday, 10 A.M.–5 P.M.; Sunday, noon–5 P.M.
   Closed Mondays and all legal holidays.

Phone: (404) 733-HIGH

When to Go: Any time. Volunteer docents conduct free 45-minute
   guided tours Tuesday–Thursday at 11 A.M. and 1:30 P.M.; and Saturday and Sunday at 1 P.M. and 3 P.M.

Special Comments: An architectural gem, the museum contributes to
   making the two blocks of Peachtree between 14th and 16th one of
   the most aesthetically pleasing walking places in the city. Good gift
   shop.

Overall Appeal by Age Group:

Pre- school	Grade School	Teens	Young Adults	Over 30	Senior Citizens
★★	★★½	★★½	★★★	★★★★	★★★★

Authors' Rating: The striking Richard Meier–designed building and
the huge Alexander Calder sculpture on the front lawn in themselves make a visit to the High worthwhile. ★★★

How Much Time to Allow: Two hours.

DESCRIPTION AND COMMENTS   Isn't it a relief to know the "High" in
"High Museum" refers to the family who gave the original collection of
art, not to the type of art displayed here? This Richard Meier building is
a striking white tile-and-glass structure on Peachtree. A giant black, yellow, and red Calder mobile decorates the front lawn. Major touring
exhibits coming to the city show here. The permanent collection is
strong in nineteenth-century American painting, photography, and decorative arts.

TOURING TIPS   Admission is free Thursday afternoon from 1–5 P.M.
Rest rooms are inside the museum and the entire facility is disabled
accessible. Parking is available at a garage under the High and at several
decked garages and surface lots along Peachtree and West Peachtree
streets.

OTHER THINGS TO DO NEARBY   This is the heart of Atlanta's Midtown.
Stroll through the rich architectural environment on 14th and 15th
streets. This is also the location of three of the most interesting bookstores in the city, including the one in the Museum Shop.

Martin Luther King Historic District and Center for Nonviolent Social Change

This memorial overlaps Zones 5 and 8. For details, see the entry
under Zone 5 attractions.

Oakland Cemetery

Type of Attraction: Guided and self-guided walking tours of Atlanta's
oldest burying ground.

Location: 248 Oakland Avenue.

Best MARTA Route: Two blocks south on Grant Street from the King
Memorial Station.

Admission: Free. Guided tours: $3 adults, $2 senior citizens, $1 children.

Hours: Cemetery: daily until about 6 P.M. or 7 P.M. Visitor Center: Monday–Friday, 9 A.M.–5 P.M.

Phone: (404) 688-2107

When to Go: Any time.

Special Comments: Gone with the Wind author Margaret Mitchell and golfer Bobby Jones are buried here, as are 23 Atlanta mayors including the first one, Moses Formwalt, 6 Georgia governors, and 5 Confederate generals.

Overall Appeal by Age Group:

Pre-school	Grade School	Teens	Young Adults	Over 30	Senior Citizens
—	★★½	★★½	★★★	★★★½	★★★½

Authors' Rating: Even if you're not a big fan of cemetery touring, this museum of Atlanta names is a place that helps the visitor understand the history, geography, and social structure of the city.
★★★★

How Much Time to Allow: Allow an hour or so to wander among the tombstones.

DESCRIPTION AND COMMENTS   Oakland Cemetery now comprises 88 acres and is the final resting place for tens of thousands of Atlantans of all colors, religions, and economic stations. But it began simply as a rural cemetery one mile from the center of town. Remarkably, it retains the flavor of its origins for anyone who chooses to take the one-mile walk from Five Points out Martin Luther King, Jr. Boulevard to the arched red brick and wrought iron entrance. To take the walk from Five Points, go south on Peachtree Street to MLK and turn left (east).

Over the years grieving relatives have erected sometimes grand, sometimes pretentious, sometimes humorous monuments to the dead. The narrow roads that wind over the hills and around large old magnolia trees are still about the right size for a horse and buggy. The one-legged, wild-eyed, long-haired Confederate General John Bell Hood watched the Battle of Atlanta from the second story of a house built on what is now gravesites covered with granite markers. Today's visitor standing at the historical marker on that same spot, looking toward the battle site to the east and then to the center of Atlanta one mile to the west, is made aware of the smaller scale, geographically speaking, on which people lived and died 130 years ago.

TOURING TIPS   Go to the Visitor Center and purchase a tour map of the cemetery for $1.25. This will show you the locations of some of the most famous graves in the cemetery and provide some useful history about the site. Regular weekend tours take place Saturday at 10 A.M. and 2 P.M. and Sunday at 2 P.M.

OTHER THINGS TO DO NEARBY   The Cyclorama and the zoo are a short distance south on Boulevard.

SCITREK, The Science and Technology Museum of Atlanta

Type of Attraction: Science attractively packaged for kids.

Location: 395 Piedmont Avenue, Plaza Level; in the same building as the Atlanta Civic Center.

Best MARTA Route: Bus #31 (Morningside) from Five Points or Peachtree Center stations.

Admission: $7.50 adults, $5 seniors and children ages 3–17, free for children under age 3.

Hours: Monday–Saturday, 10 A.M.–5 P.M.; Sunday, noon–5 P.M. Open until 8 P.M. the second Tuesday of each month. Closed Easter, Thanksgiving, Christmas, and New Year's Day.

Phone: (404) 522-5500

When to Go: Any time. During the school year, many school groups visit the museum between 10 A.M. and 2 P.M.

Special Comments: While this museum is definitely designed to appeal to children, it is also a pleasure for adults who had their problems with Physics 101.

Overall Appeal by Age Group:

Pre- school	Grade School	Teens	Young Adults	Over 30	Senior Citizens
★★★	★★★★	★★★★	★★★½	★★★½	★★★

Authors' Rating: Popular and educational. ★★★

How Much Time to Allow: Two hours.

DESCRIPTION AND COMMENTS   Over 100 interactive exhibits provide hands-on experiences for children and adults. Broad categories of exhibits include electricity and magnetism, light and perception, mechanics and simple machines. Frequent lectures, demonstrations, and rotating shows enhance the permanent exhibits. Good, high-end gift shop.

TOURING TIPS   SCITREK is free from 4 to 5 P.M. Parking at SCITREK is operated by the City of Atlanta and is a sky-high $4. The best alternative is to take MARTA to the Civic Center Station, exit south, and walk east on Ralph McGill to Piedmont, then go one block north on Piedmont to SCITREK. Total distance is about four blocks. Avoid Peachtree from Ralph McGill north to Pine Street.

OTHER THINGS TO DO NEARBY   This is a good opportunity to view the skyline of the city from the perspective of the Jackson Street Bridge. Magazine photographers and television camera crews often choose this site to record images of the city's buildings.

Telephone Museum

Type of Attraction: A small museum showing the history of telephone technology.

Location: Plaza Level, Southern Bell Center, 675 W. Peachtree Street, NE.

Best MARTA Route: Directly above the North Avenue Station.

Admission: Free.

Hours: Monday–Friday, 11 A.M.–1 P.M., except holidays.

Phone: (404) 529-7334

When to Go: Any time.

Special Comments: You may want to visit this interesting little museum as a fill-in stop between Lenox Square and downtown.

Overall Appeal by Age Group:

Pre-school	Grade School	Teens	Young Adults	Over 30	Senior Citizens
—	★★½	★★	★★	★★	★★½

Authors' Rating: Remember when a proper telephone number was Calhoun 9601 and there were no area codes? ★★

How Much Time to Allow: One-half hour.

DESCRIPTION AND COMMENTS   A collection of telephone equipment and technology to commemorate the first century of communications in the United States.

TOURING TIPS   Perhaps the best thing here is how convenient the museum is to MARTA.

OTHER THINGS TO DO NEARBY   Walk around the Fox Theater, a huge Moorish/Egyptian/Art Deco movie palace built in 1929 and saved from the wrecker's ball in the 70s by grassroots community involvement. Eat at Mary Mac's on Ponce de Leon Avenue, long an Atlanta institution for neighborly, low-key service and good southern cooking.

Tours

—— Custom Group Tours

In business for 25 years, Atlanta Arrangements (formerly Tour-Gals) is the Atlanta expert when it comes to designing custom tours for groups. The format is flexible, depending on the group's interests and time: Stone Mountain, shopping, dinner and theater, antebellum homes, Atlanta architecture, you name it. Planners will sit down with your group and come up with a tailor-made itinerary. Prices may range from $18 per person to $100 per person or more. Transportation may be a limousine or a 45-passenger motor coach. This is a la carte touring at its best, Atlanta style. Eighty-five permanent, part-time tour guides, each of whom has a southern accent and a closet full of hoop-skirted dresses, work only for Atlanta Arrangements. For information, contact Atlanta Arrangements at 2964 Peachtree Road, Suite 652, Atlanta, GA 30305; phone (404) 262-7660.

—— Bus Tours

The best way to see a quick sample of Atlanta's historic and scenic sights is by taking one of the regularly conducted city tours.

American Sightseeing Atlanta

Two half-day tours and one full-day tour cover such standard Atlanta sights and attractions as Martin Luther King, Jr. Memorial, Sweet Auburn, Georgia State Capitol, Underground Atlanta, Cyclorama, World of Coke, CNN Center, Zoo Atlanta, the Margaret Mitchell House, Stone Mountain Park, and Olympic Venues. Prices range from $26–50 for adults. For more information call (404) 233-9140 or (800) 572-3050. Custom tours arranged for a minimum of ten persons.

Civil War Tours

Jeff Dean conducts in-depth guided tours of Atlanta Campaign sites designed for persons with an interest in the Civil War. Fees are about $45–60 per person depending on the tour. For more information call (770) 980-8410.

Gray Line Tours

Half-day, full-day, and custom tours are available. Atlanta tours include Underground Atlanta and historic downtown, Inman Park, the Cyclorama, Sweet Auburn and the Martin Luther King, Jr. Center, World of Coke Museum, CNN Center, Olympic sites, Peachtree Street, and Stone Mountain. Regional tours include Callaway Gardens and Warm Springs, Madison and Westville, Dahlonega, and Chattanooga. Shopping tours include factory outlet centers, Atlanta's top malls, and historic town squares. Call for reservations and custom tours. For more information call (404) 521-3090.

—— Guided Walking Tours

The Atlanta Preservation Center offers ten guided walking tours of some of Atlanta's most interesting architecture and neighborhoods. Tours range from Historic/Birth of Atlanta to Walking Miss Daisy's Druid Hills. Call the Preservation Center at (404) 876-2041 for more information. Also see the listing under "Sights: Zone 7—Downtown West."

Amusement Parks

Atlanta has three amusement parks: American Adventures, Six Flags over Georgia, and White Water. They are described here in alphabetical order.

American Adventures (Zone 2)

Type of Attraction: Small child-oriented amusement park.

Location: 250 North Cobb Parkway. Take I-75 North, Exit #113, North Marietta Parkway, and follow signs.

Admission: $14.99 children, $5.99 adults, $4.99 children under 2.

Hours: Open daily from 11 A.M. Closing times vary seasonally.

Phone: (770) 424-9283 (recorded information).

When to Go: Any time, rain or shine.

Special Comments: The only amusement park in Atlanta that is just for children.

Overall Appeal by Age Group:

Pre-school	Grade School	Teens	Young Adults	Over 30	Senior Citizens
★★★★	★★★★	★★	★	★	★

Authors' Rating: ★★★

How Much Time to Allow: One-half day, but children may not want to leave.

DESCRIPTION AND COMMENTS   There are plenty of outdoor activities for children with two-seat go-cart racing, 18-hole miniature golf, and 15 amusement park style rides as well as indoor activities in the Penny Arcade and the four-story interactive Foam Factory. There is also a large restaurant with reasonable prices.

TOURING TIPS   Consider spending the morning at American Adventures and afternoon at White Water. Combination tickets are available.

OTHER THINGS TO DO NEARBY   Adjacent to White Water Park.

Six Flags over Georgia (Zone 1)

Type of Attraction: 331-acre amusement park with over 100 rides, attractions, and live shows for family entertainment.

Location: I-20 west of Atlanta at Six Flags exit.

Best MARTA Route: Bus transportation available. Call MARTA (404) 848-5290.

Admission: One-day ticket: $30 adults, $20 children ages 3–9, $15 senior citizens, free for children two years and under; two-day ticket: $33. Group rates available for 15 or more.

Hours: Hours vary but are generally 10 A.M.–10 P.M. It's a good idea to call; hours change during spring and fall months.

Phone: (770) 948-9290; group rates (770) 739-3430.

When to Go: Spring and fall are less crowded, but hours are limited to weekends. Most of the park is closed during winter months but "Holiday Specials" feature ice skating and special shows.

Overall Appeal by Age Group:

Pre-school	Grade School	Teens	Young Adults	Over 30	Senior Citizens
★★★	★★★★½	★★★★½	★★★½	★★½	½

Authors' Rating: Mostly for the under-thirty crowd. ★★★

How Much Time to Allow: A day, especially in summer when lines are long.

DESCRIPTION AND COMMENTS Located off I-20 just west of Atlanta, Six Flags over Georgia is one of seven theme parks operated by the Time-Warner affiliated Six Flags Corporation. The Six Flags name is derived from the respective themed areas of the company's first park in Arlington, Texas, where each section recalls a period in Texas history when a different flag flew over the statehouse. In Georgia there were not enough flags to cover the various theme areas, so a bit of poetic license was used to make up the difference. At Six Flags over Georgia, the themed areas are the USA, British, Georgia, Confederate, French, Cotton States, and Lick Skillet (whatever that is).

Larger, and a great deal more convoluted in its layout than Disneyland or the Magic Kingdom at Walt Disney World, Six Flags integrates the thrill rides of the traditional amusement park into the type of themed settings originally made popular by Disney. Rounding out the entertainment mix are live shows, restaurants, and shops. Six Flags targets children, teens, and young adults in its marketing and develops its attractions accordingly.

Roller coasters are the park's main draw, with six coasters in all. Water thrill rides are the second most abundant type of attraction, with an elaborate whitewater raft ride, two flume rides, and a water slide. There are a number of rides as well as a play area for small children, and a handful of midway rides (swings and the like) that are suitable for guests of all ages. In the main, however, those over thirty and anyone else who doesn't want to tumble upside down or get wet is basically relegated to sweating, paying for stuff, wiping noses, and watching the kids have fun. Unlike at Walt Disney World, Busch Gardens, or Sea World, there is not a whole lot at Six Flags that the entire family can enjoy doing together. Live entertainment has improved at Six Flags in the past couple of years but continues to play second fiddle to the rides.

From an engineering perspective, the rides are not designed to handle large numbers of people. Consequently, long queues build for the whitewater raft ride, the log flumes, and the roller coasters after about 11 A.M. On the positive side, however, the roller coasters and wet rides are pretty wild, with each offering a different ride experience.

When to Go. Six Flags is open weekends during the late spring and fall, and daily from mid-May to just past Labor Day in September. The least crowded days of the week are Tuesday, Monday, and Wednesday, in that order. Weekends are routinely packed.

During the spring and fall, daytime touring is pleasant. During the summer, however, Georgia days are often sweltering. Because it is situated near the Chattahoochee River, the park is especially muggy. The most comfortable time to visit the park during the summer is in the evenings. Unfortunately, the park is usually very crowded at night, and the queues for the more popular rides are long. The best time to experience the rides without long waits is during the first hour and a half the park is open in the morning.

Arriving and Getting Oriented. Parking at Six Flags cost $5, and trams are provided to transport guests to the main entrance. Because the park is a bit convoluted, the free map/guidebook provided on entry is essential to finding your way around. Unfortunately, however, the park sometimes runs out or, alternatively, fails to keep the various entry gates properly supplied. Start asking for a map/guidebook when you purchase your admission, and keep asking until someone gives you one. Six Flags employees are very apathetic about the map shortage and will sometimes direct you to a souvenir stand in the Georgia Section to buy a poster-sized map. We found, however, that if you keep bugging the entry gate employees, you will eventually be provided with a map/guidebook.

Once you have your free map/guidebook in hand, you will find a fold-out map in the front. This is your main reference for finding your way around. The remainder of the guidebook is poorly organized and difficult to use, with the various theme areas neither listed in alphabetical order nor in the sequence a guest encounters them. The most important thing to remember as you set out to tour is that the park is laid out in a rough circle with all of the premier rides located on the outside perimeter. If you pass through the main entrance and turn right, the big stuff will be on your right all the way around the park. Conversely, if you enter and turn left, all the top attractions will be on your left.

There are shops, midway "games of skill," souvenir stands, snack bars, and fast-food restaurants all over Six Flags. For the most part the food is edible, approximating but not exceeding the quality of chain fast food. Prices, however, run about twice what you would pay for the same meal at Hardee's or Burger King. Only a couple of eateries offer an indoor, air-conditioned dining space.

Six Flags Touring Plan. The following Six Flags Touring Plan is for visitors who want to enjoy the more popular attractions, specifically the roller coasters and the water rides, with a minimum of standing in line. Families with small children, or other visitors who do not care for the thrill rides, need not follow the plan. If you use the plan, bypass any rides not specifically mentioned. You will have plenty of time to return to them later. If you want to ride any of the attractions more than once, go ahead. But be mindful that you will encounter increasingly long lines as the park continues to fill with guests.

1. Call (770) 739-3400 before you go for the hours of operation on the day of your visit.

2. If you want to stay dry on the water rides, bring a large plastic garbage bag with you to the park.

3. Arrive at the park about 30 minutes before opening and purchase your admission. Wait to be admitted.

4. On entry, obtain a park map and a daily entertainment schedule.

5. Once in the park, bear left into the Georgia Section and ride the Log Flume. Cut holes for your head and arms in your plastic bag. Pull it over your head like a sack dress. After the ride, save the bag.

6. Retrace your steps back past the entrance area to the British Section. Ride the Georgia Cyclone roller coaster.

7. Exit to the right after the Cyclone and pass under the railroad tracks to the Confederate Section. Keeping hard to the right, go to the Dahlonega Mine Train and ride.

8. Exit the Mine Train to the right and consult your park map. You want to make your way to the Cotton States Section in the far upper right corner of the park (as you look at your map). You will pass Splashwater Falls, a flume ride. Skip it for the moment.

9. In the Cotton States Section, ride the Viper.

10. Exit the Viper to your right and ride the Great American Scream Machine.

11. Exit to the right. Proceed next door and ride the Ninja.

12. Exit to the right and enter the Lick Skillet Section via the vine-covered trellis. In Lick Skillet, ride Thunder River. Don't forget to put on your plastic bag.

13. After Thunder River, continue to your right into the USA Section. Bear right under the railroad tracks. Ride the Mind Bender roller coaster.

14. Exit the Mind Bender to the right, pass back under the tracks, and proceed to Free Fall, also in the USA Section.

15. This concludes the Touring Plan. If you hustled from ride to ride, you should have been able to enjoy the park's most popular rides with a minimum of time invested standing in line.

For the remainder of your day, try the rides not listed in the touring plan, and take in some of the live entertainment. The two best shows are the Batman Stunt Show in the USA Section and the country music show at the Crystal Pistol in the Confederate Section. Also worthwhile are presentations in the Majestic Theater in the USA Section, and the diving show in the French Section. All live presentations are listed in the daily entertainment schedule, available free of charge on entry.

White Water (Zone 2)

Type of Attraction: Water/swimming theme park.

Location: 250 North Cobb Parkway. Take I-75 North, Exit #113, North Marietta Parkway, and follow signs.

Best MARTA Route: None available.

Admission: $19.99 adults, $11.99 children age 3 up to 4-feet-tall, free for senior citizens and children ages 2 and under. All admissions $10.99 after 4 P.M. $2 parking.

Hours: Daily, 10 A.M.– 10 P.M.

Phone: (404) 424-WAVE

When to Go: Open weekends in May and daily Memorial Day through Labor Day.

Special Comments: Be prepared—this place is always crowded, but great on a hot day.

Overall Appeal by Age Group:

Pre-school	Grade School	Teens	Young Adults	Over 30	Senior Citizens
★★★★	★★★★	★★★★	★★★	★★★	★★

Authors' Rating: Great for kids. ★★★½

How Much Time to Allow: It depends on how wet you want to be when you leave.

DESCRIPTION AND COMMENTS   This is the largest water park in the Southeast, with more than 40 attractions including Black River Falls, The Gulf Coast Screamer, and White Water Rapids. The park also boasts the largest water play area for little children: Little Squirt's Island. The park is equipped with restaurants, snack bars, gift shops, and locker and shower facilities.

TOURING TIPS   Appropriate swimwear is required. Picnic in designated areas where tables are provided or in the parking lot.

OTHER THINGS TO DO NEARBY   Adjacent to American Adventures.

PART ELEVEN: Dining and Restaurants

Dining in Atlanta

For a perspective on how dining in Atlanta has changed over the last almost half century, a quick glance at *Gourmet* magazine's 1948 "Guide to Good Eating" reveals a city almost entirely devoted to its Southern culinary heritage. In many restaurants, alcohol was not served. The French Cafe, later known as Emile's French Cafe, probably constituted the city's most adventurous dining spot.

In the 1960s, a few Chinese restaurants appeared, serving chiefly Chinese-American food. Ding Ho, which stood on Cain Street (now International Boulevard), was probably the best of the bunch. But nothing then hinted at the current burst of Asian restaurants—authentic, good ones—lining the Buford Highway and popping up all over south and east Cobb County. Most ironically, today's plethora of Thai restaurants probably started in Gwinnett County, whose denizens are not assumed to savor extraordinary or challenging fare.

Today, Atlanta's retaurateurs win national awards. Two restaurants, Bacchanalia and Horseradish Grill, made *Bon Appétit* magazine's list of ten best new restaurants in the country the year of their respective openings. Bacchanalia's culinary team, Anne Quatrano and Clifford Harrison, has been named by *Food and Wine* magazine as among the country's best chefs. Lance Dean Velasquez of 1848 Restaurant hit the list in 1996.

Is Atlanta now culinary Nirvana? Not quite. For one thing, service hasn't kept pace with gastronomic sophistication. Too often, service personnel know nothing about the dishes on the menu, nor can they make intelligent recommendations.

Anyone interested in wine will likely find wine service maddeningly ignorant except in the most elegant of restaurants. In one supposedly sophisticated establishment, my recent request for a dry sherry as an apéritif brought the offer of a pair of vintage ports. "See me after dinner," I said.

Although by-the-glass wine lists have improved markedly, they are often still a boring pack of selections. All too rarely are wine lists constructed with the restaurant's food in mind. A few lists here and there wander into more exotic grape varietals, such as Viognier or Sangiovese, but only in the best spots.

In addition to the growth in authentic Asian restaurants, the most dramatic changes have come in the presentation of regional Southern cooking. Believe it or not, fried chicken has achieved a vogue in fine Atlanta restaurants that grandmother would never have imagined. So, too, have collard greens and black-eyed peas, made tangy with intriguing seasonings rather than the customary fat meat. (Of course, if you want the good ole dishes prepared in the down-home, standard ways, they're out there, and we've pointed the way in this chapter to some of the better sources.)

While a few cuisines are still missing in Atlanta—good Spanish, Brazilian, Portuguese, Indonesian (although one restaurant does dabble in it)—you can find just about anything your palate could possibly yearn for or your purse can pay for.

The Restaurants

We have developed detailed profiles for the best restaurants (in our opinion) in town. Each profile features an easily scanned heading that allows you, in just a second, to check out the restaurant's name, cuisine, Star Rating, cost, Quality Rating, and Value Rating.

Star Rating.   The star rating is an overall rating that encompasses the entire dining experience, including style, service, and ambience in addition to the taste, presentation, and quality of the food. Five stars is the highest rating possible and connotes the best of everything. Four-star restaurants are exceptional, and three-star restaurants are well above average. Two-star restaurants are good. One star indicates an average restaurant that demonstrates an unusual capability in some area of specialization, for example, an otherwise unmemorable place that serves great barbecued chicken.

Cost.   To the right of the star rating is an expense description that provides a comparative sense of how much a complete meal will cost. A complete meal for our purposes consists of an entree with vegetable or side dish and choice of soup or salad. Appetizers, desserts, drinks, and tips are excluded.

Inexpensive	$14 and less per person
Moderate	$15–30 per person
Expensive	Over $30 per person

Quality Rating.   On the far right of each heading appears a number and a letter. The number is a quality rating based on a scale of 0–100, with 100 being the highest (best) rating attainable. The quality rating is based expressly on the taste, freshness of ingredients, preparation, presentation, and creativity of food served. There is no consideration of price. If you are a person who wants the best food available, and cost is not an issue, you need look no further than the quality ratings.

Value Rating. If, on the other hand, you are looking for both quality and value, then you should check the value rating, expressed in letters. The value ratings are defined as follows:

A	Exceptional value, a real bargain
B	Good value
C	Fair value, you get exactly what you pay for
D	Somewhat overpriced
F	Significantly overpriced

Location. Just below the heading is a small locator map. This map will give you a general idea of where the restaurant described is located. For ease of use, we divide Atlanta into eight geographic zones.

Zone 1.	Southwest Atlanta
Zone 2.	Northwest Atlanta
Zone 3.	Buckhead/Sandy Springs
Zone 4.	Lenox/Chamblee
Zone 5.	Northeast Atlanta
Zone 6.	Southeast Atlanta
Zone 7.	Downtown West
Zone 8.	Downtown East

If you are staying downtown and intend to walk or take a cab to dinner, you may want to choose a restaurant from among those located in Zone 7 or 8. If you have a car, you might include restaurants from contiguous zones in your consideration. (See pages 15–22 for detailed zone maps.)

—— Our Pick of the Best Atlanta Restaurants

Because restaurants open and close all the time in Atlanta, we have confined our list to establishments with a proven track record over a fairly long period of time. Newer restaurants (and older restaurants under new management) are listed but not profiled. Those newer or changed establishments that demonstrate staying power and consistency will be profiled in subsequent editions. Also, the list is highly selective. Noninclusion of a particular place does not necessarily indicate that the restaurant is not good, but only that it was not ranked among the best in its genre. Note that some restaurants appear in more than one category. Detailed profiles of each restaurant follow in alphabetical order at the end of this chapter.

The Best Atlanta Restaurants

Type of Restaurant / Name	Star Rating	Price	Quality Rating	Value Rating
Adventures in Dining				
Kamogawa	★★★★★	Expensive	96	C
Little Szechuan	★★★★	Inexpensive	95	A
Garam	★★★★	Moderate	93	B
Honto	★★★★	Inexpensive	90	A
Imperial Fez	★★★★	Expensive	90	B
Zócalo	★★★	Inexpensive	95	A
American				
Bacchanalia	★★★★★	Exp/Mod	98	A
Hedgerose Heights Inn	★★★★★	Expensive	95	A
City Grill	★★★★	Expensive	95	C
Buckhead Diner	★★★★	Moderate	92	C
Luna Sí	★★★★	Moderate	90	B
The Bread Market	★★★	Inexpensive	90	C
Canoe	★★★	Moderate	90	C
Cafe Renaissance	★★★	Moderate	88	B
Zac's	★★★	Inexpensive	88	B
Palisades	★★★	Moderate	85	C
R. Thomas	★★★	Inexpensive	85	C
Barbecue				
Old South	★★★★	Inexpensive	95	B
The Rib Ranch	★★★	Inexpensive	85	B
Dusty's	★★	Inexpensive	90	A
Cajun & Creole				
A Taste of New Orleans	★★★★	Moderate	95	C
French Quarter Food Shop	★★★★	Inexpensive	88	A
Hal's	★★★	Moderate	90	B
California				
Mi Spia	★★★	Moderate	88	C
Chinese				
Little Szechuan	★★★★	Inexpensive	95	A
Honto	★★★★	Inexpensive	90	A
Hsu's Gourmet	★★★★	Moderate	90	C
Canton House	★★★	Moderate	90	B

The Best Atlanta Restaurants (continued)

Type of Restaurant / Name	Star Rating	Price	Quality Rating	Value Rating
Continental				
The Dining Room	★★★★★	Expensive	98	C
Hedgerose Heights Inn	★★★★★	Expensive	95	A
The Abbey	★★★★	Expensive	95	C
City Grill	★★★★	Expensive	95	C
Pano's & Paul's	★★★★	Expensive	94	C
The Restaurant	★★★★	Expensive	90	C
Hal's	★★★	Moderate	90	B
Van Gogh's	★★★	Moderate	90	C
Papa Pirozki's	★★★	Expensive	88	C
Palisades	★★★	Moderate	85	C
Anthonys	★★	Expensive	88	C
Cuban & Caribbean				
Coco Loco	★★★	Inexpensive	88	B
Deli				
E. 48th Street Italian Market	★★★★	Inexpensive	95	A
French				
Bacchanalia	★★★★★	Exp/Mod	98	A
Ciboulette	★★★★★	Expensive	95	C
Brasserie Le Coze	★★★★	Moderate	94	C
Riviera	★★★★	Expensive	90	D
Anis	★★★	Inexpensive	88	C
Le Giverny	★★	Moderate	85	C
Violette	★★	Inexp/Mod	80	B
Fusion				
TomTom	★★★★	Moderate	90	C
Cafe Tu Tu Tango	★★	Inexpensive	85	C
Indian				
Haveli	★★★★	Inexpensive	90	B
Himalayas	★★★	Inexpensive	85	B
Italian				
La Grotta	★★★★★	Expensive	98	C
Veni Vidi Vici	★★★★★	Moderate	98	B
Abruzzi	★★★★	Expensive	91	C

The Best Atlanta Restaurants (continued)

Type of Restaurant / Name	Star Rating	Price	Quality Rating	Value Rating
Italian (continued)				
Pricci	★★★★	Moderate	90	C
Mi Spia	★★★	Moderate	88	C
Fratelli di Napoli	★★	Moderate	88	C
Brooklyn Cafe	★★	Moderate	85	C
Japanese				
Kamogawa	★★★★★	Expensive	96	C
Hashiguchi	★★★★	Moderate	90	B
Korean				
Garam Korean Restaurant	★★★★	Moderate	93	B
Mediterranean				
Luna Sí	★★★★	Moderate	90	B
TomTom	★★★★	Moderate	90	C
Mexican, Tex-Mex, Southwestern				
Sundown Cafe	★★★★	Moderate	93	C
Zócalo	★★★	Inexpensive	95	A
Georgia Grille	★★★	Moderate	88	C
Nava	★★★	Expensive	88	D
Purple Cactus Cafe	★★	Inexpensive	85	B
Middle Eastern				
Nicola's	★★★	Inexpensive	85	B
Moroccan				
Imperial Fez	★★★★	Expensive	90	B
Russian				
Papa Pirozki's	★★★	Expensive	88	C
Seafood				
Atlanta Fish Market	★★★	Moderate	88	C
Stringer's Fish Camp	★★★	Inexpensive	85	C
Embers Seafood Grille	★★	Inexpensive	80	A
Southern				
South City Kitchen	★★★★	Moderate	95	C
Greenwood's	★★★★	Inexpensive	93	B

The Best Atlanta Restaurants (continued)

Type of Restaurant / Name	Star Rating	Price	Quality Rating	Value Rating
Southern (continued)				
Horseradish Grill	★★★★	Moderate	92	C
Mary Mac's	★★★	Inexpensive	90	A
Thelma's Kitchen	★★★	Inexpensive	88	C
Agnes & Muriel's	★★★	Inexpensive	85	B
1848 House	★★★	Expensive	85	D
Anthonys	★★	Expensive	88	C
Bobby & June's Kountry Kitchen	★★	Inexpensive	85	B
The Colonnade	★★	Inexpensive	80	B
Steak				
Bone's	★★★★★	Expensive	98	D
Sushi				
Kamogawa	★★★★★	Expensive	96	C
Hashiguchi	★★★★	Moderate	90	B
Thai				
Annie's Thai Castle	★★★★	Inexpensive	90	A
Sukhothai	★★★	Inexpensive	85	B
Vietnamese				
Bien Thuy	★★★★	Inexpensive	90	A

—— Tourist Places

These are tourist places you may have heard of, which should be considered only as a last resort. Meals here are often overpriced, and food generally falls beneath the standard of that served in lesser-known restaurants. This is not to say you won't get a lovely steak or a good meal in any of these places, but there is more creative food to be had elsewhere.

Restaurant	Cuisine	Star Rating	Price	Quality Rating	Value Rating
Coach and Six	American	★	Expensive	70	F
The Mansion	Continental	★★	Expensive	71	F
Morton's	Steak	★★★½	Expensive	89	F
Nikolai's Roof	Continental	★★	Expensive	70	F
The Palm	Steak	★★★	Expensive	85	F
Pittypat's Porch	Southern	★	Moderate	73	C
Ruth's Chris Steak House	Steak	★★★½	Expensive	89	F
Savannah Fish Company	Seafood	★★½	Moderate	78	C

—— *New and Changing Places*

Still too new to know, but very promising at press time, are the following:

Don Taco 4997 Buford Highway, (770) 458-8735. One of the best in the taquería boom, Don Taco is also one of the most approachable for anyone not familiar with the food or the language. The style is basic drive-through (available), but the food is downright smashing. Besides tacos, there are good burritos, tortas, and chicken and beef dishes that make the expatriate feel at home.

The Food Studio 887 W. Marietta Street, Studio K-102, King Plow Arts Center, (404) 815-6677. A newcomer from an experienced group (see profile for South City Kitchen), The Food Studio is an exciting, fresh operation. Dishes reflect eclectic tastes without becoming too busy. Buffalo, lamb, and fruit soup for dessert all make statements.

Les Halles 229 Peachtree Center Avenue at International Boulevard, Downtown, (404) 584-9900. The French way with steak, such as onglet, steak au poivre, entrecôte, and other French treats (cassoulet, pied de cochon, boudin).

Harvest 853 N. Highland Avenue, Virginia-Highland, (404) 876-8244. Inventive dishes sometimes work (smoked salmon on parsley-flecked potato cake with smashing fennel slaw) and sometimes don't (graceless spinach and ricotta dumplings). But this pair should get the hang of it with a little time.

McKendrick's   4505 Ashford-Dunwoody Road, Park Place, Dunwoody, (770) 512-8888. Suburban steak house with clubby comfortable interior and good wine list. Stick with the simple grilled steak or lamb chops.

Terra Cotta   1044 Greenwood Avenue at N. Highland Avenue, Virginia-Highland, (404) 853-7888. Wonderful Pacific Rim dishes, with Thai and Japanese touches flavoring many items. Terrific pork tenderloin, savory soups, an excellent wine list (with good selections by the glass), and raving popularity make this one a sure hit as the months go by. Chef changes since the opening deterred our listing it in the regular section, until the kitchen settles down. Next year.

—— *More Recommendations*

The Best Bagels

Bagelicious   Numerous locations around town. Fine bagels and extra-good spreads include an expensive but supremely savory baked salmon spread.

Goldberg's Bagel Company   4383 Roswell Road, NE, (404) 256-3751. Also a great line of sandwiches.

The New Bagel Eatery   6333 Roswell Road, NE, (404) 256-4411. The best whitefish in the city but not-so-friendly counter service.

The Royal Bagel   1544 Piedmont Avenue, NE, (404) 876-3512. One of the city's best. Good spreads, too.

The Best Bakeries

Alon's   1394 N. Highland Avenue, NE, (404) 872-6000. Try the eggplant sandwich on fresh warm bread. Mmmmm. Also the city's best croissant.

Bernie the Baker   3015 N. Druid Hills Road, NE, Toco Hills, (404) 633-1986. Atlanta's only strictly kosher baker. Wonderful poppy seed strip and breads.

The Bread Market   3167 Peachtree Road, (404) 816-8600; 1937 Peachtree Road, NE, (404) 352-5252. European breads, glorious sandwiches, espressos or light dining fare. Great owners-staff and a terrific atmosphere.

ad Company and Corner Cafe 3070 Piedmont Road, ·1978. European-style breads.

Italian Market 2462 Jett Ferry Road, Dunwoody, (770) 392-1499. Extraordinary Italian breads.

Great Harvest Bread Company 635 Atlanta Street, Roswell, (770) 594-1419; 4101 Roswell Road, Marietta, (770) 578-6160; 31 Mill Street, No. 400, Marietta, (770) 424-4490. Hearty breads and cookies. Parmesan/pepper and harvest apple are two of their best breads.

Hong Kong Bakery 5150 Buford Highway, Asian Square, (770) 452-1338. Unusual Chinese baked goods.

The Best Barbecue

Aleck's Barbecue Heaven 783 Martin Luther King, Jr. Drive, NW, (404) 525-2062. This heaven resembles a shack, so the thing to do is take-out. Terrific tangy ribs and good barbecued chicken. Sauce is tomato-y but with plenty of vim, vinegar, and pepper.

Corky's Ribs and Barbecue 1605 Pleasant Hill Road, Duluth, (770) 564-8666. Memphis-style, dry rub or wet. Good side dishes.

Down East 2289 S. Cobb Drive, SE, Smyrna, (770) 434-8887. Good ribs and pulled-pork sandwiches. Get the sandwiches with the slaw on top, North Carolina style. The owners apologize for having Georgia-style tomato-based sauce on the tables, but locals demanded it.

Dusty's 1815 Briarcliff Road, NE, (404) 320-6264; 12 Executive Park Drive, NE, (404) 325-7111. North Carolina–style 'cue with cole slaw on top and tangy, but not too hot, vinegar-pepper sauce makes your day if you like that style. At Executive Park, lots of vegetables and a daily Southern meat special are very popular with the surrounding business types who frequent the place.

Fat Matt's Rib Shack 1811 Piedmont Avenue, NE, near Cheshire Bridge Road, (404) 607-1622. Perhaps the best pulled-pork sandwich around, the big bun is thickly piled with well-flavored sauce. They also serve excellent barbecued chicken. Go next door to the sister operation (Fat Matt's Chicken Shack) for fried chicken, wings, and excellent fried fish with homemade tartar sauce. (These sandwiches are the best inexpensive eating in Atlanta.)

Holt Bros. Bar-B-Q 6539 Jimmy Carter Boulevard (at Buford Highway), Norcross, (770) 242-3984. Barbecued beef brisket, turkey, fried green tomatoes.

Lowcountry Barbecue 2000 South Pioneer Drive, Smyrna, (404) 799-8049. South Carolina–style 'cue from an old family recipe.

Old South Barbecue 601 Burbank Circle (near corner of Windy Hill Road near South Cobb Drive), Smyrna, (770) 435-4215. Splendid ribs; thick, substantial Brunswick stew; and excellent and unusual vinegar-dressed coleslaw make it worth the trip to seek this one out. The tangy Georgia-style sauce, and everything else, are closely guarded secrets.

The Rib Ranch 25 Irby Avenue, NW, Buckhead, (404) 233-7644. Succulent Texas-style beef ribs and good baby-back ribs.

The Best Bar Food and Appetizers

The Bar, Ritz-Carlton, Atlanta 181 Peachtree Street (at Ellis Street), Downtown, (404) 659-0400. Especially nice at 5 P.M. on Fridays when Francine Reed and the Jerry Lambert Trio often perform, The Bar offers complimentary nibbles and a fairly pricey bar menu with relatively inventive dishes, such as tandoori shrimp.

Cafe Tu Tu Tango 220 Pharr Road, NE, East Village Square, (404) 841-6222. Small bites reflect Italian, Hispanic, Middle Eastern, and Asian cooking on this "anything goes" nibble menu: shrimp-stuffed wontons, thin-crust pizzas, quesadillas, hummus, empanadas, and eggrolls.

Coco Loco 2625 Piedmont Road, NE, Buckhead Crossing Mall (on the Sidney Marcus Boulevard side of the shopping center), (404) 364-0212. Tapas from Spain and Cuba—croquetas, tamales, and empanadas for openers.

Fadó 3035 Peachtree Road (at Buckhead Avenue), (404) 841-0066. The wonders of the Emerald Isle come to Atlanta, in both brew and food, to take up shop in this lively new bar. Savor boxty (Irish potato crêpe with a choice of fillings), smoked salmon spread, Irish stew made with lamb, and Irish beer poured in Imperial pints (20 ounces).

Fuzzy's Place 2015 N. Druid Hills Road, NE (at Buford Highway), (404) 321-6166. Great blues and bar food. How 'bout a plate full of boiled crawfish for $3! "Seafood Patsy," one of chef Joe Dale's most popular dishes, mussels in white wine and garlic, salmon quesadilla, good oysters, and lots of interesting dishes.

Jocks & Jills   112 10th Street, NE, Midtown, (404) 873-5405. Several locations about town, but this one draws the young sports bar crowd and has a fun atmosphere. Spinach/queso dip and quesadillas get raves.

Prince of Wales   1144 Piedmont Avenue, NE, Midtown, (404) 876-0027. Take a crowd in and nibble on fine fish and chips; it's only $8.95 for a whopping plate with six fillets of flounder and a pile of straw potatoes (frozen, but still decent). Grilled sausage slices (andouille and bratwurst) with Dijon mustard are good for a single snacker. Excellent brews on tap and in the bottle, plus a good nonalcoholic selection (Haacke Beck), keep everybody satisfied.

RJ's Uptown Kitchen & Wine Bar   870 N. Highland Avenue, NE (at Drewry Street), Virginia-Highland, (404) 875-7775. More than 50 wines by the glass, some organized into "flights," so you can compare, for instance, Chardonnay against Pinot Gris and other dry white wines. New chef and new menu.

Sfuzzi   2200 Peachtree Road, NE, (404) 351-8222. The comfortable separate bar features its own menu, with specialty pizzas, such as wild mushroom and smoked chicken with caramelized onions, goat cheese, and rosemary.

TomTom: A Bistro   3393 Peachtree Road, NE, Lenox Square, Plaza Level, (404) 264-1163. Munch menu ("Bistro Bites") offered between lunch and dinner. Well-priced wine list with many wines by the glass.

Veni Vidi Vici   41 14th Street, NE, (404) 875-8424. Small dishes (antipasti piccoli) are great for grazing. This is a good spot to meet for pre-performance drinks and noshes if attending the nearby Fox Theatre.

The Best Breakfasts and/or Lunches

Grecian Gyro   855 Virginia Avenue, NE, (404) 762-1627. The best gyro in town, and, oh, that white sauce!

Rainbow Grocery   2118 N. Decatur Road, NE, (404) 636-5553. Natural foods—outstanding egg and Mexican dishes.

Silver Skillet   200 14th Street, NE, (404) 874-1388. Real country ham and red-eyed gravy.

White House 3172 Peachtree Street, (404) 237-7601. Greek diner with heaping breakfasts, fine lunches.

The Best Brew Pubs

Atlanta Beer Garden (cq) 3013 Peachtree Road (at Pharr Road), (404) 261-9898. This one will be open by the time the book is in print, but we have not been able to evaluate it. Soups, salads, sandwiches, sausages, burgers, and some German desserts (streudel) are planned for the menu. Six different beers include Lunatic Lager, Bavarian Hell-Style Beer, Buckred Ale, Buffalo Skull (a dark lager), and Scarlett's Peach Wheat. Can't wait. The company also will brew its own root beer, called "Mad Dog."

John Harvard's Brew House 3045 Peachtree Road (at Buckhead Avenue), (404) 816-2739 (BREW); 1456 Holcomb Bridge Road, Roswell, (770) 645-2739 (BREW). A slew of brews, anywhere from a half to a full dozen, comes out of this popular brew pub. Rock shrimp, ribs, and housemade sausage on skewers make excellent with-beer noshes. For dessert, the cornbread pudding is a must. Same menu at both locations.

Phoenix Brewing Co. 5600 Roswell Road, The Prado, (404) 843-2739. Serving brunch, lunch, and dinner and featuring hearty American fare, Phoenix produces five beers. Patrons may get a close-up of the gleaming copper tanks during informal, conducted tours. The company also brews its own root beer.

U.S. Border Cantina 12460 Crabapple Road, Alpharetta, (770) 772-4400. The first of the brew pubs to get up and running, Cantina produces three beers and its own root beer. Food emphasizes Southwestern/Mexican dishes, including cabrito (!), Borracho Bean Soup, and flan. The pub is open daily.

The Best Coffees and Desserts

Aurora Coffee 992 N. Highland Avenue, (404) 892-7158. Seattle-type coffee bar, with a few baked goods.

Cafe Intermezzo 4505 Ashford Dunwoody Road, NE, (770) 396-1344; 1845 Peachtree Road NE, 355-0411. Loads of desserts and pricey coffees, with some light grazing fare as well.

Coffee Plantation Toco Hill 2205-F LaVista Road, NE, (404) 636-1038; Fountain Oaks, 4920 Roswell Road, (404) 252-4686. No desserts, but fresh coffee roasted daily—huge selection, too.

Dessert Place   1000 Virginia Avenue, NE, (404) 892-8921. More desserts than coffees. Try the cream cheese brownies.

Ferrara   660 Peachtree Street, NE (at Ponce de Leon Avenue next to the Fox Theatre), (404) 870-0310; Forsyth and Luckie streets (inside the Rialto Center for the Performing Arts), (404) 651-1234. This upscale outpost of the famous coffee house established in 1892 in Manhattan dishes up coffee drinks, pastries, and light fare, often until late if there's a show going on.

Urban Coffee Bungalow   1425 Piedmont Avenue, NE, across from Ansley Mall, (404) 892-8212; 8 King's Circle, Peachtree Hills, (404) 261-1333; 1280 Peachtree Street, NW, Woodruff Arts Center, (404) 733-4545. Toothsome sandwiches and salads, baked goods from the folks at South City Kitchen.

Virginia's Coffee House   1243 Virginia Avenue, NE (at Briarcliff Road), (404) 875-4453. Very coffee house atmosphere with good sandwiches and salads.

The Best Restaurants for Kids Where Grown-Ups Can Eat Too

The Cafe, Ritz-Carlton, Atlanta and Buckhead.   Fancy places to take kids where they will be treated with respect and regard are rare. The Cafes at both Ritz-Carltons understand how to adapt dishes to children's palates, and both offer a children's menu at lunch.

California Pizza Kitchen   3393 Peachtree Road, NE, Lenox Square, (404) 262-9221; 4600 Ashford-Dunwoody Road, Dunwoody (just north of I-285), (770) 393-0390. Crayons and coloring books and kids' menu pizzas and pastas get good reviews from the little set. On Sunday, the CPK Kids' Sundae, with hot fudge sauce on a single scoop of vanilla ice cream and whipped cream and a cherry, goes for $1.95.

Camille's   1186 N. Highland Avenue, Virginia-Highland, (404) 872-7203. Kids like the deep-fried rice balls, the individual pizzas, the pastas, and even the calamari. Although there's no children's menu, every effort is made to accommodate the younger patron in this neighborhood restaurant. Be sure to get there before 7 P.M. even on weeknights, because it's really popular with nearby residents.

Dragon D. Chinese Restaurant   2333-A Peachtree Road, NE, Peachtree Battle Shopping Center, (404) 237-8729. No, it's not the most authentic Chinese restaurant you'll ever see, but they know how to treat the little patrons with affection and respect. This courtesy to the little ones is typical of Asian restaurants, but here their patience seems particularly well exercised and cheerful.

57th Fighter Group Restaurant   3829 Clairmont Road, NE, (770) 457-7757. The kids love to look at the WWII-vintage aircraft before settling down to dinner. The kids' menu offers chicken fingers and burgers, but children also enjoy nibbling the alligator bites.

Fuddruckers   Seven locations around the metro Atlanta area. Good burgers for all concerned, including kid-size ones. Freshly grilled chicken, a good salad bar, and a civilized atmosphere—a definite improvement over the fast-food scene.

Romano's Macaroni Grill   4788 Ashford-Dunwoody Road, Dunwoody (just outside I-285), (770) 394-6676; 770 Holcomb Bridge Road, Roswell (just east of GA 400), (770) 993-7115; 1565 Pleasant Hill Road, Duluth (near Gwinnett Place Mall), (770) 564-0094. Paper tablecloths, crayons, and a kids' menu with good pizza, Italian food, and excellent veal lasagne. The staff is used to kids and knows how to treat them. Family oriented, but it's not bad for dating purposes at reasonable prices for the quality of the food. Excellent dessert tray. Atmosphere is a bit boisterous, but not obnoxiously so.

Mick's   Ten locations around the metro area, many near shopping malls. In addition to kids' menus, Wednesday is a special day for the little people: They eat free at some locations; the decision rests with the on-site manager, so call ahead.

The Best Markets

99 Ranch Market   5150 Buford Highway, NE, Asian Square, Doraville, (770) 458-8899. Terrific selection of Asian staples, produce, meat (pork and duck especially good), and seafood. Oddities include quail eggs, black-skin chicken, squab.

El Rinconcito   2845 Buford Highway, Sun Tan Shopping Center, (404) 636-8714; 1000-A Cheshire Bridge Road, Cheshire Pointe Shopping Center (at Faulkner Road), (404) 636-8714. Well-displayed wide selection of Hispanic foods; Puerto Rican restaurant in rear.

Harris Teeter   3954 Peachtree Road, NE, 814-5990; 2480 Mt. Vernon Road, Dunwoody, (770) 551-0990. Atlanta's niftiest grocery store, with on-site nibbles and excellent coffee bar. A third location, due soon on Briarcliff Road near LaVista Road, will have a large kosher section.

Harry's Farmer's Market   2025 Satellite Point, Duluth, (770) 416-6900; 1180 Upper Hembree Road, Alpharetta, (770) 664-6300; 70 Powers Ferry Road, Marietta, (770) 578-4400. Impressive selection of international cheeses, meats, and breads, with an equally diverse selection of fresh vegetables and fruits.

International Farmer's Market   5193 Peachtree Industrial Boulevard, Chamblee, (770) 455-1777. Growing market with good prices, and large selection of staples.

Quality Kosher Emporium   2153 Briarcliff Road, NE, (404) 636-1114. Prepared kosher foods, meats, excellent selection kosher wines.

Pano's Food Shop   265 Pharr Road, NE (near Peachtree Road), (404) 262-3165. Attached to the only HACCP (Hazard Analysis Critical Control Point) certified restaurant in the country, the Atlanta Fish Market (see profile), Pano's Food Shop not only purveys some of the freshest sea bass, tuna, trout, and similar fare, but also dishes up good prepared foods, fine pâtés, good wines to take with, desserts, bread, and condiments to fill the earth—food for a private snuggle supper to a business bash.

Paris Market   1833 Peachtree Road, NE, (404) 351-4212. Prepared dishes, exquisite French cheeses, good breads, wines. A few tables, but mostly what's here is designed for take-out.

Sweet Auburn Curb Market   209 Edgewood Avenue, NE, Downtown, (404) 659-1665. A true farmers' market, with each stall individually owned and operated. The place offers items you can't get anywhere else. Anybody for trapped wild rabbit? One of the businesses here is Hardeman's, which specializes in pork, and is about the only place in town to get whole pigs.

Taj Mahal Imports   1594 Woodcliff Drive, NE, (404) 321-5940. Indian staples and British supplies, reflecting the influence of the Raj on Indian fare. Smells divine!

Your DeKalb Farmer's Market   3000 E. Ponce de Leon Avenue, Decatur, (404) 377-6400. Huge market, with good Asian staples.

The Best Pizza

Bertucci's Brick Oven Pizzeria   230 Peachtree Street, NW, (404) 525-2822; 3316 Piedmont Road, NE (just north of Peachtree Street), (404) 816-6566; 4380 Roswell Road, NE, Marietta, (770) 973-6999. Almost 20 different pizzas, in both small and large sizes, a "create-your-own-pizza" deal, 15 different pasta dishes, calzone, and a good kids' menu make this newcomer appealing. Decent wines by the glass, too.

California Pizza Kitchen   3393 Peachtree Road, NE, Lenox Square, (404) 262-9221; 4600 Ashford-Dunwoody Road, Dunwoody (just north of I-285), (770) 393-0390. A wide variety of intriguing toppings, plus good pastas and other dishes. Bright, high-energy atmosphere.

Everybody's Famous Pizza   1040 N. Highlands Avenue, NE, (404) 873-4545; 1593 N. Decatur Road, NE, (404) 377-7766. Try the thin, crisp-crust pizzas.

Fellini's Pizza   Multiple locations. Locals love 'em. Great choice for individual slices.

Mo's Pizza   3109 Briarcliff Road (near Clairmont Road), (404) 320-1258; also available at the Beer Mug, 1705 Peachtree Road, NE, (404) 872-5854. Nothing designer or nouvelle about these pizzas. Classic Italian-American stuff, on perhaps the best pizza crust in town. We know New Yorkers arriving in Atlanta who order one before leaving the airport so they can pick it up on the way to their destination.

Pasta Vino   2391 Peachtree Road, NE, Peachtree Battle Shopping Center, (404) 231-4946. New York–style slices, green pizzas, fresh mussels, and generously portioned salads in no-frills atmosphere.

Rocky's Brick Oven   1770 Peachtree Street, NW, (404) 876-1111; 1395 N. Highland Avenue, Virginia-Highland, (404) 870-7625. Best thin-crust pizzas—especially white and margarita.

The Best Saturday Lunches

Brasserie Le Coze   3393 Peachtree Road, NE, Lenox Square, (404) 266-1440.

The Bread Market   3167 Peachtree Road, NE (at Grandview Avenue), (404) 816-8600; 1937 Peachtree Road, NE, Brookwood Village, (404) 352-5252 (more spacious and offers prepared foods).

The Colonnade 1879 Cheshire Bridge Road, NE (near Piedmont Road), (404) 874-5642.

Hsu's Gourmet 192 Peachtree Center Avenue, NE, Downtown, (404) 659-2788.

TomTom 3393 Peachtree Road, NE, Lenox Square, Plaza Level, (404) 264-1163.

Tribeca Cafe 2880 Holcomb Bridge Road, Holcomb Center, Roswell, (770) 640-5345.

Villa Christina 45 Perimeter Summit Boulevard, at Perimeter Summit, (404) 303-0133. A quiet, relaxing, elegant atmosphere, serving fine sandwiches, soups, and salads, Villa Christina makes a good post-shopping stop after a spree at Perimeter Mall.

The Best Sunday Brunches

Babette's Cafe 471 N. Highland Avenue, NE, Poncey-Highland, (404) 523-9121. Eggs Benedict (called "Babette's Bene") and sparkling wine define luxury. Service for brunch concludes at 4:00 P.M. on Sundays, so you can take nearly all day to decide when to have it.

The Cafe The Ritz-Carlton Hotel Buckhead, 3434 Peachtree Road, NE (across from Lenox Square), (404) 237-2700. Probably the best Sunday brunch for the big appetite crowd. Grits are splendid here. Special themed brunches (Father's Day Jazz Brunch, New World Cuisine) stand out. Breakfast is a feast here any day of the week—especially the corned beef hash with poached eggs.

Flying Biscuit Cafe 1655 McLendon Avenue, NE, (404) 687-8888. It can take a while to get in on Sunday mornings, less for Saturday brunch, but the biscuits are one good reason to stand in line. Organic oatmeal pancakes keep 'em coming. Orange-vanilla French toast is another popular dish.

South City Kitchen 1144 Crescent Avenue, Midtown, (404) 873-7358. A host of brunch delights, from pancakes to French toast to grits with sausage gravy and Crab Benedict. Awesome!

Zac's 308 W. Ponce de Leon Avenue, Decatur, (404) 373-9468. Traditional egg brunch dishes don't define brunch here, although they're very good. There's also a nice collection of more nontraditional brunch items: chicken pot pie; shrimp cakes; blueberry pancakes. Saturday brunch is also available.

Zócalo   187 10TH Street, NE (at Piedmont Avenue), Midtown, (404) 249-7576. Steak and eggs over easy with tangy salsa, eggs and chorizo, fresh juices, great coffee—all enjoyed on a breezy patio. Authentic Mexican.

The Best Wee-Hours Fare

Note: Many new 24-hour operations are beginning to open in the Atlanta area, but not in time to be evaluated for this edition.

Bamboo Luau's Chinatown   2263 Cheshire Bridge Road, NE, (404) 636-9131. Close the evening (this place is open until 3 A.M.) with excellent dim sum. Insist on the Chinese menu; Occidentals are usually handed the Chinese-American menu, which is less interesting.

Cafe Tu Tu Tango   220 Pharr Road, East Village Square, (404) 841-6222. Even during the week you can eat late here, as it doesn't close until midnight on Wednesday and after that Thursday through Saturday. Small plates rule the menu, with flavors coming from Asia, Italy, Spain, and the Middle East. Good date spot.

First China   5295 Buford Highway, NE, (770) 457-6788. Good soups and noodle dishes; good, unintimidating Chinese food served until 3 A.M.

Fuzzy's Place   2015 North Druid Hills Road, NE (at Buford Highway), (404) 321-6166. Food served until 2 A.M., and that includes the nifty appetizers, such as salmon quesadilla, deep-fried oysters, mussels, and specials.

Landmark   3652 Roswell Road, Buckhead, (404) 816-9090. Service can be maddeningly indifferent and, frankly, so can the food sometimes, but it's a good place to get a substantial late dinner or early breakfast. Bright, busy, noisy, and offering a huge menu that's available in its entirety 'round the clock.

OK Cafe   1284 W. Paces Ferry Road, NW, (404) 233-2888. Breakfast served from 11 P.M.–11 A.M., then lunch takes over until 5 P.M., followed by dinner from 5–11 P.M. Note the blue plate specials at lunch and dinner, and vegetable plates are especially good. Breakfast is always substantial, featuring granola, eggs and grits, pancakes, and similar fare.

R. Thomas Deluxe Grill   1812 Peachtree Road (at Piedmont Road), (404) 881-0246. Winds down in the very early morning, so staff can clean up a bit and get ready for the next day's mobs. A good spot to wind up a late date, with an excellent burger, baked stuffed potato, or omelet and good coffee to savor with natural sugar.

Willy's Mexicana Grill   4377 Roswell Road (near Wieuca Road), Roswell-Wieuca Shopping Center, (404) 252-2235. California-style Mexican fare with salsas, guacamole, and everything freshly made. Wicked cheap. Open until 11 P.M. on weekends.

The Best Wines by the Glass

Bone's   3130 Piedmont Road, (404) 237-2663. Savor the taste of a fine Bordeaux, a first-rate Sauternes, and other exotica on the well-chosen list.

Café Intermezzo   1845 Peachtree Road, NE, (404) 355-0411. Originally a coffee bar famous for its pastries, Café Intermezzo has two locations that were separated by a common divorce some time ago. This location has added hot dishes and an expensive wine list—featuring a wide range of selections not only by the glass but also by the taste—to the menu. These tasting pours cost $1.50–3 for dry dinner wines. An extensive list of dessert wines and ports is also available. Desserts themselves are luxurious.

The Dining Room   The Ritz-Carlton Hotel Buckhead, 3434 Peachtree Road, NE (across from Lenox Square), (404) 237-2700. The chef's so knowledgeable about wines that even the award-winning sommelier doesn't worry about his selections for the four-course menu, which may be enjoyed with or without a specifically chosen glass of wine. But why have it without?

The Restaurant   The Ritz-Carlton Hotel, Atlanta, 181 Peachtree Street, NE, (404) 659-0400, ext. 6450. The wines by the glass are chosen for their ability to accompany the food served at the establishment. Look for unususal Rhône wines, Bordeaux, California wines—all excellent choices by a classically minded sommelier. Special wine-focused dinners a frequent feature to ask about when in town.

RJ's Uptown Kitchen and Wine Bar   870 N. Highland Avenue, at Drewry Street, Virginia-Highland, (404) 875-7775. Adventurous selections enable tasting in flights (several small glasses for comparison) or solo more than 50 wines by the glass. A humdinger in the "by-the-glass" department.

Toulouse   2293-B Peachtree Road, NE (near Peachtree Memorial Drive), Peachtree Walk, (404) 351-9533. The clever menu identifies a specific wine that goes well with each dish. By-the-glass options go way beyond chardonnay and cabernet sauvignon.

The Abbey

Continental ★★★★ **Expensive**

Quality	Value
95	C

163 Ponce de Leon Avenue
(404) 876-8532

Zone 8   Downtown East

Reservations: Accepted, and if conventions are in town, essential
When to go: Weekends when conventioneers are gone
Entree range: $19–28
Payment: Major credit cards
Service rating: ★★★★
Friendliness rating: ★★★
Parking: Valet
Bar: Separate lounge with full service
Wine selection: Fabulous, with many half-bottles and good selections by the glass, after-dinner wines, and excellent prices on older vintages of outstanding labels

Dress: Everything from nice tieless casual to glitter
Disabled access: Difficult
Customers: Conventioneers during the week, locals on the weekend

Dinner: Every day, with seatings from 6–10 P.M. Cocktails offered at 5 P.M.

Setting & atmosphere: Breathtaking stained glass windows lend a solemn note to the formal atmosphere in this church-turned-restaurant, an Atlanta landmark.

House specialties: Foie gras, rabbit, salmon, duck, and lamb are always prepared in interesting ways on a menu that changes seasonally. Treatments may be classic French, American, or Moroccan, depending on the chef's inclinations.

Other recommendations: Desserts are fabulous, such as tarte tatin with cinnamon ice cream and whatever flavor cheesecake is on the menu.

Entertainment & amenities: A harpist positioned in the church's choir loft plays light classics and popular tunes.

Summary & comment: This is a superior dining experience, made even more outstanding by the depth of the wine list. A must for anyone interested in fine wines, the restaurant is excellent for business as well as romantic dining.

Honors & awards: More than 12 annual awards for the wine list from *Wine Spectator;* Five-Star Diamond Award from the Academy Awards of the Restaurant Industry; *Restaurants & Institutions* magazine, Ivy Award of Distinction; American Express "Salute to Service," 1st Place Southeast Region, United States; and many more.

Abruzzi

Quality	Value
91	C

Italian ★★★★ **Expensive**

2355 Peachtree Road, NE, in Peachtree Battle Shopping Center
(404) 261-8186   Zone 3   Buckhead/Sandy Springs

Reservations: Required
When to go: Any time
Entree range: $15–27
Payment: Major credit cards
Service rating: ★★
Friendliness rating: ★★★★ if you're
known or are Italian, ★ if you're not
Parking: Fairly adequate, depending
on the season, in the shopping center lot
Bar: No separate bar, but full service
Wine selection: Wide ranging, fairly
expensive, with limited selections by the
glass
Dress: Tieless acceptable, but jacket please
Disabled access: Yes
Customers: Locals and visitors, chiefly an older crowd

Lunch: Monday–Friday, 11:30 A.M.–2 P.M.
Dinner: Monday–Thursday, 5:30–10 P.M.; Friday and Saturday,
5:30–11 P.M.; Sunday, closed.

Setting & atmosphere: Elegant and understated, the dining room is quiet and refined. If you hate the high noise level at many restaurants, you will savor the contemplative calm of Abruzzi.

House specialties: Sweetbreads in Madeira; pappardelle (broad noodles) with game or oxtail sauce; lemon sole; veal dishes (may be prepared any style); tiramisù.

Other recommendations: Baked pears.

Summary & comment: Count on the pasta to be excellent, no matter which you choose. The kitchen produces classic Italian cooking, with no attempt to be "nouvelle." Service is elegant and formal. The best seating is the banquettes that are arranged along the side of the spacious dining room.

Honors & awards: Three years ago, Delta's International Flights began using Abruzzi recipes in first and business classes. DiRoNa Award, 1996. "The award to me is my customers," says owner Nico Petrucci, a native of Abruzzi, Italy.

Agnes & Muriel's

Quality	Value
85	B

Southern ★★★ **Inexpensive**

1514 Monroe Drive, Ansley Park
(404) 885-1000   Zone 8   Downtown East

Reservations: No, but call ahead to put
your name on the waiting list
When to go: Early or late
Entree range: $8–15
Payment: Major credit cards
Service rating: ★★★
Friendliness rating: ★★★
Parking: Self
Bar: Beer and wine
Wine selection: Chiefly American,
with many good ones by the glass
Dress: Nice casual
Disabled access: Yes, ramp at the front, better than most
Customers: Neighbors, all ages, couples and theatergoers at dinner

Brunch: Saturday and Sunday, 10 A.M.–3 P.M.
Breakfast & Lunch: Saturday and Sunday, 3–5 P.M.
Lunch: Monday–Friday, 11 A.M.–5 P.M.
Dinner: Monday–Thursday, 5–11 P.M.; Friday and Saturday, 5 P.M.–
midnight; Sunday, 5–11 P.M.

Setting & atmosphere: A charming rehabilitated bungalow with appealing interior spaces is packed with tables, making patrons elbow-to-elbow. But nobody cares. The noise level is up there, but you can still easily hear your table's conversation.

House specialties: Salmon pot pie; trout; Agnes' chicken club with grilled chicken and caramelized onions; shrimp corn chowder (a special); fried green tomatoes; collard greens; green bean casserole; french-fried sweet potatoes.

Other recommendations: Chocolate chiffon pie.

Summary & comment: This is the kind of food mother prepared for bridge parties and teas, but updated by a well-trained pair who named the restaurant for their mothers.

Anis

Quality	Value
88	C

French Provençal ★★★ **Inexpensive**

2974 Grandview Avenue
(404) 233-9889

Zone 3   Buckhead/Sandy Springs

Reservations: No
When to go: Any time
Entree range: $10–15
Payment: Major credit cards
Service rating: ★★
Friendliness rating: ★
Parking: Scarce, behind the building
Bar: Separate small bar, beer and wine only
Wine selection: Mostly French (many from the south of France) with some California, and about 15 by the glass
Dress: Very casual, but preferably nice

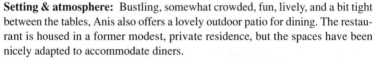

Disabled access: Best for the patio, difficult but not impossible for the interior
Customers: Mostly locals from surrounding neighborhoods

Lunch: Every day, 11:30 A.M.–2 P.M.
Dinner: Sunday–Thursday, 6–10 P.M.; Friday and Saturday, 6–10:30 P.M.

Setting & atmosphere: Bustling, somewhat crowded, fun, lively, and a bit tight between the tables, Anis also offers a lovely outdoor patio for dining. The restaurant is housed in a former modest, private residence, but the spaces have been nicely adapted to accommodate diners.

House specialties: Grilled tuna with aïoli; chicken with cèpes; chicken with olives (by request only); grilled lamb chops; bouillabaisse (Wednesday only); duck confit.

Other recommendations: Daily specials; crème brûlée.

Entertainment & amenities: Sunday night vocalist with guitar.

Summary & comment: This is the classic neighborhood French bistro transported to a posh Atlanta area. Dishes are the sort that one finds all over the south of France—casual, well prepared, not afraid of seasoning, served in good portions—and are designed to remind the expatriate Frenchman of home.

Honors & awards: *Atlanta* magazine "Best of Atlanta New Cuisine," 1994 and 1995; "Best Romantic Evening on a Budget," 1995.

Annie's Thai Castle

Quality	Value
90	**A**

Thai   ★★★★   **Inexpensive**

3195 Roswell Road
(404) 264-9546

Zone 3   Buckhead/Sandy Springs

Reservations: Recommended
When to go: Dinner
Entree range: $9–17
Payment: Major credit cards
Service rating: ★★(at lunch),
★★★(at dinner)
Friendliness rating: ★★★
Parking: Some in back
Bar: Full service
Wine selection: Limited
Dress: Nice casual
Disabled access: Easy via back door

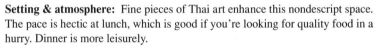

Customers: Business patrons at lunch; young couples on dates and locals at
dinner

Lunch: Tuesday–Friday, 11 A.M.–2:30 P.M.
Dinner: Tuesday–Thursday, 5:30–10:30 P.M.; Friday and Saturday,
5:30–11:30 P.M.; Sunday, 4–10 P.M.

Setting & atmosphere: Fine pieces of Thai art enhance this nondescript space.
The pace is hectic at lunch, which is good if you're looking for quality food in a
hurry. Dinner is more leisurely.

House specialties: Red curry duck; chicken or shrimp Masaman; pad thai;
whole fish dishes.

Other recommendations: Spicy Thai sausage salad; yom yai; glass noodle
salad.

Summary & comment: It's difficult to slow these folks down at lunch because
they're so used to getting business patrons in and back to their offices within 30
minutes. The small outdoor patio is comfortable for good-weather dining.

Honors & awards: "Best of Atlanta," *Atlanta* magazine, 1995.

Anthonys

Quality	Value
88	C

Southern/Continental ★★ **Expensive**

3109 Piedmont Road, NE
(404) 262-7379 Zone 3 Buckhead/Sandy Springs

Reservations: Recommended on
weekends
When to go: Any time
Entree range: $16–22; lobster, $29
Payment: Major credit cards
Service rating: ★★★
Friendliness rating: ★★★
Parking: Valet and self
Bar: Full service
Wine selection: Extensive list with
many French and California wines, a
few Italians, and several modest selec-
tions by the glass
Dress: Business attire and dresses
Disabled access: No, although yes for downstairs private party area
Customers: Out-of-towners, conventioneers

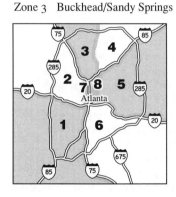

Dinner: Every day, 6 P.M. until the last customer is served.

Setting & atmosphere: The Pope-Walton House was begun in the late 18th
century near Washington, Georgia, more than 100 miles east of Atlanta. The
authentic antebellum mansion was moved over a three-year period to its present
site on an urban tract and opened as a restaurant in 1967. Portraits of stylish
19th-century dowagers adorn one dining room; romantic landscapes repose in
others.

House specialties: Veal Anthony (a form of veal Oscar), Georgia pickled
shrimp; blue crab and rock shrimp cakes; Vidalia onion fritters; fish; game.

Other recommendations: Chocolate bread pudding.

Summary & comment: Drawn from plantation sources, the food has improved
markedly over the past couple of years under the guidance of Jesse Gislason,
who enjoys perusing his collection of antebellum cookbooks looking for dishes
he can adapt.

Honors & awards: American Academy of Restaurant and Hospitality Sciences
Five-Star Diamond Award, 1990–95; *Mobil* 3-Star.

Atlanta Fish Market

Quality	Value
88	C

Seafood ★★★ **Moderate**

265 Pharr Road, NE
(404) 262-3165   Zone 3   Buckhead/Sandy Springs

Reservations: Limited, essential for weekends
When to go: Early for lunch and dinner
Entree range: $13–20
Payment: Major credit cards
Service rating: ★★★
Friendliness rating: ★★
Parking: Valet
Bar: Separate, full service
Wine selection: Mostly California with some French and Italian, several excellent, well-priced choices by the glass, including sparkling and dessert
Dress: Casual but nice
Disabled access: Easy, ramped entrance; elevator to second-level banquet room
Customers: An older crowd, many locals, some out-of-town clientele

Lunch: Monday–Saturday, 11 A.M.–2:30 P.M.
Dinner: Monday–Thursday, 5:30–11 P.M.; Friday and Saturday, 5–midnight; Sunday, 4:30–10 P.M.

Setting & atmosphere: Busy, high-energy, designed to resemble a train station, the restaurant is now distinguished by its huge and controversial 65-foot copper fish. The more sedate, separate Geechee Porch, adjacent to the dining room, is a relatively quiet space.

House specialties: Crab cakes; pecan-crusted swordfish; gumbo; New England clam chowder.

Other recommendations: Rum raisin bread pudding with vanilla crème anglaise when available.

Summary & comment: Reportedly the only HACCP (Hazard Analysis Critical Control Point) certified restaurant in the country, the Atlanta Fish Market was recognized for its special handling of seafood and the chefs' and managers' training in seafood safety.

Honors & awards: *Esquire* magazine's Top 25 Restaurants, 1994; "Best Seafood Restaurant," *Atlanta* magazine, 1994–1995.

Bacchanalia

Quality	Value
98	A

French/American ★★★★★ **Expensive/moderate**

3125 Piedmont Road, NE
(404) 365-0410   Zone 3   Buckhead/Sandy Springs

Reservations: Essential
When to go: Weekdays
Entree range: $35 fixed price for four courses, $75 with selected wines and six courses; a la carte entrees, $17–19
Payment: Major credit cards except DISC
Service rating: ★★★★
Friendliness rating: ★★★★
Parking: Ample
Bar: Beer and wine only
Wine selection: All American with excellent, fairly priced choices, but only a few by the glass
Dress: Casual
Disabled access: Partial (first floor only)
Customers: Locals and out-of-towners, couples celebrating anniversaries, businesspeople

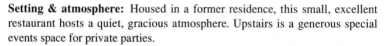

Dinner: Tuesday–Saturday, 6–10 P.M.

Setting & atmosphere: Housed in a former residence, this small, excellent restaurant hosts a quiet, gracious atmosphere. Upstairs is a generous special events space for private parties.

House specialties: Foie gras; especially fine greens from a local producer; risotto in cool weather; fish; lamb; squab; vegetarian specialties available on request.

Other recommendations: Apple Financier with cinnamon ice cream; homemade ice creams and sorbets; soups of any kind.

Summary & comment: One is hard-pressed to dine better anywhere on the planet. Chefs/owners Anne Quatrano and Clifford Harrison deserve every accolade one could attribute to them.

Honors & awards: James Beard Foundation Benefit Dinner, 1996; "Best Chefs of 1995," *Food and Wine* magazine; Aspen Food and Wine Classic, 1995; "10 Best New Restaurants of 1993," *Bon Appétit,* 1993.

Bien Thuy

Quality	Value
90	**A**

Vietnamese ★★★★ **Inexpensive**

5095 F Buford Highway, NE, Northwoods Plaza
(770) 454-9046   Zone 4   Lenox/Chamblee

Reservations: Accepted
When to go: Any time
Entree range: $5–19
Payment: Cash only
Service rating: ★★
Friendliness rating: ★★ (★★★★ if
you find Suzanne, the owner)
Parking: Self
Bar: Beer only
Wine selection: None
Dress: Casual
Disabled access: Yes

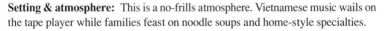

Customers: Vietnamese, locals, former servicemen who served in Vietnam

Open: Wednesday–Monday, 10 A.M.–10 P.M. Tuesday, closed.

Setting & atmosphere: This is a no-frills atmosphere. Vietnamese music wails on the tape player while families feast on noodle soups and home-style specialties.

House specialties: Grilled, stuffed jumbo shrimp (lemongrass, onion, beef stuffing); Hu Tieu (glass noodle soup with seafood); banh xeo (stuffed pancakes); cha gio (spring rolls).

Other recommendations: All kinds of noodle dishes.

Summary & comment: The authentic Vietnamese food gives the American palate no quarter, so be prepared to dine adventurously. Ask the owner's assistance in composing your meal; she is gracious and eager to explain dishes.

Honors & awards: Many "Bests" from local publications.

Bobby's & June's Kountry Kitchen

			Quality	Value
Southern	★★	**Inexpensive**	**85**	**B**

375 14th Street, NW
(404) 876-3872

Zone 7   Downtown West

Reservations: Parties of 6 or more
only
When to go: Breakfast and lunch
Entree range: $5–7
Payment: Major credit cards
Service rating: ★★★
Friendliness rating: ★★★
Parking: Self
Bar: None
Wine selection: None
Dress: Completely casual
Disabled access: Easy, ramp at
entrance

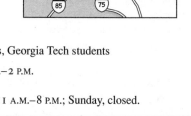

Customers: Locals, blue-collar types, Georgia Tech students

Breakfast: Monday–Saturday, 6 A.M.–2 P.M.
Lunch: Saturday, 11 A.M.–2 P.M.
Lunch & Dinner: Monday–Friday, 11 A.M.–8 P.M.; Sunday, closed.

Setting & atmosphere: This rustic, country-style establishment is a bit of the authentic old South in the middle of urban sophistication. At lunch, it's crowded with hard hats who favor basic, Southern-style comfort food.

House specialties: Breakfast, with eggs, biscuits, grits, country ham, and all the trimmings; sliced pork barbecue sandwich and cole slaw; country fried steak and gravy; fried chicken.

Other recommendations: Apple cobbler.

Summary & comment: Don't tell your doctor you ate here. Everything's cooked authentic Southern style, and that means plenty of fried food. The breakfast alone could cause cardiac arrest, but once in a while it's good for the soul. And although many vegetables and the fruit for the cobblers are canned, the dishes come out tasting pretty good.

Bone's

Quality	Value
98	**D**

Steak ★★★★★ **Expensive**

3130 Piedmont Road, NE
(404) 237-2663

Reservations: Strongly recommended
When to go: Any time
Entree range: $19–29, except Maine
lobster at $19/pound
Payment: Major credit cards
Service rating: ★★★★
Friendliness rating: ★★★
Parking: Valet
Bar: Separate, full service
Wine selection: Extensive, fairly
priced and excellent with California,
French, and Italian choices and about a
dozen by the glass
Dress: Coat and tie recommended, but not required
Disabled access: Difficult, but can be done with assistance through a side-entrance ramp to the downstairs level
Customers: Mostly male, business types, some local patrons celebrating birthdays and anniversaries

Zone 3   Buckhead/Sandy Springs

Lunch: Monday–Friday, 11:30 A.M.–2:30 P.M.
Dinner: Every day, 6–11 P.M.

Setting & atmosphere: Clubby and very masculine, with archival photographs from Atlanta's past lining the walls along with signed star photos. Secluded dining spaces are especially nice for business and romantic dining.

House specialties: Excellent filet mignon; lamb; crab cakes; and other seafood dishes.

Other recommendations: Outstanding lobster bisque.

Summary & comment: A bastion of male power dining, the restaurant feels like a clubhouse for over-the-hill fraternity types. Despite all that, the food is worth anyone's attention. Easily intimidated females should simply lunch elsewhere.

Honors & awards: Award of Excellence for the wine list, 1990–1995, *Wine Spectator;* "Best Steak House," *Atlanta* magazine, 1995; "Top 15 SteakHouses, *Wine Spectator,* 1996.

Brasserie Le Coze

Quality	Value
94	C

French Bistro   ★★★★   **Moderate**

3393 Peachtree Road, NE, Lenox Square
(404) 266-1440   Zone 3   Buckhead/Sandy Springs

Reservations: Recommended
When to go: Any time
Entree range: $12–23
Payment: Major credit cards
Service rating: ★ if dining alone,
★★★ if dining with a good-size party
Friendliness rating: ★★
Parking: Valet and self
Bar: Separate, full service with bar menu
Wine selection: Heavily French with some California and more than 30 by the glass
Dress: Casual but nice
Disabled access: Excellent

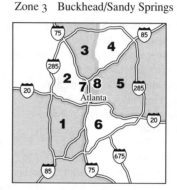

Customers: Shoppers from Lenox Square, especially at lunch; families on weekends at lunch; business and romantic diners on the weekends

Lunch: Monday–Thursday, 11:30 A.M.–2:30 P.M.; Friday, 11:30 A.M.–3 P.M.; Saturday, 11:30 A.M.–3:30 P.M.
Lunch & Dinner: Light menu, Monday–Thursday, 2:30–5:30 P.M.; Friday, 3–5:30 P.M.; Saturday, 3:30–5:30 P.M.
Dinner: Monday–Thursday, 5:30–10 P.M.; Saturday, 5:30–11 P.M.

Setting & atmosphere: Warm, gaslight-era interior with comfortable banquettes and some outside seating in good weather mark this spot as a special bistro for romantic dining and close friends reuniting.

House specialties: White bean soup with truffle oil; creamy onion soup; tuna carpaccio; coq au vin; mussels marinière; quiche; skate with brown butter; tarte tatin.

Other recommendations: All traditional French bistro dishes.

Summary & comment: Women dining alone can be ignored or given short shrift; otherwise, service is competent and quick, if not warm. A great place to relax after a heavy-duty shopping spree.

Honors & awards: "First Choice Favorite 10 Restaurants 1996," dining critic, *Atlanta-Journal Constitution.*

The Bread Market

Quality	Value
90	C

American　　　★★★　　　**Inexpensive**

3167 Peachtree Road, NE
(404) 816-8600　　　　　　　　　Zone 3　Buckhead/Sandy Springs

1937 Peachtree Road, NE, Brookwood Village
(404) 352-5252　　　　　　　　　Zone 3　Buckhead/Sandy Springs

Reservations: No
When to go: Any time
Entree range: $4–7
Payment: Major credit cards
Service rating: ★★★★
Friendliness rating: ★★★
Parking: Self, both locations
Bar: None
Wine selection: None
Dress: Casual
Disabled access: Excellent
Customers: Shoppers, locals, business types, staff and visitors from Piedmont Hospital

Breakfast: Monday–Friday, 6:30–11 A.M.; Saturday, 7 A.M.–noon; Sunday, 7:30–noon.
Lunch & Dinner: Monday–Friday, 11:30 A.M.–7:30 P.M.; Saturday and Sunday, 11:30 A.M.–6 P.M.

Setting & atmosphere: Bright, brisk, and bustling, the stores are attractive and warmly aromatic with the smells of freshly baked bread. Be careful, or you'll walk out with an armload of loaves. At the larger Brookwood Village location, prepared foods are arranged in an attractive case, and the seating is more generous.

House specialties: Specialty breads (foccacia, Greek olive, bastone); specialty sandwiches (curry chicken salad, portobello and shiitake mushrooms with fresh mozzarella cheese); desserts (yummy brownies, cookies, and cheesecake). Main-course dishes, such as grilled veggie lasagne, available to go.

Other recommendations: Fat-free muffins; breakfast burrito (weekends only); good espresso.

Summary & comment: The Bread Market also supplies bread to some of the city's best restaurants, an outstanding commendation.

Honors & awards: *Creative Loafing,* "Best Bakery," 1993.

Brooklyn Cafe

Quality	Value
85	C

Italian-American ★★ **Moderate**

220 Sandy Springs Circle
(404) 843-8377

Zone 3   Buckhead/Sandy Springs

Reservations: No, but call about an hour ahead to put your name on the waiting list
When to go: Early or late, especially on weekends
Entree range: $8–17
Payment: Major credit cards
Service rating: ★★★
Friendliness rating: ★★★★
Parking: Self, ample
Bar: Separate with TV, beer and wine only

Wine selection: Decent and fairly priced with a few good selections by the glass
Dress: Casual
Disabled access: Yes
Customers: Neighbors, Holly Berry and David Justice (when they were married and lived in Sandy Springs)

Lunch: Monday–Friday, 11:30 A.M.–2:30 P.M.
Dinner: Sunday–Thursday, 5:30–10 P.M.; Friday and Saturday, 5:30–11 P.M.

Setting & atmosphere: A neighborhood restaurant prominently positioned in a typical suburban strip center, the cafe is relaxed, comforting, and casual. An open kitchen invites patrons' inspection as the young chefs go about their business.

House specialties: Mussels; calamari; vegetarian canneloni; shrimp fra diavolo on angel hair.

Other recommendations: Zuppa inglese, good bread to be dipped in the olive oil provided at table.

Summary & comment: Substantial portions are provided for all dishes, but happily, pastas may be ordered in half orders—and even these are huge. Great for family dining.

Honors & awards: "Best of Sandy Springs," *Atlanta* magazine, 1995.

Buckhead Diner

Quality	Value
92	C

American　　　★★★★　　　**Moderate**

3073 Piedmont Road, NE
(404) 262-3336

Zone 3　Buckhead/Sandy Springs

Reservations: Not accepted
When to go: Early in each service period because the place is always packed. An hour wait is not uncommon. Midafternoon is good, especially for snacks, desserts, and coffee or late lunch
Entree range: $12–16
Payment: Major credit cards
Service rating: ★★★★
Friendliness rating: ★★★
Parking: Valet
Bar: Separate, full service
Wine selection: Extensive and well selected; mostly California, but most major wine-growing regions are represented; more than 30 available by the glass
Dress: Dressy casual to black tie
Disabled access: Excellent
Customers: Locals, tourists, movie stars—just about everybody

Lunch & Dinner: Monday–Saturday, 10:45 A.M.–midnight; Sunday, 10 A.M.–10 P.M.

Setting & atmosphere: Sumptuously designed and appointed, this neon-wrapped upscale take on the traditional American roadhouse has little in common with the original item—neither does the menu, except in one or two instances. But the place is magical, attracting glitterati and ordinary folk alike.

House specialties: Veal and wild-mushroom meat loaf with celery mashed potatoes; spicy sweet-and-sour calamari; soft-shell crab salad in season; homemade potato chips with Maytag blue cheese; white chocolate banana cream pie.

Other recommendations: Malteds and homemade ice cream.

Summary & comment: A great place to top off a fine evening at the theater or a concert, take the load off after shopping at nearby malls, or wow a date with fine food and wine. High noise level.

Honors & awards: Ivy Award, *Restaurants & Institutions,* 1994.

The Cabin

Quality	Value
85	D

American　　　★★　　**Moderate/expensive**

2678 Buford Highway, NE
(404) 315-7676　　　　　　　　　Zone 5　Northeast Atlanta

Reservations: Accepted
When to go: Any time
Entree range: $15.95–24.95
Payment: Major credit cards
Service rating: ★★
Friendliness rating: ★★
Parking: Valet
Bar: Full service
Wine selection: American, focusing
on chardonnay and cabernet sauvignon,
but with a few others as well; many
selections by the glass
Dress: Nice casual to business
Disabled access: Yes
Customers: Locals, tourists

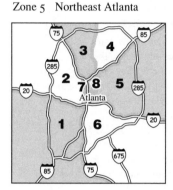

Lunch: Monday–Friday, 11:30 A.M.–2:30 P.M.
Dinner: Monday–Thursday, 5:30–10 P.M.; Friday and Saturday, 5:30–11 P.M.;
Sunday, closed.

Setting & atmosphere: The wine-dark walls are made to glow by light from
antler-based sconces. Indifferent landscapes suggest wild terrain. Well-spaced
tables make this a good business dining spot, but the neighbors like it, too, for a
night out.

House specialties: Game, steak, and fish.

Other recommendations: Corn-crab chowder; side dishes (stone-ground grits
with bacon).

Summary & comment: Farm-raised game is a permanent special, and at least
two are offered each night at dinner only. Venison is a fixture, and elk or buffalo
may constitute the second choice. The treatment is simple: grilled tenderloin of
elk comes with a demi-glace sauce.

Cafe Renaissance

American　　　★★★　　　**Moderate**

Quality	Value
88	B

7050 Jimmy Carter Boulevard, Upton's Shopping Center
(770) 441-0291　　　　　　　　Zone 4　Lenox/Chamblee

Reservations: Accepted, recommended
for lunch
When to go: Any time
Entree range: $10–20
Payment: Major credit cards
Service rating: ★★★
Friendliness rating: ★★
Parking: Self
Bar: Full service with lounge
Wine selection: Decent, with some
good ones by the glass
Dress: Nice casual
Disabled access: Yes

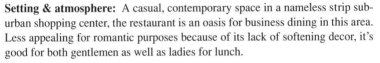

Customers: Local businesspeople at lunch; neighbors, business types, and
romantic couples at dinner

Lunch: Monday–Friday, 11:30 A.M.–3 P.M.
Dinner: Monday–Saturday, 5:30–10 P.M.

Setting & atmosphere: A casual, contemporary space in a nameless strip suburban shopping center, the restaurant is an oasis for business dining in this area.
Less appealing for romantic purposes because of its lack of softening decor, it's
good for both gentlemen as well as ladies for lunch.

House specialties: Stuffed veal chop; fresh pasta; steak salad; and specialty
sandwiches at lunch.

Other recommendations: Grilled vegetable plate.

Summary & comment: Are there better restaurants around town? Of course.
But for Norcross, this is the best for either lunch or dinner.

Café Tu Tu Tango

Quality	Value
85	C

Fusion   ★★   **Inexpensive**

---

220 Pharr Road, NE, East Village Square
(404) 841-6222   Zone 3   Buckhead/Sandy Springs

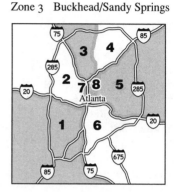

Reservations: No, but there's a pager system for waitlisted patrons
When to go: Off hours to avoid the crowds, before 7 P.M., especially on the weekends
Entree range: $4–8
Payment: Major credit cards
Service rating: ★★★
Friendliness rating: ★★★
Parking: Valet, in front (do not park within the square on Bolling Way)
Bar: Two, one on each level, full service
Wine selection: Extensive and good with several quality choices by the glass
Dress: Casual but nice
Disabled access: Yes, but not to the second level
Customers: A young, hip crowd, the heart of Generation X, usually for romantic evenings

Lunch & Dinner: Sunday–Tuesday, 11:30 A.M.–11 P.M.; Wednesday, 11:30 A.M.–midnight; Thursday, 11:30 A.M.–1 A.M.; Friday and Saturday, 11:30 A.M.–2 A.M.

Setting & atmosphere: A re-creation of an artist's attic studio, with pieces by local artists strategically positioned to enforce the point. Dimly lit, high-energy, attractive to the young-at-heart (and in chronology).

House specialties: Pizzas; Cajun chicken eggrolls; hummus with pita bread; empanadas; pot stickers; skewers.

Other recommendations: Housemade sangría (red and white).

Entertainment & amenities: Upstairs, Friday and Saturday, dancing or music or some kind of performance. Magicians and fire eaters have even had their moment of glory here.

Summary & comment: Plates are designed to be shared, unless you have a gargantuan appetite. The idea is to order a couple of items, so bring friends as this is a spot to be enjoyed with a group.

Honors & awards: "Best Hors d'oeuvres," Taste of Atlanta, 1994; "Best Appetizers," Taste of Atlanta, 1993.

Canoe

Quality	Value
90	C

American   ★★★   **Moderate**

4199 Paces Ferry Road, NW
(770) 432-2663   Zone 2   Northwest Atlanta

Reservations: Required
When to go: Before 6:30 P.M. and after
10 P.M. on the weekends
Entree range: $14–27
Payment: Major credit cards
Service rating: ★★★★
Friendliness rating: ★★★
Parking: Valet
Bar: Elegant separate space with full
service and bar menu
Wine selection: Heavy on California,
with some French and Italian; many
good ones by the glass
Dress: Nice casual to business attire
Disabled access: Excellent

Customers: Business types and leisure ladies at lunch; couples celebrating
special events and business patrons at dinner, both locals and out-of-towners

Brunch: Sunday, 10:30 A.M.–2:30 P.M.
Lunch: Monday–Friday, 11:30 A.M.–2:30 P.M.
Dinner: Monday–Thursday, 5:30–10:30 P.M., Friday and Saturday,
5:30–11:30 P.M.; Sunday, 5–9 P.M.

Setting & atmosphere: Restaurateurs would kill for this setting, along the
banks of the Chattahoochee River, where Civil War troops massed. The charming garden setting invites weddings and special events. There's been a restaurant
in this building for as long as most living Atlantans can remember.

House specialties: House-smoked salmon; rock shrimp cakes; grilled free-range
chicken; Asian-style duck; grilled vegetable plate that changes seasonally; specialty pizzas at lunch (caramelized onions and goat cheese); pappardelle and
other fresh pastas.

Other recommendations: Chocolate hazelnut praline cake.

Summary & comment: The food is controversial; some locals complain about
the cost as well as the food. After numerous visits, I can only say I have enjoyed
every bite and thought the prices appropriate. Your call.

Honors & awards: Nominated for James Beard Foundation's Best New Restaurant, 1996, one of only five chosen nationwide.

Canton House

Quality	Value
90	**B**

Chinese/Cantonese　　　★★★　　　**Moderate**

4825 Buford Highway, Chamblee
(770) 936-9030　　　　　　　　　Zone 4　Lenox/Chamblee

Reservations: Accepted only until
11:30 on Saturday and Sunday for dim
sum
When to go: Any time
Entree range: $6–24
Payment: Major credit cards
Service rating: ★★★
Friendliness rating: ★★★
Parking: Self
Bar: None
Wine selection: Limited
Dress: Nice casual
Disabled access: Access at side door
Customers: Chinese families with small children

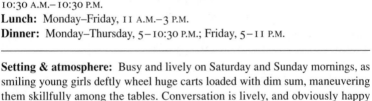

Breakfast, Lunch, & Dinner: Saturday, 10:30 A.M.–11 P.M.; Sunday,
10:30 A.M.–10:30 P.M.
Lunch: Monday–Friday, 11 A.M.–3 P.M.
Dinner: Monday–Thursday, 5–10:30 P.M.; Friday, 5–11 P.M.

Setting & atmosphere: Busy and lively on Saturday and Sunday mornings, as smiling young girls deftly wheel huge carts loaded with dim sum, maneuvering them skillfully among the tables. Conversation is lively, and obviously happy families enjoy late breakfast Chinese style.

House specialties: Dim sum; lobster and crab with ginger and scallion; whole steamed or braised fish.

Other recommendations: Barbecued pork buns.

Summary & comment: One of the most authentic Chinese restaurants in town, it eagerly welcomes Occidental patrons.

Honors & awards: A favorite of local critics and publications.

Ciboulette

Quality	Value
95	**C**

French ★★★★★ **Expensive**

1529 Piedmont Avenue, NE, Ansley Park
(404) 874-7600   Zone 8   Downtown East

Reservations: Essential, but walk-ins
may be able to sit at the counter
When to go: Any time
Entree range: $17–24
Payment: Major credit cards
Service rating: ★★★★
Friendliness rating: ★★★★
Parking: Self
Bar: Separate with full service
Wine selection: Extensive French
offerings, with good representation
from California and other wine-grow-
ing areas; about 15 good ones by the glass, plus dessert wines
Dress: Dressy casual to business attire
Disabled access: Yes, ramp on the opposite end of the shopping center, then
same-level entrance
Customers: Locals and business types

Dinner: Monday–Thursday, 6–10 P.M.; Friday and Saturday, 5:30–11 P.M.;
Sunday, closed.

Setting & atmosphere: A busy open kitchen provides the focal point for the
restaurant, a relatively tranquil space unless it's just jammed. Warm, skin-flat-
tering tones make everyone look wonderful.

House specialties: Foie gras; game (preparation varies often); fresh fish; excellent salads.

Other recommendations: Great desserts, such as flourless chocolate cake, but
these vary, too.

Summary & comment: Be very firm if you prefer rare meat, as the kitchen
tends to get meat a little overdone. No such problem, however, with the fish or
game, which always come out perfectly done.

Honors & awards: James Beard "Great Regional Chefs of America," 1995;
Zagat Guide's No. 2 Best Restaurant; *Gourmet* and *Condé Nast* have raved about
the restaurant.

City Grill

Quality	Value
95	C

American/Continental   ★★★★   **Expensive**

50 Hurt Plaza
(404) 524-2489   Zone 7   Downtown West

Reservations: Recommended
When to go: Any time
Entree range: $16–26
Payment: Major credit cards
Service rating: ★★★★★
Friendliness rating: ★★★★
Parking: Valet (dinner only); self at
adjacent pay lot (lunch)
Bar: Separate with full service
Wine selection: Excellent, with good
choices by the glass
Dress: Business attire to glitter at
dinner

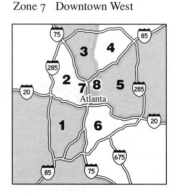

Disabled access: Hurt Plaza side entrance to building to elevators; balcony
dining
Customers: Downtowners, out-of-towners, prominent locals, business patrons

Lunch: Monday–Friday, 11:30 A.M.–2:30 P.M.
Dinner: Monday–Saturday, 5:30–10 P.M.; Sunday, closed.

Setting & atmosphere: The handsomely appointed dining room has all the
posh of a private club—sophisticated, very old-world, very chic. Through
the large windows, diners may enjoy a glimpse of the surrounding urban setting,
the bright sunshine or approaching dusk.

House specialties: Very good steak, lamb, fresh fish, quail.

Other recommendations: Crab cakes; quail with pepper cream gravy on a biscuit; housemade ice creams (chocolate Jack Daniels—yum!) and sorbets.

Summary & comment: Chef Roger Kaplan deserves the credit for crafting
food that is both provocative and approachable.

Honors & awards: Three consecutive AAA 4-Diamond awards; numerous
DiRoNa Awards; Fitness Award from *Fitness* magazine (1995) for heart-healthy
dishes.

Coco Loco Cuban & Caribbean Cafe

Quality	Value
88	B

Cuban & Caribbean ★★★ **Inexpensive**

2625 Piedmont Road, NE, Buckhead Crossing Mall
(404) 364-0212

Zone 3   Buckhead/Sandy Springs

Reservations: Required
When to go: Any time
Entree range: $6–15
Payment: Major credit cards
Service rating: ★★
Friendliness rating: ★★★★
Parking: Self
Bar: Separate with full service and tapas from main menu
Wine selection: Mostly Chilean with some Spanish and California
Dress: Casual
Disabled access: Yes
Customers: A total melting pot; baseball players of Hispanic background are practically family

Lunch: Monday–Thursday, 11 A.M.–2:30 P.M.
Lunch & Dinner: Friday, 11 A.M.–10:30 P.M.; Saturday, noon–11 P.M.
Dinner: Monday–Thursday, 6–10 P.M.; Sunday, closed.

Setting & atmosphere: A bright, lively cafe with plenty of atmospheric decor. The place packs with friends and families enjoying the home-style fare.

House specialties: Pork chunks and roast pork; Argentinian-style steak; jerked shrimp or chicken; black beans; shrimp Creole; paella.

Other recommendations: All tapas: croquetas; tostones rellenos; empanadas; conch fritters; super Cuban sandwiches.

Entertainment & amenities: Saturday salsa.

Summary & comment: Start your visit off right with a glass of chilled sangría. You will relax here from the moment you step in the door. If ordering paella for a crowd, call ahead for the big one. "Fast" paella is available nightly without prior order.

The Colonnade Restaurant

Quality	Value
80	B

Southern ★★ **Inexpensive**

1879 Cheshire Bridge Road, NE
(404) 874-5642

Zone 5   Northeast Atlanta

Reservations: No
When to go: Any time
Entree range: $6–15
Payment: Cash or check (out-of-town check OK with ID)
Service rating: ★★
Friendliness rating: ★★★
Parking: Self
Bar: Separate with full service
Wine selection: Limited but good selections, with some by the glass
Dress: Casual
Disabled access: Yes
Customers: Locals, restaurateurs on their days off

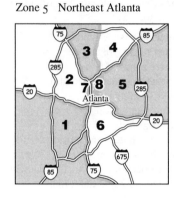

Breakfast, Lunch, & Dinner: Sunday, 11 A.M.–9 P.M.
Lunch: Monday–Saturday, 11 A.M.–2:30 P.M.
Lunch & Dinner: Monday–Saturday, 2:30–4 P.M., lunch menu in the lounge
Dinner: Monday–Thursday, 5–9 P.M.; Friday and Saturday, 5–10 P.M.

Setting & atmosphere: An ample dining room, brightly lit, with well-spaced tables and a sort of contemporary country decor, The Colonnade is where the iced-tea set mingles for lunch.

House specialties: Fried chicken; fried shrimp; prime rib.

Other recommendations: Chicken pot pie; salmon patties; bone-in center-cut ham steak; trout; all vegetables; chicken-fried steak (at lunch).

Summary & comment: After a fire nearly destroyed this landmark establishment, it came back to life in better shape than ever. It's not glossy, and shouldn't be, but the comfortable interior decor makes a perfect scene for this food.

The Dining Room, The Ritz-Carlton, Buckhead

Quality	Value
98	C

Continental   ★★★★★   **Expensive**

3434 Peachtree Road, NE
(404) 237-2700

Zone 3   Buckhead/Sandy Springs

Reservations: Essential a week or two
ahead; not taken for 8 P.M. on Friday or
Saturday
When to go: Any time
Entree range: Five-course tasting
menu with preselected wines, $99;
without wines, $70
Payment: Major credit cards
Service rating: ★★★★★
Friendliness rating: ★★★★★
Parking: Valet and self
Bar: Separate, full service; extensive
with many special vintages and selections
Wine selection: Extensive, with very fine wines by the glass
Dress: Jacket and tie, business attire to glitter
Disabled access: Via elevator
Customers: Hotel guests, appreciative locals

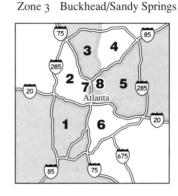

Dinner: Monday–Saturday, 6–9:30 P.M.; Sunday, closed.

Setting & atmosphere: The lobby of the Ritz-Carlton hotel prepares the visitor
for entrance into the formal, fine club atmosphere of The Dining Room. Guests
often include film and music personalities, as well as local personalities. The
open kitchen gleams and hums with activity, as chef Guenter Seeger directs his
team with close, passionate attention to detail.

House specialties: Relax, place your palate in the hands of one of the most
competent and inventive chefs on the planet. The rest is easy: Enjoy. Seeger's
minimalist approach to cooking is not for everyone. This is not the place for the
20-ounce T-bone. Instead, savor the freshest fish anywhere prepared in inventive
ways, game anointed with subtle sauces and served medium rare, and heavenly
desserts.

Other recommendations: Squab; fresh fish; duck; assorted sorbets.

Summary & comment: Seeger's restaurant in Germany was awarded a Miche-
lin Star, and no wonder. The food is too adventurous and the prices too high for
some, but if celebration with the finest is the order of the day, make it here.

Honors & awards: *Mobil* 5-Star.

Dusty's

Quality	Value
90	A

Barbecue   ★★   **Inexpensive**

1815 Briarcliff Road, NE
(404) 320-6264   Zone 5   Northeast

12 Executive Park Drive, NE
(404) 325-7111   Zone 5   Northeast

Reservations: No at *Briarcliff;* yes at *Executive Park*
When to go: Any time at *Briarcliff;* lunch only at *Executive Park*
Entree range: $4–15
Payment: Major credit cards and checks
Service rating: ★★★★
Friendliness rating: ★★★
Parking: Self
Bar: Beer and wine
Wine selection: Limited
Dress: Very casual
Disabled access: Yes
Customers: Students, business types, locals of all kinds

Lunch & Dinner: *Briarcliff:* Sunday–Thursday, 11 A.M.–9 P.M.; Friday and Saturday, 11 A.M.–10 P.M.; *Executive Park:* Monday–Friday, 11 A.M.–3 P.M.; Saturday and Sunday, closed.

Setting & atmosphere: Rustic, stylized "about-to-fall-down" charm at Briarcliff; business-park efficiency at Executive Park.

House specialties: North Carolina–style barbecue with vinegar-pepper sauce and housemade cole slaw to put on top. All sauces are housemade. At Executive Park, you'll find about 25 vegetables cooked Southern style.

Other recommendations: Ask about vegetarian items at Executive Park.

Summary & comment: Drive-through convenience at Briarcliff means you can grab a 'cue-and-slaw sandwich on the run. You'll probably have it scarfed before leaving the parking lot, however.

Honors & awards: *Creative Loafing,* "Best Barbecue Sandwich and Side Dish," 1995; Taste of Atlanta, "Best Entree" (1992) and "Best Side Dish" (1993).

E. 48th Street Italian Market

Quality	Value
95	A

Italian-American Deli ★★★★ **Inexpensive**

2462 Jett Ferry Road at Mt. Vernon Road, Williamsburg at Dunwoody Shopping Center

(770) 392-1499   Zone 4   Lenox/Chamblee

Reservations: No
When to go: Any time, but avoid busy Saturday
Entree range: $5–6
Payment: Cash or checks (out-of-town OK with ID)
Service rating: ★★★★
Friendliness rating: ★★★★★
Parking: Self
Bar: Beer and wine by the glass
Wine selection: Mostly Italian
Dress: Casual
Disabled access: Tight, but outdoor dining available
Customers: Locals, visiting expatriate New Yorkers, business people at lunch

Open: Monday–Friday, 10 A.M.–7 P.M., Saturday, 10 A.M.–6 P.M.; Sunday, closed.

Setting & atmosphere: A small shopping center space, the market would be nondescript were it not for the center shelves piled with imported dried pastas and other staples of Italian cooking. On Saturday, the place gets jammed with expatriate New Yorkers of Italian descent looking for dishes from the homeland (Brooklyn and "da" Bronx).

House specialties: Meatball hero; stofatto (Italian deli meats with house sauce on housemade bread); muffuletta; prosciutto with fresh mozzarella.

Other recommendations: Housemade biscotti with great espresso; anginetti (lemon cookies); specialty seasonal treats, such as baccalà salad; all breads.

Summary & comment: No other deli in Atlanta supplies this kind of quality, from the deli meats, homemade mozzarella, and other cheeses to the freshly baked breads. Breads are stored unwrapped on a shelf so the crusts stay fresh and crisp. The place smells great, too. Owners Charlie and Anita Augello opened their dream shop about a decade ago, and Atlantans have responded with enthusiasm.

Honors & awards: Numerous "Best of Atlanta" awards from *Atlanta* magazine and *Creative Loafing*.

1848 House

Quality	Value
85	D

Southern   ★★★   **Expensive**

780 S. Cobb Drive, SE
(770) 428-1848   Zone 2   Northwest Atlanta

Reservations: Recommended
When to go: Any time
Entree range: $14–25
Payment: Major credit cards
Service rating: ★★★★
Friendliness rating: ★★★★
Parking: Valet and self
Bar: Separate, full service
Wine selection: Chiefly California,
with a moderate by-the-glass selection
Dress: Dressy to business casual
Disabled access: Excellent

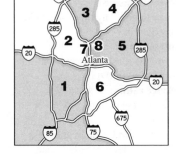

Customers: A well-heeled set, many with striking foreign accents, visitors
seeking out the Tara experience

Brunch: Sunday, 10:30 A.M.–2:30 P.M.
Dinner: Tuesday–Saturday, 6–9:30 P.M.; Sunday, 5:30–8 P.M.

Setting & atmosphere: Housed in an elegant Greek Revival antebellum built in
1848 and listed on the National Register, the restaurant is on the site of a Civil
War skirmish. The 13-acre site is dramatically lit at night. A most romantic ambience, quiet and tranquil.

House specialties: She-crab soup; spinach salad with in-house smoked trout;
saddle of venison; quail; lamb loin.

Other recommendations: Apple gratin with housemade cinnamon ice cream.

Entertainment & amenities: Jazz on Sunday at brunch.

Summary & comment: This is an excellent choice for romantic dining or for
entertaining older guests who can't deal with excessive noise levels.

Honors & awards: *Food and Wine,* "Best New Chefs," 1996, for Chef Lance
Dean Velasquez.

Embers Seafood Grille

Quality	Value
80	**A**

Seafood ★★ **Inexpensive**

---

234 Hildebrand Drive
(404) 256-0977

Zone 3   Buckhead/Sandy Springs

Reservations: Required
When to go: Any time
Entree range: $11–16
Payment: Major credit cards
Service rating: ★★★
Friendliness rating: ★★★★
Parking: Self
Bar: Separate at entrance, with full service
Wine selection: Somewhat limited, with a few good selections by the glass
Dress: Nice casual
Disabled access: Ramped
Customers: Out-of-towners, locals

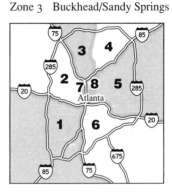

Lunch: Monday–Friday, 11:30 A.M.–2:30 P.M.
Dinner: Monday–Saturday, 6–10:30 P.M.; Sunday, closed.

Setting & atmosphere: Embers reminds you of restaurants that sit by the water's edge in isolated fishing villages—rustic, inviting, comfortable, and casual.

House specialties: Crab cakes, but they're not traditional style, thus not to everyone's taste; all grilled fish (especially swordfish and tuna); a whopping 10-ounce fillet marinated in jalapeño soy sauce. The 13-acre site is dramatically lit at night.

Other recommendations: Splendid seafood chowder; first-rate key lime pie.

Summary & comment: For more than a decade, this established landmark has held firm to the notion that fish should be simply grilled to be at its best. So don't come for eye-catching presentations and fusion-style mingling of ingredients. Just the fish, ma'am. Steaks get high marks, too, though.

Fadó

Quality	Value
90	C

Irish pub ★★★ **Moderate**

3035 Peachtree Road, NE
(404) 841-0066

Zone 3   Buckhead/Sandy Springs

Reservations: For parties of 7 or more until 6:30 P.M.
When to go: Any time, but less crowded at lunch than after work
Entree range: $8.95–13.95
Payment: Major credit cards
Service rating: ★★
Friendliness rating: ★★
Parking: Self, on street or in adjacent lots
Bar: Full service; come for the Irish beers, among others, served in Imperial pints (20 ounces)
Wine selection: Limited but decent
Dress: Nice casual to business
Disabled access: Yes
Customers: Locals, tourists

Brunch: Irish breakfast, Sunday, 9 A.M.–2 P.M.
Lunch: Sunday–Saturday, 11:30 A.M.–3 P.M.
Dinner: Monday–Friday, Sunday, 5 P.M.–2 A.M.; Saturday, 5 P.M.–3 A.M.

Setting & atmosphere: Jam-packed from day one, Fadó captures the spirit and vigor of an authentic Irish pub. With dark woods, stained glass, and intimate spaces, the place has been an instant and sustained hit.

House specialties: Boxty; potted salmon; Irish stew made with lamb as it should be; oysters fried and raw.

Other recommendations: Irish whiskey cake.

Entertainment & amenities: Irish music on Wednesday night; informal Irish music sessions with musicians sitting in as they choose on Monday night. Gaelic football is shown on the large-screen TV via satellite on Sunday morning.

Summary & comment: One of the best places in Atlanta to unwind after work, this charming Irish pub has all it takes to transport patrons to the Emerald Isle itself.

Fratelli di Napoli

Quality	Value
88	C

Italian-American   ★★   **Moderate**

2101 B Tula Street, NW
(404) 351-1533

Zone 3   Buckhead/Sandy Springs

Reservations: Only for parties of 6 or more
When to go: Before 7 P.M., especially on weekends
Entree range: $10–26
Payment: Major credit cards
Service rating: ★★★★
Friendliness rating: ★★★★
Parking: Valet and self
Bar: Separate, full service
Wine selection: Lots of California and Italian, with 15 or more by the glass
Dress: Nice casual
Disabled access: Ramp around back

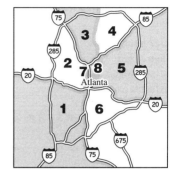

Customers: Families, especially on Sunday; groups of young people

Dinner: Monday–Thursday, 5–11 P.M.; Friday and Saturday, 5–midnight; Sunday, 4–10 P.M.

Setting & atmosphere: A high-energy place with a somewhat elevated noise level, this popular new spot has been crafted out of a warehouse-style space near a frequently running railroad line. Lighting is warm; the place is friendly; and the ambience welcomes a wide diversity of patrons.

House specialties: All pastas (rigatoni with vodka); excellent salads; snapper in basil sauce; chicken Marsala and cacciatore.

Other recommendations: Dessert platter.

Summary & comment: Family-style service on all entrees means that a single entree will serve 2–4 persons, depending on appetites. So bring a gang.

French Quarter Food Shop

Quality	Value
88	A

Cajun   ★★★★   Inexpensive

923 Peachtree Street, NE
(404) 875-2489   Zone 8   Downtown East

2144 Johnson Ferry Road
(770) 458-2148   Zone 4   Lenox/Chamblee

Reservations: No
When to go: Any time
Entree range: $7–15
Payment: Major credit cards
Service rating: ★★★
Friendliness rating: ★★★★★
Parking: Self
Bar: Beer and wine only
Wine selection: Limited
Dress: Scruffy to nice casual
Disabled access: Yes
Customers: A young local crowd

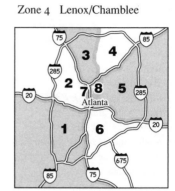

Lunch & Dinner: Monday–Thursday, 11 A.M.–10 P.M.; Friday and Saturday, 11 A.M.–11 P.M.; Sunday, closed.

Setting & atmosphere: At the Midtown location, the atmosphere is akin to that of a Lake Ponchartrain seafood house. In nice weather, sidewalk tables are a real pleasure—and may spare you from sighting the occasional uninvited insect within. The suburban location is upscale, bigger, and certainly cleaner.

House specialties: The classics of Cajun cooking: po' boys; fried oysters; muffuletta; étouffée; gumbo.

Other recommendations: Wicked bread pudding.

Summary & comment: These restaurants have enjoyed a loyal following since their establishment. "Come-as-you-are" is taken seriously. If the jeans have missing knees, so what.

Garam Korean Restaurant

Quality	Value
93	B

Korean   ★★★★   **Moderate**

5881 Buford Highway, NE
(770) 454-9198

Zone 4   Lenox/Chamblee

Reservations: Accepted
When to go: Any time
Entree range: $8–16
Payment: Major credit cards
Service rating: ★★★
Friendliness rating: ★★★
Parking: Self
Bar: Separate with full service
Wine selection: Limited
Dress: Casual
Disabled access: Yes
Customers: Koreans and other locals

Open: Every day, 10:30 A.M.–midnight.

Setting & atmosphere: Now a fixture among Atlanta's Korean restaurants, whose number grows annually, Garam greets patrons with samples of pickled vegetables, which appear before the order is taken. The decor is comfortable, suggesting Korea but not aggressively.

House specialties: Marinated grilled short ribs of beef; soups; calamari casserole.

Other recommendations: B-bim-bop with egg.

Summary & comment: The staff is accustomed to dealing with Americans who may be unfamiliar with the food, so don't hesitate to ask questions.

Georgia Grille

	Quality	Value
	88	C

Southwestern   ★★★   **Moderate**

2290 Peachtree Road, Peachtree Square Shopping Center
(404) 352-3517   Zone 3   Buckhead/Sandy Springs

Reservations: No, but waiting list preference available
When to go: Any time, but early in the dinner service is best
Entree range: $10–19
Payment: Major credit cards
Service rating: ★★★
Friendliness rating: ★★★
Parking: Self
Bar: Beer and wine (margaritas are wine based)
Wine selection: Eclectic and well chosen, with several good ones by the glass
Dress: Nice casual
Disabled access: Excellent
Customers: A young, lively set of locals

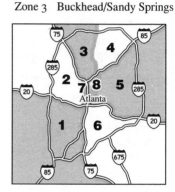

Dinner: Sunday–Thursday, 6–10 P.M.; Friday and Saturday, 6–11 P.M.

Setting & atmosphere: Colors and interior finishes reflect the warm, traditional tones of the American Southwest. The restaurant was named for artist Georgia O'Keeffe, and work by a local artist enlivens the walls.

House specialties: Lobster enchilada (an award winner); chicken corn chowder; flan.

Other recommendations: "Hot Shots," cheese-stuffed, deep-fried jalapeño peppers; black-bean cumin pancake; potato-stuffed burritos with a green chile sauce.

Summary & comment: When you want to light up your palate, take a trip to Georgia Grille. Lively flavors, yet often classically simple preparations (such as the perfect flan), bring luster to the Southwestern culinary tradition. No wonder the place stays packed.

Honors & awards: Governor's Cup, 1992, for the lobster enchilada; "Best Chocolate Dessert," *Atlanta* magazine, 1992, for the triple chocolate mousse.

Greenwood's on Green Street

Quality	Value
93	B

Southern   ★★★★   **Inexpensive**

1087 Green Street
(770) 992-5383   Zone 3   Buckhead/Sandy Springs

Reservations: No
When to go: Any time
Entree range: $6–17
Payment: Cash or check (out-of-town
check OK with ID)
Service rating: ★★★★
Friendliness rating: ★★★★★
Parking: Self
Bar: Beer and wine
Wine selection: American wines, with
several by the glass
Dress: Nice casual
Disabled access: Excellent

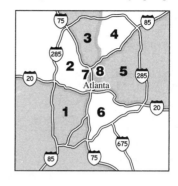

Customers: Everybody comes here, even visiting Hollywood stars; ordinary locals to glitterati

Dinner: Wednesday–Saturday, 5–10 P.M.; Sunday, 5–9 P.M.

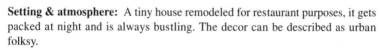

Setting & atmosphere: A tiny house remodeled for restaurant purposes, it gets packed at night and is always bustling. The decor can be described as urban folksy.

House specialties: Fried chicken; duck; Georgia trout; mashed potatoes; crayfish-tail cakes (in season).

Other recommendations: Homemade pies.

Summary & comment: Come hungry, because the portions are huge. This is food like mother used to make, only rarely did she make it this good. Entirely nonsmoking. If you're taking a cab, we suggest you inquire about the fare in advance. It could be quite a long trip.

Honors & awards: *Figaro* magazine, "A Best Restaurant" in Atlanta, 1996.

Hal's

Creole/Continental　　★★★　　**Moderate**

30 Old Ivy Road
(404) 261-0025　　　　　　　Zone 3　Buckhead/Sandy Springs

Reservations: Accepted, recommended
for later in the week and weekends
When to go: Any time, but less crowded
Monday and Tuesday or early
Entree range: $10–21.95
Payment: Major credit cards
Service rating: ★★★
Friendliness rating: ★★
Parking: Valet (except Monday)
Bar: Full service
Wine selection: Heavy on chardonnay
and cabernet sauvignon; many by the
glass
Dress: Nice casual, business, and evening
Disabled access: Yes
Customers: Locals, tourists

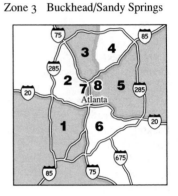

Dinner: Monday–Thursday, 5:30–10:30 P.M.; Friday and Saturday,
5:30–11:30 P.M. (flexible closing).

Setting & atmosphere: Rough-textured brick walls softened by warm lighting,
sconces with pleated glass shades, and comfortably spaced tables all make this a
popular neighborhood spot. Regulars come and go and shout their greetings to
other regulars.

House specialties: Shrimp and crab rémoulade; crab-stuffed trout; snapper
Français; duck à l'orange; bread pudding.

Other recommendations: Soft-shell crab meuniére; specials reflecting owner
Hal Nowak's New Orleans origins.

Entertainment & amenities: Piano music by Charlie Marshall Wednesday–
Saturday.

Summary & comment: There is no separate smoking section. Co-owner and
hostess Janet Walder, a smoker herself, says: "Smokers like to come here and
feel comfortable; they're not made to sit behind the dumpsters if they want to
smoke." Nevertheless, the dining room and bar are not smoke filled, a tribute to
the restaurant's ventilation system. A more casual spot, Hal's Other Place, has
been opened just in front of the restaurant, fronting Roswell Road, and serves
lunch, dinner, and Sunday brunch.

Hashiguchi Japanese Restaurant

Quality	Value
90	B

Japanese/Sushi   ★★★★   **Moderate**

3000 Windy Hill Road, NW
(770) 955-2337   Zone 3   Buckhead/Sandy Springs

3400 Wooddale Drive, NE
(404) 841-9229   Zone 3   Buckhead/Sandy Springs

Reservations: Accepted
When to go: Any time
Entree range: $15–20
Payment: Major credit cards
Service rating: ★★★
Friendliness rating: ★★★★★
Parking: Self
Bar: Beer and wine
Wine selection: Limited
Dress: Nice casual
Disabled access: Yes
Customers: Locals, Japanese

Lunch: *Windy Hill:* Monday–Friday, 11:30 A.M.–2 P.M.; *Wooddale:* Tuesday–Friday, 11:30 A.M.–2 P.M.; Saturday, noon–2:30 P.M.; Sunday, 12:30 P.M. –2:30 P.M.
Dinner: *Windy Hill:* Monday–Thursday, 5:30–10 P.M.; Friday and Saturday, 5:30–10:15 P.M.; *Wooddale:* Tuesday–Thursday, 6–10:30 P.M.; Friday and Saturday, 6–11 P.M.; Sunday, 5–9:30 P.M.

Setting & atmosphere: Simple elegance defines this long-popular Japanese restaurant, a pacesetter in the genre. Private tatami rooms offer seclusion. Children get an especially warm reception, usually the case in Japanese restaurants, but it seems especially loving at Hashiguchi. This is also a good choice when introducing anyone to the pleasures of sushi.

House specialties: Perfectly pristine sushi and sashimi; agedashi (crisply fried tofu); vegetable appetizers.

Other recommendations: Eggplant with bean paste.

Summary & comment: Warm, bright, cheerful, and altogether inviting.

Haveli Indian Restaurant

Quality	Value
90	B

Indian ★★★★ **Inexpensive**

2650 Cobb Parkway, NW
(770) 955-4525   Zone 2   Northwest Atlanta

225 Spring Street, NW
(404) 522-4545   Zone 8   Downtown East

Reservations: Not accepted on weekends
When to go: Any time
Entree range: $8–13; $6.95 (lunch buffet)
Payment: Major credit cards
Service rating: ★★
Friendliness rating: ★★
Parking: Self on *Cobb;* paid parking next door on *Spring*
Bar: Separate with full service
Wine selection: Domestic and imported, with some that go well with the food
Dress: Nice casual
Disabled access: Ramp
Customers: *Cobb:* mostly locals, some Indians; *Spring:* businesspeople and out-of-towners

Lunch: *Cobb:* Monday–Friday, 11:30 A.M.–2:30 P.M.; Saturday, noon–2:30 P.M.; *Spring:* Saturday, noon–3 P.M.
Dinner: *Cobb:* Every day, 5:30–10:30 P.M.; *Spring:* Every day, 5:30–10 P.M.

Setting & atmosphere: Quiet and serene, with light music in the air, the restaurant has become a community fixture, often participating in local restaurant charity events. Its focal point is the Tandoor oven. The Spring location is more utilitarian, serving the busy trade-show crowds from the Merchandise Mart.

House specialties: Tandoori dishes; curries; mango ice cream; saag paneer (sautéed creamy spinach with homemade cheese); chickpea dishes; stuffed breads.

Other recommendations: All vegetable dishes—a major source of inspiration for the vegetarian.

Summary & comment: The buffet lunch, a first-rate value, is a hit with businesspeople working in the area. The dishes are very approachable if you're unfamiliar with Indian food.

Honors & awards: "Best Indian Restaurant," *Atlanta* magazine, 1995.

Hedgerose Heights Inn

American/Continental ★★★★★   **Expensive**

Quality	Value
95	**A**

490 E. Paces Ferry Road, NE
(404) 233-7673

Zone 3   Buckhead/Sandy Springs

Reservations: Recommended
When to go: Weekdays
Entree range: $17–27
Payment: Major credit cards except DISC
Service rating: ★★★★★
Friendliness rating: ★★★★
Parking: Self
Bar: Full service
Wine selection: Extensive, with about a dozen by the glass
Dress: Business attire to dressy; jackets required, ties suggested
Disabled access: Yes
Customers: Well-heeled locals, some out-of-towners

Dinner: Tuesday–Saturday, 6–10:30 P.M.; Sunday and Monday, closed.

Setting & atmosphere: This early 20th-century former residence has been warmly modified to accommodate well-spaced tables. Peach tones alternate with deep green. Subdued, elegant, refined, and formal.

House specialties: Barbecued salmon Asian style; buffalo; foie gras; pheasant; desserts.

Other recommendations: All seafood preparations.

Summary & comment: This is one of the finest restaurants in Atlanta, and many out-of-towners deem it among the finest in the country.

Honors & awards: *Mobil* 4-Star; DiRoNa; frequent "Best of Atlanta" recognitions; Mimi Sheraton's "50 Best Restaurants in U.S.," 1992.

Himalayas

Quality	Value
85	**B**

Indian   ★★★   **Inexpensive**

5520 Peachtree Industrial Boulevard, NE, Chamblee Plaza
(770) 458-6557   Zone 4   Lenox/Chamblee

Reservations: Recommended
When to go: Any time, but the more interesting dishes are served at dinner
Entree range: $6–14
Payment: Major credit cards
Service rating: ★★
Friendliness rating: ★★
Parking: Self, ample
Bar: Good Indian beers
Wine selection: Decent, especially for an Asian restaurant (you can even get a Gewürztraminer—perfect for Indian food)
Dress: Casual
Disabled access: Yes
Customers: Locals

Lunch: Monday–Friday, 11:30 A.M.–2:30 P.M.; Saturday and Sunday, lunch buffet ($6.95), 11:30 A.M.–2:30 P.M.
Dinner: Tuesday–Thursday, 5:30–10 P.M.; Friday–Sunday, 5:30–10:30 P.M.

Setting & atmosphere: The dark, rather spare dining room has small tables and some side booths. Fairly no-frills.

House specialties: Garlic naan and tandoori meats.

Other recommendations: Keema naan (bread stuffed with lamb); onion bhajee (fritters); all manner of curries.

Summary & comment: Very much a neighborhood restaurant with no pretentiousness or claim to greatness. It provides a good evening out that doesn't do damage to the purse.

Honto

Quality	Value
90	A

Chinese   ★★★★   **Inexpensive**

3295 Chamblee-Dunwoody Road
(770) 458-8088   Zone 4   Lenox/Chamblee

Reservations: Required for groups of
8 or more
When to go: Any time
Entree range: $7–19
Payment: Major credit cards
Service rating: ★★★
Friendliness rating: ★★
Parking: Self, adequate
Bar: Beer (Chinese and American)
and wine
Wine selection: Dreadful
Dress: Casual
Disabled access: Yes

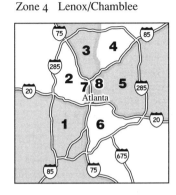

Customers: Lots of enthusiastic Chinese and other Asians, knowledgeable
locals

Lunch: Monday–Thursday, 11:30 A.M.–3 P.M.; Friday and Saturday,
11 A.M.–3 P.M.; Sunday, 11 A.M.–2 P.M.
Dinner: Sunday–Thursday, 3–9:45 P.M.; Friday and Saturday, 3–10:45 P.M.

Setting & atmosphere: The huge dining room doesn't come across as the clean-
est place on the planet. Chalkboards filled with Chinese characters announce the
daily specials to those in the know. You can eat Chinese-American here, but why
come, then? Instead, order from the Chinese menu and let the dishes roll in.

House specialties: Fish and shellfish; noodle and vegetable dishes.

Other recommendations: Salt-and-pepper squid; clams or mussels with black-
bean sauce; dim sum on the weekends.

Summary & comment: This is splendid, authentic Chinese fare at its best.
When four people eat like kings at lunch for under $40 total, you gotta believe
it's a value as well. Never mind the iffy cleanliness or the fractured English.
(Example: "Do you have a wine list handy?" "Wine list candy?" came the
quizzical reply.).

Horseradish Grill

Quality	Value
92	C

Southern ★★★★ **Moderate**

4320 Powers Ferry Road, NW
(404) 255-7277

Zone 3   Buckhead/Sandy Springs

Reservations: No
When to go: Early in any given service shift
Entree range: $15–21
Payment: Major credit cards
Service rating: ★★
Friendliness rating: ★★★
Parking: Valet
Bar: Full service with bar menu
Wine selection: Extensive and reasonably priced, with many good selections by the glass
Dress: Casual but nice to glitter
Disabled access: Excellent

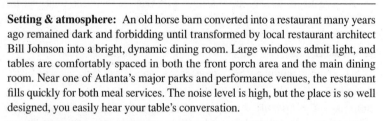

Customers: A young-at-heart crowd, families celebrating special events, locals, and out-of-towners

Brunch: Sunday, 11 A.M.–3 P.M.
Lunch: Monday–Friday, 11:30 A.M.–3 P.M.
Dinner: Monday–Thursday, 5:30–10 P.M.; Friday and Saturday, 5–11 P.M.; Sunday, 5–9 P.M.

Setting & atmosphere: An old horse barn converted into a restaurant many years ago remained dark and forbidding until transformed by local restaurant architect Bill Johnson into a bright, dynamic dining room. Large windows admit light, and tables are comfortably spaced in both the front porch area and the main dining room. Near one of Atlanta's major parks and performance venues, the restaurant fills quickly for both meal services. The noise level is high, but the place is so well designed, you easily hear your table's conversation.

House specialties: Sautéed spicy shrimp paste on grits; peanut-crusted catfish; whole grilled Georgia mountain trout; fried chicken.

Other recommendations: Pecan pie for dessert.

Summary & comment: Founding chefs Scott Peacock and Gerry Klaskala (see Canoe profile) have gone on to other enterprises, but David Berry has demonstrated his ability to continue quality.

Honors & awards: "Best New Restaurant," 1994, *Esquire;* "Best New Restaurant," 1994, *Bon Appétit*; "Best Newcomer," *Atlanta-Journal Constitution,* 1994; Catfish Institute, Nation's Ten Best Catfish Restaurants, 1996.

Hsu's Gourmet Chinese Restaurant

			Quality 90	Value C
Chinese	★★★★	**Moderate**		

192 Peachtree Center Avenue, NE
(404) 659-2788

Zone 7   Downtown West

Reservations: Recommended
When to go: Any time
Entree range: $12–20
Payment: Major credit cards
Service rating: ★★★
Friendliness rating: ★★★
Parking: Nearby parking deck (validated dinner only)
Bar: Separate, with full service
Wine selection: Respectable, with many imported and domestic choices
Dress: Nice casual to business attire
Disabled access: Yes
Customers: Non-Asian locals, out-of-towners

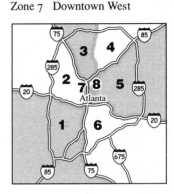

Lunch: Monday–Friday, 11:30 A.M.–4 P.M.; Saturday, noon–4 P.M.
Dinner: Monday–Saturday, 4–11 P.M.; Sunday, 5–10 P.M.

Setting & atmosphere: Straight out of elegant, sophisticated Hong Kong, the restaurant is an oasis of calm and tranquility. Highly composed surroundings showcase art objects. Guests are warmly greeted by Raymond and Anna Hsu (how does she stay so slim and lovely over the years!?).

House specialties: Chinese banquet fare and Hong Kong–style dishes, all elegantly conceived and executed.

Other recommendations: Shrimp or chicken with mango; all shrimp dishes; iceberg lettuce wrapped around seasoned minced pork; ginger ice cream.

Summary & comment: This is a knife-and-fork kind of place, perfect for entertaining a business client who might enjoy the food but is not familiar with using chopsticks and would feel uncomfortable and put down by a host's showing off. Chopsticks are available—they recline on silver rests—but they can easily be ignored as all places are set with knife and fork.

Honors & awards: *Mobil* 3 stars.

Imperial Fez

Quality	Value
90	B

Moroccan ★★★★ **Expensive**

2285 Peachtree Road, NE
(404) 351-0870

Zone 3   Buckhead/Sandy Springs

Reservations: Accepted
When to go: Any time
Entree range: $35 per person for five
courses
Payment: Major credit cards
Service rating: ★★★★
Friendliness rating: ★★★★
Parking: Self; valet on weekends
Bar: Full service
Wine selection: Wide ranging, includ-
ing some from North Africa, with
many by the glass

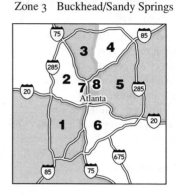

Dress: Dressy casual to business attire
Disabled access: Yes
Customers: Locals and occasional out-of-towners

Dinner: Every day, 6–11 P.M.

Setting & atmosphere: Inside the door, enter an exotic world filled with exciting aromas and sights. Park your shoes and your business cares at the front door.
You'll recline on soft cushions and be presented with warm, scented water to
wash your hands.

House specialties: Harrira (cumin-scented lentil soup); couscous; b'stella (cin-
namon-flavored pastry wrapped around Cornish hen); vegetarian dishes available every day.

Other recommendations: Dietary requirements can be handled with advance
notice. The way this works is the patron chooses a meat to top the couscous, then
soup, appetizer, salad, and dessert are part of the dinner. Thus, you might choose
lamb or chicken to top your couscous, or vegetables (a very Moroccan selection).

Entertainment & amenities: Traditional Moroccan dancing every night.

Summary & comment: Ladies may want to wear long skirts or pants to make
sitting on cushions more relaxing.

Honors & awards: Recognized by the Chaine des Rotisseurs; "Best of
Atlanta," *Creative Loafing,* 1995.

Kamogawa

Quality	Value
96	C

Japanese/Sushi   ★★★★★   **Expensive**

Hotel Nikko, 3300 Peachtree Road, NE
(404) 841-0314   Zone 3   Buckhead/Sandy Springs

Reservations: Recommended
When to go: Any time
Entree range: $17–25
Payment: Major credit cards except
DISC
Service rating: ★★★★★
Friendliness rating: ★★★★
Parking: Valet (free with validation),
self
Bar: Full service
Wine selection: Extensive and chiefly
California, with about a dozen by the
glass
Dress: Business attire to very formal
Disabled access: Yes

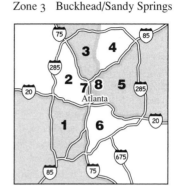

Customers: Japanese clientele, internationals, knowledgeable locals

Lunch: Monday–Friday, 11:30 A.M.–2 P.M.
Dinner: Sunday–Thursday, 6–10 P.M.; Friday and Saturday, 6–10:30 P.M.

Setting & atmosphere: Elegant, serene, formal, and exalted, Kamogawa is the place visiting Japanese businessmen choose when entertaining local guests. Guests' shoes wait patiently outside the tatami rooms until dinner is concluded. For authenticity, it's Kamogawa.

House specialties: Kaiseki Banquet (with three days' advance notice preferred); sushi and sashimi.

Other recommendations: Soft-shell crab appetizer.

Summary & comment: No one could argue with the quality or the authenticity of Kamogawa. There's no steak ceremony here, with knives tossed perilously in the air. What you do get is the pure, simple classicism of Japanese cooking at its finest.

Honors & awards: One of the critic's top 10 restaurants, *Atlanta-Journal Constitution,* 1995.

La Grotta Ristorante

Italian ★★★★★ **Expensive**

Quality	Value
98	C

2637 Peachtree Road, NE
(404) 231-1368   Zone 3   Buckhead/Sandy Springs
Ravinia Crowne Plaza Hotel, 4355 Ashford-Dunwoody Road
(770) 395-9925   Zone 4   Lenox/Chamblee

Reservations: Essential
When to go: Any time
Entree range: $16–27
Payment: Major credit cards
Service rating: ★★★★★
Friendliness rating: ★★★★★
Parking: Validated valet or self at
Ravinia; valet only at *Buckhead*
Bar: Separate with full service and
after-dinner drink list at *Buckhead;* no
separate bar, but full service at *Ravinia*
Wine selection: Extensive and well
selected, from California, Italian, and French
Dress: Business attire to black tie
Disabled access: Excellent, via elevator to the lower level
Customers: Sophisticated locals, glitterati, politicians, and folks who enjoy
good food and wine

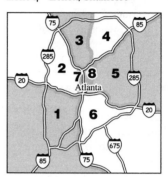

Lunch: *Ravinia:* Monday–Friday, 11:30 A.M.–2 P.M.
Dinner: *Buckhead:* Monday–Saturday, 6–10:30 P.M.; *Ravinia:* Monday–
Saturday, 5:45–10 P.M.

Setting & atmosphere: Elegant, warmly lit, quiet, and refined, La Grotta in
Buckhead demands respect, but does so without intimidating. At Ravinia, the
atmosphere is contemporary, with floor-to-ceiling glass overlooking a lush garden. Tables are well spaced, conversation easily enjoyed, and the space is very
good for business dining. This outfit also handles banquets especially well.

House specialties: Beautiful veal, seafood, and fresh pasta dishes with traditional sauces have ensured this landmark restaurant its happy repeat clientele.
Eggplant Napoleon (lunch) and Veal Mediterraneano (lunch menu and appetizer
at dinner) at Ravinia. Tiramisù.

Summary & comment: The two restaurants are very different in both atmosphere and menu, but both deliver. The original La Grotta on Peachtree Road is
old world, sophisticated, and long on attentive, correct service. The Dunwoody
La Grotta is more casual, more fun, and serves food that tastes like it comes from
the trattoria tradition.

Honors & awards: AAA 4-Diamond, 1994–1996; "Best of Atlanta," *Atlanta*
magazine, 13 years in a row.

Le Giverny

Quality	Value
85	C

French Bistro   ★★   **Moderate**

1355 Clairmont Road, Decatur
(404) 325-7252

Zone 5   Northeast Atlanta

Reservations: Accepted
When to go: Any time, although the
dinner menu is more interesting
Entree range: $10–18
Payment: Major credit cards
Service rating: ★★★★
Friendliness rating: ★★★
Parking: Self
Bar: Beer and wine only
Wine selection: French and American;
good selections appropriately priced,
with about half the list available by the
glass
Dress: Casual

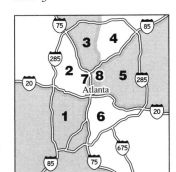

Disabled access: Through the rear of the building
Customers: Locals, especially retirees at lunch; a younger, more hip crowd
from the neighboring academic community at dinner

Lunch: Monday–Friday, 11:30 A.M.–2 P.M.
Dinner: Monday–Saturday, 5:30–10 P.M.

Setting & atmosphere: A small spot in a neighborhood strip center, Le Giverny
offers an intimate, white-linen, simple spot that is never intimidating. Posters of
Monet's work on the walls link the theme of the restaurant back to its name.
Table conversation is easy, because the noise level is very subdued.

House specialties: Boeuf bourguignonne on linguine; homemade country pâté;
fresh fish and steak dishes; chocolate pâté.

Other recommendations: Specials like sea bass and mussels on linguine in a
light cream–white wine sauce.

Summary & comment: Frenchman Rémy Kerba and his Bulgarian wife
Milena own and operate the place, so it has a definite family feel. Steady, visible
improvements in the food and its presentation have marked this neighborhood
restaurant from its earliest days. Three-course, fixed-price menus range from
$18–27; they are very good deals indeed.

Little Szechuan

Quality 95	Value A

Chinese/Szechuan ★★★★ Inexpensive

5091-C Buford Highway, NE, Northwoods Plaza
(770) 451-0192 Zone 4 Lenox/Chamblee

Reservations: Accepted for groups of
6 or more only
When to go: Any time
Entree range: $6–20
Payment: VISA, MC, D
Service rating: ★★★★
Friendliness rating: ★★★★
Parking: Self
Bar: Beer (wonderful Chinese beers)
and wine only
Wine selection: Dreadful
Dress: Casual
Disabled access: Yes

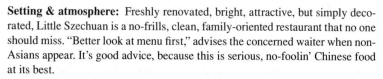

Customers: Loads of Chinese families and adventurous Occidentals

Lunch: Monday, Wednesday–Saturday, 11:30 A.M.–3 P.M.; Sunday, noon–3 P.M.
Dinner: Monday, Wednesday–Sunday, 5–9:30 P.M.; Tuesday, closed.

Setting & atmosphere: Freshly renovated, bright, attractive, but simply decorated, Little Szechuan is a no-frills, clean, family-oriented restaurant that no one should miss. "Better look at menu first," advises the concerned waiter when non-Asians appear. It's good advice, because this is serious, no-foolin' Chinese food at its best.

House specialties: String beans; shrimp egg foo yung; kung pao squid; sautéed spinach; shrimp with young garlic.

Other recommendations: For the adventurous, pig tripe soup and chicken neck stuffed with minced pork.

Summary & comment: No egg rolls or fortune cookies here. Lunch specials are very inexpensive and outstanding.

Honors & awards: Many recognitions in local press, including local Chinese language press.

Luna Sí

Quality	Value
90	B

American/Mediterranean ★★★★   **Moderate**

1931 Peachtree Road, NE, Brookwood Village Shopping Center
(404) 355-5993   Zone 3   Buckhead, Sandy Springs

Reservations: Accepted
When to go: Any time
Entree range: $15–18
Payment: Major credit cards
Service rating: ★★★★
Friendliness rating: ★★★★★
Parking: Self in back
Bar: Separate with full service
Wine selection: Extensive and well priced, with many good ones by the glass
Dress: Nice casual
Disabled access: Yes
Customers: Neighbors enjoying a really good value dining experience

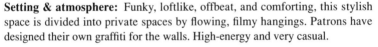

Dinner: Every day, 5:30–10:30 P.M.

Setting & atmosphere: Funky, loftlike, offbeat, and comforting, this stylish space is divided into private spaces by flowing, filmy hangings. Patrons have designed their own graffiti for the walls. High-energy and very casual.

House specialties: Salmon with ginger crust, cucumber, and citrus; foie gras; fresh pastas; roasted Cornish hen with mashed potatoes and tarragon.

Other recommendations: Daily risotto; meat and fish are always something unusual and tempting. Ask about the tasting menu.

Summary & comment: Multicourse dinners (choice of two or three courses) at fixed prices are especially inexpensive (given their quality) and popular. The tasting menu is an experience requiring some time.

Honors & awards: Lots of kudos from local press, including "Best Risotto," *Atlanta-Journal Constitution,* 1996.

Mary Mac's Tea Room

Quality	Value
90	A

Southern   ★★★   **Inexpensive**

224 Ponce de Leon Avenue, NE
(404) 876-1800   Zone 8   Downtown East

Reservations: No (for parties of 10 or
more if space permits)
When to go: For lunch, early or
between 2–5 P.M.; after 8 P.M. Mondays
are fairly slow
Entree range: $5–13
Payment: Cash or check (out-of-town
checks OK with ID)
Service rating: ★★★★★
Friendliness rating: ★★★★★
Parking: Self
Bar: Separate with full service
Wine selection: Limited, with some Georgia wineries represented
Dress: Casual
Disabled access: Excellent
Customers: Out-of-towners, celebrities, politicians (especially when the legis-
lature is in session), students from nearby colleges, business types. This is a
universally appealing Atlanta institution

Breakfast: Saturday and Sunday, 9–noon.
Lunch: Monday–Saturday, 11 A.M.–5 P.M.; Sunday, 11 A.M.–3 P.M.
Dinner: Monday–Saturday 5–9 P.M.; Sunday, closed.

Setting & atmosphere: Bright, lively, and down-home casual, the dining room
has a drill for ordering that's ages old: Pick up a pencil and fill out your form. A
waitress will call you "honey" or maybe "sugar" and take the form, returning
promptly with your plate laden with huge portions. Politicians love this place; it's
also a power lunch spot when the legislature's in session.

House specialties: Fried chicken; cornbread dressing and gravy; vegetables
(sweet potato soufflé, greens); peach cobbler. Menu changes daily.

Other recommendations: Chicken pan pie.

Entertainment & amenities: Piano does light classics, standards, and jazz in
the evenings.

Summary & comment: Now more than 50 years old, Mary Mac's is an Atlanta
institution. In the middle of the sophisticated urban setting, the visitor immediately senses what Southern hospitality and food are all about. One visit does it
all.

Mi Spia

Quality	Value
88	C

Italian/California ★★★ **Moderate**

4505 Ashford-Dunwoody Road, Park Place, Dunwoody
(770) 393-1333 Zone 4 Lenox/Chamblee

Reservations: Accepted
When to go: Any time
Entree range: $12–22
Payment: Major credit cards
Service rating: ★★★
Friendliness rating: ★★
Parking: Tight during busy hours
Bar: Full service
Wine selection: Extensive, lots of California and Italian, with good ones by the glass
Dress: Casual nice
Disabled access: Yes

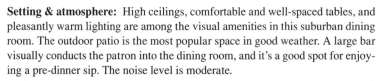

Customers: At lunch, businesspeople from the surrounding offices; at dinner, businesspeople, neighbors from area residential developments

Lunch: Monday–Friday, 11:30 A.M.–2:30 P.M.
Dinner: Sunday–Thursday, 5–10 P.M.; Friday and Saturday, 5–11 P.M.

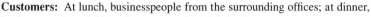

Setting & atmosphere: High ceilings, comfortable and well-spaced tables, and pleasantly warm lighting are among the visual amenities in this suburban dining room. The outdoor patio is the most popular space in good weather. A large bar visually conducts the patron into the dining room, and it's a good spot for enjoying a pre-dinner sip. The noise level is moderate.

House specialties: Veal scallopini; salmon with honey balsamic glaze; saffron fettuccine.

Other recommendations: Swordfish on white beans with Swiss chard and pancetta.

Summary & comment: Outdoor dining in nice weather makes this a real break from work for nearby office workers. The rich, faux-Tuscan interior throws off appealing, warm tones, making everyone look wonderful. This one is handy for unwinding after a shopping spree at nearby Perimeter Mall.

Nava

Quality	Value
88	D

Southwesterm   ★★★   **Expensive**

3060 Peachtree Road, NW, Buckhead Plaza
(404) 240-1984   Zone 3   Buckhead/Sandy Springs

Reservations: Accepted
When to go: Early or late
Entree range: $15–25
Payment: Major credit cards
Service rating: ★★★
Friendliness rating: ★★
Parking: Valet
Bar: Separate with full service
Wine selection: Extensive, mostly American, with some good by-the-glass offerings
Dress: Nice to dressy casual and business attire
Disabled access: Yes
Customers: Glitzy denizens of Buckhead, media types and film stars, out-of-towners

Lunch: Monday–Friday, 11:30 A.M.–2:30 P.M.
Dinner: Monday–Thursday, 5:30–11 P.M.; Friday and Saturday, 5:30 P.M.–midnight; Sunday, 5:30–10 P.M.

Setting & atmosphere: A fortune has been spent transforming this interior into a treasure trove of Southwestern American art, complete with kachina dolls in every nook.

House specialties: Corn-crusted snapper; masa chicken soup; yellowfin tuna; pork tenderloin with poblano peppers and tamarind glaze; grilled flank steak fajitas.

Other recommendations: Green chile masa taco; grilled vegetable quesadilla.

Summary & comment: Appetizers are the most interesting dishes at this multilevel, show-stopping restaurant. That makes it easy to assemble a lunch of light treats, combining, for instance, soup and quesadilla or salad.

Honors & awards: *Esquire* magazine, one of top 10 new restaurants, 1996.

Nicola's Restaurant

Quality	Value
85	B

Middle Eastern ★★★ **Inexpensive**

1602 LaVista Road, NE
(404) 325-2524   Zone 5   Northeast Atlanta

Reservations: Accepted
When to go: Any time
Entree range: $9–11
Payment: Major credit cards
Service rating: ★★★★
Friendliness rating: ★★★★
Parking: Self
Bar: Beer and wine only
Wine selection: House wine only
(French)
Dress: Casual
Disabled access: Ramped
Customers: Locals, mostly Americans

Dinner: Every day, 5:30–10:30 P.M.

Setting & atmosphere: Located in an unspectacular building and offering a no-frills interior with plain tablecloths and little decor, Nicola's doesn't go for pretense. Good food is the focus.

House specialties: Lamb shank; meza (a platter of salads and appetizers); shawarma (shredded lamb).

Other recommendations: Kibbeh (kibbeh nayee—the raw lamb version—on the weekends); stuffed grape leaves.

Summary & comment: The no-frills, value-packed dining attracts the residents of nearby middle-class neighborhoods. The staff works hard to please.

Old South Barbecue

<table>
<tr><td>Quality</td><td>Value</td></tr>
<tr><td>95</td><td>B</td></tr>
</table>

Barbecue ★★★★ **Inexpensive**

601 Burbank Circle, Smyrna
(770) 435-4215

Zone 2 Northwest Atlanta

Reservations: No
When to go: This one gets justifiably crowded, so aim for early or late
Entree range: $6–8
Payment: VISA and MC
Service rating: ★★★★
Friendliness rating: ★★★★
Parking: Ample
Bar: None
Wine selection: None
Dress: As casual as you wish
Disabled access: Good
Customers: Good ole folks, families, plenty of regulars

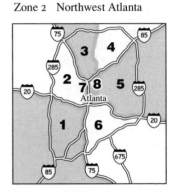

Lunch & Dinner: Tuesday–Sunday, 11 A.M.–9:30 P.M.; Monday, closed.

Setting & atmosphere: A rustic, freestanding building in the heart of bustling east Cobb County, the place is strictly no-frills. But who cares? Traditional food this good is getting real rare.

House specialties: Brunswick stew; sweet-tart cole slaw; ribs.

Other recommendations: Sliced or chopped pork sandwiches.

Summary & comment: Barbecue joints come and go, but this one deserves to outlast the planet.

Honors & awards: "Best Barbecue of Cobb," *Inside Cobb* magazine, 1995.

Palisades

Quality	Value
85	C

American/Continental   ★★★   **Moderate**

1829 Peachtree Road, NE
(404) 350-6755   Zone 3   Buckhead/Sandy Springs

Reservations: Required
When to go: Any time
Entree range: $11–26
Payment: Major credit cards
Service rating: ★★
Friendliness rating: ★★★
Parking: Self, behind restaurant
Bar: Separate with full service
Wine selection: California, French,
and Italian, with about 10 by the glass
Dress: Nice casual
Disabled access: Yes, front entrance
Customers: Residents of surrounding
upscale neighborhoods

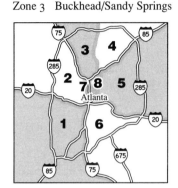

Dinner: Sunday–Thursday, 5:30–10 P.M.; Friday and Saturday, 5:30–11 P.M.

Setting & atmosphere: Warm lighting, tempered noise levels, and comfortably spaced tables fill this corner of a 1920s commercial strip. Exposed-brick walls lend texture to this casual neighborhood bistro.

House specialties: Mussels; risotto with shrimp; veal Milanese; crisp duck with sweet potato pancakes and fresh spinach melds the flavors.

Other recommendations: A three-course, fixed-price menu is offered Sunday through Thursday. Crème brûlée is splendid: a thin, light custard lies in a soup dish under a crust of melted sugar. One of the city's best.

Summary & comment: Palisades almost gets overlooked as critics and out-of-towners crowd the gourmet glitz palaces of Buckhead. But this comfortable neighborhood restaurant does itself proud, and the nearby residents treasure it.

Pano's & Paul's

Quality	Value
94	C

Continental   ★★★★   **Expensive**

1232 W. Paces Ferry Road, NW
(404) 261-3662   Zone 3   Buckhead/Sandy Springs

Reservations: Essential
When to go: Any time
Entree range: $17–34
Payment: Major credit cards
Service rating: ★★★★★
Friendliness rating: ★★★★★
Parking: Self
Bar: Separate with lounge and full service
Wine selection: Extensive, ranging across the wine-growing regions of the world, with about a dozen good ones by the glass
Dress: Suits, silk dresses, and glitter
Disabled access: Easy
Customers: The well-heeled, both out-of-towners and locals, Old Atlanta

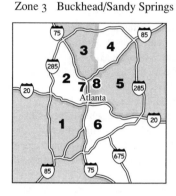

Dinner: Monday–Friday, 6–11 P.M.; Saturday, 5:30–11 P.M.; cocktails available at 5 P.M.; Sunday, closed.

Setting & atmosphere: Heavy use of fabrics creates an opulent atmosphere and tempers noise, making this one spectacular for romantic purposes. Many a question has been popped in the semicurtained banquettes along the side.

House specialties: Foie gras; soft-shell crab and pheasant any way Paul Albrecht chooses to prepare them; cold jumbo lobster tail fried in a light batter with Chinese honey mustard is a house standard from the beginning.

Other recommendations: Lemon-roasted chicken with crisp celery-potato cake; sautéed gulf red snapper fillet; lobster bisque.

Entertainment & amenities: Piano playing light classics and popular music, Friday and Saturday evenings.

Summary & comment: A classic, grand, old restaurant, the place hides an opulent, baroque interior behind a plain strip-mall exterior. Be neither alarmed nor confused; this is luxury at its zenith.

Honors & awards: *Wine Spectator* award for the wine list, 1996; one of Atlanta's ten best continental restaurants by many publications; frequent DiRoNa winner.

Papa Pirozki's

Quality	Value
88	C

Continental/Russian ★★★   **Expensive**

1447 Peachtree Road, NE
(404) 815-0100   Zone 3   Buckhead/Sandy Springs

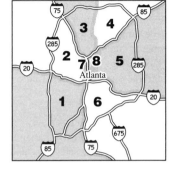

Reservations: Accepted
When to go: Any time
Entree range: $13–25
Payment: Major credit cards
Service rating: ★★★★
Friendliness rating: ★★★
Parking: Valet
Bar: Separate bar with full service and bar menu
Wine selection: Extensive, mostly California with some French; about 10 good ones by the glass
Dress: Business attire to nice casual
Disabled access: Elevator
Customers: Business patrons from surrounding office towers at lunch; business and romantic diners at dinner

Lunch: Monday–Friday, 11:30 A.M.–3 P.M.
Dinner: Monday–Saturday, 5:30–10:30 P.M.

Setting & atmosphere: The restaurant's crisp, modern design reflects nothing of czarist opulence, but what the heck. Tables are well spaced, and the noise level is low—a welcome relief from many high-din establishments.

House specialties: Caviar; pirozkis; lamb; lobster Alexandra.

Other recommendations: Choose chilled vodka with caviar, not the recommended California sparkler. Caviar service covers the range from fine Russian Beluga to golden whitefish—a unique experience.

Summary & comment: After a disastrous fire destroyed its original location, this phoenix has arisen with vigor and renewed style. Applause.

Pricci

Quality	Value
90	C

Italian　　　　★★★★　　　　**Moderate**

---

500 Pharr Road, NW
(404) 237-2941

Zone 3　Buckhead/Sandy Springs

Reservations: Accepted
When to go: Any time
Entree range: $12–25
Payment: Major credit cards
Service rating: ★★★
Friendliness rating: ★★★ (more if you're known)
Parking: Valet
Bar: Separate with full service
Wine selection: Extensive Italian list with some California selections, and many good wines by the glass
Dress: Nice, dressy casual
Disabled access: Yes
Customers: Locals, upscale residents of Buckhead

Lunch: Monday–Friday, 11 A.M.–5 P.M.
Dinner: Monday–Thursday, 5–11 P.M.; Friday and Saturday, 5 P.M.–midnight; Sunday, 5–10 P.M.

Setting & atmosphere: Patrick Kuleto (designer of sleek San Francisco establishments) did both the Buckhead Diner and this toney emporium of Italian cooking. Sleek lines and shiny surfaces don't temper the noise level, which creates the high-energy feeling the restaurant imparts.

House specialties: The daily risotto special; all seafood dishes; pastas (homemade veal agnolotti, especially); veal dishes.

Other recommendations: Scallop and spinach risotto (may be requested ahead); sea bass in parchment paper with vegetables; caciucco alla toscana (seafood stew in tomato broth).

Summary & comment: Pricci can be very diet sensitive if you request lightly prepared food. Chef John Carver operates with a definite Italian soul.

Honors & awards: *Esquire* magazine, "Best New Restaurant," 1992.

Purple Cactus Cafe

Quality	Value
85	B

Southwestern   ★★   **Inexpensive**

2142 Johnson Ferry Road
(770) 454-1050   Zone 4   Lenox/Chamblee

Reservations: For parties of 6 or more
When to go: Any time
Entree range: $8–13
Payment: Major credit cards, except
DISC and DC
Service rating: ★★★
Friendliness rating: ★★★
Parking: Valet and self
Bar: Beer and wine only
Wine selection: Modest but well
selected, with most by the glass
Dress: Scruffy to nice casual
Disabled access: Easy, especially for
the outdoor seating

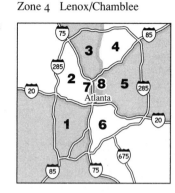

Customers: Neighbors, but out-of-towners are beginning to discover the place

Lunch: Monday–Friday, 11 A.M.–2 P.M.
Lunch & Dinner: Saturday, noon–11 P.M.
Dinner: Monday–Thursday, 5–10 P.M.; Friday, 5–11 P.M.

Setting & atmosphere: Lots of outdoor seating, a sheltered patio area, slightly makeshift but comfortable—the ideal atmosphere in a restaurant done on shoe-string.

House specialties: Chili-rubbed grilled shrimp with chutney; good guacamole; black-bean pancake; poppers (cheese-stuffed jalapeño peppers).

Other recommendations: Tropical Taco Salad, with chili-rubbed chicken breast strips and kiwi-mango chutney.

Entertainment & amenities: Blues on Wednesday and Saturday.

Summary & comment: It's been fun to watch the dynamic evolution of this neighborhood restaurant. The big boys need to watch out: here come the kids from the neighborhood.

Honors & awards: *Creative Loafing,* "Top 10 Restaurants," writers' picks, 1995.

R. Thomas Deluxe Grill

Quality	Value
85	C

American   ★★★   Inexpensive

1812 Peachtree Street, NW
(404) 881-0246
(404) 872-2942

Zone 3   Buckhead/Sandy Springs

Reservations: No
When to go: Any time, but it's very
popular for lunch and late at night
Entree range: $6–12
Payment: Major credit cards
Service rating: ★★
Friendliness rating: ★★
Parking: Self behind building
Bar: Beer and wine
Wine selection: Limited
Dress: Scruffy to nice casual
Disabled access: Yes, seating is on
outdoor sheltered space

Customers: Business types at lunch, lots of locals 'round the clock

Open: Every day, 24 hours.

Setting & atmosphere: A heated outdoor cafe with a 24-hour juice bar and a relaxed ambience, it's popular for brunch on Sunday.

House specialties: Omelets; huge burgers; stuffed baked potatoes; malteds.

Other recommendations: Breakfast dishes of all kinds; Bloody Marys with saké; all grilled items.

Summary & comment: This is a good spot to bring the kids, who enjoy burgers, salads, and malteds. The staff can ignore single diners, spending more time on large parties—a real annoyance.

The Restaurant, Ritz-Carlton, Atlanta

	Quality	Value
	90	**C**

Continental   ★★★★   **Expensive**

Ritz-Carlton Hotel Atlanta, 181 Peachtree Street, NE
(404) 659-0400, ext. 6450   Zone 8   Downtown East

Reservations: Recommended
When to go: Any time
Entree range: $26–33
Payment: Major credit cards
Service rating: ★★★★★
Friendliness rating: ★★★★
Parking: Valet
Bar: Separate with full service and bar
menu
Wine selection: Extensive with many
first-rate offerings by the glass and
flights designed to accompany specific
dishes for the tasting menu
Dress: Dressy to glitter
Disabled access: Elevator
Customers: Out-of-towners, local business regulars

Dinner: Monday–Saturday, 6–10 P.M.; Sunday, closed.

Setting & atmosphere: Hunt-themed art, both paintings and sculptures, creates a formal, but not stuffy, club setting. Waiters are in black tie, so the formality level is high.

House specialties: Foie gras; game; fish; dessert soufflées.

Other recommendations: Four-course tasting menu.

Entertainment & amenities: Jazz trio in the bar, with occasional solo vocalist on Friday afternoon.

Summary & comment: A serious power spot, serving serious food, sometimes with an Alsace touch as the chef, Daniel Schaffauser, hails from that part of France.

Honors & awards: AAA 4-Diamond; *Mobil* 4-Star; *Zagat Atlanta, Wine Spectator,* and *Food and Wine* magazine have all weighed in with honors.

The Rib Ranch

Quality	Value
85	B

Barbecue   ★★★   **Inexpensive**

---

25 Irby Avenue, NW
(404) 233-7644   Zone 3   Buckhead/Sandy Springs

Reservations: No
When to go: Any time
Entree range: $4–26
Payment: MC, VISA
Service rating: ★★★
Friendliness rating: ★★
Parking: Self across the street
Bar: Beer only, long necks, no draught
Wine selection: None
Dress: Scruffy casual to business attire
Disabled access: Ramp to the front, but
tables are tightly packed
Customers: Locals

Lunch & Dinner: Monday–Saturday, 11 A.M.–11 P.M., Sunday,
11:30 A.M.–10 P.M.

Setting & atmosphere: A shack that hums with activity in the middle of sophisticated Buckhead brings to the urbane serious barbecue Texas style. Don't glitter in here. Elbows on the table? That's manners at the Rib Ranch.

House specialties: Baby-back ribs; beef ribs; beans (all side dishes are made from scratch).

Other recommendations: Grilled smoked chicken.

Summary & comment: The huge plate of Texas-style beef ribs will easily feed two hungry honchos. Fries are about the only thing that's not done from scratch.

Honors & awards: Lots of kudos in the local press.

Riviera

Quality	Value
90	**D**

French Provençal　　★★★★　　**Expensive**

---

519 E. Paces Ferry Road, NE
(404) 262-7112　　　　　　　Zone 3　Buckhead/Sandy Springs

Reservations: Accepted
When to go: Any time
Entree range: $20–32
Payment: Major credit cards
Service rating: ★★★★
Friendliness rating: ★★★
Parking: Valet
Bar: Separate with full service
Wine selection: Extensive and mostly
French, with some good choices by the
glass; very pricey reserve list
Dress: Nice casual to business attire
Disabled access: Yes
Customers: Groups of friends, locals, romantic couples

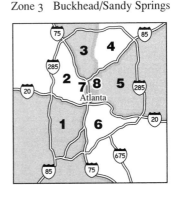

Dinner: Monday–Thursday, 6–9:30 P.M.; Friday and Saturday, 5:30–10 P.M.

Setting & atmosphere: Atlanta restaurant designer Bill Johnson completely reshaped this residence-turned-restaurant, a building that had seen far too many kitchens come and go and was decidedly tired within. Now bright with good lighting and trimmed in white, the interior actually welcomes its role as a restaurant rather than being uncomfortable with it.

House specialties: Foie gras; sweetbreads; venison in season; brandade de morue (creamed salted cod); crème brûlée.

Other recommendations: Any specials, because owner/chef Jean Banchet operates seasonally, so specials take advantage of the freshest ingredients in the marketplace.

Summary & comment: Some appetizers seemed horrendously overpriced, such as the sweetbreads for $19.95. If money is no object, the pricey reserve wine list might demand your attention. Then you, too, can have the honor of spending more than $1,000 on a Château Pétrus. If you hold on to your money clip, you can dine reasonably and very well, indeed.

South City Kitchen

Quality	Value
95	**C**

Southern ★★★★ **Moderate**

1144 Crescent Avenue, NW
(404) 873-7358

Zone 8   Downtown East

Reservations: Accepted: lunch, parties of 6 or more; dinner, all size parties
When to go: Early
Entree range: $8–22
Payment: Major credit cards
Service rating: ★★★★
Friendliness rating: ★★★★
Parking: Some in the back, on street, nearby paid lot; valet, Wednesday–Saturday evenings
Bar: Separate with full service
Wine selection: Extensive and excellent, American selections with many good ones by the glass
Dress: Jeans casual to business attire
Disabled access: No to the interior; yes for patio dining in good weather, but rest room access is impossible
Customers: Business patrons at lunch, locals in casual duds for brunch, all kinds at dinner

Brunch: Sunday, 11 A.M.–4 P.M.
Lunch & Dinner: Monday–Thursday, 11 A.M.–11 P.M.; Friday and Saturday, 11 A.M.–midnight; Sunday, 5–11 P.M.

Setting & atmosphere: The clean, bare surfaces do nothing to mitigate the noise level, so be prepared to endure a fair amount of high-energy atmosphere. A lot of work went into rescuing this former Midtown residence, whose walls are adorned with art from a local gallery.

House specialties: Crab cakes; barbecued swordfish; chocolate pecan pie.

Other recommendations: Crab hash; lamb; she-crab soup; catfish Reuben (lunch).

Summary & comment: Initial ups and downs have been replaced by sure hands in the kitchen. Consistency is more common than once was the case, and the spark to most of the dishes is supplied by the tang of Southern cooking, much of it from the coast.

Stringer's Fish Camp

Quality	Value
85	**C**

Seafood   ★★★   **Inexpensive**

3384 Shallowford Road, NE
(770) 458-7145

Zone 4   Lenox/Chamblee

Reservations: Accepted for parties of
8 or more
When to go: Any time
Entree range: $11–15
Payment: MC, VISA
Service rating: ★★★
Friendliness rating: ★★★
Parking: Self
Bar: Beer and wine
Wine selection: Unexciting and
limited
Dress: Scruffy casual
Disabled access: Yes
Customers: Locals (usually colorful)

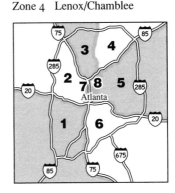

Lunch & Dinner: Monday–Thursday, 11 A.M.–9 P.M.; Friday, 11 A.M.–
10 P.M.; Saturday, noon–10 P.M.; Sunday, noon–9 P.M.

Setting & atmosphere: Feeling like a true fish camp, Stringer's takes the prize
for preserving a Southern waterfront atmosphere.

House specialties: Gumbo; fried seafood and fish, soft-shell crabs; oysters.

Other recommendations: Spicy corn salad; homemade hush puppies.

Summary & comment: The entertainment is provided by the colorful types
that frequent the place. The windows covered with scrawl announce specials.
They boast such fare as "Oysters served fried, nude, and stewed." Unpretentious
food in huge quantities is what draws everyone to Stringer's.

Sukhothai

Quality	Value
85	B

Thai ★★★ **Inexpensive**

1995 Windy Hill Road, Suite K, Windy Hill West Shopping Center
(770) 434-9276   Zone 2   Northwest Atlanta

Reservations: Accepted
When to go: Any time
Entree range: $7–18
Payment: Major credit cards
Service rating: ★★
Friendliness rating: ★
Parking: Self
Bar: Separate with full service
Wine selection: Decent, with some
wines that will complement the food,
but only a few by the glass
Dress: Nice casual
Disabled access: Yes
Customers: Locals, mostly Americans

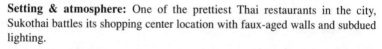

Lunch: Monday–Friday, 11:30 A.M.–2:30 P.M.
Dinner: Monday–Thursday, 6–10 P.M.; Friday and Saturday, 5:30–11 P.M.;
Sunday, 5:30–9:30 P.M.

Setting & atmosphere: One of the prettiest Thai restaurants in the city, Sukothai battles its shopping center location with faux-aged walls and subdued lighting.

House specialties: Larb (spicy mint and meat salad); pad thai; Tom Yum and Tom Kha soups; Sukhothai Salad (shrimp, squid, lettuce, and spicy lime dressing).

Other recommendations: All curries.

Summary & comment: The owners have opened Siam Palace, a new Thai restaurant on Piedmont Road, in Peachtree Piedmont Crossing Shopping Center. For more information call (404) 812-9110. It's worth looking out for.

Sundown Cafe

Quality	Value
93	C

Southwestern ★★★★ **Moderate**

2165 Cheshire Bridge Road, NE
(404) 321-1118   Zone 5   Northeast Atlanta

Reservations: No
When to go: Early
Entree range: $8–14
Payment: Major credit cards except
DISC
Service rating: ★★★★
Friendliness rating: ★★★★★
Parking: Self
Bar: Separate with full service
Wine selection: Moderately limited
Dress: Nice casual
Disabled access: Yes, with ramp
Customers: Mostly locals

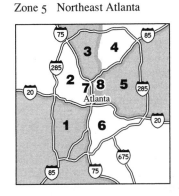

Lunch: Monday–Friday, 11 A.M.–2 P.M. (taquería)
Dinner: Monday–Thursday, 5:30–10 P.M.; Friday and Saturday,
5:30–11 P.M.

Setting & atmosphere: The clever, faux-stucco interior makes you feel like you just took a short plane ride to the American Southwest.

House specialties: Handmade tortillas; about 15 homemade salsas; green chile stew; wonderful turnip greens; divine chocolate chimichanga with tequila sauce.

Other recommendations: Specials include crab cakes, margaritas, and mashed ancho potatoes with jalapeño gravy (divine with Eddie's Pork).

Summary & comment: The lunch-time taquería was one of the first in Atlanta, starting a craze that shows no signs of abating.

Honors & awards: *Creative Loafing,* "Best Southwestern," 1995.

A Taste of New Orleans

Quality	Value
95	C

Cajun & Creole　　　★★★★　　　**Moderate**

---

889 W. Peachtree Street, NW
(404) 874-5535

Zone 8　Downtown East

Reservations: Required
When to go: Any time
Entree range: $9–18
Payment: Major credit cards
Service rating: ★★★★
Friendliness rating: ★★★★
Parking: Self
Bar: Separate with beer and wine only
Wine selection: Extensive, mostly
California with a good selection by the
glass
Dress: Casual
Disabled access: Yes
Customers: Locals, a few smart tourists

Lunch: Monday–Friday, 11:30 A.M.–2 P.M.
Dinner: Monday–Thursday, 6–10 P.M.; Friday and Saturday, 5:30–11 P.M.

Setting & atmosphere: Small, dimly lit, and intimate, this is a mecca for anyone looking for properly prepared Creole and Cajun classics. The sound system plays good music at lunch. Moderately noisy.

House specialties: Soft-shell crab in season; seafood cakes; gumbo; all the classics of Creole cooking; jambalaya (lunch); bread pudding.

Other recommendations: Cajun cordon bleu.

Summary & comment: Nobody dislikes this restaurant. The soft-shells are the biggest on the planet, but still delicious and succulent. The tables are tightly composed, but the restaurant still is relaxing.

Thelma's Kitchen

Quality	Value
88	C

Southern   ★★★   **Inexpensive**

768 Marietta Street, NW
(404) 688-5855   Zone 7   Downtown West

Reservations: No
When to go: Any time
Entree range: $6–8
Payment: Major credit cards
Service rating: ★★★★
Friendliness rating: ★★★
Parking: Self, on street
Bar: None
Wine selection: None
Dress: Very casual
Disabled access: Easy
Customers: Regulars, both black and
white, from surrounding businesses; occasional tourists

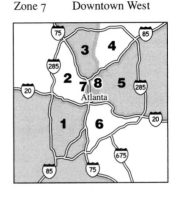

Breakfast & Lunch: Monday–Friday, 7:30 A.M.–4:30 P.M.; Saturday,
7 A.M.–3 P.M.

Setting & atmosphere: Recently reinstalled in the very modest and slightly restored Roxy Hotel, Thelma's had to move to make way for Centennial Olympic Park. This setting is much brighter and airier than the old one, with high ceilings, lots of white paint, faux ivy creeping up the latticed walls separating the kitchen from the steam tables, and plenty of natural light. Food is still dispensed from steam tables, with freshly made portions coming out at regular intervals, and the servings are huge.

House specialties: Fried catfish and fried chicken; mashed potatoes and gravy; macaroni and cheese; "cold" slaw; butter beans; greens; country steak; beef tips; okra cakes (when available).

Other recommendations: Super rich pecan pie; chocolate frosted yellow cake.

Summary & comment: Anyone looking for authentic "soul food" or Southern food (they're the same thing) need look no further, for Thelma's is its temple. Owner Thelma Grundy and her family also recently opened Thelma's Rib Shack, replacing the Auburn Avenue Rib Shack at Auburn Avenue beside the I-75/85 expressway.

Honors & awards: Plenty of local press and lots of satisfied patrons from all walks of life.

TomTom

Quality 90	Value C

Mediterranean/Fusion ★★★★ **Moderate**

3393 Peachtree Road, NE, Lenox Square, Plaza Level
(404) 264-1163 Zone 3 Buckhead/Sandy Springs

Reservations: For parties of 8 or more
When to go: Any time
Entree range: $12–20
Payment: Major credit cards
Service rating: ★★★★
Friendliness rating: ★★★
Parking: Mall lot
Bar: Separate with full service and
"Bistro Bites" menu
Wine selection: Mostly American,
with a few by the glass
Dress: Nice casual
Disabled access: Easy
Customers: Shoppers, both locals and visitors

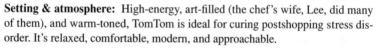

Lunch & Dinner: Monday–Thursday, 11:30 A.M.–10 P.M.; Friday and
Saturday, 11:30 A.M.–11 P.M.; Sunday, noon–9 P.M.

Setting & atmosphere: High-energy, art-filled (the chef's wife, Lee, did many
of them), and warm-toned, TomTom is ideal for curing postshopping stress dis-
order. It's relaxed, comfortable, modern, and approachable.

House specialties: Grilled tuna; barbecued salmon over white cheese grits;
whole deep-fried catfish with Asian seasonings; hot chili seafood.

Other recommendations: Pizzas and pastas; roast chicken or lamb with
mashed potatoes and haricots verts.

Summary & comment: "Bistro Bites" menu is available weekdays from 2:30
to 5 P.M. and weekends from 3 to 5 P.M., with sandwiches, soups, salads, and light
fare. Patio dining is fun in good weather.

Honors & awards: "Great Chefs Series," Discovery Channel; "Best Bistro,"
Atlanta magazine, 1995.

Van Gogh's

Quality	Value
90	C

Continental   ★★★   **Moderate**

70 W. Crossville Road, Roswell
(770) 993-1156

Zone 3   Buckhead/Sandy Springs

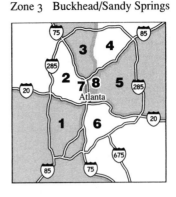

Reservations: Accepted
When to go: Weekdays
Entree range: $12–27
Payment: Major credit cards
Service rating: ★★★
Friendliness rating: ★★
Parking: Valet (dinner only) and self
Bar: Separate with full service
Wine selection: Extensive and excellent, with many by the glass; ask about the wine of the month
Dress: Nice casual to business attire
Disabled access: Easy
Customers: Neighbors

Lunch & Dinner: Monday–Thursday, 11:30 A.M.–10:30 P.M.; Friday and Saturday, 11:30 A.M.–11:30 P.M.
Dinner: Sunday, 5–10 P.M.

Setting & atmosphere: This serene space offers several separate dining rooms, warm and flattering lighting, and well-spaced tables. The noise level is not excessive.

House specialties: Crab cakes; grilled portobello mushroom sandwich (lunch); steak carpaccio; sea bass; veal special. Menu changes monthly.

Other recommendations: Smoked pork loin; rack of lamb.

Summary & comment: Wait times on the weekends can be excruciating, so plan to dine early or late on those days. This is understandable, since it's one of the best restaurants in the 'burbs.

Honors & awards: "Best Restaurant in Roswell," *Creative Loafing* and *Atlanta* magazine, 1995; *Wine Spectator,* 1995, for the wine list.

Veni Vidi Vici

Quality 98	Value B

Italian ★★★★★ **Moderate**

41 14th Street, NE
(404) 875-8424

Zone 8   Downtown East

Reservations: Recommended
When to go: Lunch is less crowded
Entree range: $11–23
Payment: Major credit cards
Service rating: ★★★★★
Friendliness rating: ★★★★
Parking: Valet
Bar: Separate with full service
Wine selection: Extensive, all Italian,
with many well priced; a few good
selections by the glass
Dress: Dressy casual to formal
Disabled access: Yes, from parking
deck
Customers: Locals, film stars, business and political figures

Lunch: Monday–Friday, 11:30 A.M.–4 P.M.
Dinner: Monday–Thursday, 5–11 P.M.; Friday and Saturday,
5 P.M.–midnight; Sunday, 5–10 P.M.

Setting & atmosphere: A stylish dining establishment in a parking garage—what will they think of next? Outdoor seating in fine weather is a real treat here, and the bacci court shifts into full swing in good weather (tournaments may be planned soon).

House specialties: Small plates with tasty morsels, such as veal meatballs in tomato sauce, braised artichoke bottoms, caponata, fresh and imported dried pastas, and rotisserie meats (duck!).

Other recommendations: Chicken with lemon; linguine with white clam sauce; scallops no matter how they're served; all desserts.

Summary & comment: Begun by Marcella Hazan, the restaurant has come under the firm direction of Pano Karatassos's and Paul Albrecht's group of restaurants (see Buckhead Diner, Pricci, Pano's & Paul's, Atlanta Fish Market). Chef Jamie Adams, who has lived in Italy, understands Italian food perfectly. Hazan would be pleased.

Honors & awards: *Mobil* 3-Star and AAA 4-Diamond; chef Jamie Adams, an Italian at heart, has been featured on "Great Chefs of America."

Violette

Quality 80	Value C

French ★★ **Inexpensive/Moderate**

3082 Briarcliff Road, NE
(404) 633-3323   Zone 5   Northeast Atlanta

2948 Clairmont Road, NE
(404) 633-3363   Zone 5   Northeast Atlanta

Reservations: Accepted
When to go: Any time
Entree range: *Briarcliff,* $6-15;
Clairmont, $9-16
Payment: Major credit cards
Service rating: ★★
Friendliness rating: ★
Parking: Self
Bar: Briarcliff Road: beer and wine
only; Clairmont: full service
Wine selection: French and California,
with some good ones by the glass
Dress: Nice casual
Disabled access: Easy
Customers: Neighbors and other locals

Lunch: *Briarcliffe:* Tuesday–Friday, 11:30 A.M.–2 P.M.; Monday, closed;
Clairmont: Monday–Friday, 11:30 A.M.–2 P.M.
Dinner: *Briarcliffe:* Tuesday–Sunday, 5:30–10 P.M.; *Clairmont:*
Monday–Thursday, 5:30–10 P.M.; Friday and Saturday, 5:30–11 P.M.;
Sunday, closed.

Setting & atmosphere: The original Violette occupies a freestanding building
that once was a bank. The new one, on Clairmont Road nearby, is a spanking
fresh structure that has a lot more room and atmosphere than the first one.

House specialties: Traditional bistro comfort fare: pâtés; chicken with lobster
sauce (Clairmont); quiche; pork with green peppercorns (Briarcliffe); salads and
soups.

Other recommendations: Crème brûlée; pear tart.

Summary & comment: If you want a special dish prepared, "we can do it,"
answers the chef with aplomb and alacrity. Neighbors still enjoy the intimate
ambiance of "Old Violette" and often fill it on the weekends.

Zac's

Quality 88	Value B

American ★★★ **Inexpensive**

308 W. Ponce de Leon Avenue, Decatur
(404) 373-9468

Zone 5   Northeast Atlanta

Reservations: No
When to go: Any time
Entree range: $8–13
Payment: MC, VISA
Service rating: ★★★★
Friendliness rating: ★★★★★
Parking: Self, limited
Bar: Beer and wine
Wine selection: Limited but decent
Dress: Casual
Disabled access: Yes
Customers: Locals, students, and
young professionals

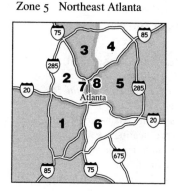

Brunch: Saturday and Sunday, 9 A.M.–3 P.M.
Lunch: Tuesday–Friday, 11:30 A.M.–2:30 P.M.
Dinner: Tuesday–Saturday, 5:30–10 P.M.

Setting & atmosphere: What was once a car sales space has been transformed into a comfortable, simple restaurant. Outdoor seating is nice in good weather. Small tables are a bit tightly packed, but we're all friends in food, right?

House specialties: Southwestern Cheesecake appetizer with blue corn chips; shrimp cakes; chicken pot pie; eggs Sardou at brunch.

Other recommendations: Fresh pastas; banana pudding (the only regular dessert); good soups.

Summary & comment: A homey, neighborhood kind of place that conveys the feeling of what Decatur is all about: a community of quiet achievers, church-goers, and students.

Zócalo

Quality	Value
95	A

Mexican ★★★ **Inexpensive**

187 10th Street, NE
(404) 249-7576 Zone 8 Downtown East

Reservations: No
When to go: Any time
Entree range: $8–13
Payment: Major credit cards
Service rating: ★★
Friendliness rating: ★★★★★
Parking: Limited
Bar: Beer and wine, even agave for the margaritas
Wine selection: Chilean, Spanish, California, with some by the glass; housemade sangría (both red and white)
Dress: Very casual
Disabled access: Excellent, with ramp to deck
Customers:

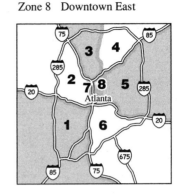

Brunch: Sunday, 11:30 A.M.–2:30 P.M.
Lunch: Tuesday–Friday, 11:30 A.M.–2:30 P.M.
Lunch & Dinner: Saturday, 2:30–11 P.M.; Sunday, 2:30–10 P.M.
Dinner: Tuesday–Thursday, 5:30–11 P.M.; Friday, 5:30–midnight.

Setting & atmosphere: Bright colors, artful and whimsical forms, and outdoor dining on a sheltered (and in cold weather, heated) deck have been popular with the neighbors ever since the restaurant opened—and way before they ever had a beer and wine license, or smooth service, or even a stable line in the kitchen.

House specialties: Tacos with chorizo and potatoes, al pastor and pork filling; black bean cakes; rajas (poblano peppers with onions and corn); mole poblano; flan.

Other recommendations: Steak with eggs and tomatillo salsa with chipotle for brunch; vegetarian specialties and soups.

Entertainment & amenities: Classic Spanish guitar on selected days.

Summary & comment: Dynamic, cheerful Lucero Martínez-Obregón flies through her tiny kitchen dispensing authenic Mexican dishes with style and flare. Don't talk to her about fajitas or any of the staples of Mexican-American cooking. She's not interested. But when it comes to classical Mexican food, the real thing, she's ready to perform. In so doing, she has provided a serious diplomatic service (dad's career, by the way).

Hotel	Room Star Rating	Zone	Street Address
Amberly Suite Hotel	★★¹/₂	5	5885 Oakbrook Parkway Norcross, GA 30093
Atlanta Airport Hilton	★★★¹/₂	1	1031 Virginia Avenue Atlanta, GA 30354
Atlanta Hilton & Towers	★★★★	7	255 Courtland Street, NE Atlanta, GA 30303
Atlanta Hilton Northwest	★★★¹/₂	2	2055 S. Park Place Atlanta, GA 30339
Atlanta Marriott Gwinnett Place	★★★¹/₂	4	1775 Pleasant Hill Road Duluth, GA 30136
Atlanta Marriott North Central	★★★¹/₂	4	2000 Century Boulevard, NE Atlanta, GA 30345
Atlanta Marriott Northwest	★★★	3	200 Interstate North Parkway Atlanta, GA 30339
Atlanta Marriott Perimeter Center	★★★★	4	246 Perimeter Center Parkway, NE Atlanta, GA 30346
Atlanta Renaissance Hotel	★★★★	8	590 W. Peachtree Street, NW Atlanta, GA 30308
Atlanta Renaissance Hotel Airport	★★★¹/₂	1	4736 Best Road College Park, GA 30337
Atlanta West Hotel	★	1	4330 Fulton Industrial Boulevard Atlanta, GA 30336
Best Western American Hotel	★★¹/₂	7	160 Spring Street, NW Atlanta, GA 30303
Best Western Bradbury Inn Norcross	★★¹/₂	5	5985 Oakbrook Parkway Norcross, GA 30093
Best Western Bradbury Suites Northlake	★★★	5	2060 Crescent Centre Boulevard Tucker, GA 30084
Best Western Bradbury Suites Windy Hill	★★★	2	4500 Circle 75 Parkway Atlanta, GA 30339
Best Western Granada Suite Hotel	★★★	7	1302 W. Peachtree Street Atlanta, GA 30309
Best Western Inn at the Peachtrees	★★¹/₂	8	330 W. Peachtree Street, NW Atlanta, GA 30308
Biltmore Peachtree Hotel	★★★	7	330 Peachtree Street, NE Atlanta, GA 30308
Biltmore Suites	★★★★	7	30 5th Street, NE Atlanta, GA 30308
Budgetel Inn Atlanta Airport	★★¹/₂	1	2480 Old National Parkway College Park, GA 30349

Local Phone	Fax	800 Reservations	Rack Rate	No. of Rooms	On-site Dining	Pool
(404) 263-0515	(404) 263-0185	(800) 365-0659	$$+	170	Yes	Yes
(404) 767-9000	(404) 768-0185	(800) HILTONS	$$$$$–	501	Yes	Yes
(404) 659-2000	(404) 522-8926	(800) HILTONS	$$$$ $$$–	1,250	Yes	Yes
(770) 953-9300	(770) 953-9315	(800) 234-9304	$$$+	222	Yes	Yes
(770) 923-1775	(770) 923-0017	(800) 228-9290	$$$$+	300	Yes	Yes
(404) 325-0000	(404) 325-4920	(800) 325-7224	$$$–	279	Yes	Yes
(770) 952-7900	(770) 952-1468	(800) 228-9290	$$$–	399	Yes	Yes
(770) 394-6500	(770) 394-4338	(800) 228-9290	$$+	400	Yes	Yes
(404) 881-6000	(404) 815-5350	(800) 228-9898	$$$$$–	504	Yes	Yes
(404) 762-7676	(404) 763-4199	(800) 228-9898	$$$$–	496	Yes	Yes
(404) 696-2274	(404) 691-4466	(800) 241-7343	$$+	150	No	Yes
(404) 688-8600	(404) 658-9458	(800) 634-1234	$$+	320	Yes	Yes
(770) 662-8175	(770) 840-1183	(800) 528-1234	$$	120	No	Yes
(770) 496-1070	(770) 939-9947	(800) 528-1234	$$$–	236	No	Yes
(770) 956-9919	(770) 955-3270	(800) 528-1234	$$$–	241	No	Yes
(404) 876-6100	(404) 875-0502	(800) 548-5631	$$$+	93	No	No
(404) 577-6970	(404) 659-3244	(800) 242-4642	$$$$–	102	Yes	No
(404) 577-1980	(404) 688-3706	(800) 241-4288	$$$–	91	No	No
(404) 874-0824	(404) 458-5384	(800) 822-0824	$$$+	61	No	No
(404) 766-0000	Ext. 142	(800) 428-3438	$$–	102	No	No

Hotel	Room Star Rating	Zone	Street Address
Budgetel Inn Atlanta Lenox	★★¹/2	4	2535 Chantilly Drive, NE Atlanta, GA 30324
Castlegate Hotel	★★¹/2	7	1750 Commerce Drive, NW Atlanta, GA 30318
Clubhouse Inn	★★★	5	5945 Oakbrook Parkway Norcross, GA 30093
Comfort Inn Atlanta Airport	★★¹/2	1	1808 Phoenix Boulevard College Park, GA 30349
Comfort Inn Buckhead	★★¹/2	3	2115 Piedmont Road, NE Atlanta, GA 30324
Comfort Inn Downtown Atlanta	★★¹/2	7	101 International Boulevard Atlanta, GA 30303
Comfort Suites Atlanta Airport	★★★	1	4820 Massachusetts Boulevard College Park, GA 30337
Courtyard Airport North	★★★¹/2	1	3399 International Boulevard Hapeville, GA 30354
Courtyard Airport South	★★★¹/2	1	2050 Sullivan Road College Park, GA 30337
Courtyard Cumberland Center	★★★¹/2	2	3000 Cumberland Circle Atlanta, GA 30339
Courtyard Executive Park	★★★¹/2	4	1236 Executive Park Drive Atlanta, GA 30329
Courtyard Gwinnett Mall	★★★¹/2	4	3550 Venture Parkway Duluth, GA 30136
Courtyard Medical Center	★★★¹/2	4	5601 Peachtree-Dunwoody Road Atlanta, GA 30342
Courtyard Midtown	★★★¹/2	7	1132 Techwood Drive Atlanta, GA 30318
Courtyard Norcross	★★★¹/2	5	6235 McDonough Drive Norcross, GA 30093
Courtyard North Lake	★★★¹/2	5	4083 La Vista Road Tucker, GA 30084
Courtyard Perimeter Center	★★★¹/2	4	6250 Peachtree-Dunwoody Road Atlanta, GA 30328
Courtyard Windy Hill	★★★¹/2	3	2045 S. Park Place Atlanta, GA 30339
Days Inn Airport	★★¹/2	1	4601 Best Road College Park, GA 30337
Days Inn Airport West	★★¹/2	1	4979 Old National Highway College Park, GA 30349

Local Phone	Fax	800 Reservations	Rack Rate	No. of Rooms	On-site Dining	Pool
(404) 321-0999	(404) 634-3384	(800) 428-3438	$$–	102	No	No
(404) 351-6100	(404) 351-6100	(800) 824-8657	$$+	365	Yes	Yes
(770) 368-9400	(770) 416-7370	(800) CLUB-INN	$$+	147	No	Yes
(770) 991-1099	(770) 991-1076	(800) 669-8888	$$+	194	Yes	Yes
(404) 876-4365	(404) 873-1007	(800) 221-2222	$$$–	182	Yes	Yes
(404) 524-5555	(404) 221-0702	(800) 535-0707	$$$$–	260	Yes	Yes
(770) 996-0000	(770) 996-9260	(800) 221-2222	$$$+	70	No	Yes
(404) 559-1043	(404) 559-1234	(800) 321-2211	$$$–	152	Yes	Yes
(770) 997-2220	(770) 994-9743	(800) 321-2211	$$$–	144	Yes	Yes
(770) 952-2555	(770) 952-2409	(800) 321-2211	$$+	182	Yes	Yes
(404) 728-0708	(404) 636-4019	(800) 321-2211	$$$$–	145	Yes	Yes
(770) 476-4666	(770) 623-0198	(800) 321-2211	$$$$–	146	No	Yes
(404) 843-2300	(404) 851-1938	(800) 321-2211	$$$+	128	Yes	Yes
(404) 607-1112	(404) 607-1020	(800) 321-2211	$$$+	168	Yes	Yes
(770) 242-7172	(770) 840-8768	(800) 321-2211	$$$+	121	No	Yes
(770) 938-1200	(770) 934-6497	(800) 321-2211	$$$+	128	No	Yes
(770) 393-1000	(770) 396-0762	(800) 321-2211	$$$$–	145	Yes	Yes
(770) 955-3838	(770) 933-0394	(800) 321-2211	$$$+	127	Yes	Yes
(404) 761-6500	(404) 763-3267	(800) 342-DAYS	$$	160	Yes	Yes
(404) 669-8616	Ext. 150	(800) 342-DAYS	$$	82	No	Yes

Hotel	Room Star Rating	Zone	Street Address
Days Inn Clairmont Road	★★¹/₂	4	2910 Clairmont Road Atlanta, GA 30329
Days Inn Downtown	★★¹/₂	7	300 Spring Street Atlanta, GA 30308
Days Inn Gwinnett Place	★★¹/₂	4	1948 Day Drive Duluth, GA 30136
Days Inn North Windy Hill	★★¹/₂	3	2767 Windy Hill Road Marietta, GA 30067
Days Inn Northlake Mall	★★¹/₂	5	2158 Ranchwood Drive Atlanta, GA 30345
Days Inn Northwest	★★¹/₂	7	1701 Northside Drive, NW Atlanta, GA 30318
Days Inn Peachtree	★★¹/₂	8	683 Peachtree Street, NE Atlanta, GA 30308
Days Inn Six Flags	★★¹/₂	1	95 South Service Road Austell, GA 30001
Days Inn Stone Mountain	★★¹/₂	5	2006 Glen Club Drive Stone Mountain, GA 30087
Doubletree Hotel at Concourse	★★★★	4	7 Concourse Parkway Atlanta, GA 30328
Econo Lodge Airport	★★	1	1360 E. Virginia Avenue Atlanta, GA 30344
Embassy Suites Airport	★★★¹/₂	1	4700 Southport Road College Park, GA 30337
Embassy Suites Buckhead	★★★★	3	3285 Peachtree Road, NE Atlanta, GA 30305
Embassy Suites Galleria	★★★★	2	2815 Akers Mill Road Atlanta, GA 30339
Embassy Suites Perimeter Center	★★★★	4	1030 Crown Pointe Parkway, NE Atlanta, GA 30338
Emory Inn	★★★	5	1641 Clifton Road Atlanta, GA 30329
Evergreen Resort at Stone Mountain	★★★¹/₂	5	1 Lakeview Drive Stone Mountain, GA 30086
Executive Inn Six Flags	¹/₂	1	305 Industrial Circle, SW Atlanta, GA 30336
Fairfield Inn Airport	★★¹/₂	1	2451 Old National Parkway College Park, Ga 30349
Fairfield Inn Gwinnett Mall	★★¹/₂	4	3500 Venture Parkway Duluth, GA 30136

Local Phone	Fax	800 Reservations	Rack Rate	No. of Rooms	On-site Dining	Pool
(404) 633-8411	(404) 633-1122	(800) 325-2525	$$+	238	No	Yes
(404) 523-1144	(404) 577-8495	(800) 633-1414	$$$	263	Yes	Yes
(770) 476-1211	(770) 623-0343	(800) 325-2525	$$$–	133	No	Yes
(770) 952-3251	Ext. 191	(800) 325-2525	$$+	193	No	Yes
(770) 934-6000	(770) 934-2535	(800) 325-2525	$$–	133	No	Yes
(404) 351-6500	Ext. 139	(800) 325-2525	$$$–	106	No	Yes
(404) 874-9200	(404) 873-4245	(800) DAYS-INN	$$$+	138	No	No
(770) 941-1400	(770) 819-9988	(800) DAYS-INN	$$$–	96	No	Yes
(770) 879-0800	Ext. 138	(800) 325-2525	$$	81	No	Yes
(770) 395-3900	(770) 395-3935	(800) 222-TREE	$$$$$–	370	Yes	Yes
(404) 761-5201	(404) 763-9534	(800) 424-4777	$$$–	100	No	Yes
(404) 767-1988	(404) 768-3507	(800) EMBASSY	$$$$$	233	Yes	Yes
(404) 261-7733	(404) 261-6857	(800) EMBASSY	$$$$$	328	Yes	Yes
(770) 984-9300	(770) 955-4183	(800) EMBASSY	$$$+	261	Yes	Yes
(770) 394-5454	(770) 396-5167	(800) EMBASSY	$$$$+	241	Yes	Yes
(404) 712-6700	(404) 712-6701	(800) 933-6679	$$$+	107	Yes	Yes
(770) 879-9900	(770) 413-9052	(800) 722-1000	$$$$$	249	Yes	Yes
(404) 691-9390	(404) 691-7068	None	$+	153	Yes	Yes
(404) 761-8371	Ext. 709	(800) 228-2800	$$+	132	No	Yes
(770) 623-9300	(770) 623-9300	(800) 228-2800	$$+	135	No	Yes

Hotel	Room Star Rating	Zone	Street Address
Fairfield Inn Midtown	★★★	7	1470 Spring Street, NW Atlanta, GA 30309
Fairfield Inn Northlake	★★¹/2	5	2155 Ranchwood Drive Atlanta, GA 30345
French Quarter Suites	★★★★¹/2	2	2780 Whitley Road Atlanta, GA 30339
Grand Hotel	★★★★★	8	75 14th Street Atlanta, GA 30309
Guest Quarters Suite Hotel	★★★★¹/2	4	6120 Peachtree-Dunwoody Road Atlanta, GA 30328
Hampton Inn Atlanta Airport	★★★	1	1888 Sullivan Road College Park, GA 30337
Hampton Inn Buckhead	★★¹/2	3	3398 Piedmont Rd., NE Atlanta, GA 30305
Hampton Inn Druid Hills	★★★	4	1975 N. Druid Hills Road Atlanta, GA 30329
Hampton Inn Northlake	★★¹/2	5	3400 Northlake Parkway Atlanta, GA 30345
Hampton Inn Stone Mountain	★★★	5	1737 Mtn Industrial Boulevard Stone Mountain, GA 30083
Harvey Hotel Airport	★★★	1	1325 Virginia Avenue East Point, GA 30344
Hawthorn Suites Northwest	★★★¹/2	3	1500 Parkwood Circle Atlanta, GA 30339
Ho Jo Inn Airport West	★★¹/2	1	5021 Old National Highway Atlanta, GA 30349
Holiday Inn Airport North	★★★	1	1380 Virginia Avenue East Point, GA 30344
Holiday Inn Airport South	★★★	1	5010 Old National Highway College Park, GA 30349
Holiday Inn at Lenox	★★★	4	3377 Peachtree Road Atlanta, GA 30326
Holiday Inn Crowne Plaza Ravinia	★★★¹/2	4	4355 Ashford-Dunwoody Road Atlanta, GA 30346
Holiday Inn Midtown North	★★★	7	1810 Howell Mill Road Atlanta, GA 30318
Holiday Inn Northlake	★★★	5	4156 La Vista Road Atlanta, GA 30084
Homewood Suites Cumberland	★★★★	2	3200 Cobb Parkway Atlanta, GA 30339

Local Phone	Fax	800 Reservations	Rack Rate	No. of Rooms	On-site Dining	Pool
(404) 872-5821	(404) 874-3602	(800) 228-2800	$$+	179	Yes	Yes
(770) 491-7444	Ext. 709	(800) 228-2800	$$+	133	No	Yes
(770) 980-1900	(770) 980-1528	(800) 843-5858	$$$$–	155	Yes	Yes
(404) 881-9898	(404) 888-8669	(800) 952-0702	$$$$$$–	246	Yes	Yes
(770) 668-0808	(770) 668-0008	(800) 424-2900	$$$$+	224	Yes	Yes
(770) 996-2220	(770) 996-2488	(800) 426-7866	$$+	130	No	Yes
(404) 233-5656	(404) 237-4688	(800) HAMPTON	$$$+	160	No	Yes
(404) 320-6600	(404) 321-2994	(800) HAMPTON	$$$–	111	No	Yes
(770) 493-1966	(770) 723-0693	(800) HAMPTON	$$+	130	No	Yes
(770) 934-0004	(770) 908-0940	(800) HAMPTON	$$$$–	129	No	Yes
(404) 768-6660	(404) 766-6121	(800) 922-9222	$$$	370	Yes	Yes
(770) 952-9595	(770) 984-2335	(800) 338-7812	$$$$	200	No	Yes
(404) 768-0040	(404) 768-0040	(800) 446-4656	$$–	50	No	Yes
(404) 762-8411	(404) 767-4963	(800) HOLIDAY	$$$$–	500	Yes	Yes
(404) 761-4000	(404) 763-0181	(800) HOLIDAY	$$$$–	230	Yes	Yes
(404) 264-1111	(404) 231-3497	(800) 526-0247	$$$$	300	Yes	Yes
(770) 395-7700	(770) 392-9503	(800) HOLIDAY	$$$$$$–	495	Yes	Yes
(404) 351-3831	(404) 352-0125	(800) 882-4828	$$–	201	Yes	Yes
(770) 938-1026	(770) 491-8113	(800) 338-9889	$$$+	187	Yes	Yes
(770 988-9449	(770) 933-9612	(800) CALLHOME	$$$+	124	Yes	Yes

Hotel	Room Star Rating	Zone	Street Address
Hotel Nikko	★★★★¹/₂	3	3300 Peachtree Road Atlanta, GA 30305
Howard Johnson Airport	★★¹/₂	1	1377 Virginia Avenue East Point, GA 30344
Howard Johnson Cumberland	★★¹/₂	2	2700 Curtis Drive Smyrna, GA 30080
Hyatt Regency Peachtree Center	★★★★	7	265 Peachtree Street, NE Atlanta, GA 30303
Hyatt Regency Suites	★★★★	3	2999 Windy Hill Road Marietta, GA 30067
J.W. Marriott at Lenox	★★★★	4	3300 Lenox Road, NE Atlanta, GA 30326
La Quinta Atlanta West	★★¹/₂	1	7377 Six Flags Drive Atlanta, GA 30001
La Quinta Motor Inn Airport	★★¹/₂	1	4874 Old National Highway College Park, GA 30337
La Quinta Norcross	★★¹/₂	5	6187 Dawson Boulevard Norcross, GA 30093
La Quinta Stone Mountain	★★★	5	1819 Mtn Industrial Boulevard Tucker, GA 30084
Lenox Inn	★★¹/₂	4	3387 Lenox Road, NE Atlanta, GA 30326
Marque of Atlanta	★★★¹/₂	4	11 Perimeter Center West Atlanta, GA 30346
Marriott Atlanta Airport	★★★¹/₂	1	4711 Best Road College Park, GA 30337
Marriott Atlanta Marquis	★★★★	7	265 Peachtree Center Avenue Atlanta, GA 30303
Marriott Suites Midtown	★★★★¹/₂	8	35 14th Street Atlanta, GA 30309
Masters Economy Inn Six Flags	★★¹/₂	1	4120 Fulton Industrial Boulevard Atlanta, GA 30336
Omni Hotel at CNN Center	★★★★	7	100 CNN Center Atlanta, GA 30335
Quality Inn Northeast	★★★	5	2960 NE Expressway Atlanta, GA 30341
Radisson Hotel Atlanta	★★¹/₂	7	165 Courtland Street Atlanta, GA 30303
Ramada Atlanta Airport North	★★★	1	1419 Virginia Avenue College Park, GA 30337

Local Phone	Fax	800 Reservations	Rack Rate	No. of Rooms	On-site Dining	Pool
(404) 365-8100	(404) 233-5686	(800) NIKKO-US	$$$$$$–	440	Yes	Yes
(404) 762-5111	Ext. 114	(800) 752-7293	$$$	189	No	Yes
(770) 435-4990	(770) 434-2573	(800) 654-2000	$$+	145	No	Yes
(404) 577-1234	(404) 588-4137	(800) 233-1234	$$$$ $$$–	1,279	Yes	Yes
(770) 956-1234	(770) 956-9479	(800) 233-1234	$$$$$+	220	Yes	Yes
(404) 262-3344	(404) 262-8689	(800) 228-9290	$$$$$+	371	Yes	Yes
(770) 944-2110	(770) 739-1698	(800) 531-5900	$$+	106	Yes	Yes
(404) 768-1241	(404) 766-3642	(800) 531-5900	$$+	122	No	Yes
(770) 448-8686	(770) 840-8924	(800) 531-5900	$$+	130	No	Yes
(770) 496-1317	(770) 493-4785	(800) 531-5900	$$+	128	No	Yes
(404) 261-5500	(404) 261-6140	(800) 241-0200	$$$–	180	Yes	Yes
(770) 396-6800	(770) 399-5514	(800) 683-6100	$$$$–	275	Yes	Yes
(404) 766-7900	(404) 209-6808	(800) 288-9290	$$$–	659	Yes	Yes
(404) 521-0000	(404) 586-6299	(800) 228-9290	$$$$–	1,671	Yes	Yes
(404) 876-8888	(404) 876-7727	(800) 228-9290	$$$+	259	Yes	Yes
(404) 696-4690	(404) 696-8432	(800) 633-3434	$$–	167	Yes	Yes
(404) 659-0000	(404) 818-4322	(800) THEOMNI	$$$$$–	466	Yes	Yes
(770) 451-5231	(770) 454-8704	(800) 228-5151	$$–	150	No	Yes
(404) 659-6500	(404) 681-5306	(800) 333-3333	$$$$	754	Yes	Yes
(404) 768-7800	(404) 767-5451	None	$$$+	245	Yes	Yes

Hotel	Room Star Rating	Zone	Street Address
Ramada Hotel Airport South	★★★	1	1551 Phoenix Boulevard College Park, GA 30349
Ramada Inn Atlanta Six Flags	★★¹/₂	1	4225 Fulton Industrial Boulevard Atlanta, GA 30336
Ramada Inn Northlake	★★★¹/₂	5	2180 Northlake Parkway Tucker, GA 30084
Red Roof Inn Airport	★★¹/₂	1	2471 Old National Parkway College Park, GA 30349
Red Roof Inn Druid Hills	★★	4	1960 N. Druid Hills Road Atlanta, GA 30329
Red Roof Inn North	★★	2	2200 Corporate Plaza Smyrna, GA 30080
Red Roof Inn Six Flags	★★	1	4265 Shirley Drive, SW Atlanta, GA 30336
Regency Suites Hotel	★★★	8	975 W. Peachtree Street Atlanta, GA 30309
Residence Inn	★★★¹/₂	4	6096 Barfield Road Atlanta, GA 30328
Residence Inn Airport North	★★★¹/₂	1	3401 International Boulevard Hapeville, GA 30354
Residence Inn Buckhead	★★★¹/₂	3	2960 Piedmont Road, NE Atlanta, GA 30305
Residence Inn Cumberland	★★★¹/₂	2	2771 Hargrove Road Smyrna, GA 30080
Residence Inn Midtown	★★★★	8	1041 W. Peachtree Street Atlanta, GA 30309
Ritz Carlton Atlanta Downtown	★★★★¹/₂	7	181 Peachtree Street, NE Atlanta, GA 30303
Ritz Carlton Buckhead	★★★★¹/₂	4	3434 Peachtree Road, NE Atlanta, GA 30326
Sheraton Colony Square Hotel	★★★★	8	188 14th Street Atlanta, GA 30361
Sheraton Gateway Atlanta Airport	★★★¹/₂	1	1900 Sullivan Road College Park, GA 30337
Sheraton Suites Cumberland	★★★★	2	2844 Cobb Parkway Atlanta, GA 30339
Shoney's Inn Northeast	★★¹/₂	4	2050 Willow Trail Parkway Norcross, GA 30093
Stone Mountain Inn	★★★¹/₂	5	Highway 78 E Stone Mountain, GA 30086

Local Phone	Fax	800 Reservations	Rack Rate	No. of Rooms	On-site Dining	Pool
(770) 996-4321	(770) 991-5795	(800) 241-3092	$$	150	Yes	Yes
(404) 691-4100	(404) 691-2117	(800) 272-6232	$$+	229	Yes	Yes
(770) 939-1000	(770) 723-0858	(800) 777-8120	$$+	163	No	Yes
(404) 761-9701	Ext. 444	(800) 843-7663	$$+	150	No	No
(404) 321-1653	Ext. 444	(800) 843-7663	$$+	115	No	No
(770) 952-6966	(770) 952-1348	(800) 843-7663	$+	137	No	No
(404) 696-4391	Ext. 444	(800) 843-7663	$$$−	120	No	No
(404) 876-5003	(404) 817-7511	(800) 642-3629	$$$+	96	No	No
(404) 252-5066	(404) 851-1723	(800) 331-3131	$$$$−	129	No	Yes
(404) 761-0511	(404) 761-0650	(800) 304-4305	$$$$	126	No	Yes
(404) 239-0677	(404) 262-9638	(800) 331-3131	$$$$$+	136	No	Yes
(770) 433-8877	(770) 436-1475	(800) 331-3131	$$$$	130	No	Yes
(404) 872-8885	(404) 872-8885	(800) 331-3131	$$$$$+	66	Yes	No
(404) 659-0400	(404) 688-0400	(800) 241-3333	$$$$ $$$−	447	Yes	No
(404) 237-2700	(404) 239-0078	(800) 241-3333	$$$ $$$+	553	Yes	Yes
(404) 892-6000	(404) 872-9192	(800) 325-3535	$$$$$	461	Yes	Yes
(770) 997-1100	(770) 997-1921	(800) 325-7224	$$$$$	397	Yes	Yes
(770) 955-3900	(770) 916-3165	(800) 325-3535	$$$$$+	279	Yes	Yes
(770) 564-0492	(770) 564-0297	(800) 222-2222	$$	144	Yes	Yes
(770) 469-3311	(770) 498-5691	(800) 277-0007	$$$	92	Yes	Yes

Hotel	Room Star Rating	Zone	Street Address
Stouffer Concourse Hotel	★★★★¹/₂	1	One Hartsfield Centre Parkway Atlanta, GA 30354
Stouffer Waverly Hotel	★★★★¹/₂	2	2450 Galleria Parkway Atlanta, GA 30339
Suite Hotel at Underground	★★★★	7	54 Peachtree Street Atlanta, GA 30303
Summerfield Suites Buckhead	★★★¹/₂	3	505 Pharr Road Atlanta, GA 30305
Summit Inn	★★¹/₂	1	3900 Fulton Industrial Blvd. Atlanta, GA 30336
Super 8 Airport	★★	1	2010 Sullivan Road College Park, GA 30337
Super 8 Motel Six Flags	★★	1	301 Fulton Industrial Circle Atlanta, GA 30336
Swissotel Atlanta	★★★★¹/₂	4	3391 Peachtree Road, NE Atlanta, GA 30326
Terrace Garden Inn Buckhead	★★★¹/₂	3	3405 Lenox Road, NE Atlanta, GA 30326
Travelodge Downtown	★★¹/₂	7	311 Courtland Street, NE Atlanta, GA 30303
Travelodge Hotel Druid Hills	★★★	4	2061 N. Druid Hills Road, NE Atlanta, GA 30329
Travelodge Marietta	★★¹/₂	3	1940 Leland Drive Marietta, GA 30067
Travelodge/Quality Inn Atlanta Airport	★★	1	4505 Best Road College Park, GA 30337
Travelodge Midtown	★★	8	1641 Peachtree Street Atlanta, GA 30309
University Inn at Emory	*★★★/ ★★★¹/₂	5	1767 N. Decatur Road Atlanta, GA 30307
Westin Peachtree Plaza	★★★¹/₂	7	210 Peachtree Street Atlanta, GA 30343
Wyndham Garden Hotel	★★★¹/₂	4	800 Hammond Drive, NE Atlanta, GA 30328
Wyndham Midtown Atlanta	★★★★	8	125 10th Street Atlanta, GA 30309

*Old rooms / new rooms

Local Phone	Fax	800 Reservations	Rack Rate	No. of Rooms	On-site Dining	Pool
(404) 209-9999	(404) 209-8934	(800) HOTELS1	$$$$ $$$–	387	Yes	Yes
(770) 953-4500	(770) 953-0740	(800) 468-3571	$$$ $$$–	521	Yes	Yes
(404) 223-5555	(404) 223-0467	(800) 477-5549	$$$+	156	Yes	No
(404) 262-7880	(404) 262-3734	(800) 833-4353	$$$$$–	88	No	Yes
(404) 691-2444	None	None	$$+	107	Yes	Yes
(770) 991-8985	Ext. 201	None	$$–	63	No	No
(404) 696-9713	(404) 696-9713	None	$$–	62	No	No
(404) 365-0065	(404) 233-8786	(800) 253-1397	$$$$+	363	Yes	Yes
(404) 261-9250	(404) 848-7301	(800) 866-7666	$$$$$	360	Yes	Yes
(404) 659-4545	(404) 659-5934	(800) 578-7878	$$$–	71	No	Yes
(404) 321-4174	(404) 636-7264	(800) 578-7878	$$$–	180	Yes	Yes
(770) 952-0052	(770) 952-0501	(800) 578-7878	$+	108	No	No
(404) 767-1224	(404) 767-0714	(800) 578-7878	$$	60	No	No
(404) 873-5731	(404) 870-5599	(800) 255-3050	$$+	55	No	Yes
(404) 634-7327	(404) 320-7023	(800) 654-8591	$$$+/ $$+	46	No	Yes
(404) 659-1400	(404) 589-7424	(800) 228-3000	$$$ $$$+	1,068	Yes	Yes
(404) 252-3344	(404) 843-1228	(800) 822-4200	$$$$–	143	Yes	Yes
(404) 873-4800	(404) 870-1530	(800) 822-4200	$$$$	191	Yes	Yes

Index

1997 Unofficial Guide **Reader Survey**

If you would like to express your opinion about Atlanta or this guidebook, complete the following survey and mail it to:

> *Unofficial Guide* Reader Survey
> P.O. Box 43059
> Birmingham, AL 35243

Inclusive dates of your visit _____

Members of your party:

	Person 1	Person 2	Person 3	Person 4	Person 5
Gender (M or F)	_____	_____	_____	_____	_____
Age	_____	_____	_____	_____	_____

How many times have you been to Atlanta? _____
On your most recent trip, where did you stay? _____

Concerning accommodations, on a scale with 100 best and 0 worst, how would you rate:

The quality of your room? _____   The value for the money? _____
The quietness of your room? _____   Check-in/checkout efficiency? _____
Shuttle service to the parks? _____   Swimming pool facilities? _____

Did you rent a car? _____   From whom? _____

Concerning your rental car, on a scale with 100 best and 0 worst, how would you rate:

Pickup processing efficiency? _____   Return processing efficiency? _____
Condition of the car? _____   Cleanliness of the car? _____
Airport shuttle efficiency? _____

Concerning your dining experiences:

How many restaurant meals (including fast food) did you average per day? _____
How much (approximately) did your party spend on meals per day? _____
Favorite restaurants in Atlanta? _____
_____

Did you buy this guide: Before leaving? _____ While on your trip? _____

How did you hear about this guide?
Loaned or recommended by a friend _____   Radio or TV _____
Newspaper or magazine _____   Bookstore salesperson _____
Just picked it out on my own _____   Library _____

What other guidebooks did you use on this trip? _____

_____

On the 100 best and 0 worst scale, how would you rate them? _____

_____

Using the same scale, how would you rate the *Unofficial Guide?* _____

Are *Unofficial Guides* readily available in bookstores in your area? _____

Have you used other *Unofficial Guides?* _____ Which one(s)? _____

Comments about your Atlanta trip or about the *Unofficial Guide:* _____

_____

_____

_____

_____

_____

_____

_____

_____

_____

_____

_____